A TEXTBOOK OF

ENGINEERING MATERIALS AND METALLURGY

A TEXTBOOK OF
ENGINEERING MATERIALS AND METALLURGY

By

A. ALAVUDEEN
Department of Mechanical Engineering
Arulmigu Kalasalingam College of Engineering
Krishnankoil
Tamil Nadu

N. VENKATESHWARAN
Department of Mechanical Engineering
Rajalakshmi Engineering College
Chennai
Tamil Nadu

DR. J.T. WINOWLIN JAPPES
Department of Mechanical Engineering
Arulmigu Kalasalingam
College of Engineering
Krishnankoil
Tamil Nadu

UNIVERSITY SCIENCE PRESS
(An Imprint of Laxmi Publications Pvt. Ltd.)
BANGALORE • CHENNAI • COCHIN • GUWAHATI • HYDERABAD
JALANDHAR • KOLKATA • LUCKNOW • MUMBAI • RANCHI
NEW DELHI

Published by :

UNIVERSITY SCIENCE PRESS

(An Imprint of Laxmi Publications Pvt. Ltd.)
113, Golden House, Daryaganj,
New Delhi-110002

Phone : 011-43 53 25 00
Fax : 011-43 53 25 28

www.laxmipublications.com
info@laxmipublications.com

Price : **Rs. 190.00** *Only.*

First Edition : 2006
Reprint : 2008, 2010

OFFICES

© **Bangalore**	080-26 61 15 61	© **Chennai**	044-24 34 47 26
© **Cochin**	0484-237 70 04, 405 13 03	© **Guwahati**	0361-254 36 69, 251 38 81
© **Hyderabad**	040-24 65 23 33	© **Jalandhar**	0181-222 12 72
© **Kolkata**	033-22 27 43 84	© **Lucknow**	0522-220 95 78
© **Mumbai**	022-24 91 54 15, 24 92 78 69	© **Ranchi**	0651-221 47 64

UEM-9525-190-ENGG MATERIAL & METALL-ALA
C—1421/010/04
Typeset at : Kalyani Computer Services, New Delhi.
Printed at : Mehra Offset Press, Delhi.

PREFACE

The primary job of an engineer in the present day of complex technology is to design, fabricate and make technology work smoothly. Hence, increasing demand of materials and newer areas of application have brought the changes in their uses. In this process, there is always the search for new material—combined with greater strength, lightweight, high reliability etc. Hence the knowledge of material science becomes an important role in the engineer's life.

The entire text of this book has been written and arranged in a systematic manner, so the readers feel comfort about the subject.

Chapter One deals with **CRYSTAL STRUCTURE AND ITS DEFECTS.** Understanding of how materials behave like they do, and why they differ in properties was only possible with the atomistic understanding allowed by quantum mechanics that first explained atoms and then solids starting in the 1930s. The combination of physics, chemistry, and the focus on the relationship between the properties of a material and its microstructure is the domain of Materials Science. The development of this science allowed designing materials and provided a knowledge base for the engineering applications.

Chapter Two is devoted to **ALLOYS AND PHASE DIAGRAM.** To know the availability of different material, phase diagram becomes unavoidable one. A phase diagram shows us the microstructure within a material as a function of the material composition (% alloying elements) and material temperature. They can help us understand the thermal history of a material and the effect of that history on material properties. They are needed to help us understand how we develop and preserve non-equilibrium microstructures. The different microstructures represented on a phase diagram produce different material properties when that microstructure is preserved in the material.

Chapter Three deals with the **HEAT TREATMENT MECHANISM** and its uses. Study of heat treatment makes us to understand how the properties of metals and alloys can be improved.

Chapter Four is the study of **FERROUS AND NON FERROUS METALS.** About three quarters of all the known chemical elements are metals. Since most of the components are made of ferrous and non-ferrous metals the basic knowledge of it becomes essential. Despite the great variety of natural metals, engineers often require materials that have properties that none of the available metals have. To fill these needs, metallurgists create alloys—metals combined with other metals, with non-metals, or both—to extend the range of a metal's properties.

Chapter Five is **MECHANICAL PROPERTIES AND TESTING.** Hardness is the property of a material that enables it to resist plastic deformation, usually by penetration. However, the term hardness may also refer to resistance to bending, scratching, abrasion or cutting.

Hardness is not an intrinsic material property dictated by precise definitions in terms of fundamental units of mass, length and time. A hardness property value is the result of a defined measurement procedure. Hence different methods are used to calculate it are dealt in lucid way.

Chapter Six consist of **NON-METALLIC MATERIALS.** As these days, the non-metallic materials application increases by replacing the conventional metals, the basic knowledge of such materials is important.

Chapter Seven briefly covers hardness and testing methods. These physical properties are discussed because sometimes physical properties other than stress strain properties may be the governing properties.

Chapter Eight consists of Isothermal Transformation and Cooling Curve Rate (CCR). The chapter attempts to summarize subjects in changes in steel structure below lower critical temperature and their effects.

Authors

FOREWORD

To prepare a textbook covering a wide range of topics in a concise form without sacrificing the details is a daunting task. In the field of **Material Science,** where the information available is scanty and scattered, comprehensive textbook of this nature is unique of its kind. The presentation is lively and candid, and the examples are taken from an array of applications. The inputs for the textbook have been drawn from extensive literature survey of several publications.

This easy-to-read and appropriately illustrated book will be used extensively by practicing engineers, consultants and by budding engineers as well. Learning **crystal structures** and mechanical properties is no means an easy task as it appears to beginners. Thus, this textbook will appeal to a wide audience of users who are to appear for the examinations and those who just want to read it and learn more about metallurgical concepts.

The authors rightly stressed the importance of sketching to correct proportions as an aid to learning structures. The book cannot fail to be extremely valuable for a beginner and will go a long way in initiating him in learning the language of engineers and in speaking the language with lucidity and preciseness.

Dr.C.Thangaraj,
Principal,
A.K.College of Engineering,
Krishnan Koil.
Tamil Nadu.

SYLLABUS

ENGINEERING MATERIALS AND METALLURGY

MH 1151 **3 0 0 100**

(Common to 4th semester Mechanical, Production, Automobile and 2nd semester Mechatronics)

Objective

To Impart knowledge on the structure, properties, treatment, testing and applications of metals and non-metallic materials so as to identify and select suitable materials for various engineering applications.

Review (Not for Exam):

Crystal structure—BCC, FCC and HCP structure—unit cell—crystallographic planes and directions, miller indices—crystal imperfections, point, line, planar and volume defects—Grain size, ASTM grain size number.

1. CONSTITUTION OF ALLOYS AND PHASE DIAGRAMS **10**

Constitution of alloys—solid solutions, substitutional and interstitial—phase diagrams, isomorphous, eutectic, peritectic, eutectoid and peritectroid reactions, iron—iron carbide equilibrium diagram. Classification of steel and cast iron microstructure, properties and application.

2. HEAT TREATMENT **11**

Definition—full annealing, stress relief, recrystallisation and spheroidizing—normalising, hardening and Tempering of steel. Isothermal transformation diagrams—cooling curves superimposed on I.T. diagram CCR—hardenability, jominy end quench test—austempering, martempering—case hardening, carburising, nitriding, cyaniding, carbonitriding—flame and induction hardening.

3. FERROUS AND NON FERROUS METALS **9**

Effect of alloying additions on steel (Mn, Si, Cr, Mo, V, Ti and W)—stainless and tool steels—HSLA—maraging steels—Gray, White malleable, spheroidal—graphite—alloy castirons.

Copper and copper alloys—brass, bronze and cupronickel—aluminum and Al-Cu—precipitation strengthening treatment—bearing alloys.

4. NON-METALLIC MATERIALS **9**

Polymers—types of polymer, commodity and engineering polymers—Properties and applications of PE, PP, PS, PVC, PMMA, PET, PC, PA, ABS, PI, PAI, PPO, PPS, PEEK, PTFE polymers—urea and phenol formaldehydes—engineering ceramics—properties and applications of Al_2O_3, SiC, Si_3, N_4, PSZ and sialon—fibre and particulate reinforced composites.

5. MECHANICAL PROPERTIES AND TESTING **6**

Mechanism of plastic deformation, slip and twinning—types of fracture—testing of materials under tension, compression and shear loads—hardness tests (Brinell, Vickers and Rockwell) impact test izod and charpy, fatigue and creep test.

TOTAL : 45

CONTENTS

1

CHAPTER

CRYSTAL STRUCTURE

1.1 HISTORICAL PERSPECTIVE

Materials are so important in the development of civilization that we associate ages with them. In the origin of human life on Earth, the stone age, people used only natural materials, like stone, clay, skins, and wood. When people found copper and how to make it harder by alloying, the bronze age started about 3000 BC. The use of iron and steel, a stronger material that gave advantage in wars started at about 1200 BC. The next big step was the discovery of a cheap process to make steel around 1850, which enabled the railroads and the building of the modern infrastructure of the industrial world. Beginning of the material science—People began to make tools from stone—Start of the Stone Age about two million years ago.

Natural materials: stone, wood, clay, skins, etc.

- The stone age ended about 5000 years ago with introduction of bronze in the far east. Bronze is an **alloy** (a metal made up of more than one element), copper + < 25% of tin + other elements.

Bronze can be hammered or cast into a variety of shapes, can be made harder by alloying, corrode only slowly after a surface oxide film forms.

- The iron age began about 3000 years ago and continues today. Use of iron and steel, a stronger and cheaper material changed drastically daily life of a common person.
- Age of advanced materials throughout the iron age many new types of materials have been introduced (ceramic, semiconductors, polymers, composites...).

A better understanding of structure-composition properties relations has lead to a remarkable progress in properties of materials. Example is the dramatic progress in the strength to density ratio of materials, that resulted in a wide variety of new products, from dental materials to tennis racquet.

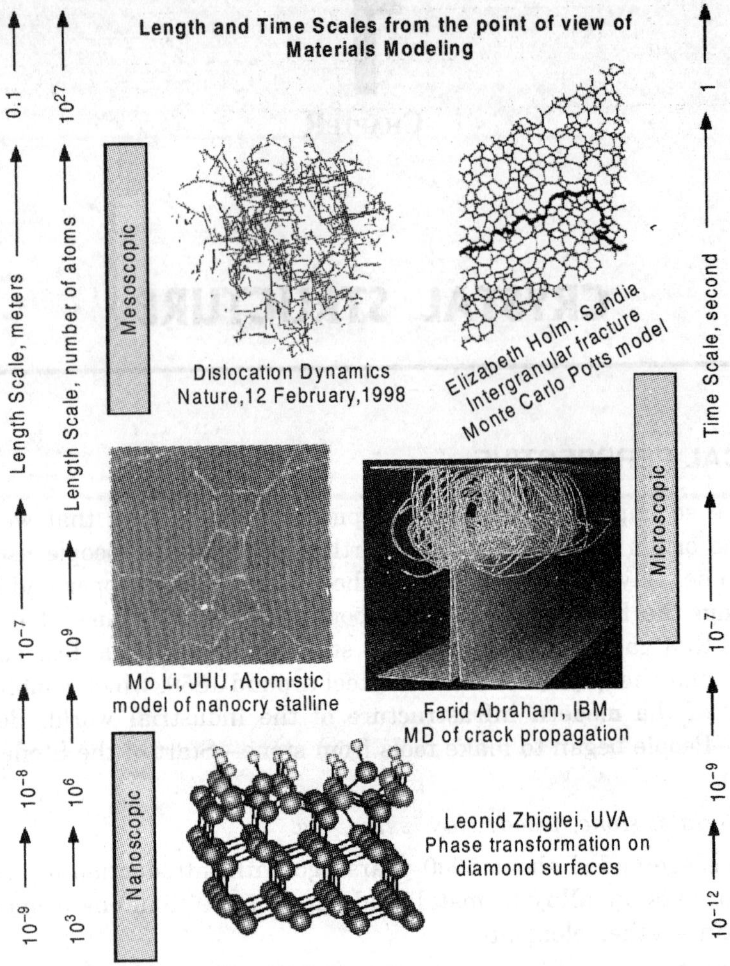

Fig. 1.1 Length and time scale of material modeling.

1.2 NEED TO STUDY MATERIALS SCIENCE AND ENGINEERING?

- To be able to select a material for a given use based on considerations of cost and performance.
- To understand the limits of materials and the change of their properties with use.
- To be able to create a new material that will have some desirable properties.

All engineering disciplines need to know about materials. Even the most "immaterial", like software or system engineering depend on the development of new materials, which in turn alter the economics, like software-hardware trade-offs. Increasing applications of system engineering are in materials manufacturing (industrial engineering) and complex environmental systems. Properties are the way the material responds to the environment and external forces.

Mechanical properties—response to mechanical forces, strength, etc.

Electrical and **magnetic** properties—response electrical and magnetic fields, conductivity, etc.

Thermal properties are related to transmission of heat and heat capacity.

Optical properties include to absorption, transmission and scattering of light.

Chemical stability in contact with the environment—corrosion resistance.

1.3 CLASSIFICATION OF MATERIALS

Like many other things, materials are classified in groups, so that our brain can handle the complexity. One could classify them according to structure, or properties, or use. The one that we will use is according to the way the atoms are bound together:

There are thousands of materials available for use in engineering applications. Most materials fall into one of three classes that are based on the atomic bonding forces of a particular material. These three classifications are metallic, ceramic and polymeric. Additionally, different materials can be combined to create a composite material. Within each of these classifications, materials are often further organized into groups based on their chemical composition or certain physical or mechanical properties. Composite materials are often grouped by the types of materials combined or the way the materials are arranged together. Below is a list of some of the commonly classification of materials within these four general groups of materials.

Metals	**Polymeric**
• Ferrous metals and alloys (irons, carbon steels, alloy steels, stainless steels, tool and die steels) • Nonferrous metals and alloys (aluminum, copper, magnesium, nickel, titanium, precious metals, refractory metals, super alloys)	• Thermoplastics plastics • Thermoset plastics • Elastomers
Ceramics	**Composites**
• Glasses • Glass ceramics • Graphite • Diamond	• Reinforced plastics • Metal-matrix composites • Ceramic-matrix composites • Sandwich structures • Concrete

Metals: valence electrons are detached from atoms, and spread in an 'electron sea' that "glues" the ions together. Metals are usually strong, conduct electricity and heat well and are opaque to light (shiny if polished). Examples: aluminium, steel, brass, gold.

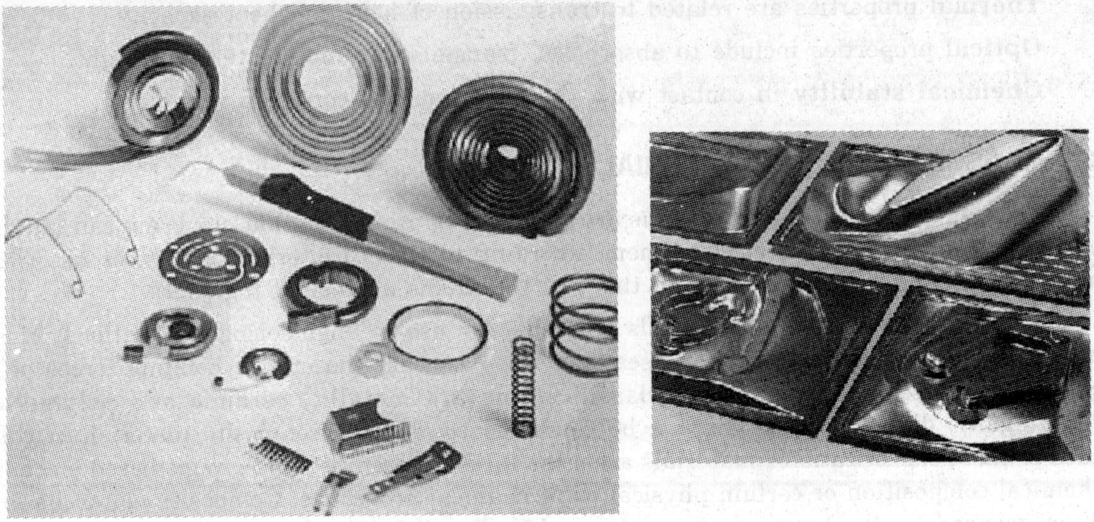

Several uses of steel and pressed aluminium.

Fig. 1.2 Examples of ceramic materials ranging from household to high performance combustion engines which utilize both metals and ceramics.

Semiconductors: the bonding is covalent (electrons are shared between atoms). Their electrical properties depend extremely strongly on minute proportions of contaminants. They are opaque to visible light but transparent to the infrared. Examples: Si, Ge, GaAs.

Micro-Electrical-Mechanical Systems (MEMS) Si wafer for computer chip devices.

Fig. 1.3 Different materials exhibit different **crystal structures** and resultant properties.

Ceramics: atoms behave mostly like either positive or negative ions, and are bound by Coulomb forces between them. They are usually combinations of metals or semiconductors with oxygen, nitrogen or carbon (oxides, nitrides, and carbides). Examples: glass, porcelain, many minerals.

Polymers: are bound by covalent forces and also by weak van der Waals forces, and usually based on H, C and other non-metallic elements. They decompose at moderate temperatures (100–400°C), and are lightweight. Other properties vary greatly. Examples: plastics (nylon, teflon, polyester) and rubber.

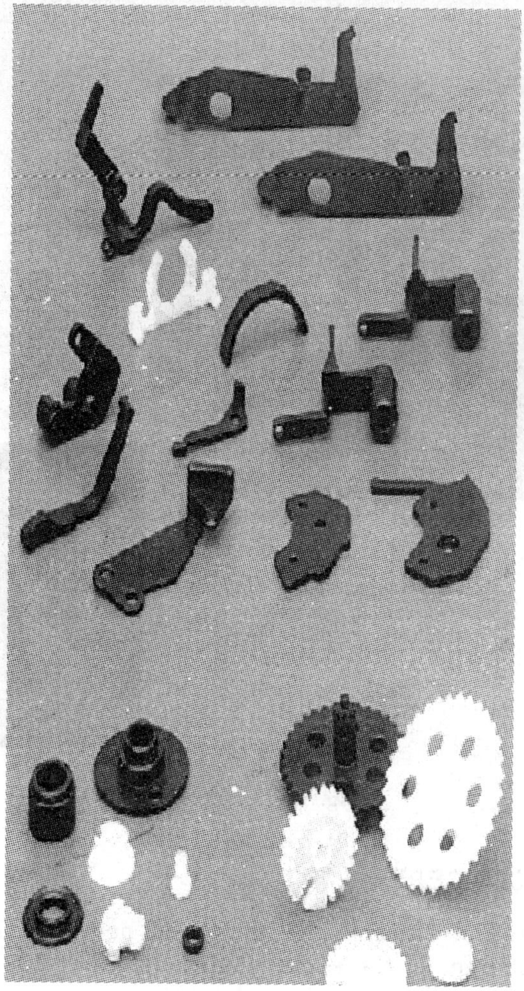

Fig. 1.4 Polymers.

Other categories are not based on bonding. A particular microstructure identifies **composites,** made of different materials in intimate contact (Examples: fiberglass, concrete, wood) to achieve specific properties. **Biomaterials** can be any type of material that is biocompatible and used, for instance, to replace human body parts.

1.4 MODERN MATERIALS' NEED

- Engine efficiency increases at high temperatures requiring high temperature structural materials.
- Use of nuclear energy requires solving problem with residues, or advances in nuclear waste processing.
- Hypersonic flight requires materials that are light, strong and resist high temperatures.
- Optical communications require optical fibers that absorb light negligibly.
- Civil construction—materials for unbreakable windows.
- Structures materials that are strong like metals and resist corrosion like plastics.

Composites

Polymer composite materials: reinforcing glass fibres in a polymer matrix.

Fig. 1.5 Composites.

1.5 FUNDAMENTAL CONCEPTS

Atoms are composed of electrons, protons, and neutrons. Electron and protons are negative and positive charges of the same magnitude, 1.6×10^{-19} Coulombs.

The mass of the electron is negligible with respect to those of the proton and the neutron, which form the *nucleus* of the atom. The unit of mass is an atomic mass unit (amu) $= 1.66 \times 10^{-27}$ kg, and equals 1/12 the mass of a carbon atom. The carbon nucleus has Z = 6, and A = 6, where Z is the number of protons, and A the number of neutrons. Neutrons and protons have very similar masses, roughly equal to 1 amu. A neutral atom has the same number of electrons and protons, Z.

A mole is the amount of matter that has a mass in grams equal to the atomic mass in amu of the atoms. Thus, a mole of carbon has a mass of 12 grams. The number of atoms in a mole is called the Avogadro number, $N_{av} = 6.023 \times 10^{23}$. Note that N_{av} = 1 gram/1 amu.

Calculating *n*, the number of atoms per cm^3 in a piece of material of density ρ (g/cm^3). $n = N_{av} \times \rho/M$.

where M is the atomic mass in amu (grams per mol). Thus, for graphite (carbon) with a density $\rho = 1.8$ g/cm^3, M = 12, we get 6×10^{23} atoms/mol × 1.8 g/cm^3/12g/mol) = 9×10^{22} C/cm^3.

For a molecular solid like ice, one uses the molecular mass, $M(H_2O) = 18$. With a density of 1 g/cm^3, one obtains $n = 3.3 \times 10^{22}$ H_2O/cm^3. Note that since the water molecule contains 3 atoms, this is equivalent to 9.9×10^{22} atoms/cm^3.

Most solids have atomic densities around 6×10^{22} atoms/cm^3. The cube root of that number gives the number of atoms per centimeter, about 39 million. The mean distance between atoms is the inverse of that, or 0.25 nm. This is an important number that gives the scale of atomic structures in solids.

1.6 ELECTRONS IN ATOMS

The forces in the atom are repulsions between electrons and attraction between electrons and protons. The neutrons play no significant role. Thus, Z is what characterizes the atom.

The electrons form a cloud around the neutron, of radius of 0.05 – 2 nanometers. Electrons do not move in circular orbits, as in popular drawings, but in 'fuzzy' orbits. We cannot tell how it moves, but only say what is the probability of finding it at some distance from the nucleus. According to quantum mechanics, only certain orbits are allowed (thus, the idea of a mini planetary system is not correct). The orbits are identified by a principal quantum number n, which can be related to the size, $n = 0$ is the smallest; $n = 1, 2$ ... are larger. (They are "quantized" or discrete, being specified by integers). The angular momentum l is quantized, and so is the projection in a specific direction m. The structure of the atom is determined by the *Pauli exclusion principle,* only two electrons can be placed in an orbit with a given n, l, m one for each spin.

1.7 THE PERIODIC TABLE

Elements are categorized by placing them in the periodic table. Elements in a column share similar properties. The noble gases have *closed shells*, and so they do not gain or lose electrons near another atom. Alkalis can easily lose an electron and become a closed shell; halogens can easily gain one to form a negative ion, again with a closed shell. The propensity to form closed shells occurs in molecules, when they share electrons to close a molecular shell. Examples are H_2, N_2, and NaCl.

The ability to gain or lose electrons is termed electronegativity or electropositivity, an important factor in ionic bonds.

1.8 BONDING FORCES AND ENERGIES

The Coulomb forces are simple attractive between electrons and nuclei, repulsive between electrons and between nuclei. The force between atoms is given by a sum of all the individual forces, and the fact that the electrons are located outside the atom and the nucleus in the center.

When two atoms come very close, the force between them is always repulsive, because the electrons stay outside and the nuclei repel each other. Unless both atoms are ions of the same charge (For example, both negative) the forces between atoms is always attractive at large internuclear distances r. Since the force is repulsive at small r, and attractive at small r, there is a distance at which the force is zero. This is the equilibrium distance at which the atoms prefer to stay.

The interaction energy is the *potential* energy between the atoms. It is negative if the atoms are bound and positive if they can move away from each other. The interaction energy is the integral of the force over the separation distance, so these two quantities are directly related. The interaction energy is a *minimum* at the equilibrium position. This value of the energy is called the *bond energy*, and is the energy needed to separate completely to infinity (the work that needs to be done to overcome the attractive force). The strongest the bond energy, the hardest is to move the atoms, for instance the hardest it is to melt the solid, or to evaporate its atoms.

1.9 PRIMARY INTERATOMIC BONDS

Ionic Bonding

This is the bond when one of the atoms is negative (has an extra electron) and another is positive (has lost an electron). Then there is a strong, direct Coulomb attraction. An example is NaCl. In the molecule, there are more electrons around Cl, forming Cl^- and less around Na, forming Na^+. Ionic bonds are the strongest bonds. In real solids, ionic bonding is usually combined with covalent bonding. In this case, the fractional ionic bonding is defined as $\%\ \text{ionic} = 100 \times [1 - \exp(-0.25\ (X_A - X_B)^2]$, where X_A and X_B are the electronegativities of the two atoms, A and B, forming the molecule.

Covalent Bonding

In covalent bonding, electrons are shared between the molecules, to saturate the valency. The simplest example is the H_2 molecule, where the electrons spend more time in between the nuclei than outside, thus producing bonding.

Metallic Bonding

In metals, the atoms are ionized, loosing some electrons from the valence band. Those electrons form an *electron sea*, which binds the charged nuclei in place, in a similar way that the electrons in between the H atoms in the H_2 molecule bind the protons.

1.10 SECONDARY BONDING (van-der-Waals)

Fluctuating Induced Dipole Bonds

Since the electrons may be on one side of the atom or the other, a dipole is formed: the + nucleus at the center, and the electron outside. Since the electron moves, the dipole fluctuates. This fluctuation in atom A produces a fluctuating electric field that is felt by the electrons of an adjacent atom, B. Atom B then polarizes so that its outer electrons are on the side of the atom closest to the + side (or opposite to the – side) of the dipole in A. This bond is called van-der-Walls bonding.

Polar Molecule-Induced Dipole Bonds

A polar molecule like H_2O (H_2 are partially +, O is partially –), will induce a dipole in a nearby atom, leading to bonding.

Permanent Dipole Bonds

This is the case of the hydrogen bond in ice. The H end of the molecule is positively charged and can bond to the negative side of another dipolar molecule, like the O side of the H_2O dipole.

Molecules

If molecules formed a closed shell due to covalent bonding (like H_2, N_2) then the interaction between molecules is weak, of the van-der-Walls type. Thus, molecular solids usually have very low melting points.

Types of Solids

Crystalline material: atoms self-organize in a periodic array.

Single crystal: atoms are in a repeating or periodic array over the entire extent of the material.

Polycrystalline material: comprised of many small crystals or **grains.**

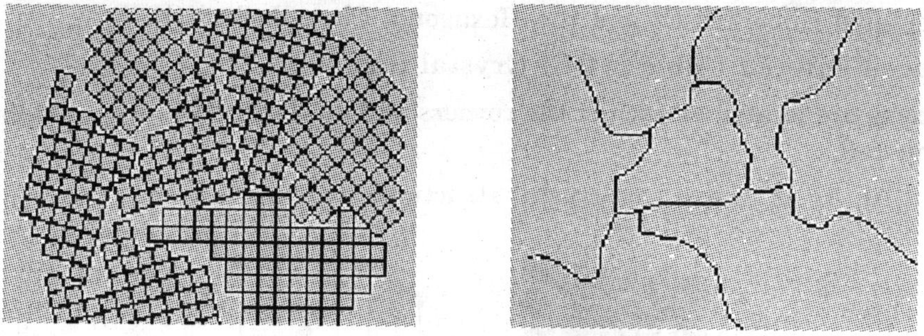

Fig. 1.6 Solids.

Amorphous: lacks a systematic atomic arrangement **Crystalline Amorphous.**
SiO_2

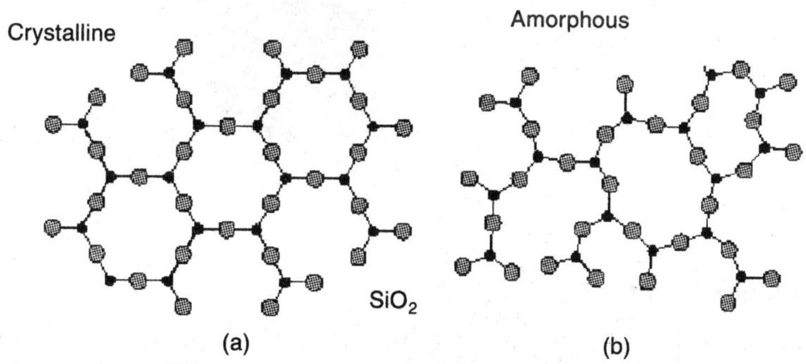

Fig. 1.7 Crystalline and amorphous.

Crystal Structure

To discuss crystalline structures it is useful to consider atoms as being hard spheres with well-defined radii. In this hard-sphere model, the shortest distance between two like atoms is one diameter. We can also consider crystalline structure as a lattice of points at atom/sphere centers.

The unit cell is the smallest structural unit or building block that can describe the crystal structure. Repetition of the unit cell generates the entire crystal.

Different choices of unit cells possible, generally choose parallelepiped unit cell with highest level of symmetry.

Metallic Crystal Structures

1. Metals are usually (poly) crystalline; although formation of amorphous metals is possible by rapid cooling.
2. As we learned in previous section, the atomic bonding in metals is non-directional. No restriction on numbers or positions of nearest-neighbor atoms. Large number of nearest neighbors and dense atomic packing.
3. **Atom (hard sphere) radius, R,** defined by ion core radius—typically 0.1–0.2 nm
4. The most common types of unit cells are the Face-Centered Cubic (FCC), the Body-Centered Cubic (BCC) and the Hexagonal Close-Packed (HCP).
5. **Face-Centered Cubic (FCC) Crystal Structure (I).**
6. Atoms are located at each of the corners and on the centers of all the faces of cubic unit cell.
7. Cu, Al, Ag, Au have this crystal structure.

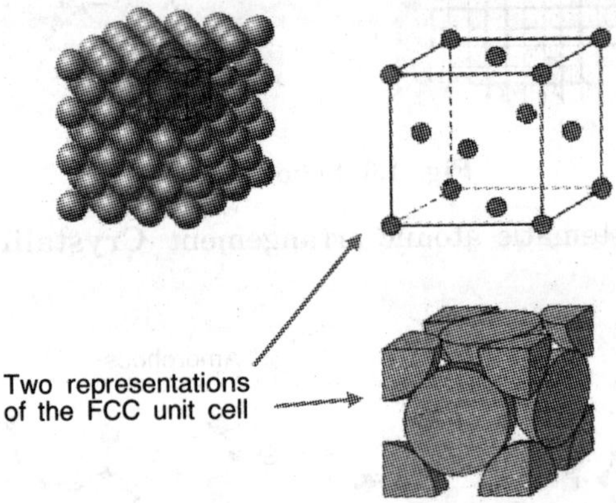

Fig. 1.8 FCC.

1.11 CRYSTALLOGRAPHY

In 1669, a Danish scientist, Nicholas Steno, discovered an important characteristic of all crystals. Steno found that, when measured at the same temperature, the angles between similar crystal faces remain constant regardless of the size or the shape of the crystal. This means that regardless of the growth conditions, the angles remains the same between corresponding faces on various crystals of the same mineral. This characteristic is called the *constancy of interfacial angels* or *Steno's law.*

Solid state physics is largely devoted to the study of crystals and their physical properties. Solids can be grouped in two basic structural categories, *amorphous* and *crystalline.* Amorphous materials have a random network of bonded atoms; there is no repeatable structure or predictable order to the atoms. An example of an amorphous material is glass where the silicon-oxygen bonds are random. Conversely, the atoms in a crystal are bonded in a regular repeating pattern that form a *lattice.* A lattice is defined as a regular spatial display of points, when refering to a crystal lattice these points represent the sites of atoms in the crystal. The smallest set of repeatable points is called a unit cell. The unit cell is an area or volume that can be translated by lattice vectors to fill space, of which there are 14 possible variations called the Bravais lattice.

An example of a crystalline material is quartz, where the silicon-oxygen bonds are repeated in exactly the same way throughout the material. One should note that glass and quartz are both composed of silicon and oxygen, in fact pure glass is often referred to as fused quartz. This shows that crystals are defined by structure and not composition. It is structure that gives crystals fascinating optical, electrical, and physical properties.

For thousands of years people have been fascinated with the beauty of crystalline materials. When most people think of crystals, they think of diamonds, quartz, ruby, or some other gem. There is something captivating about these gems, probably because they seem different from ordinary matter; however, crystals are much more than pretty stones. In fact, most solid materials are crystalline, for example, the iron exterior of a car is crystalline. Most people are oblivious to the fact that their car is crystalline because it does not look like a precious stone. The reason your car and many other solids don't look like a diamond is that they are not one big crystal as a diamond is, rather most materials are *polycrystalline.* If something is polycrystalline it is composed of many tiny interlocking crystals, these small crystals are generally randomly oriented. In the macroscopic regime, polycrystalline materials are treated as amorphous due to this random orientation, but microscopically most solids are crystalline. It is only occasionally that the individual crystals are large enough to catch our attention.

The term lattice refers to an infinite array of discrete points with an arrangement and orientation that appears exactly the same when viewed from any point of the array. The regular arrangement of atoms in a crystal constitutes a lattice; in 1848, Auguste Bravais demonstrated that in a 3-dimensional system there are fourteen possible lattices and no more. The unit cell of a Bravais lattice must meet the following criteria. For his efforts, the term bravais lattice is often used in place of point lattice.

Atoms can be gathered together as an aggregate through a number of different processes, including condensation, pressurization, chemical reaction, electro deposition, and melting. The process usually determines, at least initially, whether the collection of atoms will take to form of a gas, liquid or solid. The state usually changes as its temperature or pressure is changed. Melting is the process most often used to form an aggregate of atoms. When the temperature of a melt is lowered to a certain point, the liquid will form either a crystalline solid or and amorphous solid.

1.12 AMORPHOUS SOLIDS

A solid substance with its atoms held apart at equilibrium spacing, but with no long-range periodicity in atom location in its structure is an amorphous solid. Examples of amorphous solids are glass and some types of plastic. They are sometimes described as super cooled liquids because their molecules are arranged in a random manner some what as in the liquid state. For example, glass is commonly made from silicon dioxide or quartz sand, which has a crystalline structure. When the sand is melted and the liquid is cooled rapidly enough to avoid crystallization, an amorphous solid called a glass is formed. Amorphous solids do not show a sharp phase change from solid to liquid at a definite melting point, but rather soften gradually when they are heated. The physical properties of amorphous solids are identical in all directions along any axis so they are said to have isotropic properties.

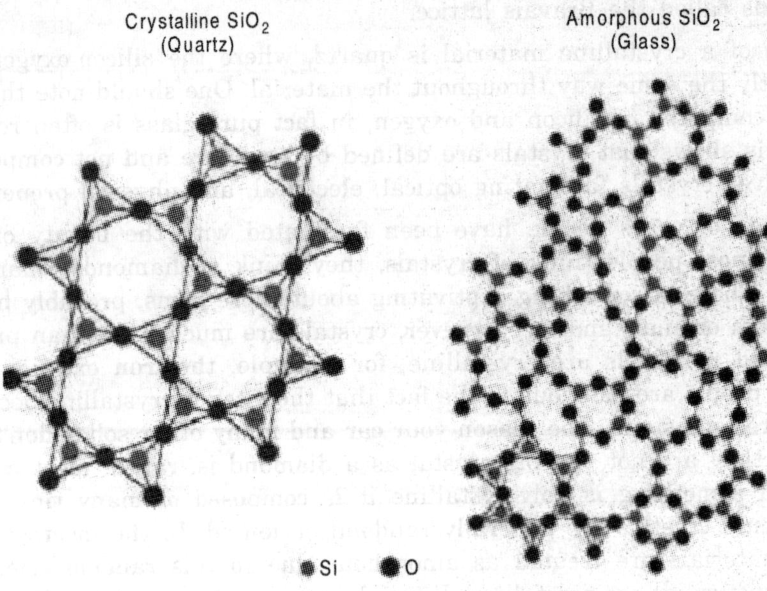

Fig. 1.9 Crystalline SiO_2.

An **amorphous solid** is a solid in which there is no long-range order of the positions of the atoms. (Solids in which there is long-range atomic order are called crystalline solids.) Most classes of solid materials can be found or prepared in an amorphous form. For instance, common window glass is a ceramic, most polymers are amorphous, and even some amorphous metallic alloys can be prepared under special processing conditions (such as rapid solidification and ion implantation). Glass is often referred to as a 'super-cooled' liquid.

There are many ways in which amorphous solids can be made. If a liquid is cooled rapidly enough to avoid crystallization, an amorphous solid called a glass is formed below the glass transition temperature. Amorphous solids produced by other routes, such as ion implantation are, technically speaking, not glasses. In common parlance, the term glass refers to amorphous oxides, and especially silicates (compounds based on silicon and oxygen). To avoid confusion, other types of glass often are referred to with a modifier, such as the term 'metallic glass' to refer to amorphous metallic alloys.

It is difficult to make a distinction between truly amorphous solids and crystalline solids in which the size of the crystals is very small (less than two nanometers). Even amorphous materials have some short-range order among the atomic positions (over length scales of about one nanometer). Furthermore, in very small crystals a large fraction of the atoms are located at or near the surface of the crystal; relaxation of the surface and interfacial effects distort the atomic positions, decreasing the structural order. Even the most advanced structural characterization techniques, such as x-ray diffraction and transmission electron microscopy, have difficulty in distinguishing between amorphous and crystalline structures on these length scales.

The transition from the liquid state to the glass, at a temperature below the equilibrium melting point of the material, is called the glass transition. From a practical point of view, the glass transition temperature is defined empirically as the temperature at which the viscosity of the liquid exceeds a certain value (commonly 10^{13} Pascal-seconds). The transition temperature depends on cooling rate, with the glass transition occurring at higher temperatures for faster cooling rates. The precise nature of the glass transition is the subject of ongoing research. While it is clear that the glass transition is not a first-order thermodynamic transition (such as melting), there is debate as to whether it is a higher-order transition, or merely a kinetic effect. Some examples of amorphous solids are glass and plastic

1.13 CRYSTALLINE SOLIDS

More than 90% of naturally occurring and artificially prepared solids are crystalline. Minerals, sand, clay, limestone, metals, carbon (diamond and graphite), salts (NaCl, KCl etc.), all have crystalline structures. A crystal is a regular, repeating arrangement of atoms or molecules. The majority of solids, including all metals, adopt a crystalline arrangement because the amount of stabilization achieved by anchoring interactions between neighboring particles is at its greatest when the particles adopt regular (rather than random) arrangements. In the crystalline arrangement, the particles pack efficiently together to minimize the total intermolecular energy.

The regular repeating pattern that the atoms arrange in is called the crystalline lattice. The scanning tunneling microscope (STM) makes it possible to image the electron cloud associated individual atoms at the surface of a material. Below is an STM image of a platinum surface showing the regular alignment of atoms.

1.14 CRYSTAL STRUCTURE

Crystal structures may be conveniently specified by describing the arrangement within the solid of a small representative group of atoms or molecules, called the 'unit cell.' By multiplying identical unit cells in three directions, the location of all the particles in the crystal is determined. In nature, 14 different types of crystal structures or lattices are found. The simplest crystalline unit cell to picture is the cubic, where the atoms are lined up in a square, 3D grid. The unit cell is simply a box with an atom at each corner. Simple cubic crystals are relatively rare, mostly because they tend to easily distort. However, many crystals form body-centered-cubic (bcc) or face-centered-cubic (fcc) structures, which are cubic with either an extra atom centered in the cube or centered in each face of the cube. Most metals form bcc, fcc or hexagonal close packed (hcp) structures; however, the structure can change depending on temperature. Crystalline structure is important because it contributes to the properties of a material. For example, it is easier for planes of atoms to slide by each other if those planes are closely packed. Therefore, lattice structures with closely packed planes allow more plastic deformation than those that are not closely packed. Additionally, cubic lattice structures allow slippage to occur more easily than non-cubic lattices. This is because their symmetry provides closely packed planes in several directions. A face-centered cubic crystal structure will exhibit more ductility (deform more readily under load before breaking) than a body-centered cubic structure. The bcc lattice, although cubic, is not closely packed and forms strong metals. Alpha-iron and tungsten have the bcc form. The fcc lattice is both cubic and closely packed and forms more ductile materials. Gamma-iron, silver, gold, and lead have fcc structures. Finally, HCP lattices are closely packed, but not cubic. HCP metals like cobalt and zinc are not as ductile as the fcc metals.

Characteristic Features of a Crystal Structure

What does it mean to know the crystal structure of a compound?

It means that we know the location (with respect to each other) and identity of all atoms in the compound.

How do we specify the crystal structure of a compound?

In an exact sense the complete crystal structure is specified by the crystallographic description, which includes the space group, unit cell parameters, occupied Wyckoff sites and fractional coordinates. For example, consider the crystal structure of LiF:

Space Group = Fm`3m

Atom	Site	x	y	z
Li	4a	0	0	0
F	4b	1/2	1/2	1/2

In a more approximate and descriptive sense we often describe a compound's structure by its structure type. In this case LiF adopts the rock salt (or NaCl) structure type. By this statement we mean that LiF has the same space group and occupied Wyckoff sites as all other rock salt compounds (including NaCl). If we know what the rock salt structure looks like, this description gives us an immediate image of the crystal structure, including the local environment and symmetry of each ion. However, it does not provide any specific is about the size of the unit cell, nor of the bond distances. Part of what we will be concerned with in this section of the course is identifying and describing some of the more important crystal structures in solid state chemistry.

Unit Cell

A unit cell is a spatial arrangement of atoms which is tiled in three-dimensional space to describe the crystal. The positions of the atoms inside the unit cell are described by the asymmetric unit or **basis**, the set of atomic positions (x_i, y_i, z_i) measured from a lattice point. For each crystal structure there is a *conventional unit cell*, usually chosen to make the resulting lattice as symmetric as possible. However, the conventional unit cell is not always the smallest possible choice. A **primitive unit cell** of a particular crystal structure is the smallest possible unit cell one can construct such that, when tiled, it completely fills space

1.15 SIMPLE CUBIC UNIT CELL

The simple cubic unit cell is a cube (all sides of the same length and all face perpendicular to each other) with an atom at each corner of the unit cell. The unit cell completely describes the structure of the solid, which can be regarded as an almost endless repetition of the unit cell. The volume of the unit cell is readily calculated from its shape and dimensions. This calculation is particularly easy for a unit cell that is cubic. The dimensions of the unit cell are dictated by the size of the atoms in the cell. In the case of the simple cubic unit cell the atom lying on a corner is in contact with each atom on a neighboring corner. Thus the side of the unit cell has a length of $2r$, where r is the radius of an atom.

Atoms, of course, do not have well-defined bounds, thus the radius of an atom is somewhat ambiguous. In the context of crystal structures, the diameter ($2r$) of an atom can be defined as the center-to-center distance between two atoms packed as tightly together as possible. This provides a type of effective radius for the atom and is sometime called the atomic radius. A more challenging task is to determine the number of atoms that lie in the unit cell. As described above, an atom is centered on each corner. In this case, however, none of these atoms lies completely within the cell. Part of each atom lies within the unit cell and the remainder lies outside the unit cell. In determining the number of atoms inside the unit cell, one must count only that portion of an atom that actually lies within the unit cell. The density of a solid is the mass of all the atoms in the unit cell divided by the volume of the unit cell.

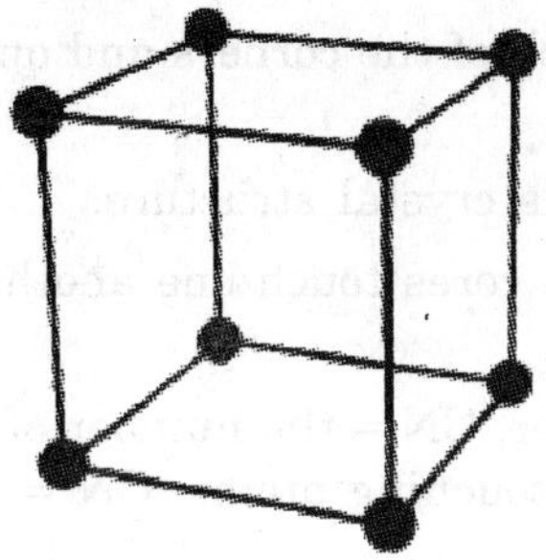

Fig. 1.10 Simple cubic unit cell.

1.16 FACE-CENTERED CUBIC UNIT CELL

Silver crystallizes in a cubic closest-packed structure. The unit cell for this structure is cubic (all sides of the same length and all face perpendicular to each other) with a silver atom at each corner of the unit cell and a silver atom in the center of each face of the unit cell. This unit cell is also called a face-centered cubic (fcc) unit cell. The unit cell completely describes the structure of the solid, which can be regarded as an almost endless repetition of the unit cell.

The volume of the unit cell is readily calculated from its shape and dimensions. This calculation is particularly easy for a unit cell that is cubic. The dimensions of the unit cell are dictated by the size of the atoms in the cell. In the case of the fcc unit cell the atoms lying along the diagonal of each face are in contact with each other. Thus the diagonal of the face of the unit cell has a length of $4r$, where r is the radius of a silver atom.

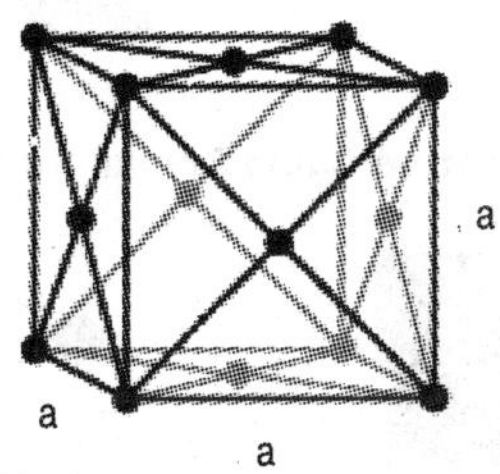

Fig. 1.11 Face centered cubic unit cell.

Atoms, of course, do not have well-defined bounds, thus the radius of an atom is somewhat ambiguous. In the context of crystal structures, the diameter ($2r$) of an atom can be defined as the center-to-center distance between two atoms packed as tightly together as possible. This provides a type of effective radius for the atom and is sometime called the atomic radius. A more challenging task is to determine the number of atoms that lie in the unit cell. As described above, an atom is centered on each corner and in the middle of each face of the fcc unit cell. In this case, however, none of these atoms lies completely within the cell. Part of each atom lies within the unit cell and the remainder lies outside the unit cell. In determining the number of atoms inside the unit cell, one must count only that portion of an atom that actually lies within the unit cell. The density of a solid is the mass of all the atoms in the unit cell divided by the volume of the unit cell.

Face-Centered Cubic (FCC) Crystal Structure (I)

1. Atoms are located at each of the corners and on the centers of all the faces of cubic unit cell.
2. Cu, Al, Ag, Au have this crystal structure.
3. The hard spheres or ion cores touch one another across a face diagonal. The cube edge length, $a = 4R/\sqrt{2}$
4. The co-ordination number, CN = the number of closest neighbors to which an atom is bonded = number of touching atoms, CN = 12.

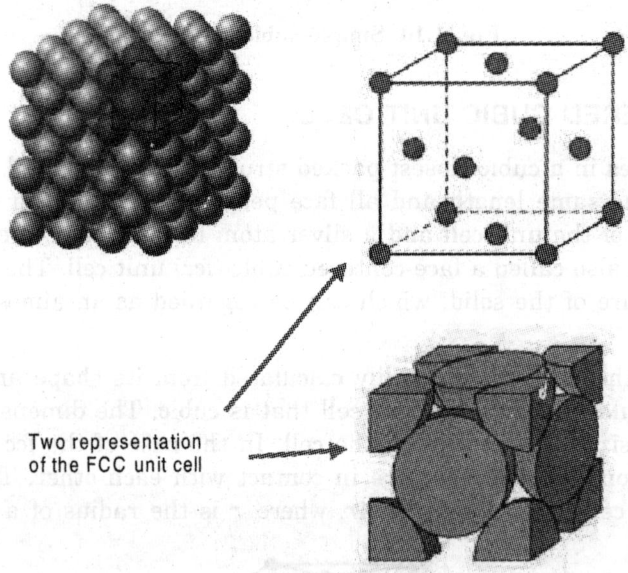

Face-Centred Cubic Crystal Structure (II)

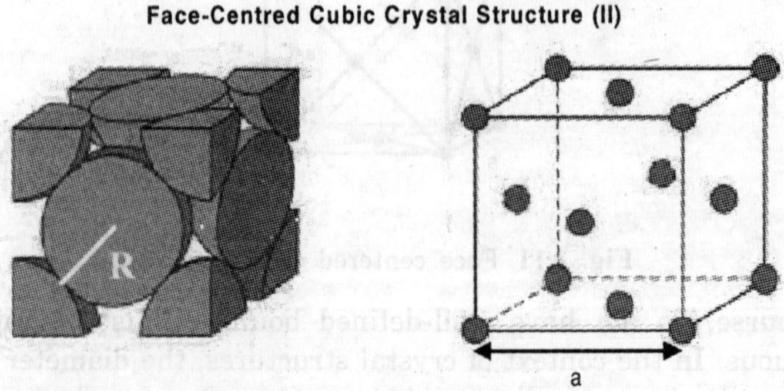

Fig. 1.12 FCC structure.

5. Number of atoms per unit cell, $n = 4$. (For an atom that is shared with m adjacent unit cells, we only count a fraction of the atom, 1/m). In FCC unit cell we have:
6. 6 face atoms shared by two cells: $6 \times 1/2 = 3$.
7. 8 corner atoms shared by eight cells: $8 \times 1/8 = 1$.

   Atomic packing factor, APF = fraction of volume occupied by hard spheres = (Sum of atomic volumes)/(Volume of cell) = 0.74 (maximum possible).

   Corner and face atoms in the unit cell are equivalent.
8. FCC crystal has APF of 0.74, the maximum packing for.
9. A system equal-sized spheres. FCC is a close-packed structure.
10. FCC can be represented by a stack of close-packed planes (planes with highest density of atoms).

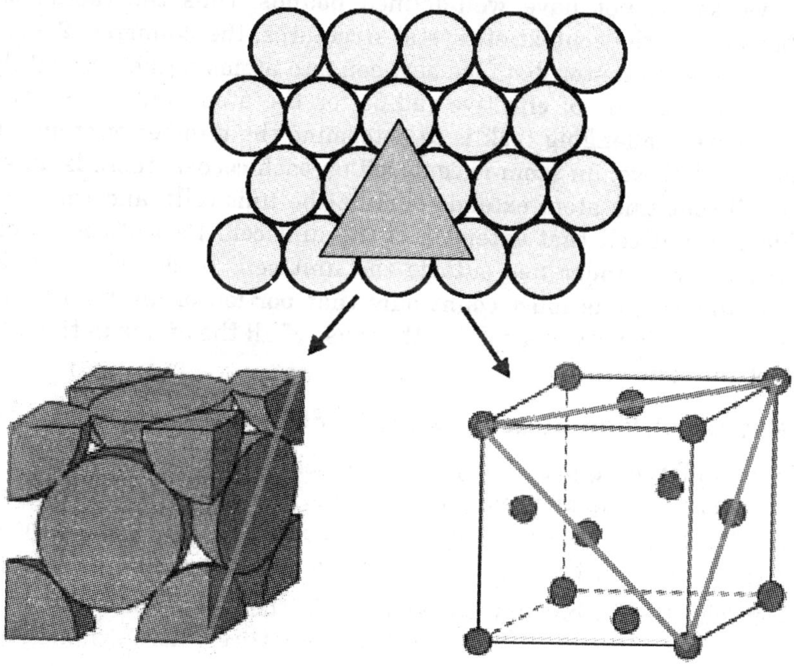

Fig. 1.13 FCC Structure.

Hexagonal Closest-Packed Structure

The unit cell for the hexagonal closest-packed structure has a diamond-shaped or hexagonal base with sides of equal length. The base is perpendicular to the longest side of the unit cell. An atom is centered on each corner of the unit cell. In addition, an atom is centered inside the unit cell, and there are two other atoms whose centers lie outside the unit cell but whose bodied penetrate the unit cell. The unit cell completely describes the structure of the solid, which can be regarded as an almost endless repetition of the unit cell.

The volume of the unit cell is readily calculated from its shape and dimensions. The volume is the product of the area of the base and the height of the cell. The lengths of the sides of the base are the same: $a = b$. The height of the unit cell is c. Because the atoms are in "physical contact", these lengths are directly related to the atomic radius, r. Atoms on adjacent corners of the base are in contact, thus $a = b = 2r$. The height of the unit cell, which more challenging to calculate, is $c = 4r(2/3)^{1/2}$. See if you can derive this value.

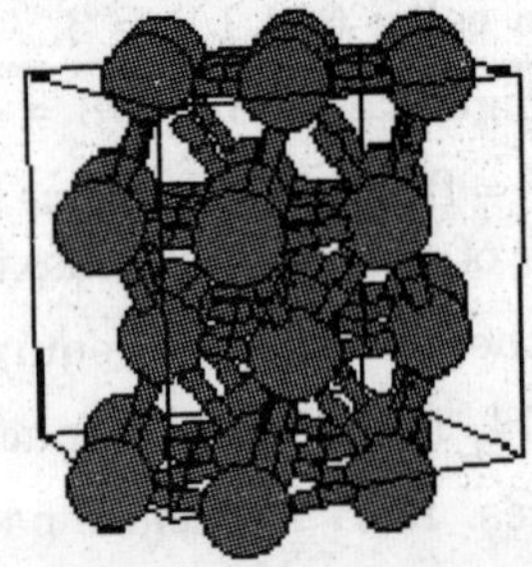

Fig. 1.14 Hexagonal closed packed unit cell.

Atoms, of course, do not have well-defined bounds, thus the radius of an atom is somewhat ambiguous. In the context of crystal structures, the diameter ($2r$) of an atom can be defined as the center-to-center distance between two atoms packed as tightly together as possible. This provides a type of effective radius for the atom and is sometime called the atomic radius. A more challenging task is to determine the number of atoms that lie in the unit cell. As described above, an atom is centered on each corner, there is an atom centered inside the unit cell (but this atom extends outside the unit cell), and there are two atoms centered outside the unit cell that extend into the unit cell. Part of each atom lies within the unit cell and the remainder lies outside the unit cell. In determining the number of atoms inside the unit cell, one must count only that portion of an atom that actually lies within the unit cell. The density of a solid is the mass of all the atoms in the unit cell divided by the volume of the unit cell.

Primary Metallic Crystalline Structures (BCC, FCC, HCP)

There are 14 different types of crystal unit cell structures or lattices are found in nature. However, most metals and many other solids have unit cell structures described as body center cubic (bcc), face centered cubic (fcc) or hexagonal close packed (hcp). Since these structures are most common, they will be discussed in more detail.

In crystalography the **cubic crystal system** is the most symmetric of the 7 crystal system. The system is composed of the three Bravais lattice whose symmetry group is that of a cube.

The three Bravais lattices that form the cubic crystal system are:

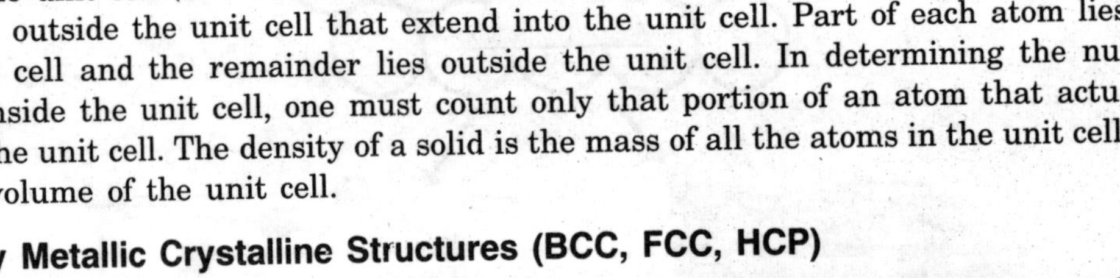

Fig. 1.15 (*a*) Simple cubic structure (*b*) Body centered cubic (*c*) Face centered cubic.

Body-Centered Cubic (BCC) Structure

The body-centered cubic unit cell has atoms at each of the eight corners of a cube (like the cubic unit cell) plus one atom in the center of the cube (left image below). Each of the corner atoms is the corner of another cube so the corner atoms are shared among eight unit cells. It is said to have a *co-ordination number of 8*. The bcc unit cell consists of a net total of two atoms; one in the center and eight eighths from corners atoms as shown in the middle image below (middle image below). The image below highlights a unit cell in a larger section of the lattice.

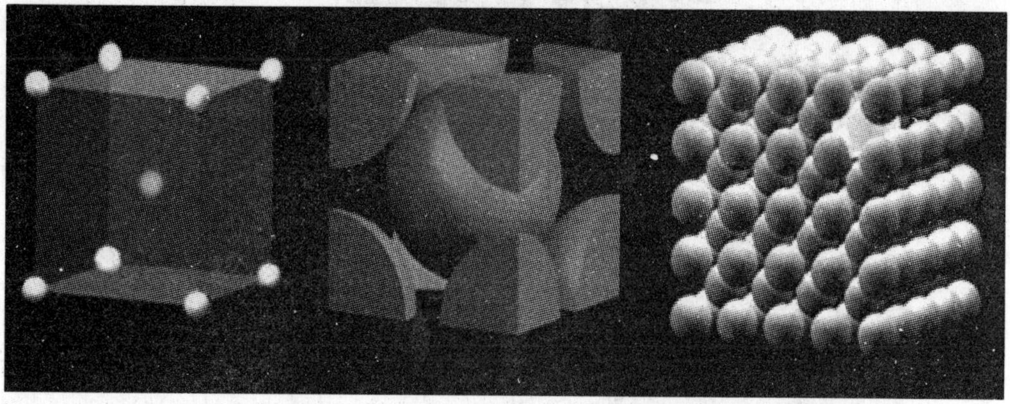

Fig. 1.16 BCC.

The bcc arrangement does not allow the atoms to pack together as closely as the fcc or hcp arrangements. The bcc structure is often the high temperature form of metals that are close-packed at lower temperatures. The volume of atoms in a cell per the total volume of a cell is called the **packing factor.** The bcc unit cell has a packing factor of 0.68.

Some of the materials that have a bcc structure include lithium, sodium, potassium, chromium, barium, vanadium, alpha-iron and tungsten. Metals which have a bcc structure are usually harder and less malleable than close-packed metals such as gold. When the metal is deformed, the planes of atoms must slip over each other, and this is more difficult in the bcc structure. It should be noted that there are other important mechanisms for hardening materials, such as introducing impurities or defects which make slipping more difficult. These hardening mechanisms will be discussed latter.

Body-Centered Cubic (BCC) Crystal Structure (I)

Atom at each corner and at center of cubic unit cell Cr, α-Fe, Mo have this crystal structure.

1. The hard spheres touch one another along cube diagonal,
2. The cube edge length, $a = 4r/\sqrt{3}$
3. The co-ordination number, CN = 8
4. Number of atoms per unit cell, $n = 2$
5. Center atom (1) shared by no other cells: $1 \times 1 = 1$
6. 8 corner atoms shared by eight cells: $8 \times 1/8 = 1$
7. Atomic packing factor, APF = 0.68.

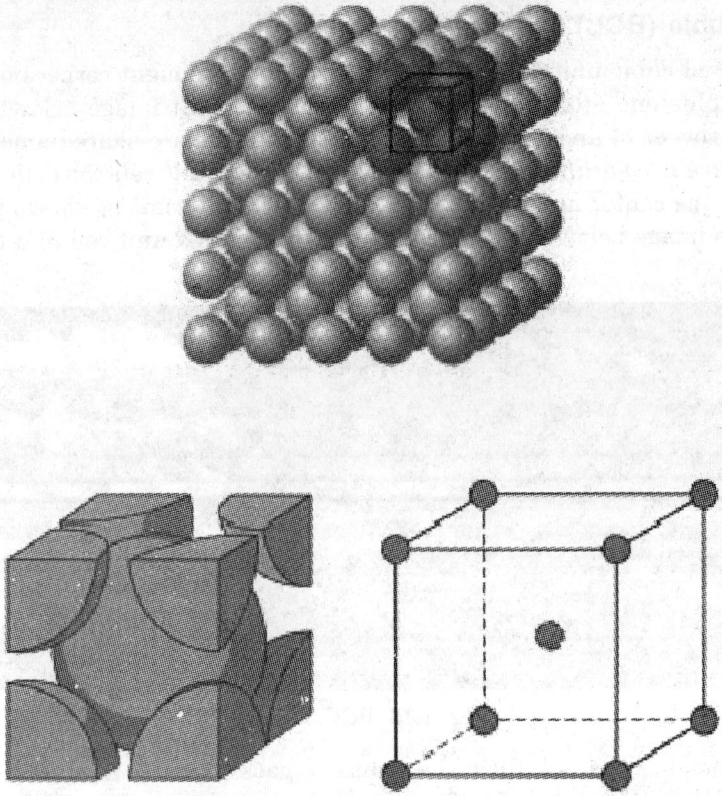

Fig. 1.17 BCC Structure.

Face Centered Cubic (FCC) Structure

The face centered cubic structure has atoms located at each of the corners and the centers of all the cubic faces (left image below). Each of the corner atoms is the corner of another cube so the corner atoms are shared among eight unit cells. Additionally, each of its six face centered atoms is shared with an adjacent atom. Since 12 of its atoms are shared, it is said to have a *co-ordination number of 12*. The fcc unit cell consists of a net total of four atoms; eight eighths from corners atoms and six halves of the face atoms as shown in the middle image above. The image below highlights a unit cell in a larger section of the lattice.

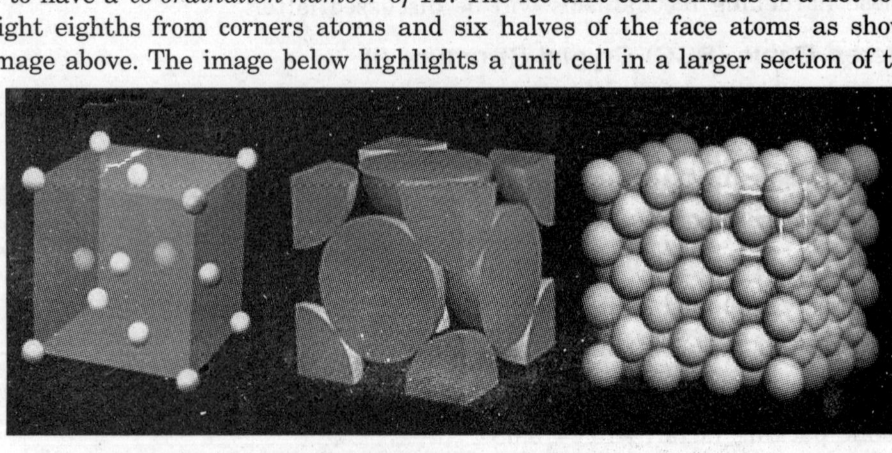

Fig. 1.18 FCC Structure.

In the fcc structure (Fig. 1.18) (and the hcp structure) the atoms can pack closer together than they can in the bcc structure. The atoms from one layer nest themselves in the empty space between the atoms of the adjacent layer. To picture packing arrangement, imagine a box filled with a layer of balls that are aligned in columns and rows. When a few additional balls are tossed in the box, they will not balance directly on top of the balls in the first layer but instead will come to rest in the pocket created between four balls of the bottom layer. As more balls are added they will pack together to fill up all the pockets. ***The packing factor*** (the volume of atoms in a cell per the total volume of a cell) is ***0.74*** for fcc crystals. Some of the metals that have the fcc structure include aluminium, copper, gold, iridium, lead, nickel, platinum and silver.

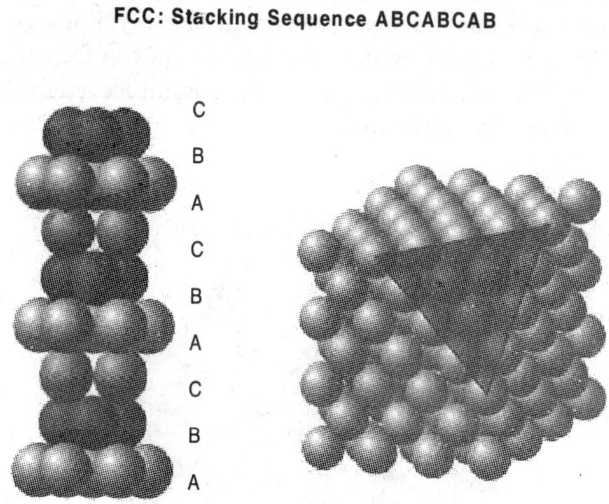

Fig. 1.19 FCC ABCABCABC.

Hexagonal Close Packed (HCP) Structure

Another common close packed structure is the hexagonal close pack. The hexagonal structure of alternating layers is shifted so its atoms are aligned to the gaps of the preceding layer. The atoms from one layer nest themselves in the empty space between the atoms of the adjacent layer just like in the fcc structure. However, instead of being a cubic structure, the pattern is hexagonal. (See image below). The difference between the HCP and FCC structure is discussed later in this section.

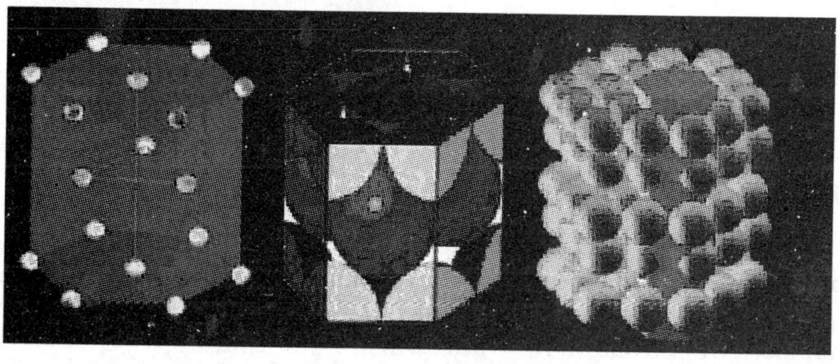

Fig. 1.20 HCP.

The hcp structure has three layers of atoms. In each the top and bottom layer, there are six atoms that arrange themselves in the shape of a hexagon and a seventh atom that sits in the middle of the hexagon. The middle layer has three atoms nestle in the triangular "grooves" of the top and bottom plane. Note that there are six of these "grooves" surrounding each atom in the hexagonal plane, but only three of them can be filled by atoms.

As shown in the middle image above, there are six atoms in the hcp unit cell. Each of the 12 atoms in the corners of the top and bottom layers contribute 1/6 atom to the unit cell, the two atoms in the center of the hexagon of both the top and bottom layers each contribute ½ atom and each of the three atom in the middle layer contribute 1 atom. The image on the right above attempts to show several hcp unit cells in a larger lattice.

The *co-ordination number* of the atoms in this structure is *12*. There are six nearest neighbors in the same close packed layer, three in the layer above and three in the layer below. The **packing factor is 0.74,** which is the same as the fcc unit cell. The hcp structure is very common for elemental metals and some examples include beryllium, cadmium, magnesium, titanium, zinc and zirconium.

HCP: Stacking Sequence ABABAB

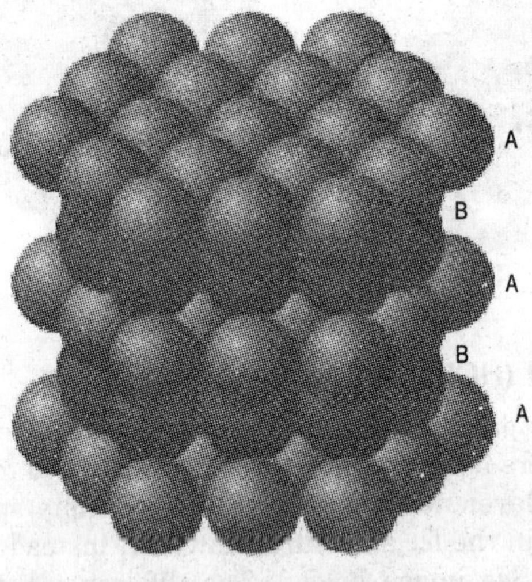

Fig. 1.21 HCP ABABA.

Third plane is placed directly above the first plane of atoms. Since the entire crystal can be generated by the repetition of the unit cell, the density of a crystalline material = the density of the unit cell ρ = (atoms in the unit cell, *n*) . (mass of an atom, M)/(the volume of the cell, Vc)

Density Computations

Atoms in the unit cell, n = 2 (BCC); 4 (FCC); 6 (HCP)

Mass of an atom, M = Atomic weight, A, in amu (or g/mol) is given in the periodic table. To translate mass from amu to grams we have to divide the atomic weight in amu by the Avogadro number NA = 6.023×10^{-23} atoms/mol.

The volume of the cell, $V_c = a^3$ (FCC and BCC)

$a = 2r\sqrt{2}$ (FCC); $a = 4r/\sqrt{3}$ (BCC)

where R is the atomic radius

Thus, the formula for the density is:

$$\rho = nA/(V_c\, N_A)$$

Hexagonal Close-Packed Crystal Structure (I)

1. HCP is one more common structure of metallic crystals
2. Six atoms form regular hexagon, surrounding one atom in center. Another plane is situated halfway up unit cell (*c*-axis), with 3 additional atoms situated at interstices of hexagonal (close-packed) planes
3. Cd, Mg, Zn, Ti have this crystal structure.
4. Unit cell has two lattice parameters *a* and *c*. Ideal ratio $c/a = 1.633$
5. The co-ordination number, CN = 12 (same as in FCC)
6. Number of atoms per unit cell, $n = 6$, mid-plane atoms shared by no other cells: $3 \times 1 = 3$
7. 12 hexagonal corner atoms shared by 6 cells: $12 \times 1/6 = 2$ top/bottom plane center atoms shared by 2 cells: $2 \times 1/2 = 1$
8. Atomic packing factor, APF = 0.74 (same as in FCC)
9. All atoms are equivalent

Hexagonal Close-Packed Crystal Structure (II)

1. Unit cell has two lattice parameters *a* and *c*. Ideal ratio $c/a = 1.633$
2. The co-ordination number, CN = 12 (same as in FCC)
3. Number of atoms per unit cell, $n = 6$, mid-plane atoms shared by no other cells: $3 \times 1 = 3$
4. 12 hexagonal corner atoms shared by 6 cells: $12 \times 1/6 = 2$ top/bottom plane center atoms shared by 2 cells: $2 \times 1/2 = 1$
5. Atomic packing factor, APF = 0.74 (same as in FCC)
6. All atoms are equivalent

Bravais Lattices

In geometry and crystallography, a **Bravais lattice** is an infinite set of points generated by a set of discrete translation operations. A Bravais lattice looks exactly the same no matter from which point one views it.

The position vectors of a Bravais lattice in three dimensions are given by

$$R = n_1\, a_1 + n_2\, a_2 + n_3\, a_3$$

where n_1, n_2, and n_3 are integers and a_1, a_2, and a_3 are three non-coplanar vectors, called *primitive vectors*. The Bravais lattices were studied by M. L. Frankenheim in 1842 who found that there were 15 Bravais lattices. This was corrected to 14 by A. Bravais in 1845.

When classified by spacegroup, there are 14 unique Bravais lattices in three dimensions. These can be grouped according to their crystal system, or crystallographic point group.

Table 1.1. Discription of the 14 Bravais lattices among the seven crystal systems

Crystal System	*No.*	*Unit Cell*	*Coordinate Description*
Triclinic	1	Primitive	**a** ≠ **b**≠ **c** α ≠ β≠ γ
Monoclinic	2	Primitive	**a** ≠ **b**≠ **c**
	3	Body Centered	α = β = 90°≠ γ
	4	Primitive	**a** ≠ **b** ≠ **c**
Orthorhombic	5	Base Centered	α = β = γ = 90°
	6	Body Centered	
	7	Face Centered	
	8	Primitive	**a** ≠ **b**≠ **c**
Tetragonal	9	Body Centered	α = β = γ = 90° **a** = **b** ≠ **c**
Trigonal	10	Primitive	α = β = γ < 120°, ≠ 90°
Hexagonal	11	Primitive	**a** = **b** ≠ **c** α = β = 90°, γ = 120°
	12	Primitive	**a** = **b** ≠ **c**
Cubic	13	Body Centered	α = β = γ = 90°
	14	Face Centered	

where the three primitive lattice vectors a_i are not all in the same plane, and the n's are integers. The primitive lattice vectors can be used to generate the lattice by varying the integers. The smallest parallelepiped with a lattice point at each corner is called the primitive unit cell of the crystal. There is only one lattice point per unit cell since the points at the eight corners are shared by eight adjacent unit cells.

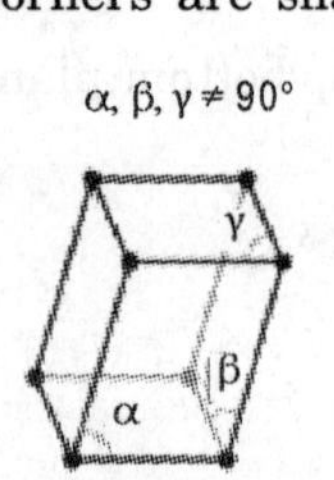

Triclinic

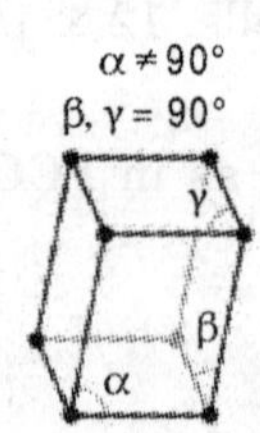

Monoclinic-simple

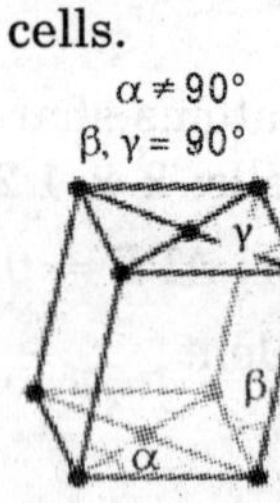

Monoclinic-centered

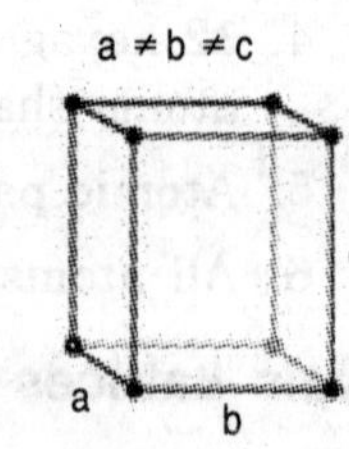

Orthorhombic-simple

Orthorhombic-base centered

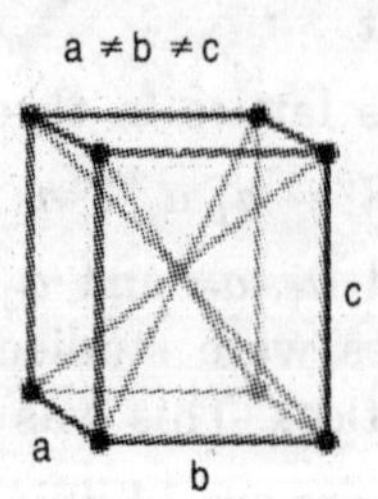

Orthorhombic-body centered

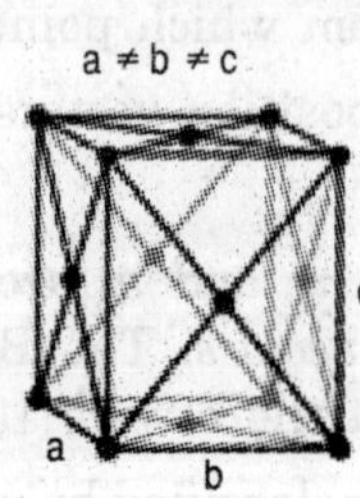

Orthorhombic-face centered

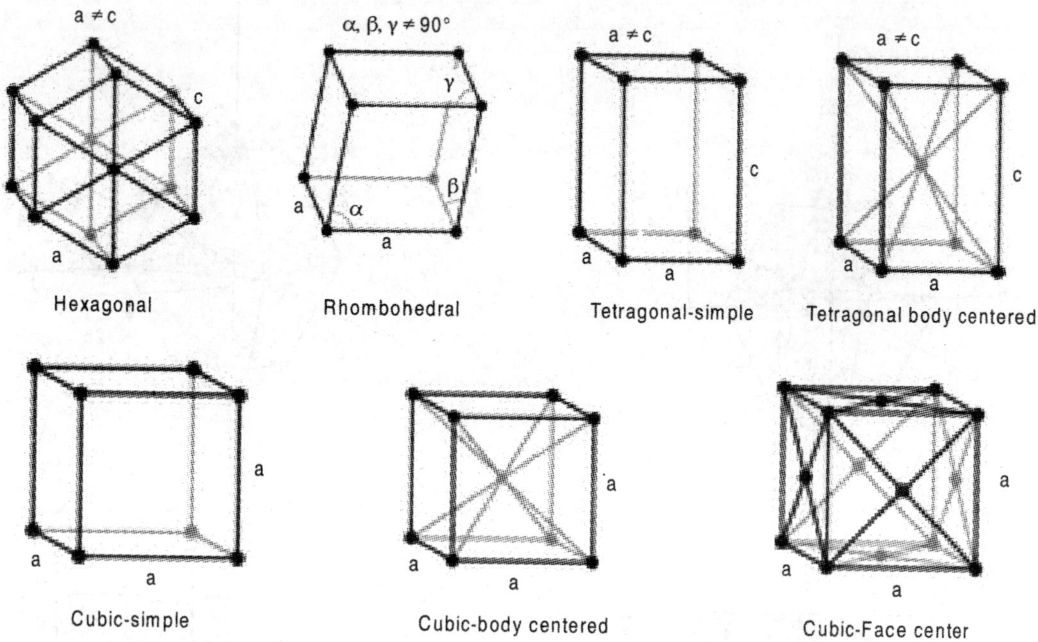

Fig. 1.22 Unit cell.

1.17 MILLER INDICES

It is often necessary to convey information about a particular crystal face, or crystal form, or other spatial information about crystals and their symmetry. The scheme employed is to imagine how a face intersects, or doesn't intersect, the crystal's axes. The relative intersection ratios are inverted to create a Miller index. It is important to specify the orientation of crystal planes and directions because crystals may have different properties along different directions. A crystal plane is specified by its Miller indices.

Rules for Miller Indices

- Determine the intercepts of the face along the crystallographic axes, *in terms of unit cell dimensions.*
- Take the reciprocals
- Clear fractions
- Reduce to lowest terms

For example, if the *x*-, *y*-, and *z*- intercepts are 2, 1, and 3, the Miller indices are calculated as:

- Take reciprocals: 1/2, 1/1, 1/3
- Clear fractions (multiply by 6): 3, 6, 2
- Reduce to lowest terms (already there)

Thus, the Miller indices are 3, 6, 2. If a plane is parallel to an axis, its intercept is at infinity and its Miller index is zero. A generic Miller index is denoted by (*hkl*).

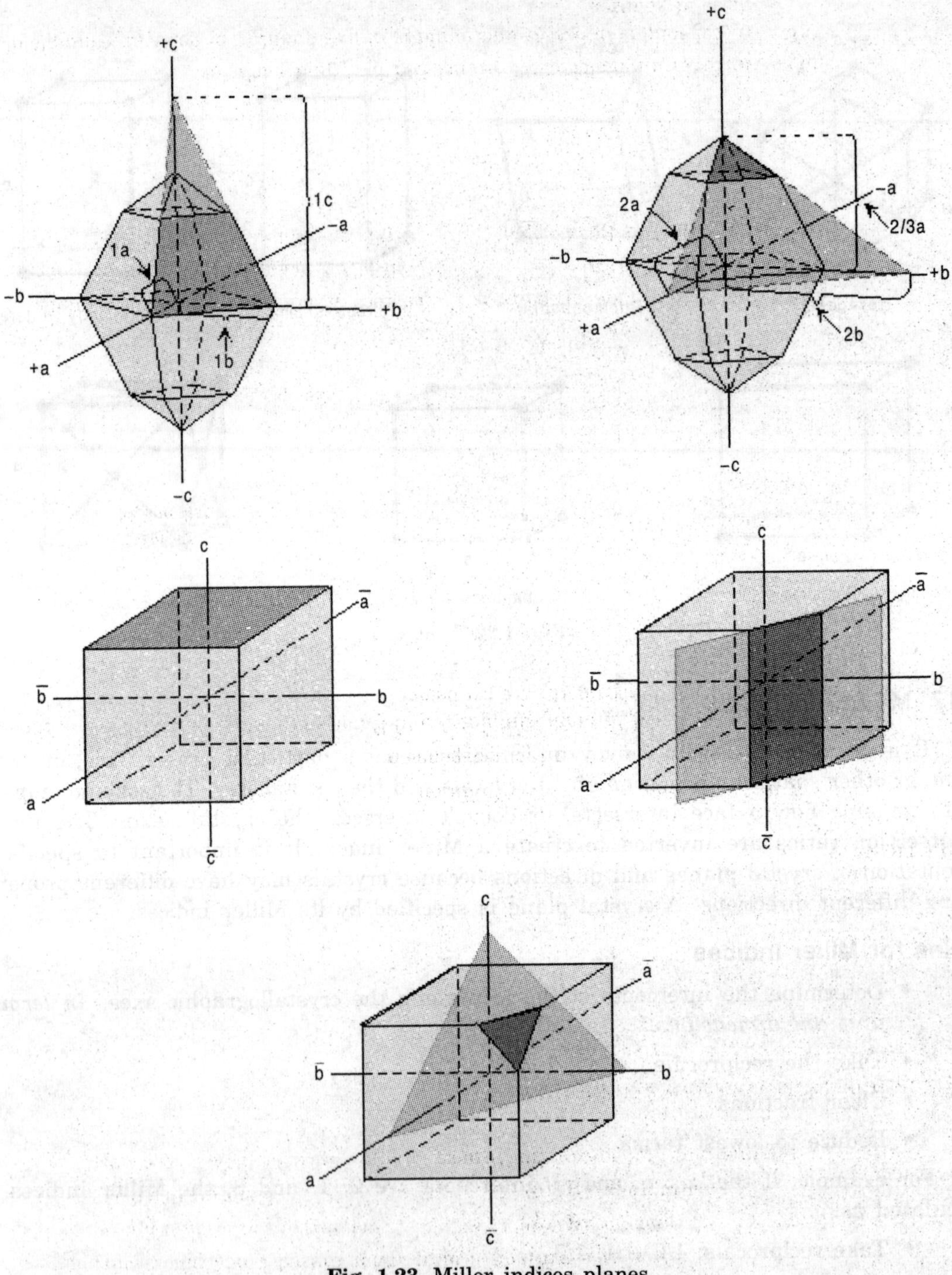

Fig. 1.23 Miller indices planes.

The method by which indices are determined is best shown by example. Recall, that there are three axes in crystallographic systems (*except sometimes in the hexagonal system adopts a convention where there are four axes). Miller indices are represented by a set of 3 integer numbers.

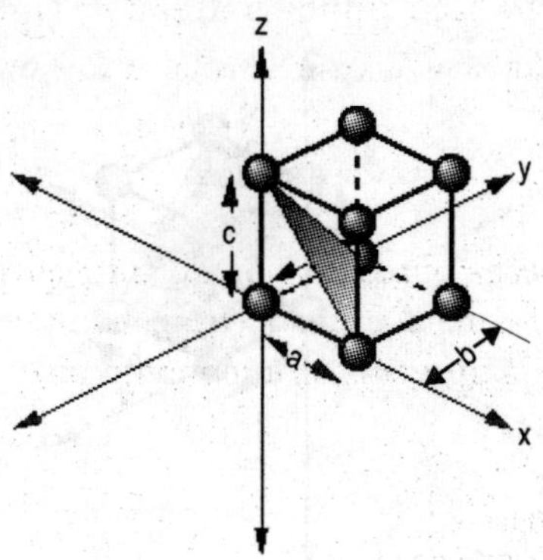

	a	b	c
Intercept length	1	1	1
Reciprocal	$\frac{1}{1}$	$\frac{1}{1}$	$\frac{1}{1}$
Cleared fraction	1	1	1
Miller indice		(111)	

Fig. 1.24 111 Miller indices planes.

If you want to describe the orientation of a crystal face or a plane of atoms within a crystal lattice, then there are series of steps that will lead you to its notation using Miller indices.

1. The first thing that must be ascertained are the fractional intercepts that the plane/face makes with the crystallographic axes. In other words, how far along the unit cell lengths does the plane intersect the axis. In the figure above the plane intercepts each axis at exact one unit length.
2. Step two involves taking the reciprocal of the fractional intercept of each unit length for each axis. In the figure above the values are all 1/1.
3. Finally the fractions are cleared (*i.e.*, make 1 as the common denominator).
4. These integer numbers are then parenthetically enclosed and designate that specific crystallographic plane within the lattice. Since the unit cell repeats in space, the notation actually represents a family of planes, all with the same orientation. In the figure above the Miller indices for the plane is (111).

Example of the (101) Plane

This becomes immediately apparent when we consider the case of the (101) plane. In this case the plane intercepts the *a* axis at one unit length and also the *c* axis at one unit length. The plane however, never intersects the *b* axis. In other words, it can be said that the intercept to the *b* axis is infinity. The intercepts are then designated as 1, infinity, 1. The reciprocals are then 1/2, 1/infinity, 1/1. Knowing 1/infinity = 0 then the indices become (101).

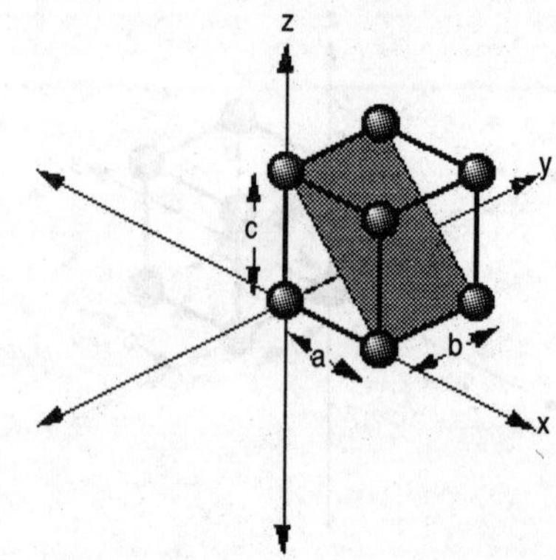

	a	b	c
Intercept length	1	∞	1
Reciprocal	$\frac{1}{1}$	$\frac{1}{\infty}$	$\frac{1}{1}$
Cleared fraction	1	0	1
Miller indice		(101)	

Fig. 1.25 101 Miller indices planes.

If a plane has negative intercept, the negative number is denoted by a bar above the number. *Never alter negative numbers.* For example, do not divide –1, –1, –1 by –1 to get 1, 1, 1. This implies symmetry that the crystal may not have.

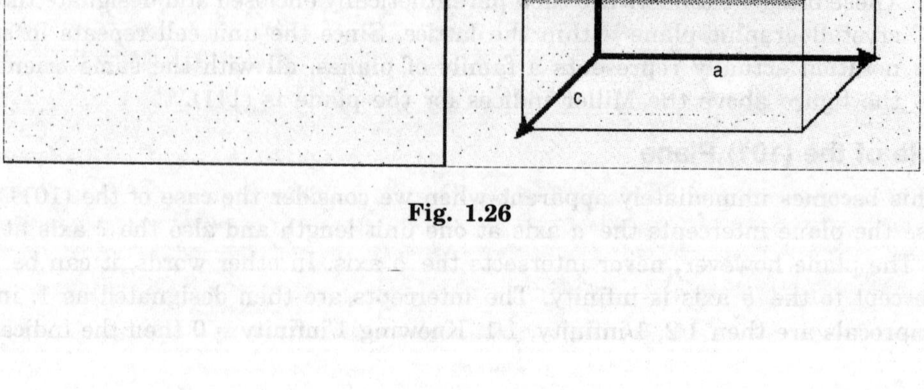

Fig. 1.26

Example of the (102) plane

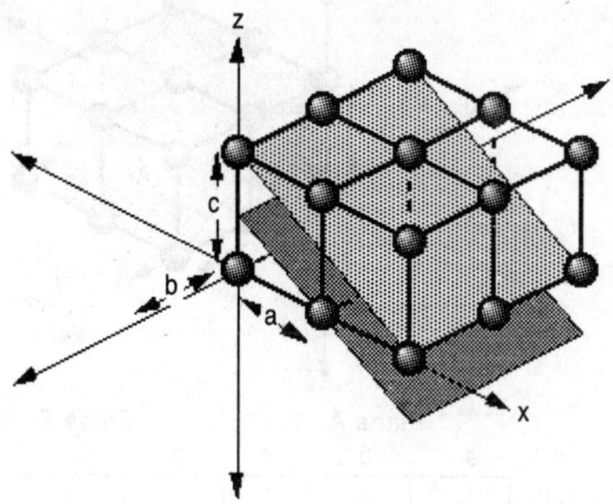

	a	b	c
Intercept length	1	∞	1/2
Reciprocal	$\frac{1}{1}$	$\frac{1}{\infty}$	$\frac{1}{1/2}$
Cleared fraction	1	0	1
Miller indice		(102)	

(a) 102 Miller indices planes.

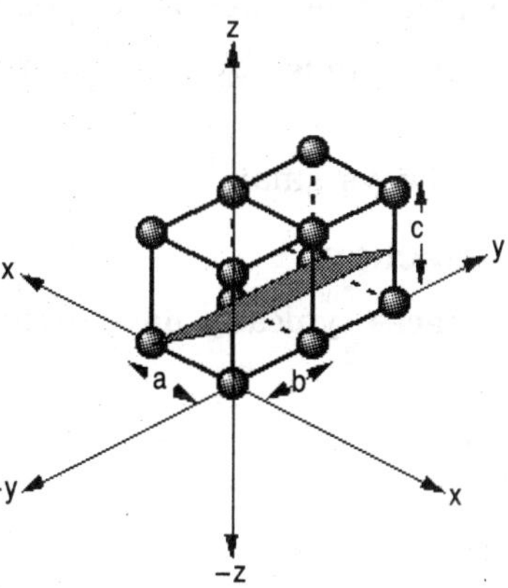

	a	b	c
Intercept length	–1	∞	$\frac{1}{2}$
Reciprocal	$\frac{1}{-1}$	$\frac{1}{\infty}$	$\frac{1}{1/2}$
Cleared fraction	–1	0	2
Miller indice		(102)	

(b) Miller indices (–102) planes.

Fig. 1.27

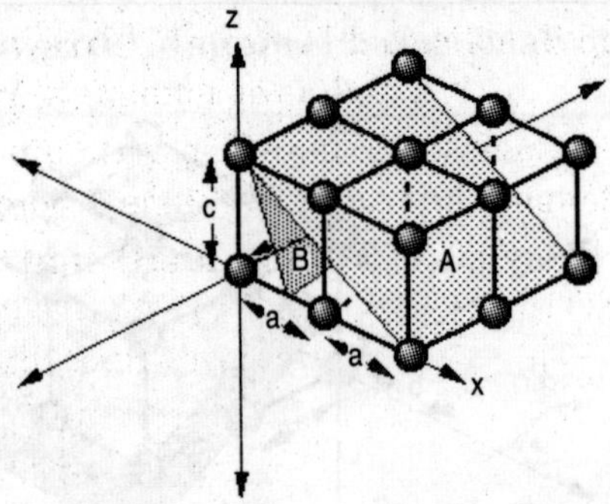

	Plane A			Plane B		
	a	b	c	a	b	c
Intercept length	1	∞	$\frac{1}{2}$	$\frac{1}{2}$	∞	1
Reciprocal	$\frac{1}{1}$	$\frac{1}{\infty}$	$\frac{1}{1/2}$	$\frac{1}{1/2}$	$\frac{1}{\infty}$	$\frac{1}{1}$
Cleared fraction	1	0	2	2	0	1
Miller indice	(102)			(201)		

Fig. 1.28 102 and 201 Miller indices planes.

Some General Principles

- If a Miller index is zero, the plane is parallel to that axis.
- The smaller a Miller index, the more nearly parallel the plane is to the axis.
- The larger a Miller index, the more nearly perpendicular a plane is to that axis.
- Multiplying or dividing a Miller index by a constant has no effect on the orientation of the plane.
- Miller indices are almost always small.

Assigning Miller Indices by Inspection

- Prominent (and common) faces typically have small integers in Miller indices
  – relate to unit cell
- Face that cuts only one axis:
  – (100), (010), (001) etc.
- Face that cuts two axes:
  – (110), (101), (011) etc.
- Face that cuts all three axes:
  – (111) etc.
  – called unit face.

Why Miller Indices?

- Using reciprocals spares us the complication of infinite intercepts.
- Formulas involving Miller indices are very similar to related formulas from analytical geometry.

Specifying dimensions in unit cell terms means that the same label can be applied to any face with a similar stacking pattern, regardless of the crystal class of the crystal. Face 111 always steps the same way whether the crystal is isometric or triclinic.

Example: *Find the Miller indices for the crystal planes shown in figure below. Assume the lattice constant is unity.*

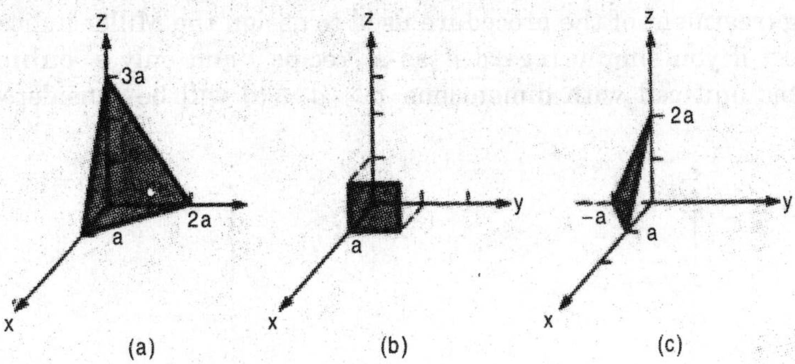

Fig. 1.29 Sampe cubic crystal planes (1).

In the figure above the plane intercepts the three crystal axes at (1, 0, 0), (0, 2, 0) and (0, 0, 3) or simply (1, 2, 3). The reciprocals are 1/1, ½ , 1/3.

Multiplying by 6, these fractions are reduced to 6, 3, 2 that are the Miller indices. The plane is known as the (6, 3, 2) plane.

Find the Miller indices for the crystal planes in Fig. 1.30 (b) and (c).

- Note that the direction of a crystal plane is normal to the plane itself and is designated by brackets of the same Miller indices. For example the direction of the (111) plane is written as [111].
- Using braces can show families of equivalent planes. The notation {100} refers to the six planes on the cube faces.
- Using angle brackets can show families of equivalent vectors. The notation <100> refers to the six directions ±x, ± and ±z.

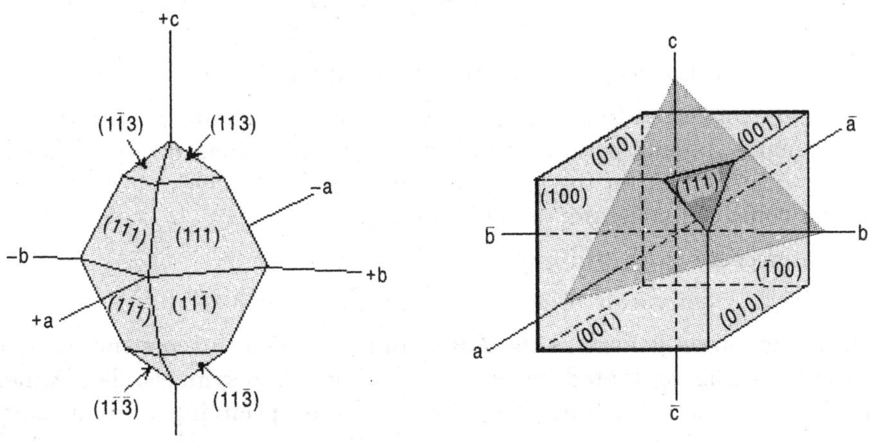

Fig. 1.30 Various Miller indices.

Miller Indices (hkl)

The orientation of a surface or a crystal plane may be defined by considering how the plane (or indeed any parallel plane) intersects the main crystallographic axes of the solid. The application of a set of rules leads to the assignment of the Miller indices, (hkl); a set of numbers which quantify the intercepts and thus may be used to uniquely identify the plane cr surface.

The following treatment of the procedure used to assign the Miller indices is a simplified one (it may be best if you simply regard it as a "recipe") and only a **cubic** crystal system (one having a cubic unit cell with dimensions $a \times a \times a$) will be considered.

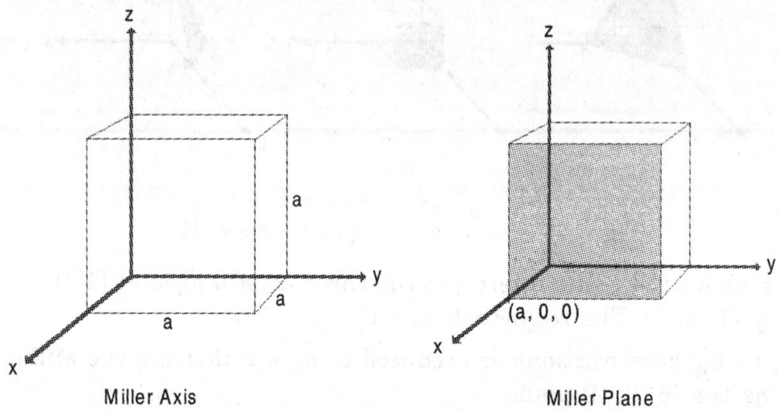

Fig. 1.31 Miller axis and plane.

The procedure is most easily illustrated using an example so we will first consider the following surface/plane:

Step 1 : Identify the intercepts on the x-, y- and z-axes.

In this case the intercept on the x-axis is at $x = a$ (at the point $(a, 0, 0)$), but the surface is parallel to the y- and z-axes-strictly therefore there is no intercept on these two axes but we shall consider the intercept to be at infinity (∞) for the special case where the plane is parallel to an axis. The intercepts on the x-, y- and z-axes are thus

Intercepts : a, ∞ , ∞

Step 2 : Specify the intercepts in fractional co-ordinates.

Co-ordinates are converted to fractional co-ordinates by dividing by the respective cell-dimension–for example, a point (x, y, z) in a unit cell of dimensions $a \times b \times c$ has fractional co-ordinates of $(x/a, y/b, z/c)$. In the case of a cubic unit cell each co-ordinate will simply be divided by the cubic cell constant, a. This gives

Fractional Intercepts : $a/a, \infty/a, \infty/a$ *i.e.* $1, \infty, \infty$

Step 3 : Take the reciprocals of the fractional intercepts.

This final manipulation generates the Miller indices which (by convention) should then be specified without being separated by any commas or other symbols. The Miller indices are also enclosed within standard brackets (....) when one is specifying a unique surface such as that being considered here.

The reciprocals of 1 and ∞ are 1 and 0 respectively, thus yielding

Miller Indices : (100)

So the surface/plane illustrated is the (100) plane of the cubic crystal.

Other Examples :

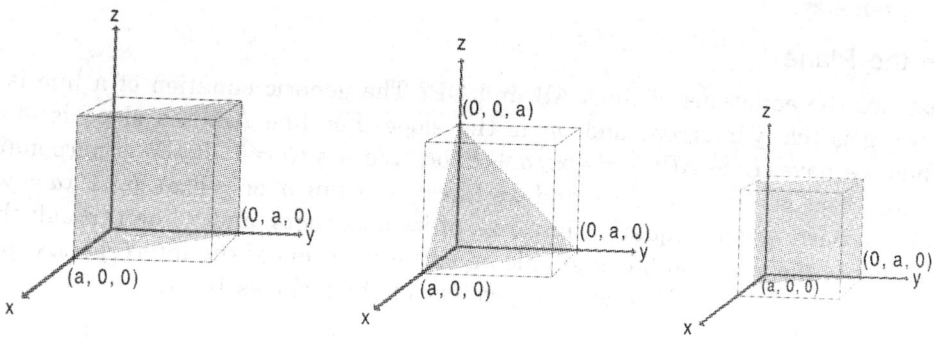

Fig. 1.32

The (100), (110) and (111) surfaces considered above are the so-called low index surfaces of a cubic crystal system (the "low" refers to the Miller indices being small numbers – 0 or 1 in this case). These surfaces have a particular importance but there an infinite number of other planes that may be defined using Miller index notation. We shall just look at one more.

Further Notes

(*i*) In some instances the Miller indices are best multiplied or divided through by a common number in order to simplify them by, for example, removing a common factor. This operation of multiplication simply generates a parallel plane which is at a different distance from the origin of the particular unit cell being considered.

e.g., (200) is transformed to (100) by dividing through by 2.

(*ii*) If any of the intercepts are at negative values on the axes then the negative sign will carry through into the Miller indices; in such cases the negative sign is actually denoted by over-striking the relevant number.

e.g., (00 –1) is instead denoted by $(00\bar{1})$.

(*iii*) In the *hcp* crystal system there are four principal axes; this leads to four Miller indices *e.g.*, you may see articles referring to an *hcp* (0001) surface. It is worth noting, however, that the intercepts on the first three axes are necessarily related and not completely independent; consequently the values of the first three Miller indices are also linked by a simple mathematical relationship.

What are symmetry-equivalent surfaces ?

In the above diagram the three highlighted surfaces are related by the symmetry elements of the cubic crystal—they are entirely equivalent.

In fact there are a total of 6 faces related by the symmetry elements and equivalent to the (100) surface—any surface belonging to this set of symmetry related surfaces may be denoted by the more general notation {100} where the Miller indices of one of the surfaces is instead enclosed in curly-brackets.

Final important note : in the cubic system the (*hkl*) plane and the vector (*hkl*), defined in the normal fashion with respect to the origin, are normal to one another **but** this characteristic is unique to the cubic crystal system and does **not** apply to crystal systems of lower symmetry.

Lines in the Plane

What are the equations of lines AB and OP? The generic equation of a line is $y = mx + b$, where b is the y-intercept and m is the slope. For line AB, the slope is $-\tan q$, or $-b/a$. Thus we have: Line AB: $y = -bx/a + b$, or, $x/a + y/b = 1$. If OP is perpendicular to AB, its y-intercept is obviously zero, and we have $y = x \tan p$, or $y = xa/b$, or $xa = yb$. Thus, a general line has a simple equation in terms of its intercepts, and a line through the origin perpendicular to the line also has a simple equation in terms of the intercepts. As a general rule, if two lines are perpendicular, the product of their slopes is –1.

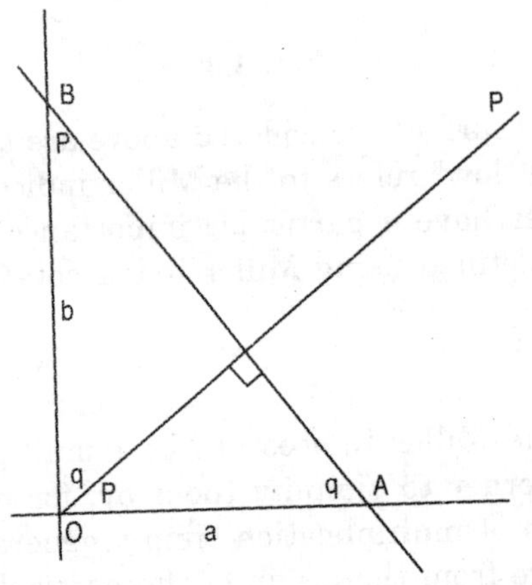

Miller Indices and Lines

The Miller index of a line is about as simple as it can be: if the line passes through (h, k, l), its Miller index is (*hkl*), written in brackets to distinguish it from a face.

Zones

A family of faces all parallel to some particular line is called a *zone*, and the line is called the *zone axis*. Two faces (*hkl*) and (*pqr*) belong to zone [*kr-lq*, *lp-hr*, *hq-kp*]. Note the similarity of this formula to the cross-product formula from vector mechanics. Any other face (*def*) belongs to the same zone if its indices are some linear combination of (*hkl*) and (*pqr*), for example, $d = 2h–3p$, $e = 2k–3q$, etc.

For example, faces (110) and (010) belong to [1*0–0*1, 0*0–1*0, 1*1–1*0], or [001]. The final zero in the face indices is a tipoff that they are both parallel to the z-axis, and the zone index [001] is the z-axis. Any other face whose index is some linear combination of (110) and (010) is also a member of that zone. Obviously the final index must be zero.

What about faces (211) and (124)? Their zone axis is [1*4–1*2, 1*1–2*4, 2*2–1*1] or [2, –7, 1]. Faces (335), (546), (1, –1, –3), etc. also belong to this zone.

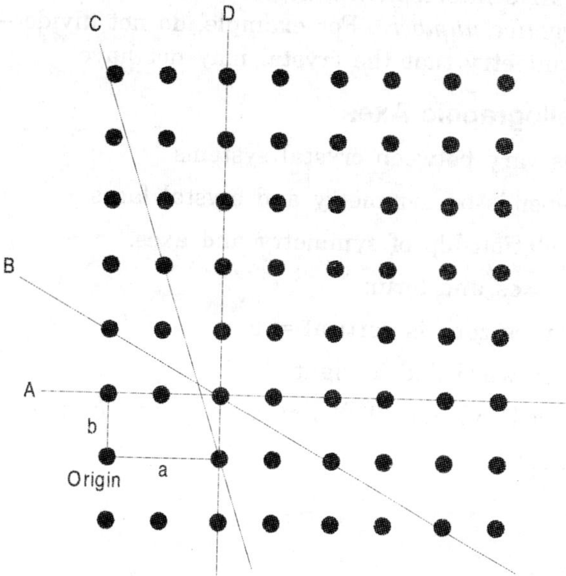

Fig. 1.33 Characterization of a two dimensional lattice in terms of set of planes.

Lines and Planes in Three Dimensions

The equation for a plane in three dimensions is exactly analogous for the line in two dimensions: $x/a + y/b + z/c = 1$. If line OP is perpendicular to the plane, its equation is also analogous to the two-dimensional case: $xa = yb = zc$. If we know a plane, we know the line through the origin perpendicular to it, called the *pole* to the plane. Quantities a, b and c are termed the *direction numbers* of the line. Line OP makes angles A, B, and C with the axes. The angles are related as follows: $\cos^2 A + \cos^2 B + \cos^2 C = 1$.

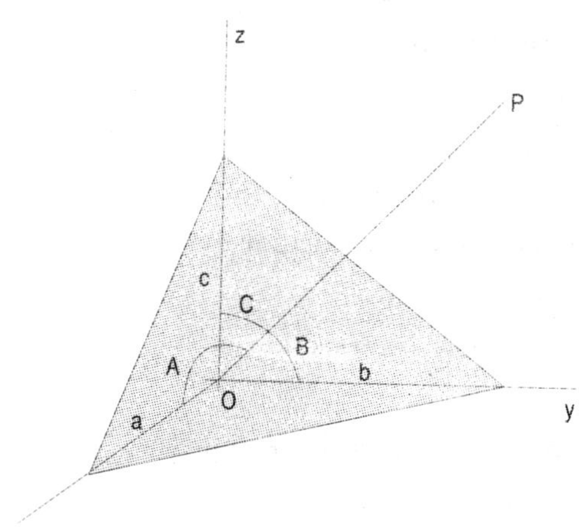

Cos A, cos B and cos C are called the *direction cosines* of the line. They are obviously also direction numbers. If you know any arbitrary direction numbers a, b and c, then cos A = a/s, cos B = b/s and cos C = c/s, where $s^2 = a^2 + b^2 + c^2$.

If a plane has negative intercept, the negative number is denoted by a bar above the number. *Never alter negative numbers.* For example, do not divide –1, –1, –1 by –1 to get 1, 1, 1. This implies symmetry that the crystal may not have!

Orientation of Crystallographic Axes

Orientation of axes vary between crystal systems

- Orientation depends on symmetry and crystal faces.
- Triclinic—no relationship of symmetry and axes.
- Orientation of axes and form:
  - Most pronounces zone is vertical = c
  - {001} slopes forward and to right
  - Intersection of {100} and {010} represent a and b axes
  - b axis is longest
  - $c < a < b$
- Monoclinic
  - 2 fold axis is b
  - mirror is vertical and includes a and c
- Orientation and crystal form
  - elongate crystal have c in long direction
  - prominent sloping plane parallels a
  - if 1 prominent cleavage parallel to b is perpendicular to c
  - if 2 prismatic cleavages, their intersection parallels c
- Orthorhombic
  - 2 fold axis coincides with the crystallographic axis
- Orientation and crystal form
  - lengths are $c < a < b$ (convention)
  - axis to be c depends on habit
  - elongate minerals in c direction
  - tabular minerals have c perpendicular
  - one cleavage, c perpendicular
  - two cleavages, c parallels intersection
- Tetragonal
  - crystallographic axes controlled by symmetry
  - 4—fold axis = c (c < or > a)
  - 2nd Hermann-Mauguin symbol (if present) is symmetry in $a1$ and $a2$ direction
  - 3rd Hermann-Mauguin symbol (if present) is symmetry 45° to $a1$ and $a2$ direction

- **Hexagonal**
  - 6 or 3 fold axis = c
  - 2nd H-M symbol (if present) = symmetry axes parallel to $a1$, $a2$, and $a3$
  - 3rd H-M symbol (if present) = symmetry perpendicular (but in same plane to $a1$, $a2$, and $a3$
- Isometric
  - 1st H-M notation = $a1$, $a2$, and $a3$
  - 2nd H-M notation = 4 diagonals of 3 fold symmetry (corner of cube)
  - 3rd H-M notation = 6 directions between edges of cube.

1.18 CRYSTAL DEFECTS

Crystal defects

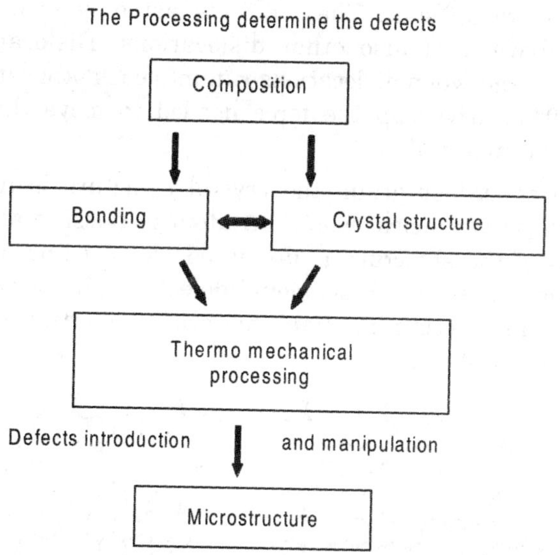

A perfect crystal, with every atom of the same type in the correct position, does not exist. All crystals have some defects. Defects contribute to the mechanical properties of metals. In fact, using the term "defect" is sort of a misnomer since these features are commonly intentionally used to manipulate the mechanical properties of a material. Adding alloying elements to a metal is one way of introducing a crystal defect. Nevertheless, the term "defect" will be used, just keep in mind that crystalline defects are not always bad. There are basic classes of crystal defects:

Types of Defects

Defects may be classified into four categories depending on their dimension:

0D, Point defects: atoms missing or in irregular places in the lattice (vacancies, interstitials, impurities)

1D, Linear defects: groups of atoms in irregular positions (*e.g.*, screw and edge dislocations)

2D, Planar defects: the interfaces between homogeneous regions of the material (grain boundaries, external surfaces)

3D, Volume defects: extended defects (pores, cracks)

- *Point defects*, which are places where an atom is missing or irregularly placed in the lattice structure. Point defects include lattice vacancies, self-interstitial atoms, substitution impurity atoms, and interstitial impurity atoms.
- *Linear defects*, which are groups of atoms in irregular positions. Linear defects are commonly called dislocations.
- *Planar defects*, which are interfaces between homogeneous regions of the material. Planar defects include grain boundaries, stacking faults and external surfaces.

It is important to note at this point that plastic deformation in a material occurs due to the movement of dislocations (linear defects). Millions of dislocations result for plastic forming operations such as rolling and extruding. It is also important to note that any defect in the regular lattice structure disrupts the motion of dislocation, which makes slip or plastic deformation more difficult. These defects not only include the point and planer defects mentioned above, and also other dislocations. Dislocation movement produces additional dislocations, and when dislocations run into each other it often impedes movement of the dislocations. This drives up the force needed to move the dislocation or, in other words, strengthens the material.

Within a single crystal or grain, the crystal structure is not perfect. The structure contains defects such as vacancies, where an atom is missing altogether, and dislocation, where the perfection of the structure is disrupted along a line. Grain boundaries in polycrystals can be considered as two-dimensional defects in the perfect crystal lattice. Crystal defects are important in determining many material properties, such as the rate of atomic diffusion and mechanical strength.

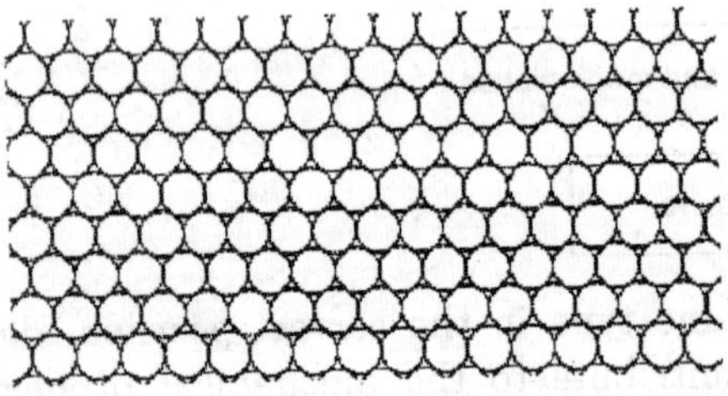

(a) Closed pack plane

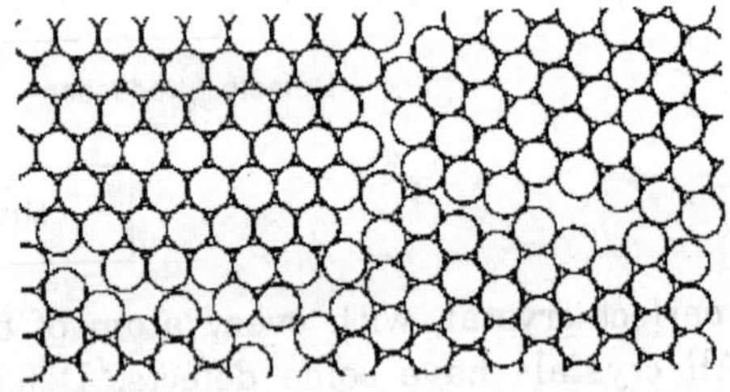

(b) Polycrystalline form

Fig. 1.34

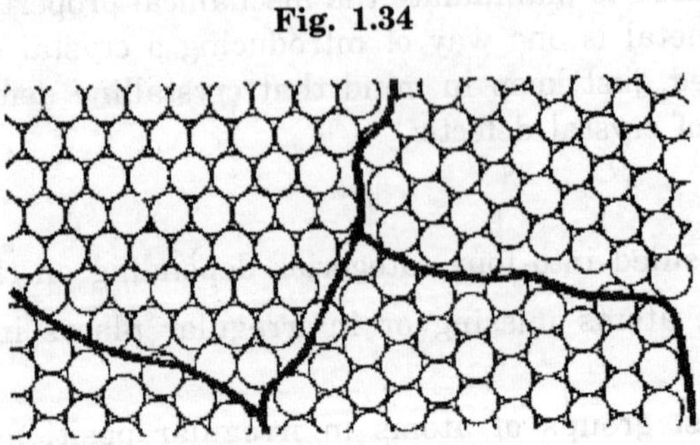

Fig 1.35 Grains bounded by disordered grain boundaries.

1.18.1 Point Defects

Point defects are where an atom is missing or is in an irregular place in the lattice structure. Point defects include *self interstitial atoms, interstitial impurity atoms, substitutional atoms and vacancies.* A self interstitial atom is an extra atom that has crowded its way into an interstitial void in the crystal structure. Self interstitial atoms occur only in low concentrations in metals because they distort and highly stress the tightly packed lattice structure.

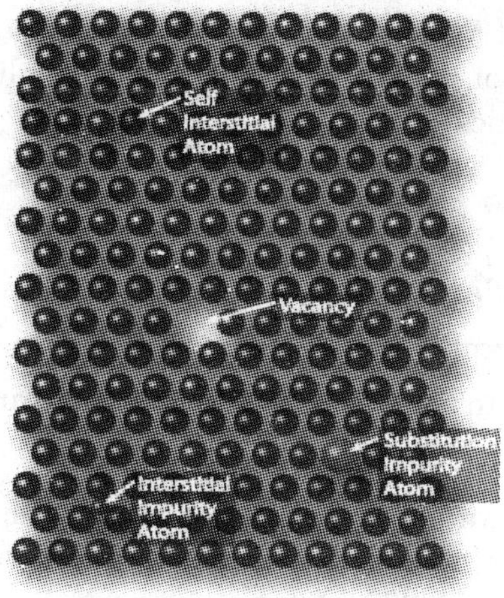

Fig. 1.36 Point defects.

A *substitutional impurity* atom is an atom of a different type than the bulk atoms, which has replaced one of the bulk atoms in the lattice. Substitutional impurity atoms are usually close in size (within approximately 15%) to the bulk atom. An example of substitutional impurity atoms is the zinc atoms in brass. In brass, zinc atoms with a radius of 0.133 nm have replaced some of the copper atoms, which have a radius of 0.128 nm.

Interstitial impurity atoms are much smaller than the atoms in the bulk matrix. Interstitial impurity atoms fit into the open space between the bulk atoms of the lattice structure. An example of interstitial impurity atoms is the carbon atoms that are added to iron to make steel. Carbon atoms, with a radius of 0.071 nm, fit nicely in the open spaces between the larger (0.124 nm) iron atoms.

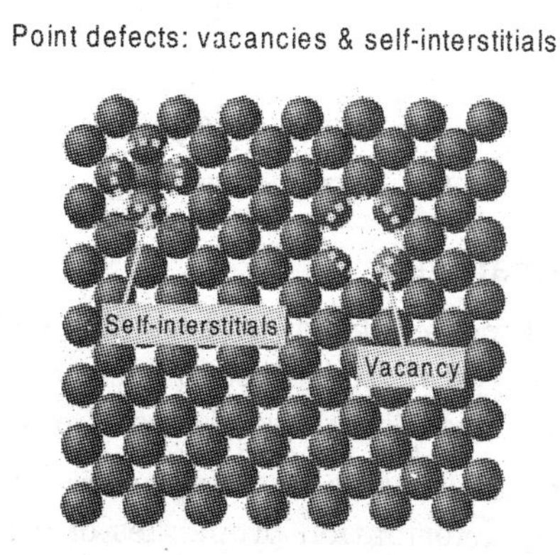

Fig. 1.37 Point defects.

Vacancy. A lattice position that is vacant because the atom is missing. Vacancies are empty spaces where an atom should be, but is missing. They are common, especially at high temperatures when atoms are frequently and randomly change their positions leaving behind empty lattice sites. In most cases diffusion (mass transport by atomic motion) can only occur because of vacancies.

Interstitial. An atom that occupies a place outside the normal lattice position. It may be the same type of atom as the other (self interstitial) or an impurity interstitial atom.

Howmany vacancies are there ?

The equilibrium number of vacancies formed as a result of thermal vibrations may be calculated from thermodynamics :

$$N_v = N_s\,(-Qv/k_bT)$$

Where,

N_s is the number of regular lattice,

K_b is the boltzman constant

Q_v is the energy needed to form a vacant lattice site in a perfect crystal

T is the temperature in Kelvin

Using this equation we can estimate that at room temperature in copper there is one vacancy per 10^{15} lattice atoms, whereas at high temperature, just below the melting point there is one vacancy for every 10,000 atoms.

Let us estimate the number of vacancies in Cu at room temperature,

$$N_v = N_s\,(-Qv/k_bT) \quad \text{...(a)}$$

$$K_b = 1.38 \times 10^{-23}\ \text{J/atom-K} = 8.62 \times 10^{-5}\ \text{eV/atom–K}$$

$$\text{Temperature T in Kelvin T} = 27^{\circ}\text{C} + 273 = 300\text{K}$$

$$K_bT = 300\text{K} \times 8.62 \times 10^{-5}\ \text{eV/K} = 0.026\ \text{eV}$$

The energy for vacancy formation

$$Q_v = 0.9\ \text{eV/atom}$$

$$\text{The no.of regular lattice sites } N_s = N_a\,\rho/A_{cu}$$

$$N_a = 6.023 \times 10^{23}\ \text{atoms/mol}$$

$$\rho = 8.4\ \text{g/cm}^3,\ A_{cu} = 63.5\ \text{g/mol}$$

Substitutingin (a) we get

$$N_s = 8 \times 10^{22}\ \text{atoms/cm}^3$$

$$N_a = 7.4 \times 10^{7}\ \text{vacancies/cm}^3$$

1.18.2 Linear Defects–Dislocations

Dislocations are another type of defect in crystals. Dislocations are areas were the atoms are out of position in the crystal structure. Dislocations are generated and move when a stress is applied. The motion of dislocations allows slip—plastic deformation to occur.

Before the discovery of the dislocation by Taylor, Orowan and Polyani in 1934, no one could figure out how the plastic deformation properties of a metal could be greatly changed by solely by forming (without changing the chemical composition). This became even bigger mystery when in the early 1900's scientists estimated that metals undergo plastic deformation at forces much smaller than the theoretical strength of the forces that are holding the metal atoms together. Many metallurgists remained skeptical of the dislocation theory until the development of the transmission electron microscope in the late 1950's. The TEM allowed experimental evidence to be collected that showed that the strength and ductility of metals are controlled by dislocations.

There are two basic types of dislocations, *the edge dislocation and the screw dislocation.* Actually, edge and screw dislocations are just extreme forms of the possible dislocation structures that can occur. Most dislocations are probably a hybrid of the edge and screw forms but this discussion will be limited to these two types.

Dislocations—Linear Defects

Dislocations are linear defects: the inter atomic bonds are significantly distorted only in the immediate vicinity of the dislocation line. This area is called the **dislocation core.**

Dislocations also create small elastic deformations of the lattice at large distances.

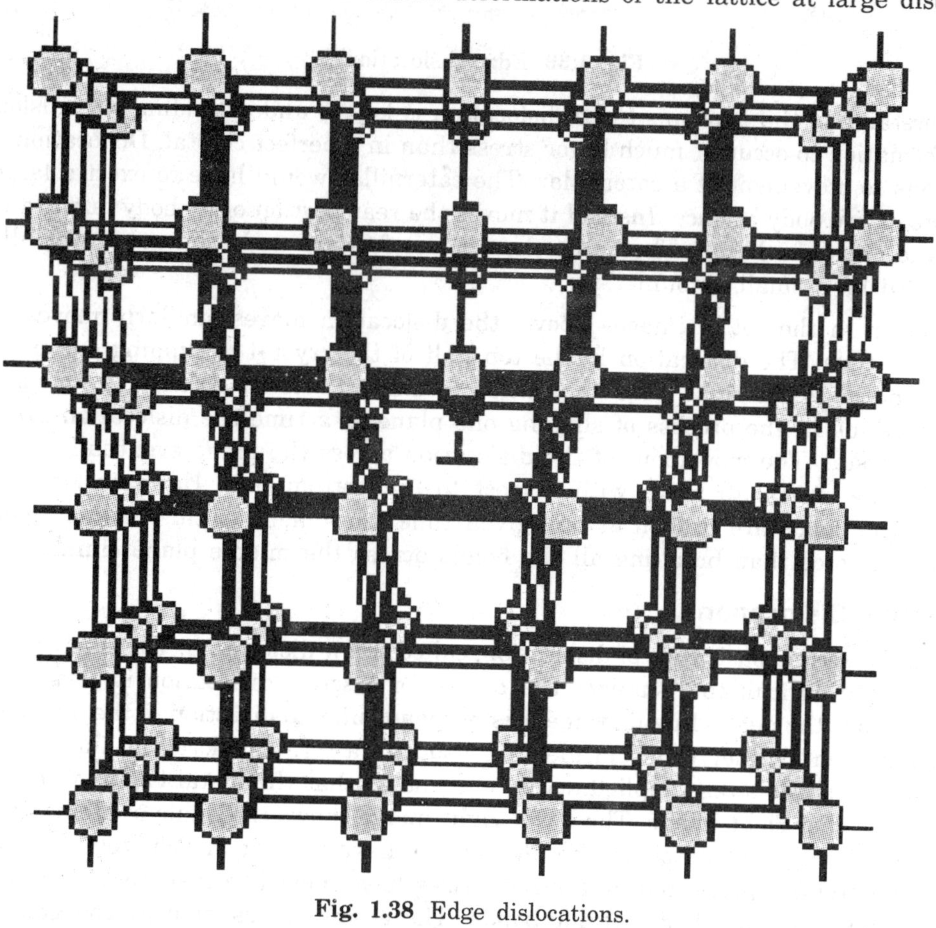

Fig. 1.38 Edge dislocations.

1.18.3 Edge Dislocations

The edge defect can be easily visualized as an extra half-plane of atoms in a lattice. The dislocation is called a line defect because the locus of defective points produced in the lattice by the dislocation lie along a line. This line runs along the top of the extra half-plane. The inter-atomic bonds are significantly distorted only in the immediate vicinity of the dislocation line.

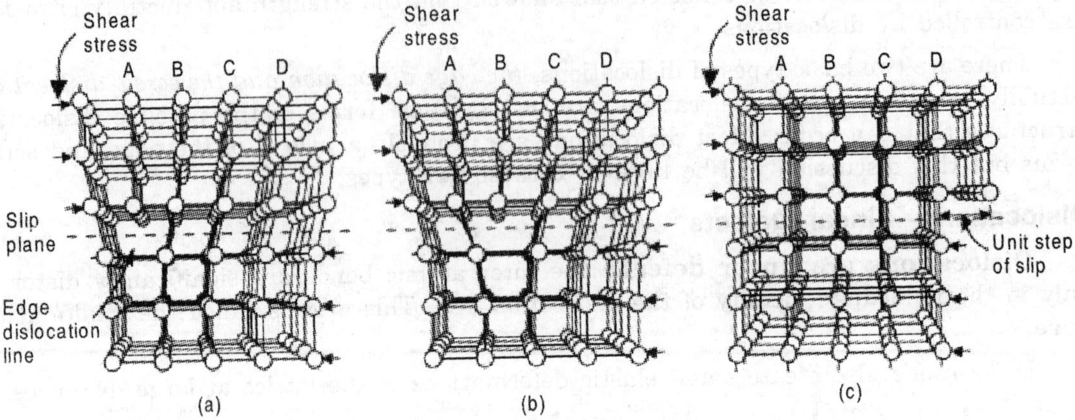

Fig. 1.39 Edge dislocations.

Understanding the movement of a dislocation is key to understanding why dislocations allow deformation to occur at much lower stress than in a perfect crystal. Dislocation motion is analogous to movement of a caterpillar. The caterpillar would have to exert a large force to move its entire body at once. Instead it moves the rear portion of its body forward a small amount and creates a hump. The hump then moves forward and eventual moves all of the body forward by a small amount.

As shown in the set of images above, the dislocation moves similarly moves a small amount at a time. The dislocation in the top half of the crystal is slipping one plane at a time as it moves to the right from its position in image (a) to its position in image (b) and finally image (c). In the process of slipping one plane at a time the dislocation propagates across the crystal. The movement of the dislocation across the plane eventually causes the top half of the crystal to move with respect to the bottom half. However, only a small fraction of the bonds are broken at any given time. Movement in this manner requires a much smaller force than breaking all the bonds across the middle plane simultaneously.

1.18.4 Screw Dislocations

There is a second basic type of dislocation, called screw dislocation. The screw dislocation is slightly more difficult to visualize. The motion of a screw dislocation is also a result of shear stress, but the defect line movement is perpendicular to direction of the stress and the atom displacement, rather than parallel. To visualize a screw dislocation, imagine a block of metal with a shear stress applied across one end so that the metal begins to rip. This is shown in the upper right image. The lower right image shows the plane of atoms just above the rip. The atoms represented by the blue circles have not yet moved from their original position. The atoms represented by the red circles have moved to their new position in the lattice and have reestablished metallic bonds. The atoms represented by the green circles are in the process of moving. It can be seen that only a portion of the bonds are broke at any given time. As was the case with the edge dislocation, movement in this manner requires a much smaller force than breaking all the bonds across the middle plane simultaneously.

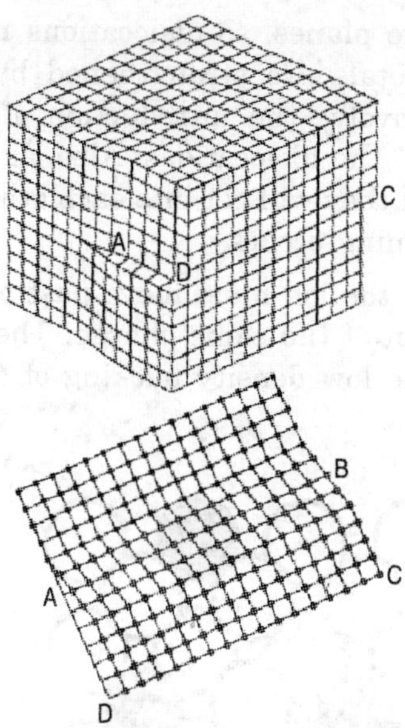

Fig 1.40 Screw dislocations.

If the shear force is increased, the atoms will continue to slip to the right. A row of the green atoms will find there way back into a proper spot in the lattice (and become red) and a row of the blue atoms will slip out of position (and become green). In this way, the screw dislocation will move upward in the image, which is perpendicular to direction cf the stress. Recall that the edge dislocation moves parallel to the direction of stress. As shown in the image below, the net plastic deformation of both edge and screw dislocations is the same, however.

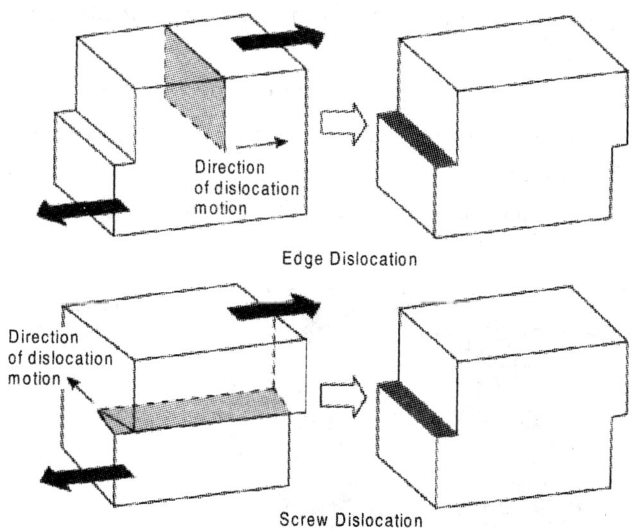

Fig. 1.41 Screw and edge dislocation.

The dislocations move along the densest planes of atoms in a material, because the stress needed to move the dislocation increases with the spacing between the planes. FCC and BCC metals have many dense planes, so dislocations move relatively easy and 'these materials have high ductility. Metals are strengthened by making it more difficult for dislocations to move. This may involve the introduction of obstacles, such as interstitial atoms or grain boundaries, to "pin" the dislocations. Also, as a material plastically deforms, more dislocations are produced and they will get into each others way and impede movement. This is why strain or work hardening occurs.

In ionically bonded materials, the ion must move past an area with a repulsive charge in order to get to the next location of the same charge. Therefore, slip is difficult and the materials are brittle. Likewise, the low density packing of covalent materials makes them generally more brittle than metals.

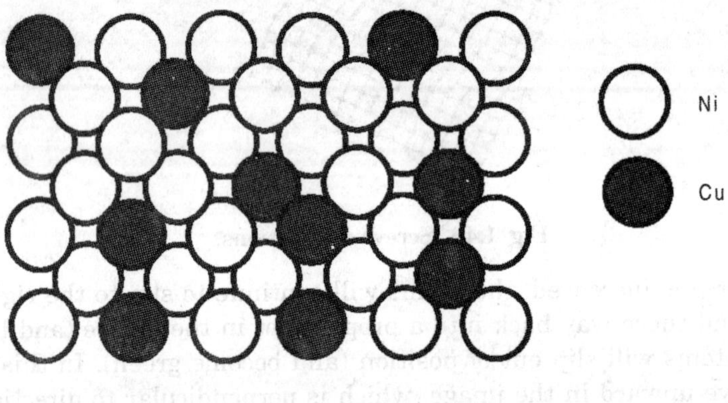

Fig. 1.42 Substitutional solid solutions.

Factors for High Solubility

Atomic size factor—atoms need to "fit". Solute and solvent atomic radii should be within ~ 15%.

Crystal structures of solute and solvent should be the same.

Electro-negativities of solute and solvent should be comparable (otherwise new inter-metallic phases are encouraged).

Generally more solute goes into solution when it has higher valency than solvent.

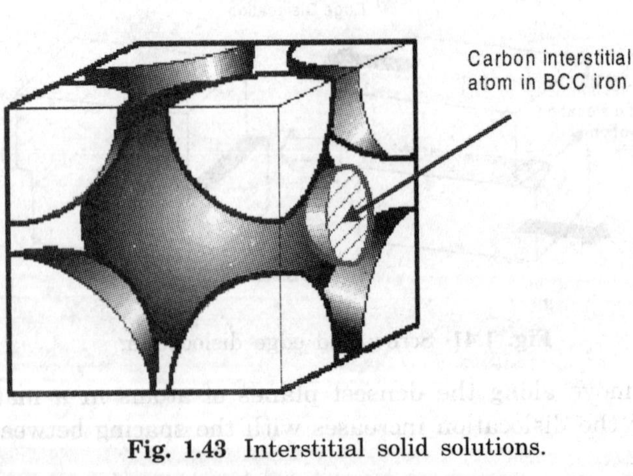

Fig. 1.43 Interstitial solid solutions.

Factors for High Solubility

For fcc, bcc, hcp structures the voids (or interstices) between the host atoms are relatively small atomic radius of solute should be significantly less than solvent normally, max. Solute concentration = 10%, (2% for C-Fe). Interstitial solid solution of C in α-Fe. The C atom is small enough to fit, after introducing some strain into the BCC lattice.

1.19 PLANAR DEFECTS

Stacking Faults and Twin Boundaries

A disruption of the long-range stacking sequence can produce two other common types of crystal defects: (1) a stacking fault and (2) a twin region. A change in the stacking sequence over a few atomic spacing produces a stacking fault whereas a change over many atomic spacing produces a twin region.

A stacking fault is a one or two layer interruption in the stacking sequence of atom planes. Stacking faults occur in a number of crystal structures, but it is easiest to see how they occur in close packed structures. For example, it is know from a previous discussion that face centered cubic (fcc) structures differ from hexagonal close packed (hcp) structures only in their stacking order. For hcp and fcc structures, the first two layers arrange themselves identically, and are said to have an AB arrangement. If the third layer is placed so that its atoms are directly above those of the first (A) layer, the stacking will be ABA. This is the hcp structure, and it continues ABABABAB. However, it is possible for the third layer atoms to arrange themselves so that they are in line with the first layer to produce an ABC arrangement which is that of the fcc structure. So, if the hcp structure is going along as ABABAB and suddenly switches to ABABABCABAB, there is a stacking fault present.

Alternately, in the fcc arrangement the pattern is ABCABCABC. A stacking fault in an fcc structure would appear as one of the C planes missing. In other words the pattern would become ABCABCAB_ABCABC.

If a stacking fault does not corrects itself immediately but continues over some number of atomic spacings, it will produce a second stacking fault that is the twin of the first one. For example if the stacking pattern is ABABABAB but switches to ABCABCABC for a period of time before switching back to ABABABAB, a pair of twin stacking faults is produced. The red region in the stacking sequence that goes ABCABCACBACBABCABC is the twin plane and the twin boundaries are the A planes on each end of the highlighted region.

Grain Boundaries in Poly Crystals

Another type of planer defect is the grain boundary. Up to this point, the discussion has focused on defects of single crystals. However, solids generally consist of a number of crystallites or grains. Grains can range in size from nanometers to millimeters across and their orientations are usually rotated with respect to neighboring grains. Where one grain stops and another begins is know as a grain boundary. Grain boundaries limit the lengths and motions of dislocations. Therefore, having smaller grains (more grain boundary surface area) strengthens a material. The size of the grains can be controlled by the cooling rate when the material cast or heat treated. Generally, rapid cooling produces smaller grains whereas slow cooling result in larger grains. For more information, refer to the discussion on solidification.

Polycrystalline material comprised of many small crystals or grains. The grains have different crystallographic orientation. There exist atomic mismatch within the regions where grains meet. These regions are called *grain boundaries.*

Surfaces and interfaces are reactive and impurities tend to segregate there. Since energy is associated with interfaces, grains tend to grow in size at the expense of smaller grains to minimize energy. This occurs by diffusion (Chapter 5), which is accelerated at high temperatures.

High and Low Angle Grain Boundaries

Depending on misalignments of atomic planes between adjacent grains we can distinguish between the low and high angle grain boundaries.

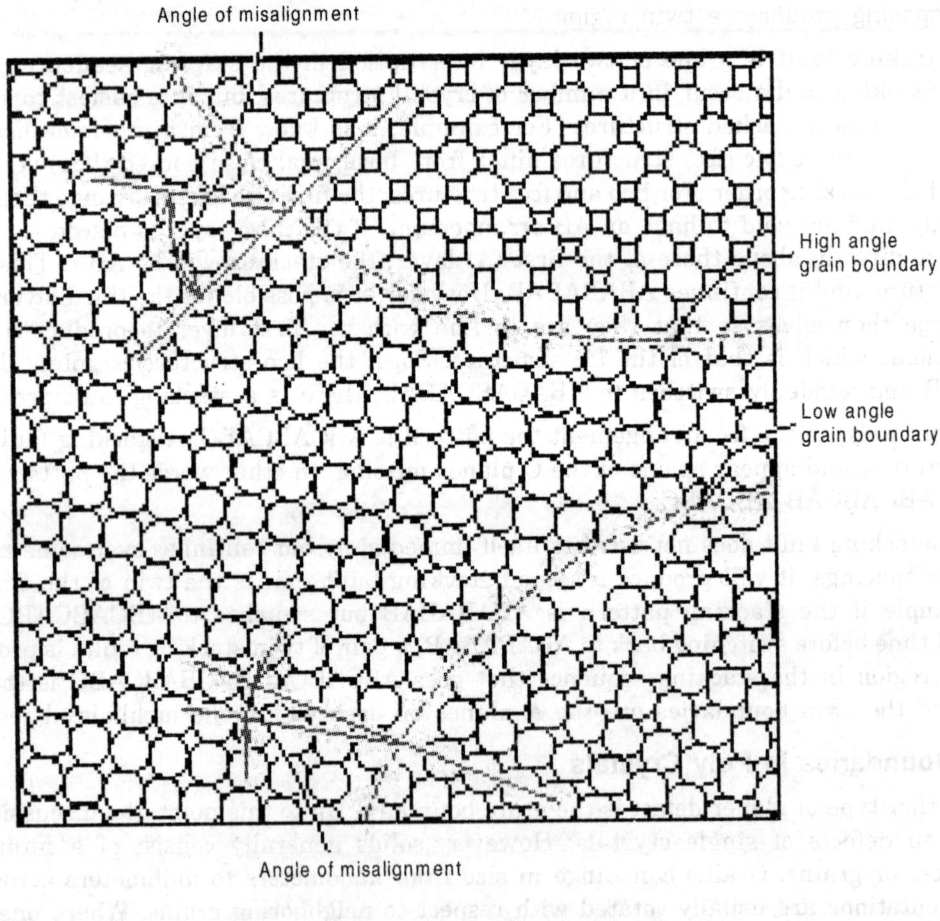

Fig. 1.44 Grain boundary.

Tilt and Twist Grain Boundaries

Low angle grain boundary is an array of aligned edge dislocations. This type of grain boundary is called **tilt boundary** (consider joint of two wedges).

Transmission electron microscope image of a small angle tilt boundary in Si. The dark lines mark the edge dislocations, the light lines indicate the tilt angle.

Fig. 1.45 Tilt boundary.

Twist boundary—The boundary region consisting of arrays of screw dislocations (consider joint of two halves of a cube and twist an angle around the cross section normal).

Low-energy **twin boundaries** with mirrored atomic positions across boundary may be produced by deformation of materials. This gives rise to **shape memory metals,** which can recover their original shape if heated to a high temperature. Shape-memory alloys are twinned and when deformed they untwin. At high temperature the alloy returns back to the original twin configuration and restore the original shape.

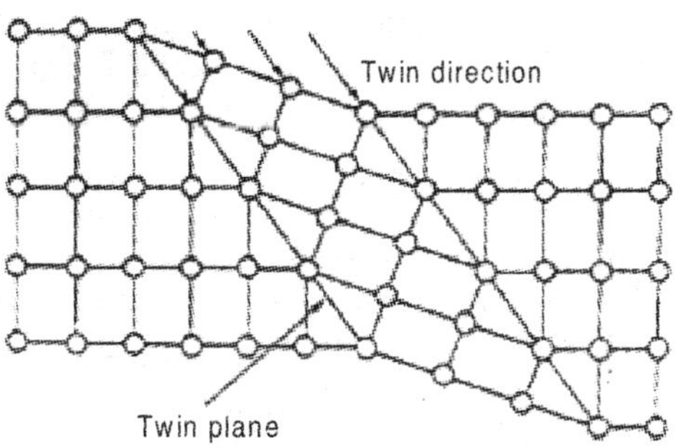

Fig. 1.46 Twin boundary.

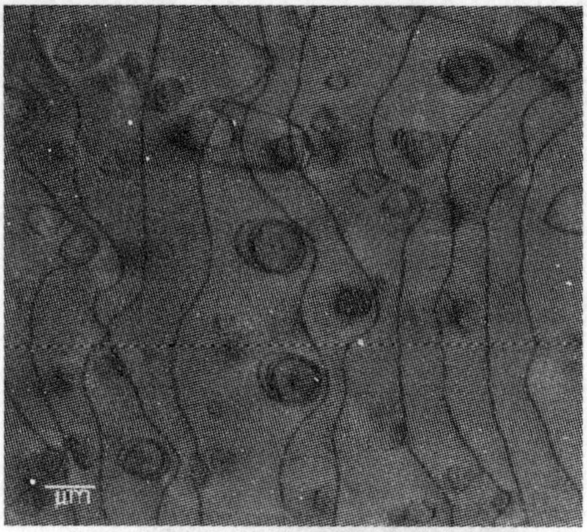

Fig. 1.47 Electron microscopy.

Dislocations in Nickel (the dark lines and loops),transmission electron microscopy image, Manchester Materials Science Center.

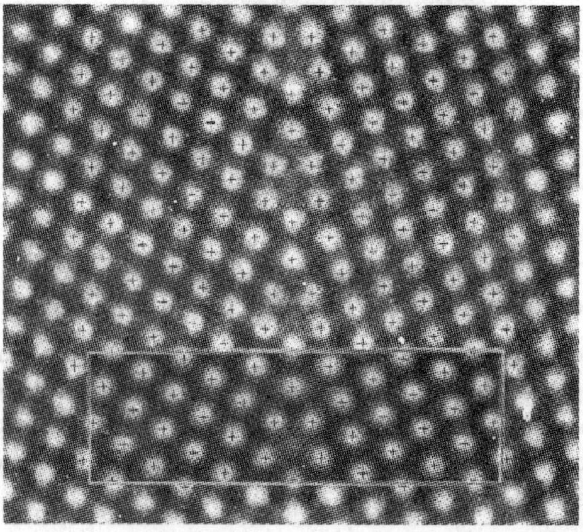

Fig. 1.48 High-resolution transmission electron microscope image of a tilt grain boundary in aluminium, Sandia national lab.

1.20 BULK DEFECTS

Bulk defects occur on a much bigger scale than the rest of the crystal defects discussed in this section. However, for the sake of completeness and since they do affect the movement of dislocations, a few of the more common bulk defects will be mentioned. Voids are regions where there are a large number of atoms missing from the lattice. The image to the right is a void in a piece of metal. The image was acquired using a Scanning Electron Microscope (SEM). Voids can occur for a number of reasons. When voids occur due to air bubbles becoming trapped when a material solidifies, it is commonly called porosity. When a void occurs due to the shrinkage of a material as it solidifies, it is called cavitation.

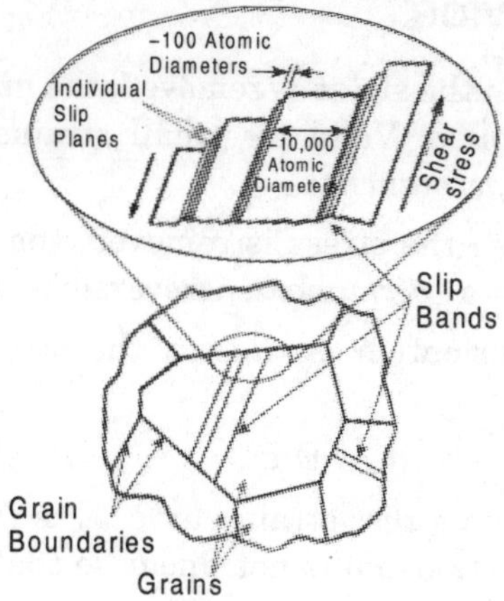

Fig. 1.49 Bulk defects.

Another type of bulk defect occurs when impurity atoms cluster together to form small regions of a different phase. The term 'phase' refers to that region of space occupied by a physically homogeneous material. These regions are often called precipitates.

Mechanical Properties of Metal

Often materials are subject to forces (loads) when they are used. Mechanical engineers calculate those forces and material scientists how materials deform (elongate, compress, twist) or break as a function of applied load, time, temperature, and other conditions.

Materials scientists learn about these mechanical properties by testing materials. Results from the tests depend on the size and shape of material to be tested (specimen), how it is held, and the way of performing the test. That is why we use common procedures, or *standards*, which are published by the ASTM.

Concepts of Stress and Strain

To compare specimens of different sizes, the load is calculated per unit area, also called normalization to the area. Force divided by area is called stress. In tension and compression tests, the relevant area is that perpendicular to the force. In shear or torsion tests, the area is perpendicular to the axis of rotation.

$$\sigma = F/A_0 \text{ tensile or compressive stress}$$

$$\tau = F/A_0 \text{ shear stress}$$

$$\text{The unit is the Megapascal} = 10^6 \text{ Newtons/m}^2.$$

There is a change in dimensions, or deformation elongation, ΔL as a result of a tensile or compressive stress. To enable comparison with specimens of different length, the elongation is also normalized, this time to the length L. This is called strain, ε.

$$\varepsilon = \Delta L/L$$

The change in dimensions is the reason we use A_0 to indicate the initial area since it changes during deformation. One could divide force by the actual area, this is called true stress.

For torsional or shear stresses, the deformation is the angle of twist, and the shear strain is given by:

$$\gamma = tg\ \theta$$

1.21 STRESS-STRAIN BEHAVIOR

Elastic deformation. When the stress is removed, the material returns to the dimension it had before the load was applied. Valid for small strains (except the case of rubbers). Deformation is *reversible, non permanent.*

Plastic deformation. When the stress is removed, the material does not return to its previous dimension but there is a *permanent,* irreversible deformation.

In tensile tests, if the deformation is *elastic,* the stress-strain relationship is called Hooke's law:

$$\sigma = E\,\varepsilon$$

That is, E is the slope of the stress-strain curve. E is *Young's modulus* or *modulus of elasticity*. In some cases, the relationship is not linear so that E can be defined alternatively as the local slope:

$$E = d\sigma/d\varepsilon$$

Shear stresses produce strains according to:

$\tau = G\gamma$ where G is the *shear modulus.*

Elastic moduli measure the *stiffness* of the material. They are related to the *second* derivative of the inter-atomic potential, or the first derivative of the force vs. internuclear distance (Fig. 6.6). By examining these curves we can tell which material has a higher modulus. Due to thermal vibrations the elastic modulus decreases with temperature. E is large for ceramics (stronger ionic bond) and small for polymers (weak covalent bond). Since the inter-atomic distances depend on direction in the crystal, E depends on direction (i.e., it is anisotropic) for single crystals. For *randomly* oriented polycrystals, E is isotropic.

Anelasticity

Here the behavior is elastic but not the stress-strain curve is not immediately reversible. It takes a while for the strain to return to zero. The effect is normally small for metals but can be significant for polymers.

Elastic Properties of Materials

Materials subject to tension shrink laterally. Those subject to compression, bulge. The ratio of lateral and axial strains is called the *Poisson's ratio* ν.

$$\nu = \frac{\text{lateral strain}}{\text{axial strain}}$$

The elastic modulus, shear modulus and Poisson's ratio are related by $E = 2G(1+\nu)$

Tensile Properties

Yield point. If the stress is too large, the strain deviates from being proportional to the stress. The point at which this happens is the *yield point* because there the material yields, deforming permanently (plastically).

Yield stress. Hooke's law is not valid beyond the yield point. The stress at the yield point is called *yield stress,* and is an important measure of the mechanical properties of materials. In practice, the yield stress is chosen as that causing a permanent strain of 0.002.

The yield stress measures the resistance to plastic deformation.

The reason for plastic deformation, in normal materials, is not that the atomic bond is stretched beyond repair, but the motion of dislocations, which involves breaking and reforming bonds.

Plastic deformation is caused by the motion of dislocations.

Tensile strength. When stress continues in the plastic regime, the stress-strain passes through a maximum, called the *tensile strength* (σ_{TS}) , and then falls as the material starts to develop a *neck* and it finally breaks at the *fracture point.*

Note that it is called strength, not stress, but the units are the same, MPa.

For structural applications, the yield stress is usually a more important property than the tensile strength, since once the it is passed, the structure has deformed beyond acceptable limits.

Toughness

The quality known as *toughness* describes the way a material reacts under sudden impacts. It is defined as the work required to deform one cubic inch of metal until it fractures. Toughness is measured by the Charpy test or the Izod test.

Ductility. The ability to deform before braking. It is the opposite of **brittleness.** Ductility can be given either as percent maximum elongation ε_{max} or maximum area reduction.

$$\%EL = \varepsilon_{max} \times 100\%$$

$$\%AR = (A_0 - A_f)/A_0$$

These are measured after fracture (repositioning the two pieces back together).

Ductility is more commonly defined as the ability of a material to deform easily upon the application of a tensile force, or as the ability of a material to withstand plastic deformation without rupture. Ductility may also be thought of in terms of bendability and crushability. Ductile materials show large deformation before fracture. The lack of ductility is often termed brittleness. Usually, if two materials have the same strength and hardness, the one that has the higher ductility is more desirable. The ductility of many metals can change if conditions are altered. An increase in temperature will increase ductility. A decrease in temperature will cause a decrease in ductility and a change from ductile to brittle behavior. Irradiation will also decrease ductility, cold-working also tends to make metals less ductile. Cold-working is performed in a temperature region and over a time interval to obtain plastic deformation, but not relieving the strain hardening. Minor additions of impurities to metals, either deliberate or unintentional, can have a marked effect on the change from ductile to brittle behavior. The heating of a cold-worked metal to or above the temperature at which metal atoms return to their equilibrium positions will increase the ductility of that metal. This process is called *annealing.* Ductility is desirable in the high temperature malleable deformation of a cylinder under uniform axial compression high pressure applications in reactor plants because of the added stresses on the metals. High ductility in these applications helps prevent brittle fracture, here ductility is the ability of a material to deform easily upon the application of a tensile force.

Malleability

Malleability is the ability of a metal to exhibit large deformation or plastic response when being subjected to compressive force. Uniform compressive force causes deformation. The material contracts axially with the force and expands laterally. Restraint due to friction at the contact faces induces axial tension on the outside. Tensile forces operate around the circumference with the lateral expansion or increasing girth. Plastic flow at the center of the material also induces tension.

Resilience. Capacity to absorb energy *elastically*. The energy per unit volume is the *area under the strain-stress curve in the elastic region.*

Toughness. Ability to absorb energy up to fracture. The energy per unit volume is the *total area under the strain-stress curve.* It is measured by an impact test.

True Stress and Strain

When one applies a constant tensile force the material will break after reaching the tensile strength. The material starts necking (the transverse area decreases) but the stress cannot increase beyond σ_{TS}. The ratio of the force to the initial area, what we normally do, is called the engineering stress. If the ratio is to the actual area (that changes with stress) one obtains the *true stress.*

Elastic Recovery During Plastic Deformation

If a material is taken beyond the yield point (it is deformed plastically) and the stress is then released, the material ends up with a permanent strain. If the stress is reapplied, the material again responds elastically at the beginning up to a new yield point *that is higher than the original yield point.* The amount of elastic strain that it will take before reaching the yield point is called *elastic strain recovery.*

Compressive, Shear, and Torsional Deformation

Compressive and shear stresses give similar behavior to tensile stresses, but in the case of compressive stresses there is no maximum in the σ-ε curve, since no necking occurs.

Hardness

Hardness is the resistance to plastic deformation (*e.g.*, a local dent or scratch). Thus, it is a measure of *plastic* deformation, as is the tensile strength, so they are well correlated. Historically, it was measured on an empirically scale, determined by the ability of a material to scratch another, diamond being the hardest and talc the softer. Now we use standard tests, where a ball, or point is pressed into a material and the size of the dent is measured. There are a few different hardness tests: Rockwell, Brinell, Vickers, etc. They are popular because they are easy and non-destructive (except for the small dent). The Brinell is one of the more popular types of machines for measuring hardness. It provides a Brinell Hardness Number (BHN), which is in kilograms per square millimeter based on the load applied to the hardened ball in kilograms and divided by the area of the impression left by the ball in square millimeters.

There is several other hardness measuring systems. A popular machine is the Rockwell hardness tester, which utilizes a diamond that is forced into the surface of the specimen. Different loads are used to provide different scaled. Smaller loads are used for softer materials. Another method is by means of the Vickers hardness machine, which reads directly, as a diamond is pressed into the surface of the metal. Another way is the Shore scleroscope, which utilizes a small dropped weight which will bounce from the surface of the metal providing a hardness measure.

Variability of Material Properties

Tests do not produce exactly the same result because of variations in the test equipment, procedures, operator bias, specimen fabrication, etc. But, even if all those parameters are controlled within strict limits, a variation remains in the materials, due to uncontrolled variations during fabrication, non homogenous composition and structure, etc. The measured mechanical properties will show scatter, which is often distributed in a Gaussian curve (bell-shaped), that is characterized by the mean value and the standard deviation (width).

Design/Safety Factors

To take into account variability of properties, designers use, instead of an average value of, say, the tensile strength, the probability that the yield strength is above the minimum value tolerable. This leads to the use of a safety factor $N > 1$ (typ. 1.2 – 4). Thus, a working value for the tensile strength would be $\sigma_W = \sigma_{TS} / N$.

The mechanical properties of metals determine the range of usefulness of the metal and establish the service that can be expected. Mechanical properties are also used to help specify and identify metals. The most common properties considered are strength, hardness, ductility, and impact resistance.

Strength

The strength of a metal is its ability to withstand the action of external forces without breaking. Tensile strength, also called ultimate strength, is the maximum strength developed in a metal in a tension test. The tension test is a method for determining the behavior of a metal under an actual stretch loading. This test provides the elastic limit, elongation, yield point, yield strength, tensile strength, and the reduction in area. Tensile tests are normally taken at standardized room temperatures but may also be made at elevated temperatures.

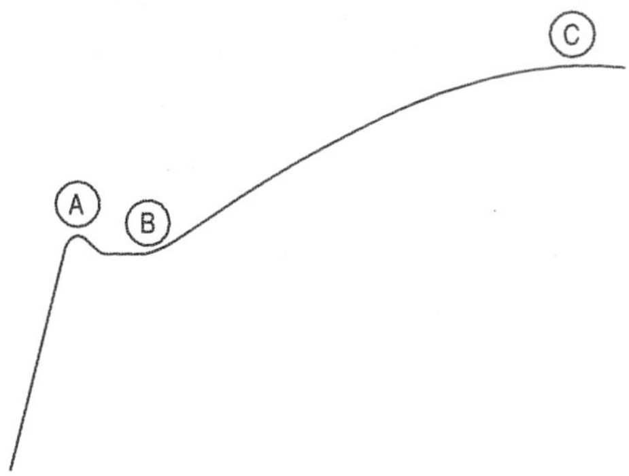

Many tensile testing machines are equipped to plot a curve which shows the load or stress and the strain or movement that occurs during the test operation. In the testing operation the load is increased gradually and the specimen will stretch or elongate in proportion to the tensile load.

The specimen will elongate in direct proportion to the load during the elastic portion of the curve to point A. At this point, the specimen will continue to elongate but without an increase in the load. This is known as the yield point of the steel and is the end of the elastic portion. At any point up to point A if the load is eliminated, the specimen will come back to its original dimension.

Yielding occurs from point A to point B and this is the area of plastic deformation. If the load were eliminated at point B the specimen would not go back to its original dimension but instead take a permanent set. Beyond point B the load will have to be increased to further stretch the specimen.

The load will increase to point C, which is the ultimate strength of the material. At point C the specimen will break and the load is no longer carried. The ultimate tensile strength of the material is obtained by dividing the ultimate load by the cross-sectional area of the original specimen. This provides the ultimate tensile strength in Newtons per square millimeter (Mega Pascals, MPa) or pounds per square inch.

The yield stress or yield point is obtained by dividing the load at yield or at point A by the original area. This provides a figure in pounds per square inch or MPa. Extremely ductile metals do not have a yield point. They stretch or yield at low loads. For these metals the yield point is determined by the change in elongation. Two tenths of one percent elongation is arbitrarily set as the yield point. The yield point is the limit upon which designs are calculated.

Ductility

The ductility of a metal is the property that allows it to be stretched or otherwise changed in shape without breaking and to retain the changed shape after the load has been removed.

The ductility of a metal can be determined from the tensile test. This is done by determining the percent of elongation. Gauge marks are made two inches apart across the point where fracture will occur. The increase in gauge length related to the original length times 100 is the percentage of elongation. This is done by making center punch marks two inches apart at the reduced section of the test coupon, testing the coupon, tightly holding the two pieces together and re-measuring the distance between the center punch marks. The original two inches is subtracted from the measured length and the difference is divided by two and multiplied by 100 to obtain percentage of elongation.

Reduction of Area

Reduction of area is another measure of ductility and is obtained from the tensile test by measuring the original cross-sectional area of the specimen and relating it to the cross-sectional area after failure.

For a round specimen the diameter is measured and the cross-sectional area is calculated. After the test bar is broken the diameter is measured at the smallest point. The cross-sectional area is again calculated. The difference in area is divided by the original area and multiplied by 100 to give the percentage reduction of area. This figure is of less importance than the elongation but is usually reported when the mechanical properties of a metal are given.

The tensile test specimen also provides another property of metal known as its modulus of elasticity, also called Young's modulus. This is the ratio of the stress to the elastic strain. It relates to the slope of the curve to the yield point. The modulus of elasticity is important to the designers and is incorporated in many design formulas.

Impact Resistance

Resistance of a metal to impacts is evaluated in terms of impact strength. A metal may possess satisfactory ductility under static loads but may fail under dynamic loads or impact.

Impact strength is most often determined by the Charpy test. It is sometimes measured by the Izode test. Both types of tests use the same type of pendulum-testing machine. The Charpy test specimen is a beam supported at both ends and contains a notch in the center. The specimen is placed on supports and struck with a pendulum on the side opposite the notch. The accuracy and location of the notch is of extreme importance. There are several types of Charpy specimens; the V-notch type is the most popular.

The impact strength of a metal is determined by measuring the energy absorbed in the fracture. This is equal to the weight of the pendulum times the height at which the pendulum is released and the height to which the pendulum swings after it has struck the specimen. In standard metric practice, impact resistance is measured two ways. One, in Joules based on energy absorbed and, two, in Joules per square centimeter of the area of the fractured surface or the cross-sectional area under the notch. In Anglo-Saxon terms the impact strength is the foot pounds of energy absorbed.

1.22 EFFECT OF ALLOY ON PHYSICAL PROPERTIES

Nickel is an important alloying element. In concentrations of less than 5%, nickel will raise the toughness and ductility of steel without raising the hardness. It will not raise the hardness when added in these small quantities because it does not form carbides, solid compounds with carbon.

Chromium in steel forms a carbide that hardens the metal. The chromium atoms may also occupy locations in the crystal lattice, which will have the effect of increasing hardness without affecting ductility. The addition of nickel intensifies the effects of chromium, producing a steel with increased hardness and ductility.

Copper is quite similar to nickel in its effects on steel. Copper does not form a carbide, but increases hardness by retarding dislocation movement.

Strengthening Mechanisms

Ability to deform plastically depends on ability of dislocations to move. Strengthening consists in hindering dislocation motion. We discuss the methods of grain-size reduction, solid-solution alloying and strain hardening. These are for single-phase metals. We discuss others when treating alloys. Ordinarily, strengthening reduces ductility.

Strengthening by Grain Size Reduction

This is based on the fact that it is difficult for a dislocation to pass into another grain, especially if it is very misaligned. Atomic disorder at the boundary causes discontinuity in slip planes. For high-angle grain boundaries, stress at end of slip plane may trigger new dislocations in adjacent grains. Small angle grain boundaries are not effective in blocking dislocations.

The finer the grains, the larger the area of grain boundaries that impedes dislocation motion. Grain-size reduction usually improves toughness as well. Usually, the yield strength varies with grain size "*d*" according to:

$$\sigma_y = \sigma_0 + k_y/d^{1/2}$$

Grain size can be controlled by the rate of solidification and by plastic deformation.

Solid-Solution Strengthening

Adding another element that goes into interstitial or substitutional positions in a solution increases strength. The impurity atoms cause lattice strain which can "anchor" dislocations. This occurs when the strain caused by the alloying element compensates that of the dislocation, thus achieving a state of low potential energy. It costs strain energy for the dislocation to move away from this state (which is like a potential well). The scarcity of energy at low temperatures is why slip is hindered. Pure metals are almost always softer than their alloys.

Strain Hardening

Ductile metals become stronger when they are deformed plastically at temperatures well below the melting point **(cold working)**. (This is different from hot working is the shaping of materials at high temperatures where large deformation is possible). Strain hardening (work hardening) is the reason for the elastic recovery discussed in Chapter 2.

The reason for strain hardening is that the dislocation density increases with plastic deformation (cold work) due to multiplication. The average distance between dislocations then decreases and dislocations start blocking the motion of each one.

The measure of strain hardening is the percent cold work (%CW), given by the relative reduction of the original area, A_0 to the final value A_d :

$$\%CW = 100\,(A_0 - A_d)/A_0$$

Recovery, Recrystallization and Grain Growth

Plastic deformation causes (1) change in grain size, (2) strain hardening, (3) increase in the dislocation density. Restoration to the state before cold-work is done by heating through two processes: recovery and recrystallization. These may be followed by grain growth.

Recovery

Heating → increased diffusion → enhanced dislocation motion → relieves internal strain energy and reduces the number of dislocation. The electrical and thermal conductivity are restored to the values existing before cold working.

Recrystallization

Strained grains of cold-worked metal are replaced,. upon heating, by more regularly-spaced grains. This occurs through short-range diffusion enabled by the high temperature. Since recrystallization occurs by diffusion, the important parameters are both temperature and time.

The material becomes softer, weaker, but more ductile.

Recrystallization temperature: is that at which the process is complete in one hour. It is typically 1/3 to 1/2 of the melting temperature. It falls as the %CW is increased. Below a "critical deformation", recrystallization does not occur.

Grain Growth

The growth of grain size with temperature can occur in all polycrystalline materials. It occurs by migration of atoms at grain boundaries by diffusion, thus grain growth is faster at higher temperatures. The "driving force" is the reduction of energy, which is proportional to the total area. Big grains grow at the expense of the small ones.

Polymorphism and Allotropy

Some materials may exist in more than one crystal structure, this is called **polymorphism.** If the material is an elemental solid, it is called allotropy.

An example of allotropy is carbon, which can exist as diamond, graphite, and amorphous carbon.

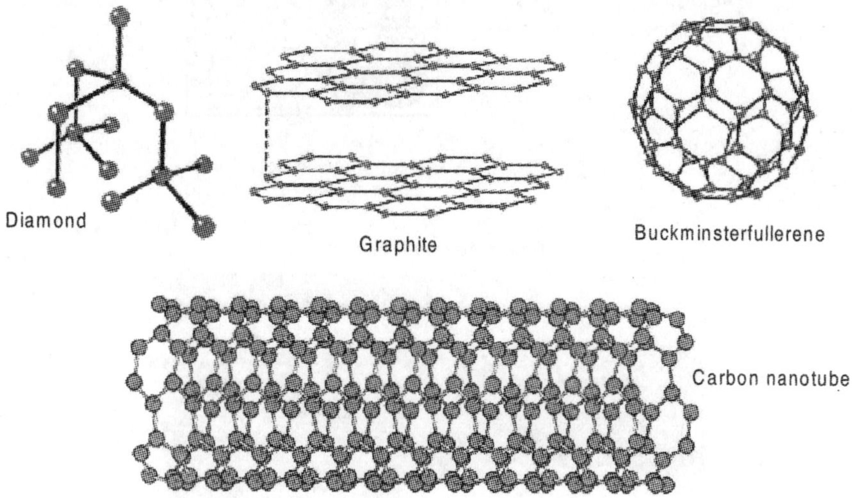

Fig. 1.50 Diamond, graphite, carbon nanotube.

Pure, solid carbon occurs in three crystalline forms—diamond, graphite; and large, hollow fullerenes. Two kinds of fullerenes are shown here: buckminsterfullerene (bucky ball) and carbon nanotube.

Single Crystals and Polycrystalline Materials

Single crystal: atoms are in a repeating or periodic array over the entire extent of the material

Polycrystalline material: comprised of many small crystals or **grains.** The grains have different crystallographic orientation. There exist atomic mismatch within the regions where grains meet. These regions are called **grain boundaries.**

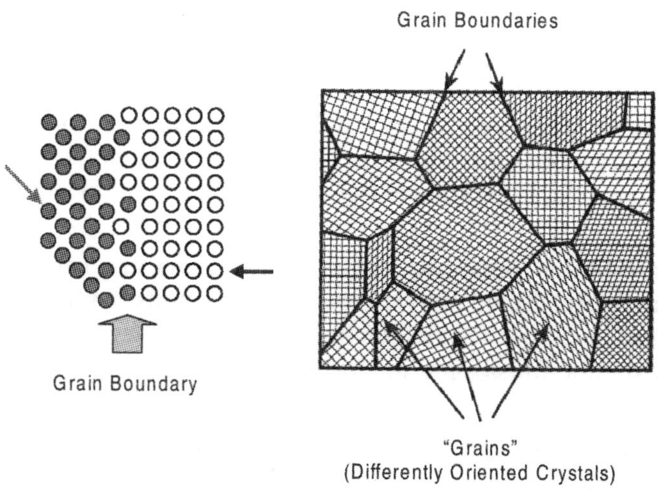

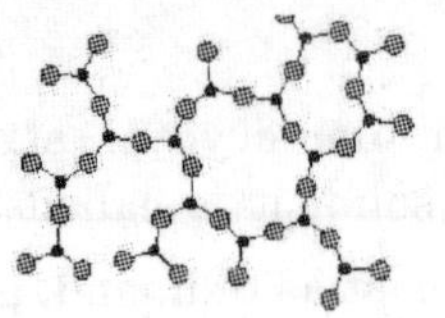

Schematic picture of amorphous SiO_2 structure

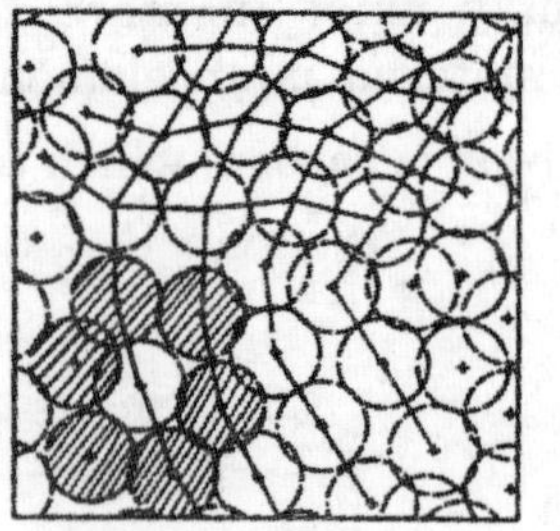

Amorphous structure from simulations by E.H. Brandt

Polycrystalline Materials

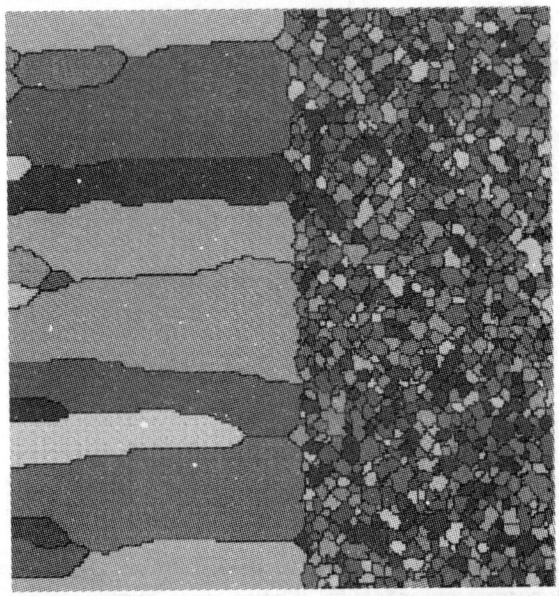

Simulation of annealing of a polycrystalline grain structure

Fig. 1.51

Anisotropy

Different directions in a crystal have a different packing. For instance, atoms along the edge of FCC unit cell are more separated than along the face diagonal. This causes **anisotropy** in the properties of crystals, for instance, the deformation depends on the direction in which a stress is applied.

In some polycrystalline materials, grain orientations are random, so bulk material properties are **isotropic.** Some polycrystalline materials have grains with preferred orientations (**texture**), so properties are dominated by those relevant to the texture orientation and the material exhibits anisotropic properties.

Non-Crystalline (Amorphous) Solids

In amorphous solids, there is no long-range order. But amorphous does not mean random, in many cases there is some form of short-range order.

REVIEW QUESTIONS

1. Classify materials.
2. What are the different types of solids ?
3. What is unit cell ?
4. What is crystalline and amorphous solid ?
5. With the help of neat sketch explain different types of crystal structure.
6. List some examples of BCC FCC and HCP structure.
7. What is co-ordination number ?
8. What is atomic packing factor ?
9. What is bravais lattice ?
10. Explain different kinds of bravais lattice structure.
11. What is Miller indices and its uses ?
12. What are the steps to be followed in Miller indices ?
13. Why defect in crystal occurs ?
14. Explain different kinds of crystal defects.
15. Briefly explain different mechanical properties of metals.
16. What are the effects of alloy on physical properties ?
17. Explain different strengthening mechanism.
18. What is primitive unit cell ?
19. Explain the process of grain growth.
20. Draw the direction and planes for the following F.C.C Structures (112), (321), (111).
21. Explain the uses of grain.
22. Explain various ASTM grain size number.

2
CHAPTER

IRON CABON EQUILIBRIUM DIAGRAM

2.1 PHASE DIAGRAMS

A phase diagram shows us the microstructure within a material as a function of the material composition (% alloying elements) and material temperature.

Why are phase diagrams important?

- They can help us understand the thermal history of a material and the effect of that history on material properties.
- They are needed to help us understand how we develop and preserve non-equilibrium microstructures.
- The different microstructures represented on a phase diagram produce different material properties when that microstructure is preserved in the material.

The properties of a material depend on the type, number, amount, and form of the phases present, and can be changed by altering these quantities. In order to make these changes, it is essential to know the conditions under which these quantities exist and the conditions under which a change in phase will occur.

The best method to record the data related to phase changes in many alloy systems is in the form of *phase diagrams*, also known as *equilibrium diagrams* or *constitutional diagrams.*

In order to specify completely the state of a system in equilibrium, it is necessary to specify three independent variables. These variables, which are externally controllable, are *temperature, pressure* and *composition*. With pressure assumed to be constant at atmospheric value, the equilibrium diagram indicates the structural changes due to variation of temperature and composition. Phase diagrams show the phase relationships under equilibrium conditions, that is, under conditions in which there will be no change with time. Equilibrium conditions may be approached by extremely slow heating and cooling, so that if a phase change is to occur, sufficient time is allowed.

Phase diagrams are usually plotted with temperature as the ordinate, and the alloy composition as the abscissa as shown in Fig. 2.1.

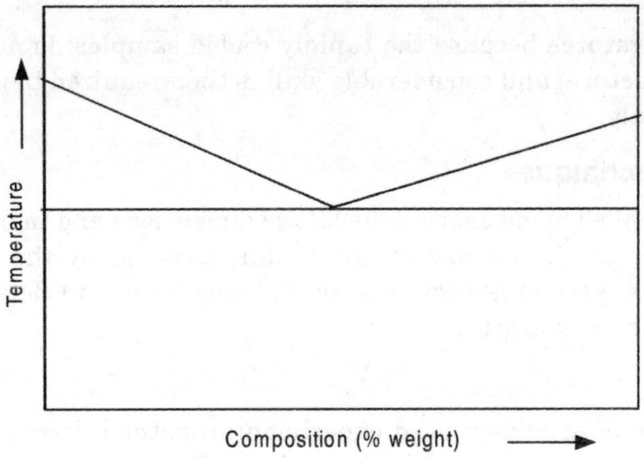

Fig. 2.1 Sample phase diagram.

Definitions

Component: Pure metal or compound (*e.g.*, Cu, Zn in Cu-Zn alloy, sugar, water, in a syrup.)

Solvent: Host or major component in solution.

Solute: Dissolved, minor component in solution.

System: Set of possible alloys from same component (*e.g.*, iron-carbon system.)

Solubility Limit: Maximum solute concentration that can be dissolved at a given temperature.

Phase: Part with homogeneous physical and chemical characteristics.

2.2 INTERPRETATION OF PHASE DIAGRAMS

The information that we can find from a phase diagram includes:

1. The phases present
2. The composition of the phases
3. The percentages or fractions of the phases.

Experimental Methods

The data for the construction of equilibrium diagrams are determined experimentally by a varicty of mcthods, the most common methods are:

1. Metallographic methods
2. X-ray diffraction technique
3. Thermal analysis.

Metallographic Methods

This method is applied by heating samples of an alloy to different temperatures, waiting for equilibrium to be established, and then quickly cooling to retain their high-temperature structure. The samples then examined microscopically. This method is difficult to apply to metals at high temperatures because the rapidly cooled samples do not always retain their high-temperature structure, and considerable skill is then required to interpret the observed microstructure correctly.

X-ray Diffraction Technique

This method is applied by measuring the lattice dimensions and indicating the appearance of a new phase either by the change in lattice dimension or by the appearance of a new crystal structure. This method is very precise and very useful in determining the changes in solid solubility with temperature.

Thermal Analysis

This is by far the most widely used experimental method. It relies on the information obtained from the cooling diagrams. In this method, alloys mixed at different compositions are melted and then the temperature of the mixture is measured at a certain time interval while cooling back to room temperature.

A cooling diagram for each mixture is constructed and the initial and final phase change temperatures are determined. Then these temperatures are used for the construction of the phase diagrams.

2.3 COOLING CURVE OF A PURE METAL

Under equilibrium conditions, all metals exhibit a definite melting or freezing point. If a cooling curve is plotted for a pure metal. It will show a horizontal line at the melting or freezing temperature.

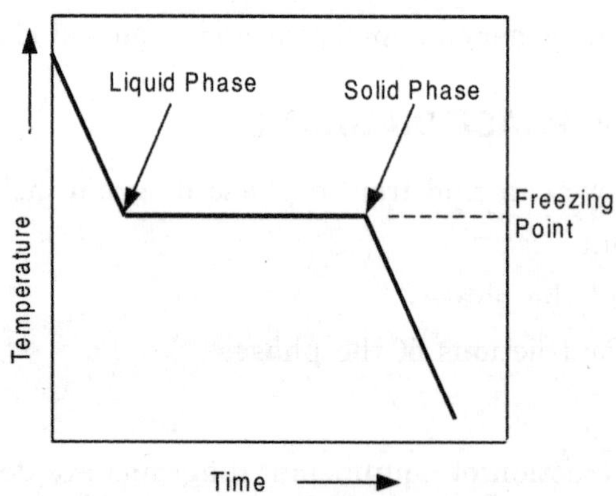

Fig. 2.2 Cooling curve for the solidification of pure metal.

Cooling Curve of a Solid Solution

A solid solution is a solution in the solid state and consists of two kinds of atoms combined in one type of space lattice. A solution is composed of two parts: a solute and a solvent. The solute is the minor part of the solution or the material which is dissolved, while the solvent constitutes the major portion of the solution. When solidification of the solution starts, the temperature may be higher or lower than the freezing point of the pure solvent. Most solid solutions solidify over a range in temperature. Fig. 2.3 below shows the cooling curve for the solidification of a solid solution.

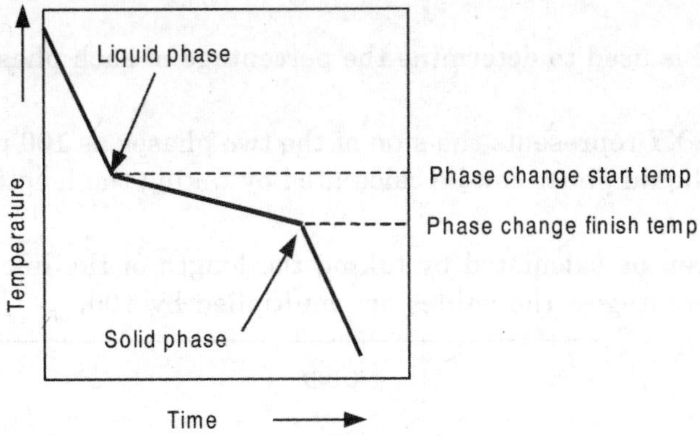

Fig. 2.3 Cooling curve for solid solution.

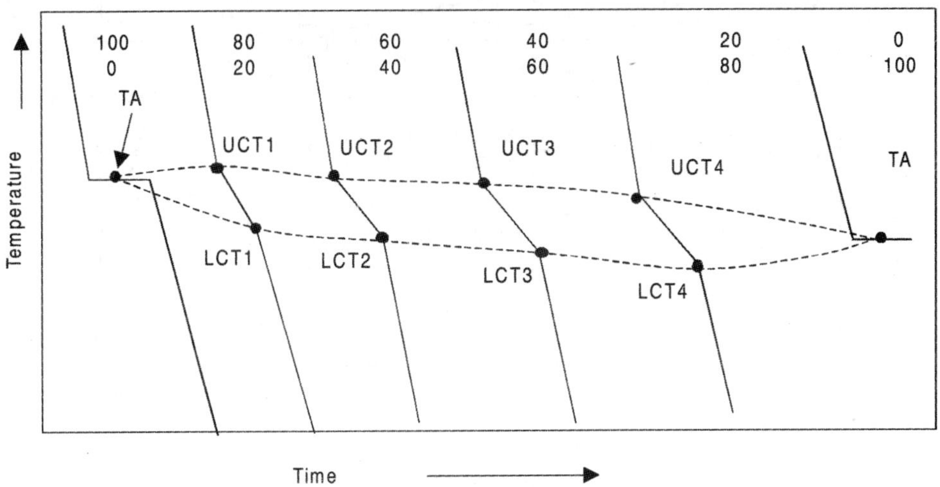

Fig. 2.4 Cooling curve.

Fig. 2.5 below shows the series of cooling curves for different alloys in a completely soluble system. The dotted lines indicate the form of the phase diagram

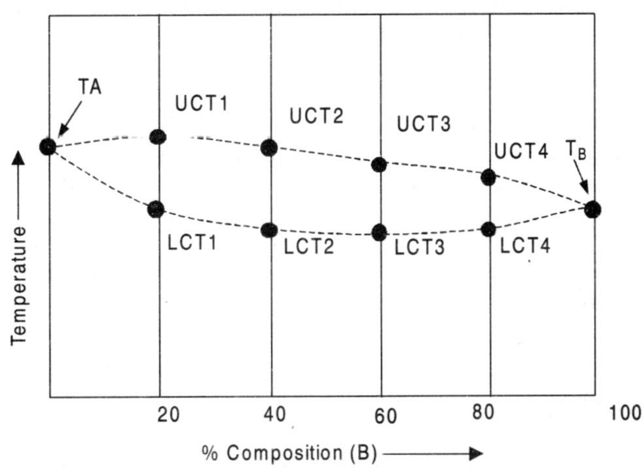

Fig. 2.5 Phase Diagram for alloy A + B.

Inverse Lever Rule

Inverse lever rule is used to determine the percentage of each phase that is present at various temperatures.

The length of line XY represents the sum of the two phases as 100 percent. The inverse lever rule states that liquid phase can be calculated by taking the length of the line XZ and dividing this by XY.

The solid phase can be calculated by taking the length of the line ZY and dividing it by XY. To get the percentages, the values are multiplied by 100.

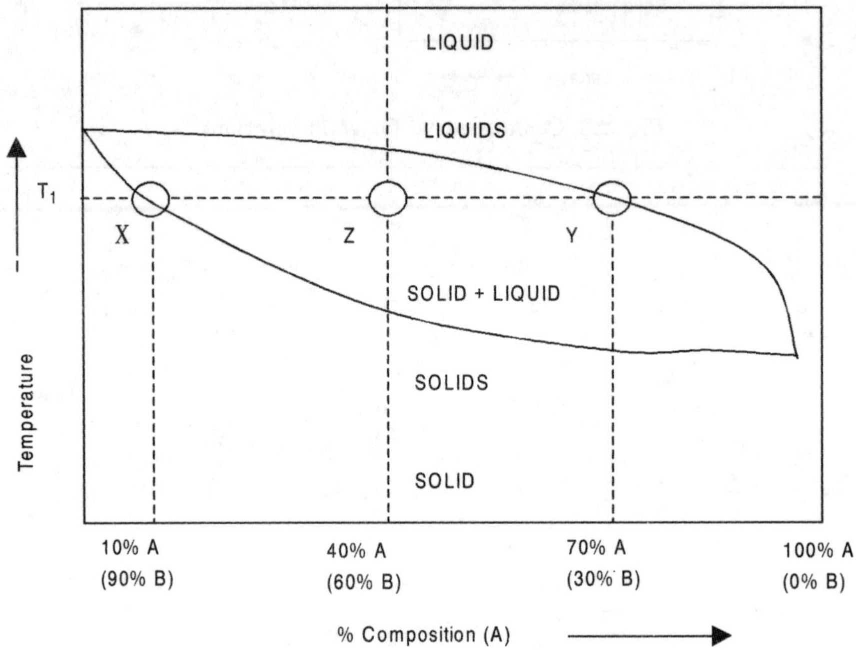

Fig. 2.6 Phase diagram of a mixture with complete solubility in liquid and solid states.

Sample Calculation

Alloy with 40% A and 60% B at room temperature is heated to a temperature T_1. Calculate the liquid and solid phase and indicate the composition of each phase.

Liquid Phase = (XZ/XY) × 100 = [(40 – 10) / (70 – 10)] × 100 = 50%

Solid Phase = (ZY/XY) × 100 = [(70 – 40) / (70 – 10)] × 100 = 50%

At temperature T_1, the solid composition is found by the intersection (point X) of isothermal line T_1 and the solidus curve.

Solid composition: 10% A and 90% B.

The liquid composition at temperature T_1 is found by the intersection (point Y) of isothermal line T_1 and the liquidus curve.

Liquid composition: 70% A and 30% B.

2.4 EUTECTIC SYSTEM

Eutectic system is a phase transformation that takes place when a single-phase liquid transforms directly to a two-phase solid.

L —> S1 + S2

Liquid —> Solid 1 + Solid 2

(This is a reversible phase transformation)

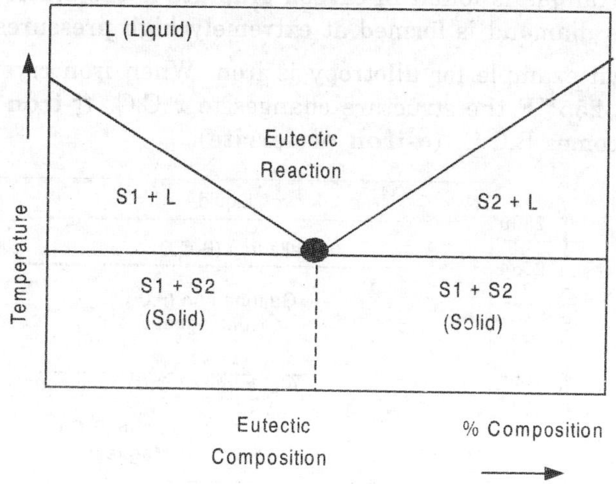

Fig. 2.7 Eutectic phase transformation.

2.5 EUTECTOID SYSTEM

The eutectoid phase transformation occurs when a single-phase solid transforms directly to two-phase solid.

S1 —> S2 + S3

Solid 1 —> Solid 2 + Solid 3

(This is a reversible phase transformation)

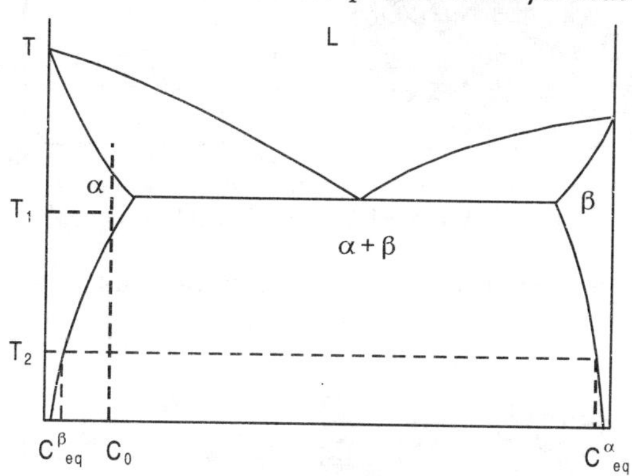

Fig. 2.8 Eutectoid phase transformation.

2.6 POLYMORPHISM AND ALLOTROPY

Polymorphism is a physical phenomenon where a material may have more than one crystal structure. A material that shows polymorphism exists in more than one type of space lattice in the solid state. If the change in structure is reversible, then the polymorphic change is known as ***allotropy.*** The prevailing crystal structure depends on both the temperature and the external pressure.

One familiar example is found in carbon graphite is the stable polymorph at ambient conditions, whereas diamond is formed at extremely high pressures.

The best known example for allotropy is iron. When iron crystallizes at 2800°F it is B.C.C. (**δ-iron**), at 2554°F the structure changes to F.C.C. (**γ-iron or austenite**), and at 1670°F it again becomes B.C.C. (**α-iron or ferrite**).

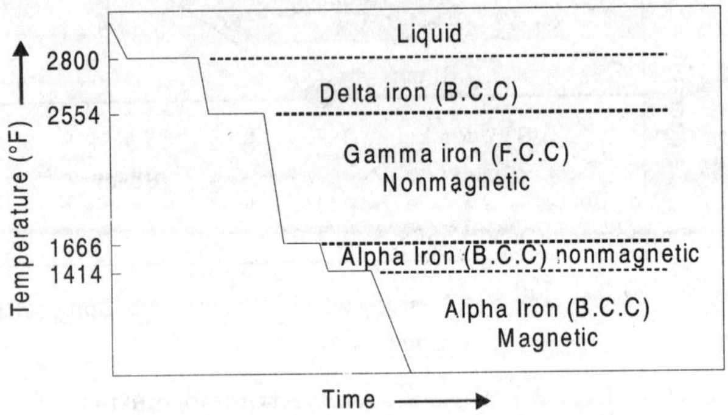

Fig. 2.9 Cooling curve for pure iron. (Allotropic behavior of pure iron)

α-iron (alpha)

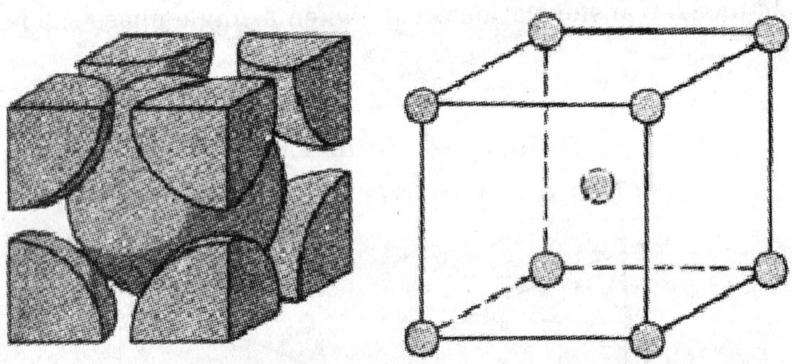

Fig. 2.10 Alpha iron (B.C.C) unit cell.

The other name for α-iron is ferrite. This crystal has body centered cubic structure.

γ-iron (Gamma)

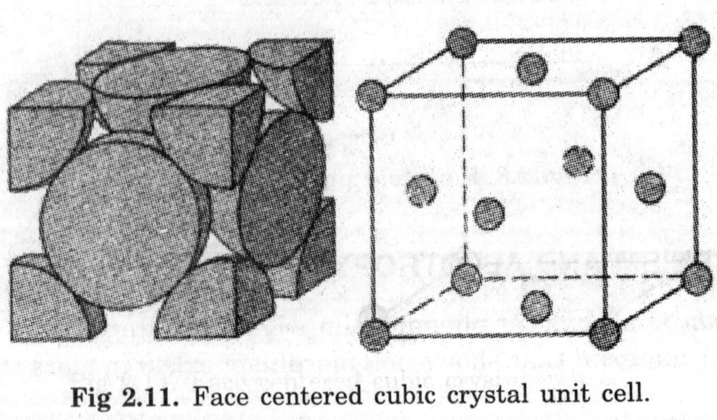

Fig 2.11. Face centered cubic crystal unit cell.

The other name for γ-iron is austenite. This crystal has face centered cubic (F.C.C) structure.

2.7 IRON-CARBON EQUILIBRIUM DIAGRAM

This is one of the most important alloys for structural applications. The diagram Fe-C is simplified at low carbon concentrations by assuming it is the Fe-Fe_3C diagram. Concentrations are usually given in weight percent. The possible phases are:

- α-ferrite (BCC) Fe-C solution
- γ-austenite (FCC) Fe-C solution
- δ-ferrite (BCC) Fe-C solution
- Liquid Fe-C solution
- Fe_3C (iron carbide) or cementite. An intermetallic compound.

The maximum solubility of C in α-ferrite is 0.022 wt%. δ-ferrite is only stable at high temperatures. It is not important in practice. Austenite has a maximum Carbon concentration of 2.14 wt%. It is not stable below the eutectic temperature (727°C) unless cooled rapidly. Cementite is in reality metastable, decomposing into α-Fe and C when heated for several hours between 650° and 770°C.

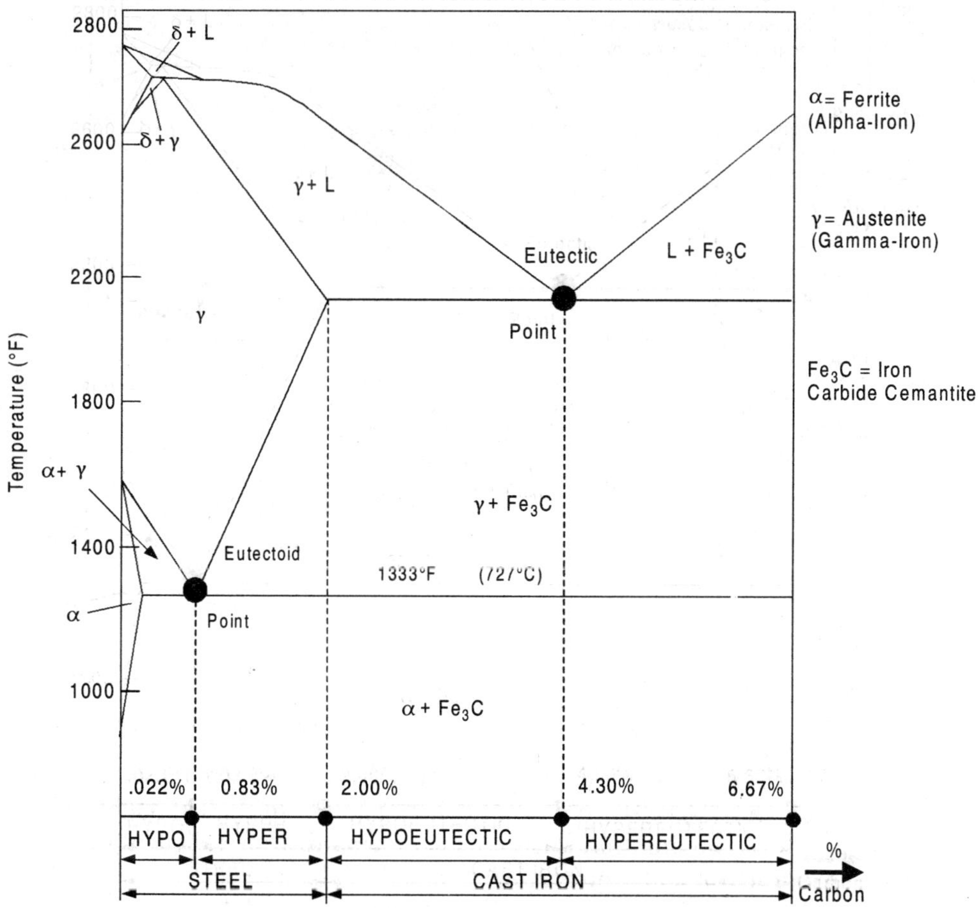

Fig. 2.12 Iron-carbon equilibrium diagram.

For their role in mechanical properties of the alloy, it is important to note that

Ferrite is soft and ductile.

Cementite is hard and brittle.

Thus, combining these two phases in solution an alloy can be obtained with intermediate properties. (Mechanical properties also depend on the microstructure, that is, how ferrite and cementite are mixed.)

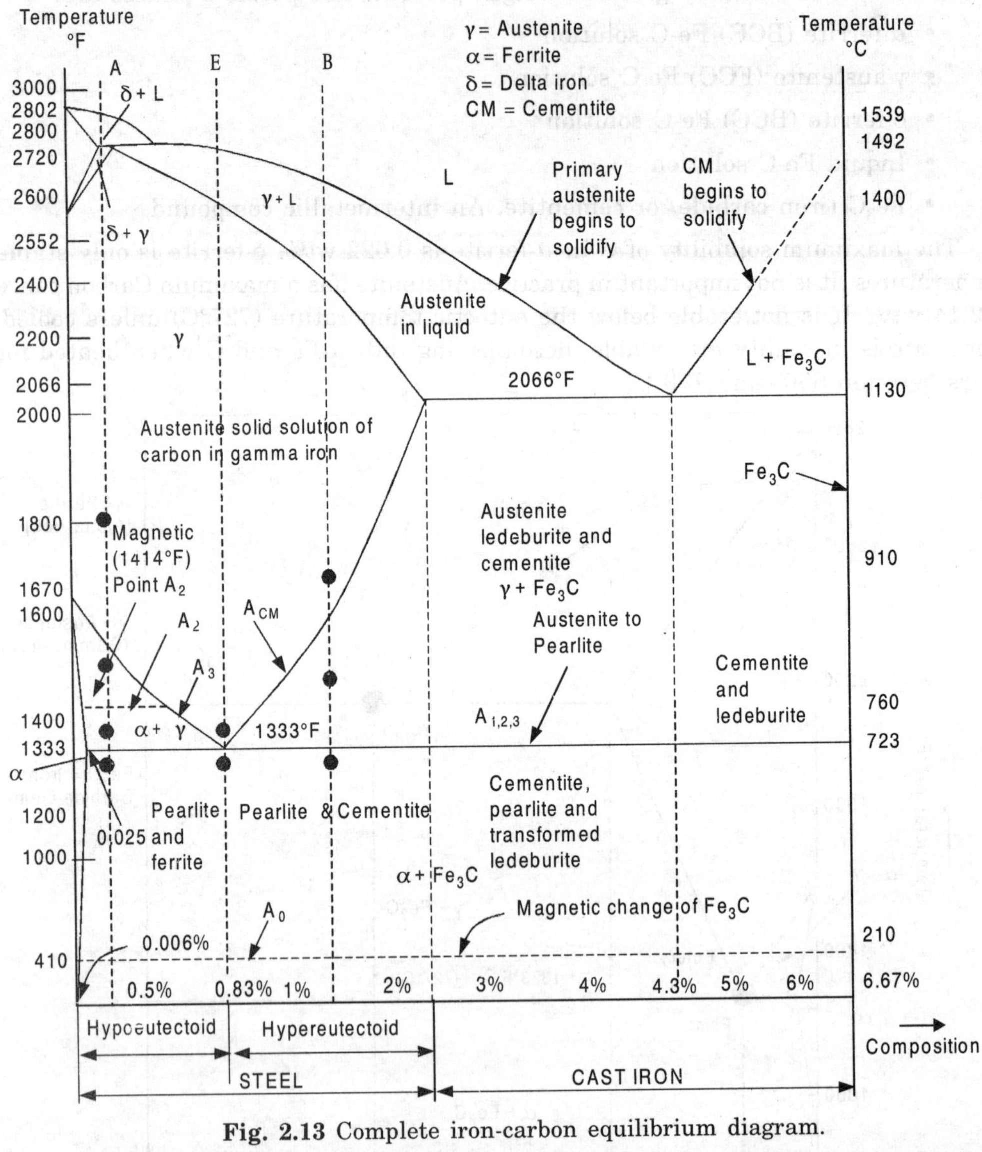

Fig. 2.13 Complete iron-carbon equilibrium diagram.

Three significant regions can be made relative to the steel portion of the diagram. They are the *Eutectoid*, the *Hypoeutectoid* , and the *Hypereutectoid* . The right side of the pure iron line is carbon in combination with various forms of iron called alpha iron (**ferrite**), gamma iron (**Austenite**), and **deltairon.**

Allotropic changes take place when there is a change in crystal lattice structure. From

2802°–2552°F the delta iron has a **body-centered** cubic lattice structure. At 2552°F, the lattice changes from a body-centered cubic to a **face-centered** cubic lattice type. At 1400°F, the curve shows a plateau but this does not signify an allotropic change. It is called the Curie temperature, where the metal changes its magnetic properties.

Two very important phase changes take place at 0.83% C and at 4.3% C. At 0.83% C, the transformation is eutectoid, called pearlite.

δ iron (austenite) → α iron + Fe_3C (cementite)

At 4.3% C and 2066°F, the transformation is eutectic, called ledeburite.

L(liquid) → γ iron (austenite) + Fe_3C (cementite)

The Eutectoid Reaction

The eutectoid reaction describes the phase transformation of one solid into two different solids. In the Fe-C system, there is a eutectoid point at approximately 0.8 wt% C, 723°C. The phase just above the eutectoid temperature for plain carbon steels is known as austenite or gamma. We now consider what happens as this phase is cooled through the eutectoid temperature (723°C).

The phase diagram which we will be considering throughout this section is shown below:

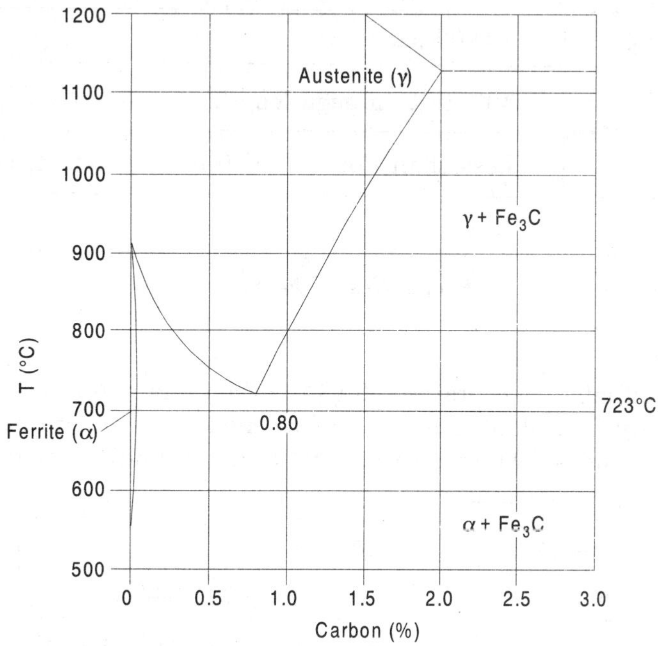

Fig. 2.14 The eutectoid reaction.

Cementite (Fe_3C)

Cementite is also known as iron carbide which has a chemical formula, Fe_3C. It contains 6.67 % Carbon by weight. It is a typical hard and brittle interstitial compound of low tensile strength (approximately 5,000 psi) but high compressive strength. Its crystal structure is orthorhombic.

Austenite (γ iron)

It is also known as (γ) gamma-iron, which is an interstitial solid solution of carbon dissolved in iron with a Face Centered Cubic (F.C.C) crystal structure. Average properties of austenite are:

Tensile strength	150,000 psi.
Elongation	10% in 2 in gage length.
Hardness	Rockwell C 40
Toughness	High

Properties of Austenite

Austenite is normally unstable at room temperature. Under certain conditions it is possible to obtain austenite at room temperature.

Ferrite (α iron)

It is also known as (α) alpha-iron, which is an interstitial solid solution of a small amount of carbon dissolved in iron with a Body Centered Cubic (B.C.C.) crystal structure. It is the softest structure on the iron-iron carbide diagram. Average properties are:

Tensile strength	40,000 psi
Elongation	40% in 2 in gage length
Hardness	Less than Rockwell C 0 or less than Rockwell B 90.
Toughness	Low

Properties of Ferrite

Pearlite (α + Fe_3C)

It is the eutectoid mixture containing 0.83% carbon and is formed at 1333°F on very slow cooling. It is very fine plate like or lamellar mixture of ferrite and cementite. The structure of pearlite includes a white matrix (ferritic background) which includes thin plates of cementite. Average properties are:

Tensile strength	120,000 psi
Elongation	20% in 2 in gage length
Hardness	Rockwell C 20 or BHN 250–300

Properties of Pearlite

A fixed amount of carbon and a fixed amount of iron are needed to form cementite (Fe_3C). Also, pearlite needs fixed amounts of cementite and ferrite.

If there is not enough carbon, that is less than 0.83%, the carbon and the iron will combine to form Fe_3C until all the carbon is consumed. This cementite will combine with the required amount of ferrite to form pearlite. The remaining amount of ferrite will stay in the structure as free ferrite. Free ferrite is also known as proeutectoid ferrite. The steel that contains proeutectoid ferrite is referred to as hypoeutectoid steel.

If, however, there is an excess of carbon above 0.83% in the austenite, pearlite will form, and the excess carbon above 0.83% will form cementite. The excess cementite deposits in the grain boundaries. This excess cementite is also known as proeutectoid cementite.

Ledeburite ($\alpha + Fe_3C$)

It is the eutectic mixture of austenite and cementite. It contains 4.3% carbon and represents the eutectic of cast iron. Ledeburite exists when the carbon content is greater than 2%, which represents the dividing line on the equilibrium diagram between steel and cast iron.

(δ) Delta Iron

Delta iron exists between 2552 and 2802°F. It may exist in combination with the melt to about 0.50% carbon, in combination with austenite to about 0.18% carbon and in a single phase state out to about 0.10% carbon. Delta iron has the Body Centered Cubic (B.C.C) crystal structure and is magnetic.

2.8 EXAMPLES OF IRON-IRON CARBIDE PHASE TRANSFORMATIONS ON THE T-T-T DIAGRAM

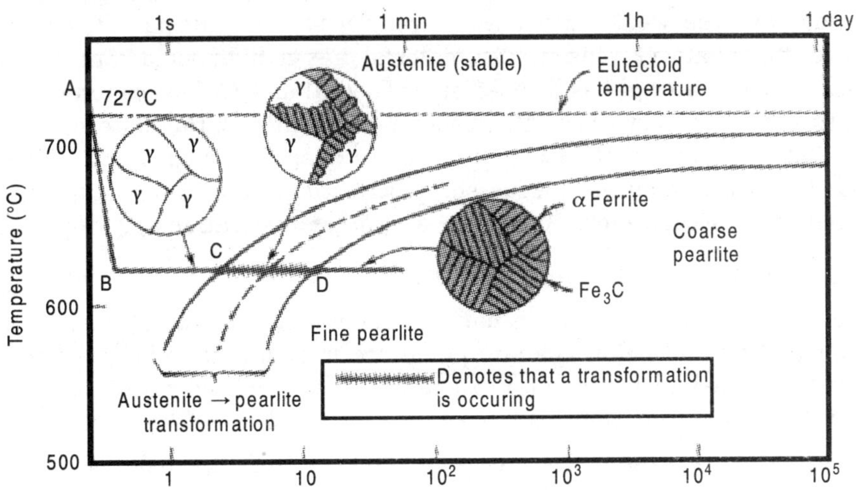

Fig. 2.15 Fe-Fe_3C T-T-T diagram.

The time-temperature transformation curves correspond to the start and finish of transformations which extend into the range of temperatures where **austenite** transforms to **pearlite.** Above 550°C, austenite transforms completely to pearlite. Below 550°C, both pearlite and bainite are formed and below 450°C, only bainite is formed. The horizontal line C-D that runs between the two curves marks the beginning and end of isothermal transformations. The dashed line that runs parallel to the solid line curves represents the time to transform half the austenite to pearlite.

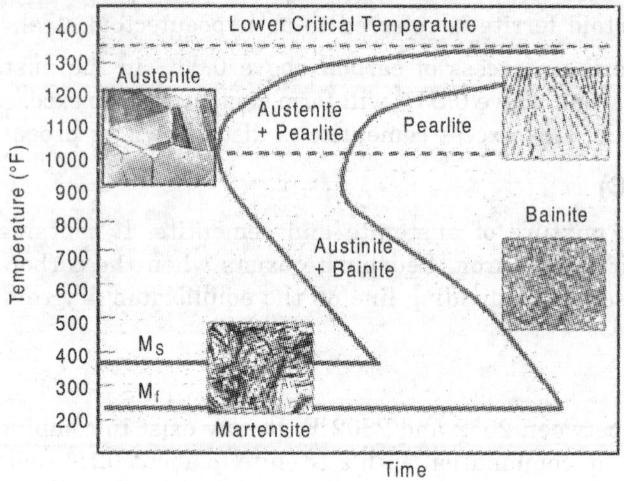

Fig. 2.16 TTT diagram and microstructures obtained by different types of cooling rates.

2.9 STRENGTHENING MECHANISMS

Plastic deformation in a crystal usually occurs by the movement of dislocations. As such, dislocations are the weak link in the strength of the material. If dislocations are unable to move, for whatever reason, the material has a high yield stress and will not deform plastically. The material has been strengthened. If dislocations can move easily, then only a small stress is necessary to start a dislocation gliding and the material is soft. There are many ways of *pinning* a dislocation, in order to keep it from moving. Three types of obstacles to dislocation motion are discussed: substitutional and interstitial solute atoms, precipitates and other second-phase particles, and other dislocations.

Intrinsic Lattice Resistance to Deformation

Let us begin by considering a pure metal without any alloy additions. In the perfect lattice, all atoms above and below the slip plane are in minimum energy positions. When a shear stress is applied to the crystal, all atoms are displaced from their equilibrium positions creating a force that opposes the applied stress. The deformation is elastic.

When a dislocation is present, the atoms far removed from the dislocation are still very close to their equilibrium positions and any deformation arising from an external stress will induce a deformation in the atomic structure that will oppose the applied forces. The atoms in the immediate vicinity of the dislocation are not in their equilibrium positions, but are in a higher energy state. Although the net force acting on a straight dislocation is zero, the stress field around the dislocation will still interact with the external stress field.

The glide force acting on a dislocation in the pure metal as a result of an external load. However, we know from experiment that a characteristic shear stress, or *critical resolved shear stress*, $[\sigma]_{crss}$, is required for slip to commence; resolved stresses less than the critical resolved shear stress result in elastic deformation that is recovered when the external load is removed. A minimum shear stress is required because most crystals have an *intrinsic strength* caused by the bonds between the atoms which must be broken and reformed as the dislocation moves. We designate the shear stress necessary to overcome the intrinsic stress, $[\sigma]_{intr}$. Thus, in a pure metal, $\sigma_{crss} = [\sigma]_{intr}$.

An external shear stress is applied to the crystal so as to cause the dislocation to move to the right. In order to do so, the atomic bonds of the atoms in the atomic plane to the right of the dislocation must first be broken. (See arrow in middle sketch.) Although the movement of the dislocation from one position to the adjacent position involves only a small rearrangement of the atomic bonds near the dislocation, breaking the bonds still requires that an activation barrier be surmounted. A sufficiently large applied stress must be applied before the dislocation is able to overcome the barrier. The stronger the bonds between atoms, the larger the applied stress that must be applied in order to move the dislocation. For this reason, the yield stress is usually very large in materials with strong directional or covalent bonding, such as many ceramic materials including diamond, carbides and nitrides. Metals, on the other hand, possess a very low intrinsic resistance to dislocation motion and are very soft. It is even possible to bend a properly heat-treated rod of pure copper with your hands.

In summary, pure metals possess an intrinsic resistance to dislocation motion which requires a critical resolved shear stress to be applied to the material before a dislocation will move or glide. Intrinsic resistance results from the necessity of breaking atomic bonds to move the dislocation. In a pure metal, $[\sigma]_{crss} = [\sigma]_{intr}$. In a single crystal, the force required to move a dislocation depends on crystal orientation.

2.10 SOLID-SOLUTION STRENGTHENING

Now consider the addition of an alloying element or *solute* to the pure metal discussed above to form a solid solution. A substitutional solid solution is one in which the alloying element occupies the same lattice sites as the atoms of the host matrix, as when copper is dissolved in aluminium. In contrast, an *interstitial solid solution* occurs when the alloying element occupies one or several different interstitial sites, such as when carbon is dissolved in iron to form steel. Examples of substitutional and interstitial solid solutions are shown in Fig. 2.17 below.

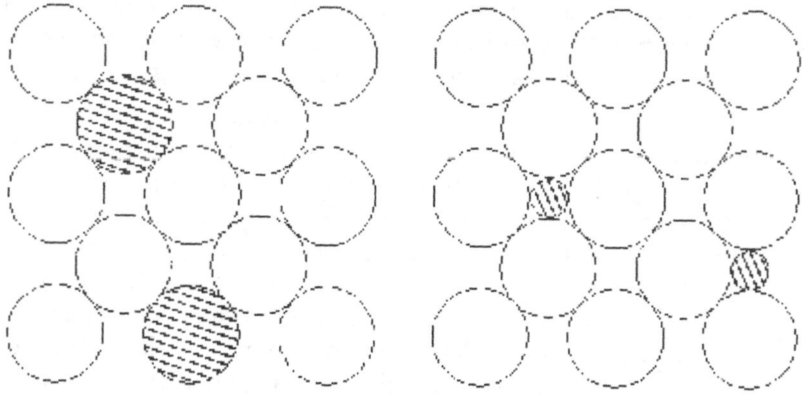

(a) (b)

Fig.2.17 The solute atoms replace the solvent atoms in a substitutional solid solution in (*a*). In an interstitial solid solution, (*b*) The solute atoms occupy interstitial sites in the lattice.

For both interstitial and substitutional solid solutions, the solute atom distorts the surrounding lattice. This deformation occurs on account of the solute and solvent atoms possessing different atomic sizes. For example, if the atomic volume of a substitutional solute atom is greater than that of the host solvent atom, it will tend to push on the surrounding atoms creating a compressive stress field in the vicinity of the solute atom. If the solute atom is smaller than the solvent atom, the solute atom will engender a state of tension in the surrounding lattice as the atoms adjacent to the solute tend to collapse towards the smaller solute atom. To a first approximation, a substitutional atom can be thought of as a center of expansion or contraction.

The stress state associated with an interstitial atom is usually more complex than that associated with a substitutional atom. Since an interstitial site rarely has a spherical symmetry, stresses in one direction are often much stronger than stresses in other directions. One example already encountered is the large tetragonal distortion associated with a carbon interstitial atom in a BCC iron lattice. Significant shear stresses also accompany interstitial atoms. Interstitial atoms act not only as a center of expansion or contraction, but also produce shear stresses in the lattice.

The stress field produced by a solute atom will interact with the elastic stress field of a dislocation. The elastic interaction between solute and dislocation can either increase or decrease the elastic energy of the crystal, depending on the type of dislocation, the type of solute atom and the relative position of the two. For example, consider a solute atom with an atomic volume greater than the atomic volume of the solvent atoms. The solute acts as a center of expansion, compressing the surrounding atoms in the lattice. If the solute atom is in the vicinity of an edge dislocation, then the compressive and tensile stresses produced by the dislocation will interact with the compressive stresses of the solute atom. If the solute atom is located above the slip plane, the stress field of the dislocation is compressive. When the compressive elastic field of the solute atom is added to the compressive field of the dislocation, the lattice is even more highly compressed. This increases the elastic energy of the system in comparison to its elastic energy when the solute atom and dislocation are far apart. The *interaction energy* is positive, meaning that the energy of the system increases when the solute atom is located near the edge dislocation at a point above the slip plane, as compared to the system energy when the solute atom and dislocation are infinitely far apart. Solute atoms usually diffuse to the dislocation if the interaction energy is negative and diffuse away from the dislocation when the interaction energy is positive.

The lattice is in a state of tension for points below the slip plane of the edge dislocation shown. If the large solute atom is located at a point below the slip plane, the compressive state of the solute atom and the tensile stresses produced by the dislocation would tend to push one another, resulting in a lattice that is less deformed than if the solute atom or dislocation were there alone. In this case, the interaction energy is negative; the energy of the system is decreased when the solute atom is located below the slip plane. Since a shear stress will not interact with a center of expansion or contraction, a screw dislocation interacts only weakly with a substitutional atom (There are other sources of elastic interaction between a dislocation and solute atom. For example, there is a *modulus effect* when solute and solvent possess different shear moduli). The more negative the interaction energy, the stronger the solute-dislocation interaction.

If solute atoms are able to diffuse, or dislocations are able to move to the solute atom, the energy of the system will be lowered when such rearrangement reduces the elastic energy of the system. A non-uniform distribution of solute atoms will also result in the vicinity of the dislocation. Fig.2.18 shows the type of heterogeneous distribution of solute atoms that can result for solute atoms that are centers of expansion in the vicinity of an edge dislocation, as in the above discussion. The largest concentration of solute atoms is found immediately below the dislocation where the tensile stresses are largest. Although no solute atoms are found immediately above the dislocation, a net segregation of solute atoms to the dislocation can result. The equilibrium concentration of solute atoms is recovered, as the distance from the dislocation center increases. For comparison, the equilibrium distribution of vacancies, which act as a center of contraction, around an edge dislocation is also shown. The stress-induced redistribution of solute atoms around a dislocation is termed a *Cotrell atmosphere*.

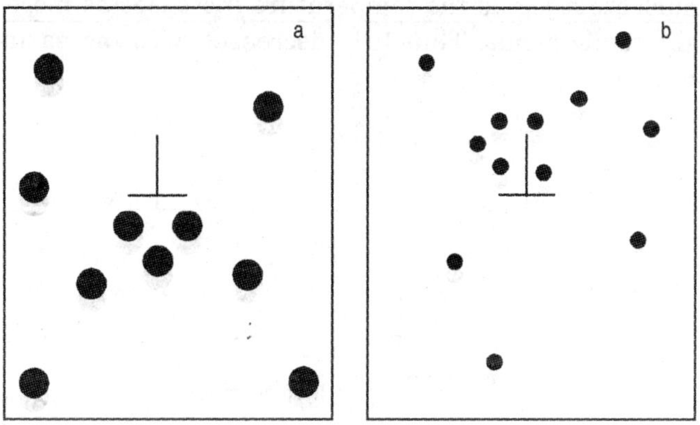

(a) (b)

Fig. 2.18 The distribution of solute atoms that are centers of expansion (oversized atoms) near an edge dislocation is shown in (*a*). The distribution of atoms is much different when the atomic volume of the solute is less than the atomic volume of the solvent atoms, as shown in (*b*).

For sufficiently high temperatures, solute atoms will diffuse to achieve an equilibrium distribution around a dislocation. If a stress is subsequently applied to the material, the dislocation will have to overcome the interaction energy between the dislocation and solute atoms, in addition to the intrinsic stress, before it is able to move. The dislocation is said to be *pinned* by the solute atoms.

The magnitude of the stress, above and beyond the intrinsic stress, required to separate the dislocation from the solute atmosphere is termed solid-solution hardening or strengthening and is here designated as $[\sigma]_{ss}$. The critical resolved shear stress of the solid solution is the sum of the contributions of the intrinsic stress and the increment in stress owing to solid-solution hardening, $[\sigma]_{crss} = [\sigma]_{intr} + [\sigma]_{ss}$. The critical resolved shear stress and hence, yield stress, depends upon the number, type and distribution of solute atoms at the dislocation and the manner in which the dislocation separates from the solute atoms. An estimate of this unlocking stress can be obtained by considering the interaction energy between the dislocation and some density of solute atoms. For straight dislocations, the interaction energy is proportional to the strain induced by the solute atom and inversely proportional to the distance of separation between dislocation core and solute atom. The dislocation-solute interaction energy, which can usually be written in analytic form for simple cases, is differentiated with respect to the solute-dislocation distance of separation to obtain the force on the dislocation. If the dislocation is required to remain straight as it moves, then the incremental force needed to be overcome in order for the dislocation to glide is the maximum force exerted between the solute atom and dislocation.

Experiments indicate that the method used above to calculate the increase in yield stress owing to solid-solution hardening, $[\sigma]_{ss}$, provides a reasonable estimate for temperatures near absolute zero but is too large at elevated temperatures. This is because dislocations do not remain straight and parallel to the solute atmosphere when they move. Rather, if the dislocation is flexible, local thermal fluctuations can provide sufficient energy for small segments of the dislocation to move from one lattice plane to the adjacent plane. These small segments, shown in figure, are called *dislocation jogs.* Once a jog has been nucleated, it is possible for the jog to extend, or become wider, by pulling the rest of the dislocation along. It becomes easier to nucleate a jog as the temperature increases as more thermal energy is available to help break atomic bonds. Thus $[\sigma]_{ss}$ decreases with increasing temperature, all other factors held constant.

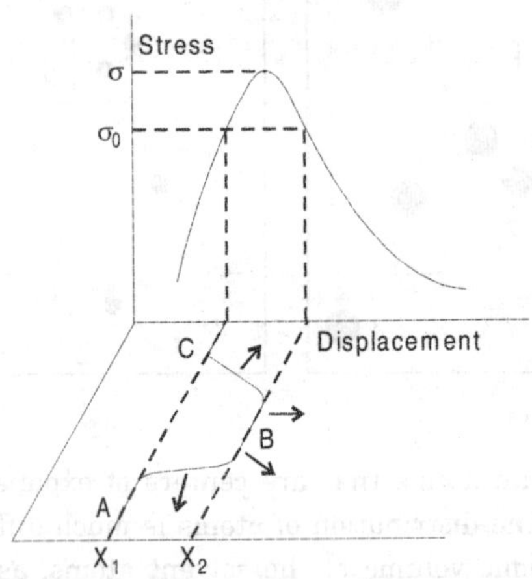

Fig. 2.19 A schematic drawing of a dislocation Jog, ABC, formed by a thermal fluctuation, that is in the process of breaking away from atomic plane x_1 and the associated stress.

As temperature increases, the jogs are easier to nucleate, and it is easier for the dislocation to escape its atmosphere of solute atoms. The increment in yield stress owing to solid-solution hardening, $[\sigma]_{ss}$, decreases with increasing temperature.

As the concentration of solute atoms increases, we would expect a larger number of solute atoms to segregate to the dislocations. The enhanced segregation would, in turn, pin the dislocation more strongly and thereby increase the critical resolved shear stress. This is indeed observed experimentally. The critical resolved shear stress increases as

$$\sigma_{crss} = \sigma_{intr} + \sigma_{ss}$$

or

$$\sigma_{crss} = \sigma_{intr} + CC^{1/2}$$

where C is the concentration of solute atoms in solid solution, [epsilon] is a materials constant and $[\sigma]_{intr}$ is the intrinsic stress. This relationship between critical resolved shear stress (yield stress) and solute concentration for solid solutions is shown for a copper-zinc alloy and has been verified experimentally for many other, but not all, alloy systems.

In summary, dislocation-solute interactions lead to solid-solution hardening or strengthening. The magnitude of the increase depends on the type of deformation induced

by the solute atom and decreases with increasing temperature. The increase in critical resolved shear stress, and therefore yield stress, is proportional to the square-root of the solute atom concentration.

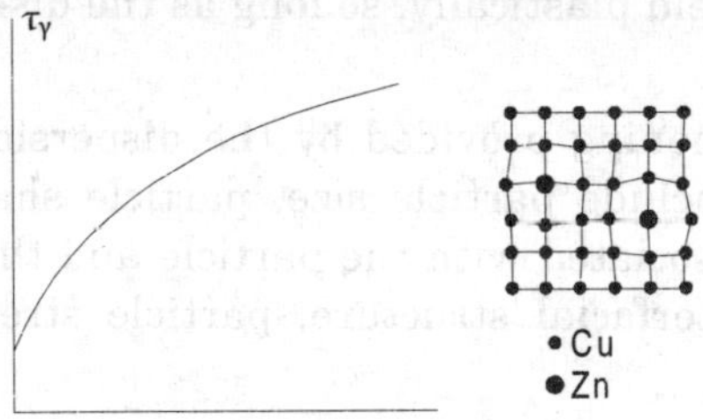

Fig. 2.20 The yield stress increases approximately proportional to the square-root of the concentration of solute in a solid solution.

2.11 PRECIPITATE OR DISPERSION STRENGTHENING

Most structural alloys are multiphase systems with at least one phase dispersed in the other. Over a wide range of temperatures and applied load, multiphase systems also deform plastically by the flow of dislocations. The precipitates act as obstacles to dislocation motion. In this section, we examine how second-phase particles or precipitates affect the yield stress by impeding dislocation glide and some of the mechanisms by which the dislocation circumvents the precipitate. Using precipitates or second-phase particles as a source of strength is known as precipitate hardening or dispersion strengthening.

Particle Hardening

Small particles dispersed in a matrix (Precipitates are second-phase particles that from by a nucleation and growth process. "Particle" is a more generic term and refers to any second-phase addition.) can increase significantly the matrix yield strength even when the volume fraction of particles is quite low (less than 10%.) This is not unexpected as we would expect an aggregate of solute atoms, which is what a precipitate is, to be more effective in pinning a dislocation than an isolated solute atom.

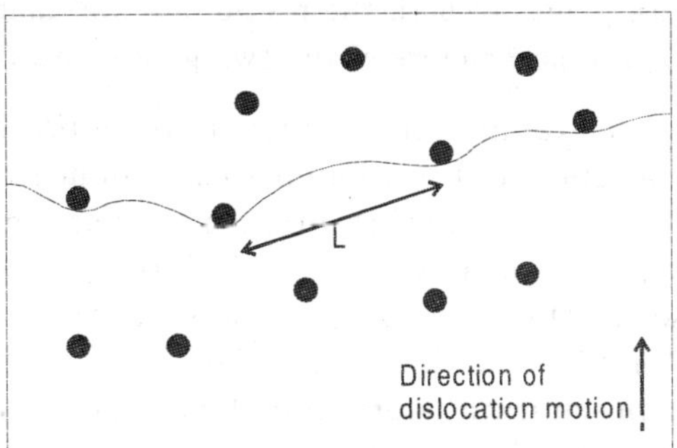

Fig. 2.21 A schematic illustration of a dislocation in an external stress field that is pinned by a dispersion of particles. The applied stress required to break the dislocation free from the particles depends upon many factors.

Fig. 2.21 depicts a dislocation that has been impeded by a dispersion of particles. A shear stress has been applied to the system to cause the dislocation to move in the indicated direction. The dislocation is pinned at the particles but bows out between the particles. The extent of bowing depends upon the magnitude of the applied stress and the dislocation line tension, discussed earlier, which resists dislocation bowing. The dislocation remains pinned, and the material does not yield plastically, so long as the dislocation is unable to bypass the particles.

The amount of strengthening provided by the dispersion of particles depends upon a number of factors. These include particle size, particle shape, average distance between particles, the stress field associated with the particle and the nature of the particle-matrix interface. The effects of interfacial structure, particle stress state and particle size are discussed below.

2.12 PRECIPITATE-MATRIX INTERFACIAL STRUCTURE

Second-phase particles possess crystal structures and compositions different from those of the parent phase. As a result, they can, in principle, generate stresses and strains in much the same manner as solute atoms in solid solution. Whether they actually do depends strongly on the structure of the precipitate-matrix interface.

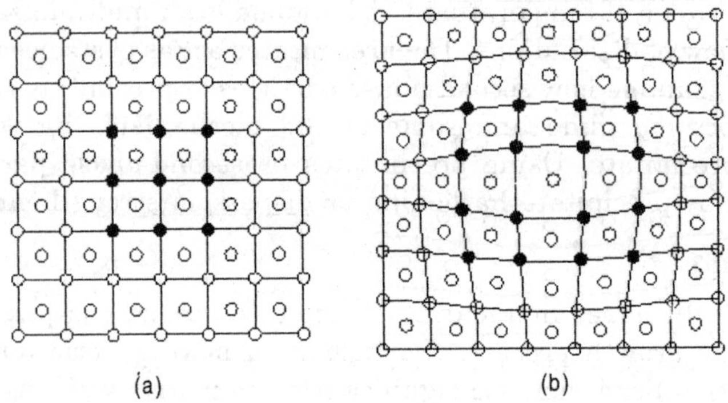

Fig. 2.22 A coherent interface between a precipitate (dark spheres) and matrix phase is indicated by the dashed line in (*a*). There is complete continuity between the lattice planes of both phases. The lattice planes of both the precipitate and matrix phases are elastically distorted when the lattice parameters of the two phases are fifferent, as shown in (*b*).

Fig. 2.22 (*a*) shows an example of a *coherent precipitate.* The lattice planes of the precipitate are perfectly aligned and in complete coincidence with the lattice planes of the matrix phase. There are no extra or missing lattice planes at the precipitate-matrix interface. In almost all cases, the lattice parameter of an isolated precipitate will be different from that of the matrix phase. In this example, the precipitate has a lattice parameter larger than the lattice parameter of the cubic matrix when it is imagined to be removed from the matrix phase. When the precipitate is embedded coherently in the matrix, as depicted in Fig. 2.22 (*b*), it acts as a center of expansion. To a first approximation, both the precipitate and matrix phases are in a state of compression and the stress field engendered by the precipitate is similar to the stress field of a solute atom which acts as a center of expansion.

If there is not perfect continuity in the stacking of the lattice planes between precipitate and matrix, the precipitate-matrix interface is termed *semi-coherent* or *in-coherent.* An example is shown in Fig. 2.23. Incoherent precipitates usually occur when the crystal structures of the precipitate and matrix do not permit a coherent structure or when the difference in lattice parameters between the phases is too large. Since incoherent interfaces are regions of disregistry between phases and contain lattice planes that end at the interface, different types of dislocations can be found at the interface. These dislocations help to relieve the elastic stress fields that arise because of the different crystal structures or lattice parameters between phases. Sometimes the precipitate stresses will be totally relieved and the precipitate will not produce any stresses.

It is also possible that a precipitate will nucleate initially as a coherent particle and then lose coherency, as the particle grows larger. The loss of coherency occurs when the elastic energy associated with the coherent precipitate becomes too large, and it becomes energetically favorable to introduce a dislocation into the interface. The new dislocation increases the energy of the system by an amount equal to its self-energy, but this increase in energy is more than offset by the accompanying decrease in the self-energy of the precipitate. If the stress fields around the precipitate are large enough, dislocations can be generated at the interface. Sometimes dislocations in the matrix phase will be attracted to the interface by the elastic stresses of the precipitate in order to relieve the misfit strains of the precipitate. This loss of coherency with increasing particle size has a strong influence on the yield stress.

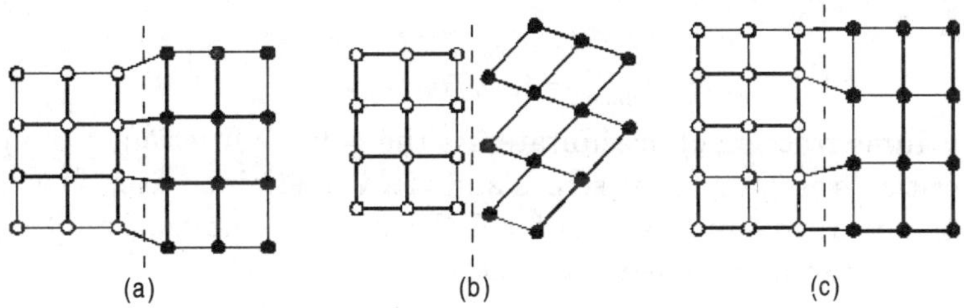

Fig. 2.23 Each of the three sketches represent a portion of a precipitate-matrix interface. The Interface is coherent in *(a)*, Incoherent in *(b)* and Semicoherent in C. A precipitate will often be coherent when it is small, Becoming Semicoherent and eventually incoherent as it grows larger. The dislocations at the interface help to relieve the stresses associated with the precipitate.

The stress field of a misfitting precipitate interacts with a dislocation in the same manner as a solute atom that has a different size from the surrounding solvent atoms. When the stress fields of the dislocation and precipitate overlap, there is an elastic interaction energy that is either positive or negative, depending upon the misfit strain of the particle, type of dislocation, materials parameters, and the relative positions of the precipitate and dislocation. Whether the interaction energy is negative or positive, the precipitate still exerts a retarding force on the dislocation. When the interaction energy is negative, the dislocation is attracted to the particle and it is difficult to pull the dislocation away from the particle. If the interaction energy is positive, an additional external stress must be applied just to move the dislocation up to the particle.

As mentioned, a coherent precipitate will usually have the largest stress field associated with it and, therefore, offer the greatest resistance to dislocation glide owing to the elastic dislocation-precipitate interaction. As the precipitate grows it reaches a point where it will lose coherency, relieving some or all of the misfit strains associated with the precipitate. As a consequence, there is a decrease in the degree of precipitation hardening when the particles lose coherency.

2.13 DISLOCATION SHEARING OF DEFORMABLE PARTICLES

There are two primary methods by which a dislocation can circumvent a precipitate. The first method is by *precipitate shearing* or *cutting*, in which the dislocation cuts through the precipitate. Precipitate shearing usually occurs with deformable particles, at least when they are small. The second method involves the dislocation circumventing the precipitate by moving around the precipitate in one manner or another. This method is called dislocation bypass and usually leaves a dislocation loop around the precipitate. Dislocation bypass often occurs when the particles do not deform.

Figure below depicts the dislocation shearing mechanism. In (a), the dislocation approaches the precipitate. If the applied stress is sufficiently large, the dislocation enters the precipitate phase displacing one half of the precipitate with respect to the other half. The entire displacement process produces a new interphase surface of approximate area *2[π]rb*, where *r* is the precipitate radius and *b* the Burgers vector. The increase in energy associated with this new area is *2[π]rb[γ]*, where [gamma] is the interfacial energy density. If $b << r$, then half of the energy increase takes place as the dislocation first cuts the precipitate. The corresponding increase in the critical resolved shear stress, τ_{chem} can be estimated to be:

$$\tau_{chem} = \tau \, \gamma f / b$$

where *f* is the volume fraction of precipitate. As the volume fraction of the precipitate phase increases, the critical resolved shear stress and yield stress increase, if the particle shearing mechanism is the operative mechanism for dislocation circumvention of a precipitate. This is because there is a greater density of obstacles to shear.

The above expression for [τ_{chem}] was derived assuming the Burgers vector is much smaller than the precipitate radius. For systems in which this assumption is not valid, the energy increase as a function of dislocation passage is not as great as assumed in the derivation, and the incremental hardening owing to the shearing process is consequently less than that predicted by above equation. Thus, for a given volume fraction, very small precipitates are not as effective strengtheners as very large precipitates. Thus, in addition to the volume fraction dependence of above equation, there is an implicit particle size dependence as well.

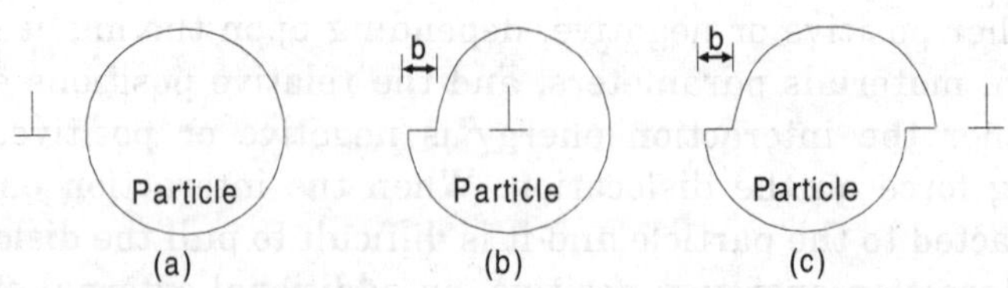

Fig. 2.24 Schematic depiction of an edge dislocation bypassing a precipitate by shear of the precipitate. An additional shear stress τ_{chem}, must be applied to the dislocation to overcome the interfacial energy created by the dislocation in the shearing process.

The strengthening mechanism which dominates will depend upon the alloy system studied. It is usually assumed that the various contributions to hardening are additive, but this is just a working hypothesis for most alloy systems. Nevertheless, the general relationship between the magnitude of particle strengthening obtained from a dispersion of *deformable* particles and the particle's strength, size and volume fraction, can be summarized in the plot of Fig. 2.24 below and the relation, $[\sigma]_{crss} = [\sigma]_{intr} + [\sigma]_{ss} + \tau_{chem}$. At small particle sizes, $[\tau_{chem}]$ increases proportional to the square-root of the particle radius, $r^{(1/2)}$. This reflects the increasing resistance of larger particles to dislocation cutting or shearing. For a fixed particle volume fraction, however, the spacing between particles becomes progressively larger and, eventually, the particles do not present as effective an obstacle to dislocation cutting. This latter effect is sometimes due to a loss of the particle's coherency. Furthermore, when the precipitates become very large and widely spaced, other methods of particle circumvention, such as the dislocation bypass mechanism to be discussed in the following section, become operative. The most important point is that the hardness reaches a maximum value at a certain precipitate radius. This maximum value increases with increasing precipitate volume fraction or precipitate strength.

In summary, deformable particles act as obstacles to dislocation motion. If the particles are not too large, dislocations can shear or cut the precipitate. Larger particles offer greater resistance to shearing than very small particles.

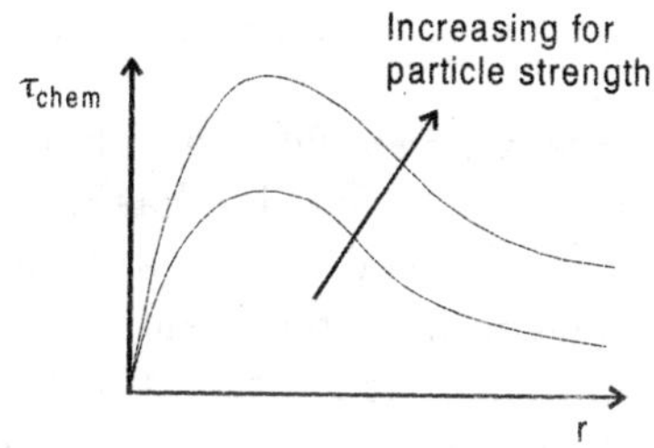

Fig. 2.25 Schematic of the incremental stress required for a dislocation to cut through deformable precipitates as a function of precipitate Radius, r.

Particle Bypass-Non-deforming Particles

If a precipitate is sufficiently hard, it cannot be readily sheared by a dislocation. In these cases, the dislocation will sometimes bow around the particle. This bowing process is depicted in figure below.

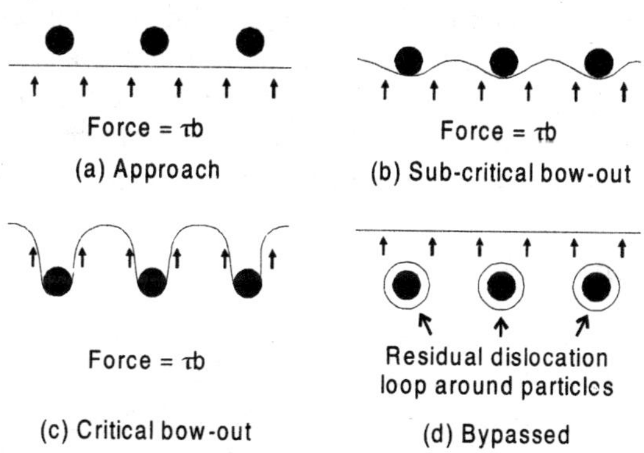

Fig. 2.26 Schematic of a dislocation bowing about a line of precipitates. Eventually, the dislocation line from adjacent loops will touch, allowing the dislocation to glide and leaving behind a dislocation loop.

The applied stress exerts a force on the dislocation causing it to move. Points along the dislocation are pinned by strong precipitates that are resistant to dislocation penetration and shearing. The dislocation is able to bow out between the precipitates, but the bowing process is resisted by the dislocation tension. (Remember, the bowing of the dislocation creates more dislocation line and increases the energy of the system.) Eventually, the edges of adjacent dislocation loops touch, join and pinch-off. The dislocation is able to continue gliding and a dislocation loop is left behind circling the precipitate. This process of circumventing a particle is called *Orowan looping* or *dislocation bypass*.

Analysis of the incremental shear stress necessary to allow the dislocation to loop the precipitate, $[\sigma]_B$, predicts that, to first-order,

$$[\sigma]_B = Gb/(L-2r)^{\sim}\ Gb/L \text{ for } r << L$$

where *G* is the matrix shear modulus, *r* the precipitate radius, and *L* is the average interparticle spacing. For a given interparticle spacing, the larger the precipitate, the more difficult it is for the dislocation to bow around the precipitate. The dislocation loop that is left behind can decrease the misfit strain of the precipitate or can impede the motion of subsequent dislocations that encounter the precipitate.

2.14 WORK HARDENING

Work hardening refers to the increase in yield stress that accompanies plastic deformation in a material. A material that does not work harden has a yield stress that does not change with increasing plastic strain of the material. There are many origins of work hardening, depending upon the controlling mechanism for yielding. The underlying cause of work hardening, however, is dislocation-dislocation interactions, the dislocations formed in the initial yielding process act as barriers to the movement of other dislocations, making the subsequent movement of dislocations more difficult and, thereby, increasing the yield stress.

For our purposes, it is necessary only to realize that there are many types of dislocation-dislocation interactions. These include the elastic interaction of individual dislocations and the interaction of a dislocation with a group of dislocations, such as those found in grain boundaries. Dislocations interact with one another through their stress fields in the same manner as dislocations and solute atoms or dislocations and precipitates.

In summary, we have considered two primary mechanisms of strengthening in crystals, solid-solution strengthening and particle hardening. Solid-solution strengthening occurs as a result of dislocation-solute atom elastic interactions and is proportional to the square-root of the concentration of solute atoms *in solution*. Particle hardening is a result of precipitates acting as obstacles to dislocation motion. Deformable precipitates are usually cut or sheared by the dislocations while dislocations circumvent non-deformable precipitates by Orowan looping.

2.15 PRECIPITATION HARDENING

In this section, we use the above analysis in combination with our understanding of the precipitation process to explain why a material's hardness will often change with aging time and how these changes can be connected to the material's microstructure.

With reference to the phase diagram, consider an alloy of composition C_o at the temperature T_o. For purposes of illustration, we assume that the alloy forms a substitutional solid solution. The system in its equilibrium state is homogeneous $[\alpha]$ phase. If the alloy is quenched to the temperature T_1, the equilibrium state consists of a two-phase mixture of $[\alpha]$

and [β]. In this simple system, we can divide the precipitation process into three stages. The first stage is the nucleation of the second-phase precipitates, [β], in the [α] matrix. The nucleated precipitates are, for the most part, isolated from one another and have compositions near their equilibrium value. The composition of the [α] matrix is near the bulk composition, C_o. During this stage, the number of precipitates increases drastically with time. The second stage of the precipitation process entails the *growth* of the initially isolated precipitates into the supersaturated matrix phase. During this stage, the size of the particles increases and the composition of the matrix phase steadily decreases, approaching the equilibrium value, $C_{eq}\alpha$. The final stage is termed *coarsening*. The volume fraction of the precipitates has just about reached its equilibrium value. Likewise, the composition of the matrix phase is close to its equilibrium value, $C_{eq}\alpha$. During coarsening, the number of precipitates decrease with time as the average size of the precipitates increases at constant volume fraction.

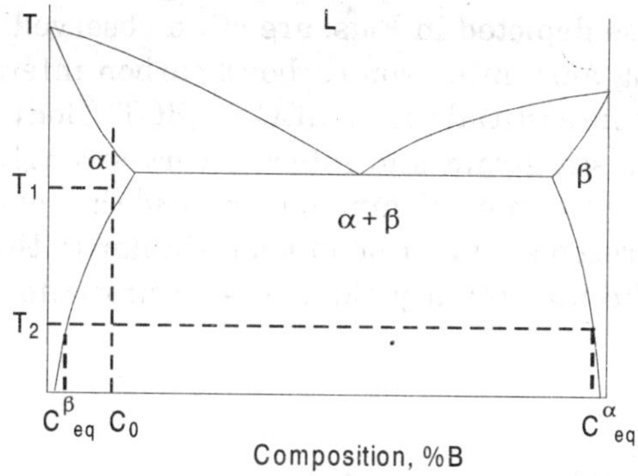

Fig. 2.27 A binary phase diagram with a eutectic point.

We can imagine performing a series of hardness tests taken at various times during the precipitation process. At time t=0, there has been insufficient time for precipitates to nucleate in the quenched alloy. The measured yield stress would reflect contributions from the intrinsic stress and solid-solution hardening. A hardness measurement taken in the early stages of nucleation would show an increase in the yield stress resulting from a small amount of dispersion hardening. The hardness would continue to increase through the nucleation stage as the number and volume fraction of precipitates increase and there is little change in the matrix super saturation.

The hardness continues to increase through the growth stage as the volume fraction of the particles continues to increase. The precipitates are becoming larger and more difficult to shear, if the dislocation cutting mechanism is operative, or more difficult to bypass, if the Orowan looping mechanism is operative. This tends to increase the critical resolved shear stress and yield stress of the material. As the growth process proceeds, however, the super saturation in the matrix phase decreases. This decrease in the concentration of solute atoms in the matrix results in a decrease in the solid-solution hardening. The increase in hardening owing to dispersion hardening is more than offset by the decrease in hardening owing to solid-solution hardening and the material's yield strength continues to increase with time. By the end of the growth stage, there is a fine dispersion of [β] precipitates in the [α] matrix.

The strength of the material continues to increase in the initial stages of coarsening as the particles continue to increase in size at constant volume fraction. There is no further decrease in strength owing to a decrease in the concentration of solute in the matrix, as it has essentially reached its equilibrium value. As the particles become larger, coherent particles will lose their coherency and the dislocation-precipitate elastic interaction will be diminished. In addition, the decreasing number of particles and the concomitant increase in mean intercenter spacing between particles will cause a decrease in the particle strengthening and an overall decrease in the strength of the material. Thus, the strength of the material will reach a maximum value and begin to decrease. As coarsening continues, the material's strength will continue to decrease. The yield stress for this material is plotted as a function of aging time in Fig. 2.28. The relative contributions of the solid-solution hardening and dispersion hardening are shown in figure respectively. This example is relevant to many aluminium-and nickel-based alloys.

The yield stress as a function of aging time for a hypothetical binary alloy. The contributions of solid-solution hardening, and dispersion hardening, to the yield stress of the hypothetical alloy of Fig. 2.29 are shown as a function of aging time in (*a*) and (*b*), respectively. Aging curves other than those depicted in Figs. are often observed. In an earlier laboratory, we learned that in quenching austenite (iron-carbon), carbon interstitial atoms do not have time to diffuse. The carbon interstitials in a BCC or BCT (Body Centered Cubic.) lattice possess a large tetragonal misfit strain and interact very strongly with dislocations. Thus the contribution of the solid-solution hardening may exceed that of the precipitate hardening and the evolution of yield stress as a function of time similar to those seen in Fig. 2.30 can be observed. In this case, the maximum yield stress occurs immediately after quenching.

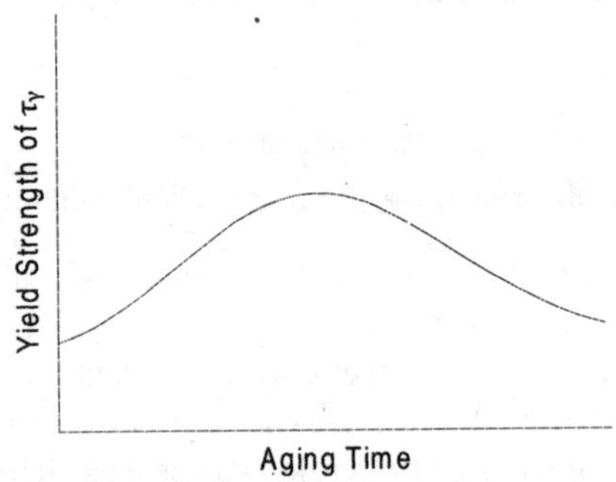

Fig. 2.28 The yield stress as a function of aging time for a hypothetical binary alloy.

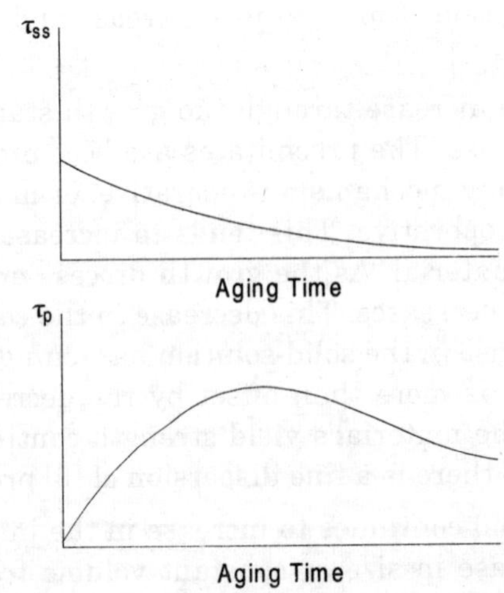

Fig. 2.29 The contributions of solid-solution hardening, $[tau]_{ss}$, and dispersion hardening, $[tau]_B$, to the yield stress of the hypothetical alloy shown as a function of aging time in (*a*) and (*b*), respectively.

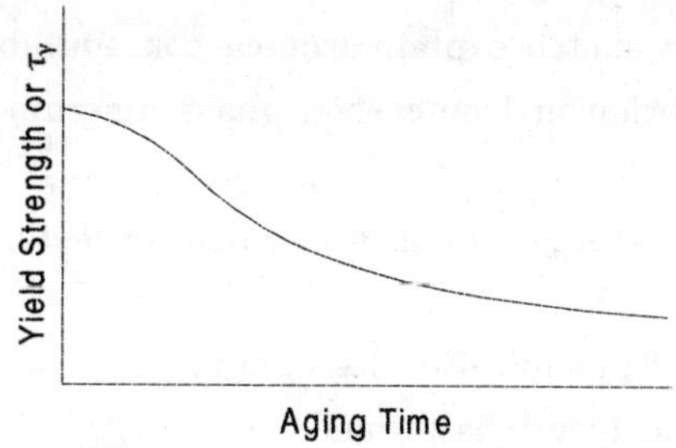

Fig. 2.30 The yield stress as a function of aging time for a hypothetical interstitial alloy with strong solid-solution hardening.

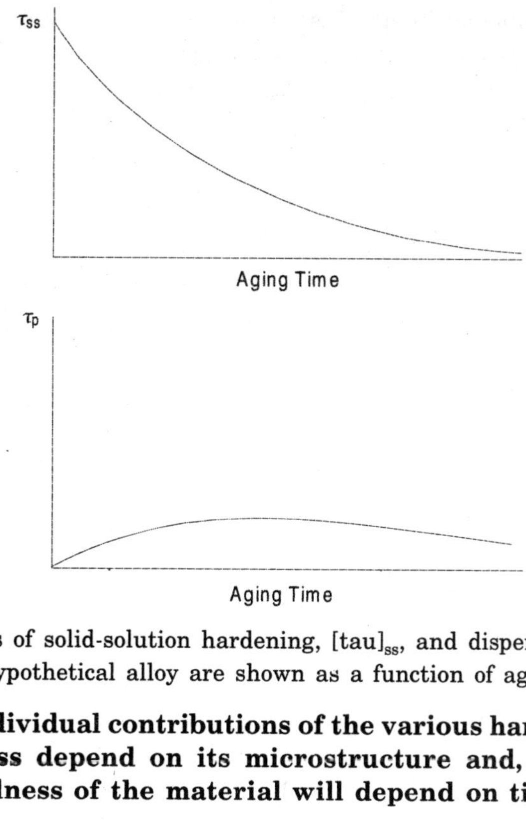

Fig. 2.31 The contributions of solid-solution hardening, [tau]$_{ss}$, and dispersion hardening, [tau]$_B$, to the yield stress of the hypothetical alloy are shown as a function of aging time in (*a*) and (*b*).

In summary, the individual contributions of the various hardening mechanisms to a material's hardness depend on its microstructure and, therefore, on time. Consequently, the hardness of the material will depend on time.

REVIEW QUESTIONS

1. What are alloys?
2. What is phase diagram and what are its uses?
3. Explain the methods available to construct the phase diagram.
4. What is the use of inverse rule?
5. Define polymorphism and allotropy.
6. Explain the availability of iron in various forms.

7. What is an equilibrium diagram?
8. With the help of neat sketch explain Iron-carbon equilibrium diagram.
9. Explain different reaction in Iron-carbon phase diagram.
10. What is TTT diagram?
11. Explain the different strengthening mechanism of metals.
12. What is work hardening?
13. Explain the process of precipitation hardening.
14. What is cementite and how it is formed?
15. What is austenite and how it is formed?
16. What is martensite and at what temperature its is formed?
17. Classify various types of steel.
18. Explain the different kinds of cast iron.
19. List out the application of various types of steel.
20. List out the application of various types of cast iron.

3 CHAPTER

HEAT TREATMENT

3.1 INTRODUCTION

The term 'heat treatment' may be defined as an operation or a combination of operations, in the manufacturing process of machine parts and tools. As a matter of fact, the heat treatment of a metal or an alloy is carried out first by heating it in solid state and then cooling it. It is possible to impart the required or desirable mechanical properties to steel or alloys for normal operations by heat treatment.

3.2 OBJECTIVES OF HEAT TREATMENT

Though there are innumerable objectives, which are achieved by heat treatment, yet the following are important from the subject point of view:

1. To relieve internal stresses, which are set up in the metal due to cold or hot working.
2. To soften the metal.
3. To improve hardness of the metal surface.
4. To improve machinability.
5. To refine grain structure.
6. To improve mechanical properties like tensile strength, ductility and shock resistance.

3.3 PROCESS OF HEAT TREATMENT

The process of heat treatment is carried out first by heating the metal and then cooling it. In fact, this process consists of:

1. Heating the metal to a specified temperature.
2. Holding the metal at that temperature for a specified period *i.e.*, (Soaking Period).
3. Cooling the metal (*i.e.*, quenching) according to specified process. It will be interesting to know that the true heat treatment does not involve any chemical change. But it essentially involves time temperature cycle, which means the range and rate of heating and cooling.

The temperature to which a metal or an alloy is heated depends upon its grade, grain size as well as type and shape. In general, the metal is never heated much beyond its upper critical temperature. As a result of this, some plastic deformation of the grains of the metal takes place. This deformation depends upon the chemical composition of the metal or alloy and the temperature to which it is heated.

The metal or alloy is now held at the increased temperature to ensure uniformity of temperature throughout the mass. The period of heating depends upon the size and shape of the component. In general, time required for heating a component is approximately 1 minute to 3 minutes for 1 mm thickness of the largest section.

The main transformation in the properties of a component takes place in the cooling process of the metal. It depends mostly upon the rate at which the cooling takes place. It also depends upon the medium in which the cooling takes place. It may be noted that these days only five quenching medias adopted are caustic soda solution, brine, water, oil and air.

3.4 TYPES OF HEAT TREATMENT PROCESSES

Though there are many types of heat treatment processes, yet the following are important from the subject point of view:

1. Annealing
2. Spheroidizing
3. Normalising
4. Hardening
5. Tempering and
6. Case hardening techniques like Carburising, Nitriding Cyaniding, Induction hardening and Flame hardening.

Steel often requires heat treatment to obtain improved properties *e.g.*, increase hardness or strength, or to neutralize negative effects resulting from previous manufacturing processes *e.g.*, remove internal stresses generated by fabrication processes.

3.4.1 Annealing

Annealing is one of the heat treatment processes in which a material is taken to an elevated temperatures kept there for a specific time and then quenched.

The main objectives of annealing heat treatment are:

1. To soften the steel, so that it may be more easily machined or cold worked.
2. To refine the grain-size and structure to improve mechanical properties like strength and ductility.
3. To relieve internal stresses which may have been caused by hot or cold working or by unequal contraction in casting.
4. To alter electrical, magnetic or other physical properties.
5. To remove the gases, trapped in the metal, during initial casting.

The process of annealing is of the following two types:

Full annealing. The main objective of full annealing is to softer metal, to refine its grain structure, to relieve the stresses and to remove gases trapped in the metal. This process consists of heating the steel 30°C to 50°C above the upper critical temperature for hypo eutectoid steel .The steel is then held at this temperature for sometime to enable the internal changes to take place. The time allowed is approximately 3 to 4 minute each millimeter of thickness of the largest section, and then slowly cooled in the furnace.

The rate of cooling varies from 30°C to 200°C per hour, depending upon the composition of steel. The cooling is, usually, carried out in the furnace. The objects may also be taken out of the furnace and cooled in ashes is to prolong the cooling time.

Process annealing. The main objective of process annealing is to relieve the metal internal stresses set up in the metal and for increasing the machinability of the steel. In this process, the steel is heated to a temperature below or close to the lower critical temperature, held at this temperature for specific time and then cooled slowly. This causes complete recrystallisation of materials. Which have been severely cold worked and a new grain structure is formed. The process of annealing is commonly used in the sheet and wire industries. Anealing is reheating steel followed by slow cooling. It is completed *(a)* to remove internal stress or to soften or *(b)* to refine the crystalline structure (This involves heating to above the upper-critical temperature).

The steel is heated about 25°C above the upper critical temperature, held for a set time and then cooled slowly in the furnace. This process is used to remove internal stresses built up as a result of cold working and fabrication processes. Following annealing the dislocations are rearranged into a lower energy configuration, new strain free grains are formed and grain growth is encouraged.

Stages of Annealing

- Heating to required temperature
- Holding ("soaking") at constant temperature
- Cooling.

The time at the high temperature (soaking time) is long enough to allow the desired transformation to occur. Cooling is done slowly to avoid warping/cracking of due to the thermal gradients and thermo-elastic stresses within the or even cracking the metal piece.

Purposes of Annealing

- It used to relieve internal stresses
- Increase ductility, toughness, softness
- Produce specific microstructure.

Proccss Annealing–used to revert effects of work hardening (by recovery and recrystallization) and to increase ductility. Heating is usually limited to avoid Excessive grain growth and oxidation.

Stress Relief Annealing–used to eliminate/minimize stresses arising from

- ❖ Plastic deformation during machining
- ❖ Non uniform cooling
- ❖ Phase transformations between phases with different densities.

Stress relief annealing allows these stresses to relax. Annealing temperatures are relatively low so that useful effects of cold working are not eliminated.

Internal residual stresses may develop in metal pieces in response to the following:

(1) plastic deformation processes such as machining and grinding; (2) nonuniform cooling of a piece that was processed or fabricated at an elevated temperature, such as a weld or a casting; and (3) a phase transformation that is induced upon cooling wherein parent and product phases have different densities. Distortion and warpage may result if these residual stresses are not removed. They may be eliminated by a stress relief annealing heat treatment in which the piece is heated to the recommended temperature, held there long enough to attain a uniform temperature, and finally cooled to room temperature in air. The annealing temperature is ordinarily a relatively low one such that effects resulting from cold working and other heat treatments are not affected.

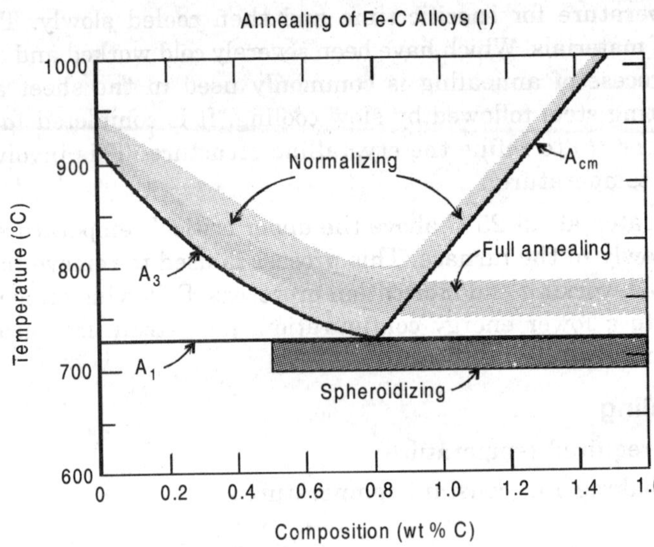

Fig. 3.1 Thermal processing of metal alloy (I).

- **Lower critical temperature** A_1 below which austenite does not exist
- **Upper critical temperature** lines, A_3 and A_{cm} above which all material is austenite

Normalizing: an annealing heat treatment just above the upper critical temperature to reduce grain sizes (of pearlite and proeutectoid phase) and make more uniform size distributions. After complete transformation to austenite (austenitizing) the treatment is completed by cooling to the required microstructure.

Full annealing

A heat treatment known as **full annealing** is often utilized in low- and medium-carbon steels that will be machined or will experience extensive plastic deformation during a forming operation. The alloy is austenitized by heating to 15 to 40°C (30 to 70°F) above the lines as indicated in Fig. 3.2 until equilibrium is achieved. The alloy is then furnace cooled; that is, the heat-treating furnace is turned off and both furnace and steel cool to room temperature at the same rate, which takes several hours. The microstructural product of this anneal is coarse pearlite (in addition to any proeutectoid phase) that is relatively soft and ductile. The full-anneal cooling procedure is time consuming; however, a microstructure having small grains and a uniform grain structure results. Austenizing and slow cooling (several hours) produces coarse pearlite (and possible proeutectoid phase) that is relatively soft and ductile.

Is used to soften pieces which have been hardened by plastic deformation, and which need to undergo subsequent machining/forming.

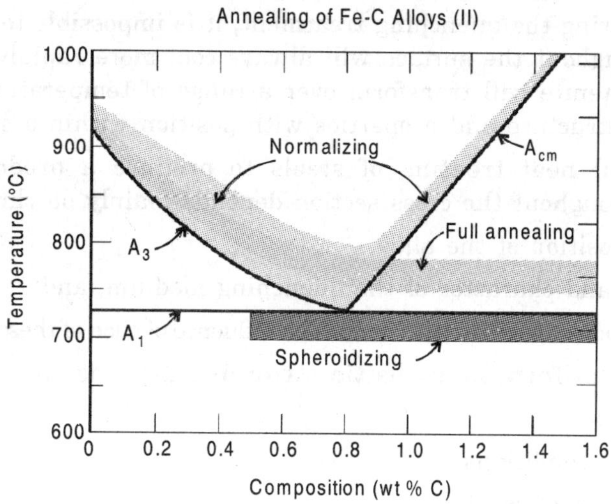

Fig. 3.2 Annealing of Fe-C alloys (II)

3.4.2 Spheroidizing

Prolonged heating just below the eutectoid temperature, which results in the soft spheroidite structure discussed in end of this chapter. This achieves maximum softness needed in subsequent forming operations. Martensite has the strongest microstructure and can be made more ductile by tempering. Therefore the optimum properties of quenched and tempered steel are realized if high content of martensite is produced.

The process applies more to the hypereutectoid steels (above 0, 8% C). The process involves heating the metal to between 600°C and 650°C and holding it at the selected temperature for a period of time the cementite changes from a lamella formation to a formation based on an alpha ferrite matrix with particles of spheroidal cementite (Fe_3C) are embedded. This resulting steel has improved ductility and toughness compared to the original steel with reduced hardness and strength.

Medium-and high-carbon steels having a microstructure containing even coarse pearlite may still be too hard to conveniently machine or plastically deform. These steels, and in fact any steel, may be heat treated or annealed to develop the spheroidite structure as described in this chapter. Spheroidized steels have a maximum softness and ductility and are easily machined or deformed. The **spheroidizing** heat treatment consists of heating the alloy at a temperature just below the eutectoid in the $a + Fe_3C$ region of the phase diagram. If the precursor microstructure contains pearlite, spheroidizing times will ordinarily range between 15 and 25 hr. During this annealing there is a coalescence of the Fe_3C to form the spheroid particles.

Still other annealing treatments are possible. For example, glasses are annealed, as outlined in previous section, to remove residual internal stresses that render the material excessively weak.

Quenching medium, such as water, oil, or air. The optimum properties of a steel that has been quenched and then tempered can be realized only if, during the quenching heat treatment, the specimen has been converted to a high content of martensite; the formation of any pearlite and/or bainite will result in other than the best combination of mechanical characteristics. During the quenching treatment, it is impossible to cool the specimen at a uniform rate throughout the surface will always cool more rapidly than interior regions. Therefore, the austenite will transform over a range of temperatures, yielding a possible variation of microstructure and properties with position within a specimen.

The successful heat treating of steels to produce a predominantly martensitic microstructure throughout the cross section depends mainly on three factors:

(1) The composition of the alloy,

(2) The type and character of the quenching medium, and

(3) The size and shape of the specimen. The influence of each of these factors is now addressed.

Production of **uniform martensitic structure** depends on

(1) Composition

(2) Quenching conditions

(3) Size + shape of specimen.

3.4.3 Normalising

Normalising involves heating the steel to about 40°C above its upper critical limit. The steel is then held at this temperature for a period of time and is then cooled in air. It is desireable that the temperature of the steel shall be maintained for a time period more than 2 minutes per mm of section thickness and shall not exceed the upper critical temperature by more than 50°C. The structure produced by this process is pearlite (eutectoid) or pearlite in a ferrite matrix (hypoeutectoid) or pearlite in a cementite matrix (hypereutectoid). Because the steel is cooled in air the process results in a fine pearlite formation with improved mechanical properties compared to the full annealing process below

Normalising is used to

- To refine the grain structure and to create a more homogeneous austenite when a steel is to be reheated for quench hardening or full annealing.
- To encourage reduced grain segregation in castings and forgings and provide a more uniform structure.
- To provide moderate hardening.
- To remove strains caused by cold working processes like hammering, rolling, bending etc., which makes the metal brittle and unreliable.
- To remove dislocations caused in the internal structure of the steel due to hot working.
- To improve certain mechanical and electrical properties.

Hardening involves heating a steel to its normalising temperature and cooling (Quenching)rapidly in a suitable fluid *e.g.*, oil, water or air. Steel is basically an alloy iron and carbon some steels alloys have various other elements in solution. When steel is heated above the upper critical temperature (about 760°C), the iron crystal structure will change to face centered cubic (FCC), and the carbon atoms will migrate into the central position formerly occupied by an iron atom. This form of red-hot steel is called austentite (γ iron). If this steel form cools slowly, the iron atoms move back into the cube forcing the carbon atoms back out, resulting in soft steel called pearlite. If the sample was formerly hard, this softening process is called annealing. If the steel is cooled quickly (quench) by immersing it in oil or water, the carbon atoms are trapped, and the result is a very hard, brittle steel. This steel crystal structure is now a body centered tetragonal (BCT) form called martensite.

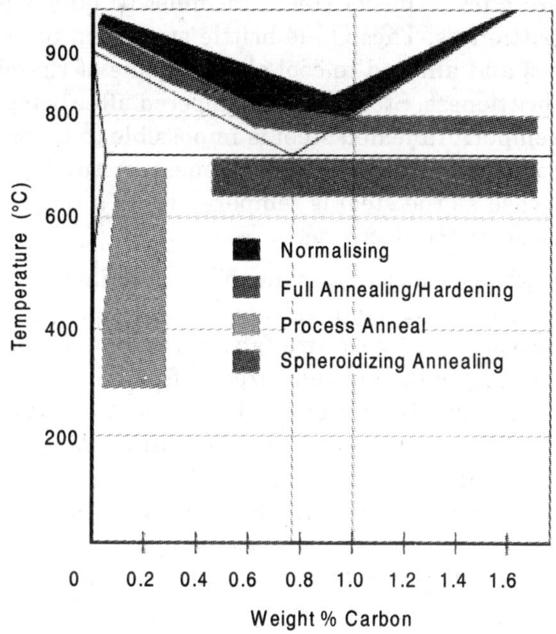

Fig. 3.3 Temperature Vs. weight % carbon.

3.4.4 Tempering

After the hardening treatment is applied, steel is often harder than needed and is too brittle for most practical uses. Also, severe internal stresses are set up during the rapid cooling from the hardening temperature. To relieve the internal stresses and reduce brittleness, you should temper the steel after it is hardened. Tempering consists of heating the steel to a specific temperature (below its hardening temperature), holding it at that temperature for the required length of time, and then cooling it, usually instill air. The resultant strength, hardness, and ductility depend on the temperature to which the steel is heated during the tempering process.

The purpose of tempering is to reduce the brittleness imparted by hardening and to produce definite physical properties within the steel. Tempering always follows, never precedes, the hardening operation. Besides reducing brittleness, tempering softens the steel. That is un-avoidable, and the amount of hardness that is lost depends on the temperature that the steel is heated to during the tempering process. That is true of all steels except high-speed steel. Tempering increases the hardness of high-speed steel. Tempering is always conducted at temperatures below the low-critical point of the steel. In this respect, tempering differs from annealing, normalizing, and hardening in which the temperatures are above the upper critical point. When hardened steel is reheated, tempering begins at 212°F and continues as the temperature increases toward the low-critical point.

By selecting a definite tempering temperature, you can predetermine the resulting hardness and strength. The minimum temperature time for tempering should be 1 hour. If the part is more than 1 inch thick, increase the time by 1 hour for each additional inch of thickness. Normally, the rate of cooling from the tempering temperature has no effect on the steel. Steel parts are usually cooled in still air after being removed from the tempering furnace; however, there are a few types of steel that must be quenched from the tempering temperature to prevent brittleness. These blue brittle steels can become brittle if heated in certain temperature ranges and allowed to cool slowly. Some of the nickel chromium steels are subject to this temper brittleness. Steel may be tempered after being normalized, providing there is any hardness to temper. Annealed steel is impossible to temper. Tempering relieves quenching stresses and reduces hardness and brittleness. Actually, the tensile strength of a hardened steel may increase as the steel is tempered up to a temperature of about 450°F. Above this temperature it starts to decrease.

Tempering increases softness, ductility, malleability, and impact resistance. Again, high-speed steel is an exception to the rule. High-speed steel increases in hardness on tempering, provided it is tempered at a high temperature (about 1550°F). Remember, all steel should be removed from the quenching bath and tempered before it is completely cold. Failure to temper correctly results in a quick failure of the hardened part. Permanent steel magnets are made of special alloys and are heat-treated by hardening and tempering. Hard- ness and stability are the most important properties in permanent magnets. Magnets are tempered at the minimum tempering temperature of 212°F by placing them in boiling water for 2 to 4 hours. Because of this low-tempering temperature, magnets are very hard. Case-hardened parts should not be tempered at too high a temperature or they may loose some of their hardness. Usually, a temperature range from 212°F to 400°F is high enough to relieve quenching stresses. Some metals require no tempering.

The design of the part helps determine the tempering temperature. Color tempering is based on the oxide colors that appear on the surface of steel, as it is heated. When you slowly heat a piece of polished hardened steel, you can see the surface turn various colors as the temperature changes. These colors indicate structural changes are taking place within the metal. Once the proper color appears, the part is rapidly quenched to prevent further structural change. In color tempering, the surface of the steel must be smooth and free of oil. The part may be heated by a torch, in a furnace, over a hot plate, or by radiation.

3.5 SURFACE HARDENING OR CASE HARDENING

Case hardening produces a hard, wear-resistant surface or case over a strong, tough core. The principal forms of casehardening are carburizing, cyaniding, and nitriding. Only ferrous metals are case-hardened. Case hardening is ideal for parts that require a wear-resistant surface and must be tough enough internally to withstand heavy loading. The steels best suited for case hardening are the low-carbon and low-alloy series. When high-carbon steels are case-hardened, the hardness penetrates the core and causes brittleness. In case hardening, you change the surface of the metal chemically by introducing a high carbide or nitride content. The core remains chemically unaffected. When heat-treated, the high-carbon surface responds to hardening, and the core toughens.

In many engineering applications, it is desirable that a steel to be used should have a hardened surface to resist wear and tear. At the same time, it should have soft and tough interior or core so that it is able to absorb any shocks etc. This is achieved by hardening the surface layers of the article, while the rest of it is left as such. This type of treatment is applied to gears, hall bearings, railway wheels, etc.

Following are the various surface or case hardening processes by means of which the surface layer is hardened:

1. Carburising.
2. Cyaniding.
3. Nitriding.
4. Induction hardening.
5. Flame hardening.

The primary purpose of case hardening is to produce a surface which is resistant to wear while maintaining the overall toughness and strength of the steel core. This type of process is normally used on a steel with a low carbon content and introduces carbon by diffusion (carburising) into the local surfaces requiring treatment. Subsequent heat treatment develops the desired combination of high surface hardness and internal toughness. Another process called Nitriding consists of the diffusion of nitrogen.

3.5.1 Flame Hardening

Flame hardening is another procedure that is used to harden the surface of metal parts. When you use an oxyacetylene flame, a thin layer at the surface of the part is rapidly heated to its critical temperature and then immediately quenched by a combination of a water spray and the cold base metal. This process produces a thin, hardened surface, and at the same time, the internal parts retain their original properties. Whether the process is manual or mechanical, a close watch must be maintained, since the torches heat the metal rapidly and the temperatures are usually determined visually. Flame hardening may be either manual or automatic. Automatic equipment produces uniform results and is more desirable. Most automatic machines have variable travel speeds and can be adapted to parts of various sizes and shapes. The size and shape of the torch depends on the part. The torch consists of a mixing head, straight extension tube, 900 extension head, an adjustable yoke, and a water-cooled tip. Practically any shape or size flame-hardening tip is available (Fig. 3.4).

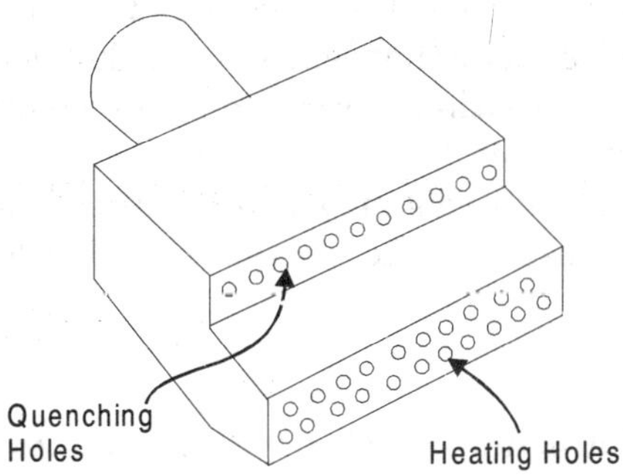

Fig. 3.4 Progressive hardening torch tip.

Tips are produced that can be used for hardening flats, rounds, gears, cams, cylinders, and other regular or irregular shapes. In hardening localized areas, you should heat the metal with a standard hand-held welding torch. Adjust the torch flame to neutral for normal heating; however, in corners and grooves, use a slightly oxidizing flame to keep the torch from sputtering. You also should particularly guard against overheating in corners and grooves. If dark streaks appear on the metal surface, this is a sign of overheating, and you need to increase the distance between the flame and the metal. For the best heating results, hold the torch with the tip of the inner cone about an eighth of an inch from the surface and direct the flame at right angles to the metal. Sometimes it is necessary to change this angle to obtain better results; however, you rarely find a deviation of more than 30 degrees. Regulate the speed of torch travel according to the type of metal, the mass and shape of the part, and the depth of hardness desired. In addition, you must select the steel according to the properties desired. Select carbon steel when surface hardness is the primary factor and alloy steel when the physical properties of the core are also factors.

Plain carbon steels should contain more than 0.35% carbon for good results in flame hardening. For water quenching, the effective carbon range is from 0.40% to 0.70%. Parts with a carbon content of more than 0.70% are likely to surface crack unless the heating and quenching rate are carefully controlled. The surface hardness of a flame-hardened section is equal to a section that was hardened by furnace heating and quenching. The decrease in hardness between the case and the core is gradual. Since the core is not affected by flame hardening, there is little danger of spalling or flaking while the part is in use. Thus flame hardening produces a hard case that is highly resistant to wear and a core that retains its original properties. Flame hardening can be divided into five general methods: stationary, circular band progressive, straight line progressive, spiral band progressive, and circular band spinning.

Sometimes, a particular portion (or portions) of an article is required to be hardened. This is generally done in case of a portion subject to wear, abrasion or shocks. This type of local hardening is done by a process, known as flame hardening. In this process, the portion, to be hardened, is heated with the help of a flame of oxyacetylene torch above its critical temperature. The heated portion is then immediately quenched by means of spray of water, which is directed towards heated portion. Since the heating is localised, therefore no stresses are developed. As a result of this, the chances of distortion or cracking are reduced.

This is a surface hardening process resulting in a hard surface layer of about 2 mm to 6 mm deep. The main difference between this process and other surface hardening processes is that the composition of the steel being hardened is not changed. The steel must itself have sufficient hardenability . This limits this process to steels having carbon contents of above 0, 35%. Steels with carbon contents of 0, 4%–0, 7% are most suitable for this process. Steels with higher content and high alloy steels may not be suitable as they a liable to cracking. This process produces similar result to the conventional hardening process but with less hardness penetration.

3.5.2 Induction Hardening

It is a process of surface hardening in which the surface, to be hardened, is surrounded by an inductor block which acts as a primary coil of a transformer. The inductor block, should not touch the surface to be hardened. A high frequency current is passed through this block. The heating effect is due to induced eddy currents and hysteresis losses in the surface material. The inductor block, surrounding the heated surface, has water connections and numerous small holes on its inside surface. As soon as the surface reaches to the proper temperature (750°C to 760°C for 0.5 per cent carbon steel and 790°C to 800°C for alloy steel), it is automatically spray-quenched under pressure.

An important feature of this method of hardening is its rapidity of action, because it requires only a few seconds to heat the steel to a depth of 3 mm. The actual time depends upon the frequency used, power input and depth of hardening required. The induction hardening is widely used for wearing surfaces of crankshafts, camshafts, gear teeth etc Induction hardening provides a similar surface treatment regime to flame hardening. The steel component is located inside a water cooled copper coil which has (AC) alternating current through it. This causes the outer surface of the component to heat up. Depending on the AC frequency and current, the rate of heating as well as the depth of heating can be controlled. This process is well suited for surface heat treatment.

3.5.3 Pack Carburising

Carburizing is a case-hardening process by which carbon is added to the surface of low-carbon steel. This results in a carburized steel that has a high-carbon surface and a low-carbon interior. When the carburized steel is heat-treated, the case becomes hardened and the core remains soft and tough. Two methods are used for carburizing steel. One method consists of heating the steel in a furnace containing a carbon monoxide atmosphere. The other method has the steel placed in a container packed with charcoal or some other carbon-rich material and then heated in a furnace. To cool the parts, you can leave the container in the furnace to cool or remove it and let it air cool. In both cases, the parts become annealed during the slow cooling. The depth of the carbon penetration depends on the length of the soaking period. With today's methods, carburizing is almost exclusively done by gas atmospheres.

3.5.4 Pack or Solid Carburising

In this process, the article to be carburised is placed in a carburising box of proper design made of special heat resisting alloy, cast steel or steel sheet. The space between the article and the box is filled with a solid carburising compound.

The layer of compound between the article and the box should be as uniform as possible to give uniform transfer of heat from the under surface of the box to the article. The box is covered with a lid and sealed with clay to eliminate the entry of air. The box is now gradually heated in a furnace to the selected carburising temperature and maintained there for a specified period.

During heating, carbon monoxide gas is formed which reacts with the article to form carbon and carbon dioxide gas. This process is the simplest and earliest carburising process based on placing the components to be treated in metal containers with the carburising mixture,based on powdered charcoal and 10% barium carbonate, packed around the components. The containers are then heated to a constant temperature 850°C for a time period to ensure an even temperature throughout and sufficient to enable the carbon to diffuse into the surface of the components to sufficient depth. Because this process is difficult to control case depths of less than 0, 6 mm are not viable and the normal case depths produced are 0, 25 mm to 6 mm.

3.5.5 Cyaniding

The cyaniding (also called liquid carburising) is a case of surface hardening process in which both carbon and nitrogen are absorbed by the metal surface to get it hardened. In this process, the piece of low carbon steel is immersed in a bath of cyanide salt, such as sodium cyanide or potassium cyanide maintained at 850 to 950°C. The process applied to the low carbon steel parts of automobiles (oil pump gear, drive worm gear, change over switch shaft).

This process is a type of case hardening that is fast and efficient. Preheated steel is dipped into a heated cyanide bath and allowed to soak. Upon removal, it is quenched and then rinsed to remove any residual cyanide. This process produces a thin, hard shell that is harder than the one produced by carburizing and can be completed in 20 to 30 minutes vice several hours. The major drawback is that cyanide salts are a deadly poison.

Gas carburising

Gas carburising is accurate control of the process temperature and carburising atmosphere. The components are brought to a uniform temperature in a neutral atmosphere. Gas carburising uses a gaseous atmosphere in a sealed furnace usually containing propane (C_3H_8) or butane (C_4H_{10}). Sometimes the generated carbon dioxide, water vapour, and oxygen are controlled at low levels by purifying using activated carbon filters at high temperatures.

An alternative carburising atmosphere is sometime generated by using a drip feed system by feed an organic fluid based on methyl, ethyl or isopropyl achohol + benzene or equivalent is fed into the carburising chamber at a controlled rate. In this process there are generally internal fans working to ensure and even gas in the chamber. After carburising, the work is either slow cooled for later quench hardening, or quenched directly into various liquid quenches.

3.5.6 Nitriding

It is a process of case or surface hardening in which nitrogen gas is employed in order to obtain hard surface of the steel. This process is commonly used for those steels, which are alloyed with chromium, molybdenum, aluminium, manganese etc. The steel articles, usually, well machined and finished are placed in an air tight container made of high nickel chromium, steel and provided with inlet and outlet tubes through which the ammonia gas is circulated. The nitriding process is generally carried out in the electric furnace, where the temperature in the range of 450°C to 550°C is maintained. The container with the articles is placed in the furnace and ammonia gas is passed through it. The ammonia gas, when comes in contact with steel articles, gets dissociated in the form of nascent nitrogen, which reacts with the surface of the articles and form nitrides which is very hard. This process can give surface hardness up to a depth of 0.8 mm.

The nitriding process is used in the production of machine parts, which require high wear resistance at elevated temperatures such as automobile and air valves and valve parts, piston pins, crank shafts and cylinder liners. It also finds some application in the production of ball and roller bearing parts, or other parts to withstand high pressure steam services die-casting dies, wire-drawing dies etc.

Note: The core should be brought to its original toughness before nitriding by quenching in oil from about 900°C and tempering from about 600°C to 650°C.

Certain steel alloys can absorb nitrogen with a resulting extremely hard surface layer. The process consists of maintaining the steel component at a carefullly controlled temperature of 490°C to 530°C under the action of nascent of active nitrogen produced on the surface of the component by the decomposition of gaseous ammonia. The resulting surface is extremely hard and extremely thin but very brittle.The process time is relatively long compared to the carburising process at about 90 hours. The temperature of the furnace has to be maintained within ± 5°C and therefore electrical heating is generally used. The components are generally stacked in gas-tight boxes supported on nickel mesh trays. The boxes include a inlet and outlet pipes for the ammonia gas circulation flow. Quenching is not normally required following nitriding and therefore is normal to machine the components to size before nitriding nitrided surfaces retain hardness even if cycled for short periods at temperatures of up to 500°C. Carburised hardened surfaces lose their hardness under similar circumstances. Steel subject to nitriding is generally hardened and tempered and finished machined. The components are often stress relieved prior to final machining.

This case-hardening method produces the hardest surface of any of the hardening processes. It differs from the other methods in that the individual parts have been heat-treated and tempered before nitriding. The parts are then heated in a furnace that has an ammonia gas atmosphere. No quenching is required so there is no worry about warping or other types of distortion. This process is used to case harden items, such as gears, cylinder sleeves, camshafts and other engine parts, that need to be wear resistant and operate in high-heat areas.

3.6 WORK (STRAIN) HARDENING

Work hardening is when a metal is strained beyond the yield point. An increasing stress is required to produce additional plastic deformation and the metal apparently becomes stronger and more difficult to deform. Stress-strain curves are discussed in Chapter 2. The gradient of the straight part of the line is known as the strain hardening coefficient or work hardening coefficient, and is closely related to the shear modulus (about proportional). Therefore, a metal with a high shear modulus will have a high strain or work hardening coefficient (for example, molybdenum). Grain size will also influence strain hardening. A material with small grain size will strain harden more rapidly than the same material with a larger grain size. However, the effect only applies in the early stages of plastic deformation, and the influence disappears as the structure deforms and grain structure breaks down. Work hardening is closely related to fatigue. In the example on fatigue given above, bending the thin steel rod becomes more difficult the farther the rod is bent. This is the result of work or strain hardening. Work hardening reduces ductility, which increases the chances of brittle failure.

REVIEW QUESTIONS

1. What is heat treatment and how it is help full to metal?
2. Explain briefly the heat treatment process.
3. What are the different types of heat treatment process?
4. Explain the process of annealing heat treatment.
5. Explain the process of normalizing heat treatment.
6. Explain the process of tempering.
7. What are the different types of case hardening?
8. Explain the process of case hardening.

9. Explain the process of strain hardening.
10. Explain the uses of various kinds of heat treatment process.
11. Explain isothermal transformation diagram.
12. What is hardenability and how it will be found in metals?
13. Explain Jominy end quench test.
14. Explain the flame hardening process.
15. Explain induction hardening method.

4
CHAPTER

FERROUS AND NON FERROUS METALS

4.1 INTRODUCTION

There is no one material called steel, just as there is no one material called plastic. There are thousands of different kinds of steel. Steel is the general name given to a large family of alloys of iron with carbon and a variety of different elements. Ferrous (Iron) with maximum of 2% of carbon is called steel. Even small differences in the composition of the steel can have a dramatic effect on its properties. The properties of the steel can also be modified by different mechanical and heat treatments.

Why steel is so versatile?

Steel is such a versatile material because we can adjust its composition and internal structure to tailor its properties. So we can produce a steel for paperclips, a steel for bridges, thin strips of steel for razor blades and large beams for columns and skyscrapers.

4.2 STEEL CLASSIFICATION

Listed in this are two of the methods used in the classification of steels. One is a system devised by the *American Iron and Steel Institute (AISI)* in cooperation with the *Society of Automotive Engineers (SAE)*. This system groups tool steels by their purpose or unique properties. The second method, called the *Unified Numbering System (UNS)* uses a series of 4 to 5 digits to classify steels according to their primary alloying element, the approximate content of the primary alloying element, and the approximate carbon content in hundredths of one percent.

SAE Classification of Steel

The Society of Automotive Engineers (SAE) has established standards for specific analysis of steels. In the 10XX series, the first digit indicates a plain carbon steel. The second digit indicates a modification in the alloys. 10XX means that it is a plain carbon steel where the second digit (zero) indicates that there is no modification in the alloys. The last two digits denote the carbon content in points. For example SAE 1040 is a carbon steel where 40 points represent 0.40% carbon content. Alloy steels are indicated by 2XXX, 3XXX, 4XXX, etc. The American Iron and Steel Institute (AISI) in co-operation with the Society of Automotive

Engineers (SAE) revised the percentages of the alloys to be used in the making of steel, retained the numbering system, and added letter prefixes to indicate the method used in steel making. The letter prefixes are:

A = alloy, basic open hearth

B = carbon, acid bessemer

C = carbon, basic open hearth

D = carbon, acid open hearth

E = electric furnace

If the prefix is omitted, the steel is assumed to be open hearth. Example: AISI C1050 indicates a plain carbon, basic open hearth steel that has 0.50% carbon content. Another letter is the hardenability or H-value. Example: 4340H

General Representation of Steels

SAE 1 0 4 0

- 40 → Carbon content 0.40%
- 0 → Modification in the alloy (None) plain carbon
- 1 → Indicate whether it is a carbon steel or alloy steel (1–Carbon steel, 2–alloy steel)

SAE 2 5 1 5

- 15 → Carbon Content 0.15%
- 5 → Major alloying element content (5% Nickel)
- 2 → Indicate whether it is a carbon steel or alloy steel (2–Nickel Steel)

SAE 5 1 2 0

- 20 → Carbon content 0.2%
- 1 → Major alloying element content (1% Cr)
- 5 → Indicate whether it is a carbon steel or alloy steel (5–Chromium steel)

Table 4.1. SAE classification of steel

SAE-AISI Number	*Classification*
1XXX	Carbon steels Low carbon steels: 0 to 0.25% C Medium carbon steels: 0.25 to 0.55% C High carbon steels: Above 0.55% Carbon
2XXX	Nickel steels 5% Nickel increases the tensile strength without reducing ductility. 8 to 12% Nickel increases the resistance to low temperature impact 15 to 25% Nickel (along with Al, Cu and Co) develop high magnetic properties. (Alnico metals) 25 to 35 % Nickel create resistance to corrosion at elevated temperatures.
3XXX	Nickel-chromium steels These steels are tough and ductile and exhibit high wear resistance hardenability and high resistance to corrosion.
4XXX	Molybdenum steels Molybdenum is strong carbide former. It has a strong effect on hardenability and high temperature hardness. Molybdenum also increases the tensile strength of low carbon steels.
5XXX	Chromium steels Chromium is a ferrite strengthener in low carbon steels. It increases the core toughness and the wear resistance of the case in carburized steels.
86XX 87XX 93XX 94XX 97XX 98XX	Triple alloy steels which include Nickel (Ni), Chromium (Cr), and Molybdenum (Mo). These steels exhibit high strength and also high strength to weight ratio, good corrosion resistance.

4.3 EFFECTS OF ALLOYING ELEMENTS

4.3.1 Effect of Carbon on the Physical Properties of Steel

In general, as the carbon content increases the hardness of the steel also increases. The tensile strength and the yield strength also increase to about 0.83% carbon. Thereafter, they level out. This is shown in Fig. 4.1 below:

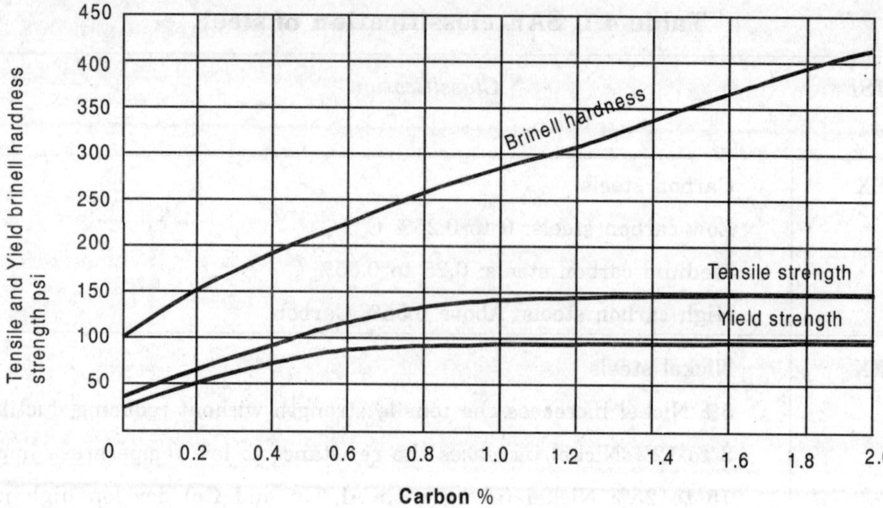

Fig. 4.1 Effect of carbon on hardness, tensile strength and yield strength of steels.

The tensile strength and hardness are affected as the ratio of ferrite to cementite in the structure of steel changes. As the percentage of pearlite increases in the hypoeutectoid steels, the tensile strength increases. The hardness does not increase dramatically. The hypereutectoid steels show only a slight increase in strength as the cementite-to-ferrite ratio increases.

The elongation and the reduction in area represent how ductile or brittle a material is indicates the effect of carbon on the ductility and impact resistance (toughness) of steels. The elongation and the reduction in area drop sharply with increase in carbon content, going almost to zero at about 1.5% carbon. This indicates that the carbon content of 1.5% or more will cause high brittleness. The impact resistance also decreases very sharply up to about 0.83% carbon and then levels out.

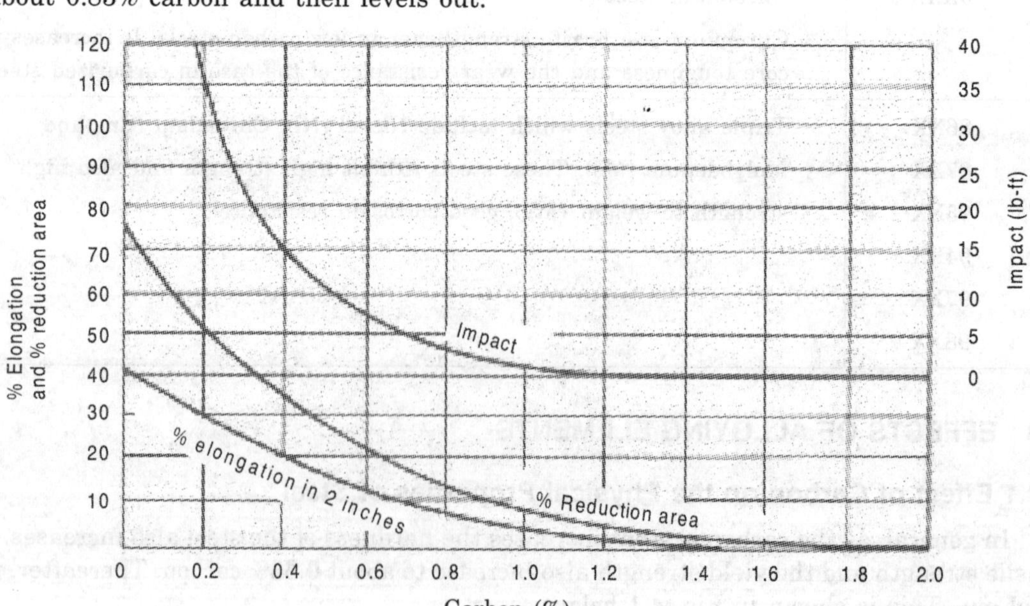

Fig. 4.2 Effect of carbon on the impact resistance and ductility of steels.

Usually only a small amount of alloying element are added to steels (usually less than 5%). Mostly the purpose is to improve the hardenability and strength corrosion resistance, stability at high/low temperatures, control grain size.

The other effects of adding specific elements into Steel are:

Manganese-increases ductility, hardenability, high strain hardening capacity, slightly strengthens, excellent wear resistance

Sulphur-if carefully proportioned can add machinability without imparting embrittlement.

Nickel-increases toughness and impact resistance, good properties at low temperatures. With other alloys imparts excellent corrosion resistance. With certain alloys it has a small thermal expansion and used for sensitive measuring devices. Increase strength with little loss of ductility.

Chromium-if added in large enough amounts can impart corrosion resistance and heat resistance and wear resistance and hardenability. Otherwise for amounts (less than 2.11%) it is used to slightly increase hardenability and strength.

Molybdenum-improves hardenability and increases strength primarily under dynamic and high temperature conditions. Extremely stable at elevated temperatures. It helps to retains fine grain sizes which provides strength and creep resistance at elevated temperatures. Molybdenum carbides are used in hot work tool steels and forging dies to impart hardness even at red heat.

Vanadium-like molybdenum, forms strong carbides at elevated temperatures. Also limits grain size.

Tungsten-used in tool steels to maintain their hardness at elevated temperatures.

Copper-increases the corrosion resistance. Limits have to be controlled or it'll sacrifice surface quality and hot-working behavior.

Silicon-increases strength without limiting grain size. Used to promote large grain sizes used in magnetic applications. Used in spring steels.

Boron - very important harden ability agent being several hundred times better than nickel, molybdenum and chromium. Used more for low carbon steels. Also improve machinability and cold forming.

Table 4.2. The effect of alloying elements on the properties of steel

Element	*Effect*
Aluminium	1. Ferrite hardener 2. Graphite former 3. Deoxidizer
Chromium	1. Mild ferrite hardener 2. Moderate effect on hardenability 3. Graphite former 4. Resists corrosion 5. Resists abrasion
Cobalt	1. High effect on ferrite as a hardener 2. High red hardness

Molybdenum	1. Strong effect on hardenability 2. Strong carbide former 3. High red hardness 4. Increases abrasion resistance
Manganese	Strong ferrite hardener
Nickel	1. Ferrite strengthener 2. Increases toughness of the hypoeutectoid steel 3. With chromium, retains austenite 4. Graphite former
Copper	1. Austenite stabilizer 2. Improves resistance to corrosion
Silicon	1. Ferrite hardener 2. Increases magnetic properties in steel
Phosphorus	1. Ferrite hardener 2. Improves machinability 3. Increases hardenability

The addition of small amounts of other metals to make alloy steels changes the properties of the material even further and means that a steel can be manufactured that has exactly the right properties for its purpose.

Table 4.3. Alloying element and its uses

Alloying element	Properties given to steel	Uses
Cobalt	High magnetic permeability	Magnets
Manganese	Strong and hard	Heavy duty railway crossings.
Molybdenum	Maintains high strength at high temperature	High speed drill tips
Nickel and chromium	Resists corrosion	Surgical instruments
Titanium	Increased hardness and tensile strength	High speed tool steels, permanent magnets
Tungsten	High melting temperature, tough	Cutting and drilling tools
Vanadium	Strong, hard	Tools

4.4 MECHANICAL PROPERTIES OF STEEL

The way in which a material behaves is described as its **mechanical properties.** When the forces tend to stretch a material it is said to be in tension. When the forces squash the material it is said to be under compression. When forces tend to twist the material or to make one part of it move relative to another part it is described as being in shear.

Properties

The main properties that we can test are:

- Stress
- Tensile strength
- Strain
- Stiffness
- Hardness

Stress

Stress and strain are the quantities we use to compare fairly the effects of a force on a material. Instead of the applied force we use stress; and instead of extension (or compression), we use strain.

Stress is the force per unit area.

What does stress mean?

Stress allows us to get a fair comparison of the effects of a force on different samples of a material. A tensile force will stretch and, possibly, break the sample. However, the force needed to break a sample will vary—depending on the cross-sectional area of the sample. If the cross-sectional area is bigger, the breaking force will be bigger. However, the breaking *stress* will always be the same because the stress is the force per unit area. So breaking **stress** is a more useful measurement than breaking **force** because it is constant for a given material. It allows us to fairly compare the strengths of different materials.

Tensile strength

A tensile test is used to find out what happens when a material such as steel is stretched. A steel bar is placed in a device that pulls one end away from the other fixed end. The **tensile strength** is the maximum stress that the bar can withstand before breaking.

Stretching

So far, we have looked at only the *breaking* stress of a material. But what about the stretching effect of a force. We would expect that different samples of the same material would stretch in the same way when we apply the same stress to them. However, in order to compare the amount they stretch, we need to think of more than simply their extension. This is **strain**.

Hardness

The **hardness** of a material is a measure of how hard it is to change its shape. A hard material is difficult to scratch or dent, but *it* will scratch or dent a softer material. The relative hardness of some materials are:

Table 4.4. Hardness of various elements

Material	*Relative Hardness*
Diamond	10.0
Steel	7.0
Glass	5.5
Tin	1.5

4.5 STAINLESS STEELS

Stainless steel is a generic term for a family of corrosion resistant alloy steels containing 10.5% or more chromium. All stainless steels have a high resistance to corrosion. This resistance to attack is due to the naturally occurring chromium-rich oxide film formed on the surface of the steel. Although extremely thin, this invisible, inert film is tightly adherent to the metal and extremely protective in a wide range of corrosive media. The film is rapidly self repairing in the presence of oxygen, and damage by abrasion, cutting or machining is quickly repaired.

Stainless steel was discovered by accident in 1913 by a sheffield chemist called Harry Brearley. He was trying to solve the problem of rapid wear of the inside of rifle barrels and decided to try out a steel containing a high proportion of chromium. Routine analysis of steel at that time involved dissolving it in acid. The high chromium steel, however, would not dissolve and also stayed shiny when left around in the laboratory. Brearley immediately realized the potential his steel had for making cutlery that would not rust. Progress by accidental discovery in this way in not uncommon in science. Sometimes it is referred to as serendipity.

Benefits of Stainless Steel

Corrosion resistance

All stainless steels have a high resistance to corrosion. Low alloyed grades resist corrosion in atmospheric conditions, highly alloyed grades can resist corrosion in most acids, alkaline solutions, and chloride bearing environments, even at elevated temperatures and pressures.

High and low temperature resistance

Some grades will resist scaling and maintain high strength at very high temperatures, while others show exceptional toughness at cryogenic temperatures.

Ease of fabrication

The majority of stainless steels can be cut, welded, formed, machined and fabricated readily.

Strength

The cold work hardening properties of many stainless steels can be used in design to reduce material thickness and reduce weight and costs. Other stainless steels may be heat treated to make very high strength components.

Aesthetic appeal

Stainless steel is available in many surface finishes. It is easily and simply maintained resulting in a high quality, pleasing appearance.

Hygienic properties

The cleanability of stainless steel makes it the first choice in hospitals, kitchens, food and pharmaceutical processing facilities.

Life cycle characteristics

Stainless steel is a durable, low maintenance material and is often the least expensive choice in a life cycle cost comparison.

Today, there is a range of steels from the plain chromium variety to those containing up to six alloying elements in addition to the usual impurities.

Classification of steel

A simple classification of the steels are follows :

Hardenable alloys

1. 12–14% of chromium, iron and steels, whose mechanical properties are largely dependent on the carbon content. High strength is combined with considerable corrosion resistance:

   (a) *Stainless iron,*

   (b) *Stainless steel, (mild, medium and hard)*

2. Secondary hardening, 10–12% of chromium, 0.12% C, with small additions Mo, V, Nb, Ni; a steel with ultimate stress of 927 MPa is used for gas turbine blades.
3. High chromium steel 17% Cr, 0.15% C, 2.5% Ni (431 S29). It has a higher resistance to corrosion than iron, due to higher chromium content. It is used for pump shafts, valves and fittings subjected to high temperature and high-pressure steam, but is unsuitable for acid conditions.

High carbon, 0.8 C, 16.5 Cr, 0.5 Mo steel (oil quenched at 1025°C and tempered at 1000°C to give hardness of 700 HB) is used for stainless ball bearings and instruments such as scalpels.

Stainless steels contain sufficient amounts of chromium that they are not considered low alloy steels. These require reduced cutting speeds (approx 1/2, finer feeds, lighter cuts, and sharp carbide tooling. Because the thermal conductivity of stainless steel is 1/3 that of carbon steel, the *heat is held in a localized area when welding.* This tends to localize the stress. The metal that is hot wants to expand but is hemmed in by the cold adjacent metal. When the material cools and contracts, the cooler metal does not move, with the result that cracks form during the solidification. Methods of dealing with these problems are available.

The corrosion resistance is imparted by the formation of a strong adherent chromium oxide on the surface of the metal. Good resistance to corrosive media encountered in the chemical industry can be obtained by the addition of 4 to 6% chromium to low carbon steel.

AISI classes these with a three digit number for stainless

- 200 series = chromium, nickel, manganese (Structure is austenitic)
- 300 series = chromium and nickel (Structure is austenitic)
- 400 series = chromium only (Structure is ferritic or martensitic)
- 500 series = low chromium (<12%) martensitic.

4.6 TYPES OF STAINLESS STEELS

In addition to chromium, nickel, molybdenum, titanium, niobium and other elements may also be added to stainless steels in varying quantities to produce a range of stainless steel grades, each with different properties. There are a number of grades to chose from, but all stainless steels can be divided into five basic categories:

1. Austenitic
2. Ferritic
3. Martensitic
4. Duplex

4.6.1 Austenitic Stainless Steels

When nickel is added to stainless steel in sufficient amounts the crystal structure changes to "austenite". The basic composition of austenitic stainless steels is 18% chromium and 8% nickel. Austenitic grades are the most commonly used stainless steels accounting for more than 70% of production (type 304 is the most commonly specified grade by far).

Basic properties of austenitic steels

1. Excellent corrosion resistance in organic acid, industrial and marine environments
2. Excellent weldability (all processes)
3. Excellent formability, fabricability and ductility
4. Excellent cleanability, and hygiene characteristics
5. Good high and excellent low temperature properties (high toughness at all temperatures)
6. Non magnetic (if annealed)
7. Hardenable by cold work only (These alloys are not hardenable by heat treatment)

Common uses of austenitic steels

1. Computer floppy disk shutters (304)
2. Computer keyboard key springs (301)
3. Kitchen sinks (304D)
4. Food processing equipment
5. Architectural applications
6. Chemical plant and equipment

Table 4.5. Chemical composition of austenitic steels

	302	*304*	*316*
Carbon	0.15% max.	0.08% max	0.08% max.
Chromium	17.00 to 19.00%	18.00 to 20.00%	16.00 to 18.00%
Manganese	2.0% max.	2.0% max.	2.0% max.
Silicon	1.0% max.	1.0% max.	1.0% max.
Nickel	8.00 to 10.00%	8.00 to 10.50%	10.00 to 14.00%
Molybdenum	----	----	2.00 to 3.00%

Table 4.6. Mechanical properties of austenitic stainless steels

	302	*304*	*316*
Tensile strength (Ksi)	90–185	84–185	84–185
Yield strength (Ksi)	40–140	42–140	42–140
Elongation in 2 inches (Annealed)	50%	55%	50%
Modulus of elasticity (psi)	28×10^6	28×10^6	28×10^6
Hardness (Annealed)	R_B 75–R_B 90	R_B 75–R_B 90	R_B 75–R_B 90
Hardness (Cold work)	R_C 25–R_C 39	R_C 25–R_C 39	R_C 25–R_C 39

Advantages

- Best corrosive resistance
- Highest of all for strength at high temperatures
- Best of all for ductility at low temperatures
- Nonmagnetic
- Highly resistant to chemical corrosion (except one), mirror polish
- Attractive appearance
- Formability is outstanding characteristic of the fcc
- Strengthen drastically when cold worked.

Disadvantages

- Corrosive in hydrochloric acid and other halide acids and salts
- Most expensive
- Water quench cold rolled
- Yield strength 38 ksi 117 ksi
- Tensile strength 90 ksi 140 ksi
- Elongation in 2" 68% 11%.

4.6.2 Ferritic Stainless Steels

This group of alloys generally containing only chromium, with the balance mostly Fe. These alloys are somewhat less ductile than the austenitic types and again are not hardenable by heat treatment. These are plain chromium stainless steels with varying chromium content between 12 and 18%, but with low carbon content. 16/18% chromium rustless iron with low carbon content (430 S15). It has high resistance to corrosion but low impact and cannot be refined by heat-treatment alone. Prolonged service at 480°C can cause embrittlement. Used for trim moldings and decorative applications and where buffing to a mirror finish is important.

Forms sigma phase additions of "Nb" and "Mo" prevent excessive grain growth. When chromium is added an increase in temperature range is seen by which ferrite is the stable structure. That is, ferrite is at all temperatures below solidification. Has low amount of carbon to chromium ratio; therefore hardening by heat-treating is not done.

Basic properties

1. Moderate to good corrosion resistance increasing with chromium content
2. Not hardenable by heat treatment and always used in the annealed condition magnetic
3. Weldability is poor
4. Formability not as good as the austenitic

Common uses

1. Computer floppy disk hubs
2. Automotive trim
3. Automotive exhausts
4. Colliery equipment
5. Hot water tanks

Advantages

- Readily weldable (no martensite can form at the welds because)
- Chromium retards the bcc martensite
- Cheapest of the stainless steels
- Magnetic
- Easiest of all to machine.

Disadvantages

- Poor ductility
- Poor formability because of the bcc crystal structure.

4.6.3 Martensitic Stainless Steels

Martensitic stainless steels were the first stainless steels commercially developed (as cutlery) and have relatively high carbon content (0.1–1.2%) compared to other stainless steels. They are plain chromium steels containing between 12 and 18% chromium. High amount of carbon to chromium ratio therefore can be heat treated. More corrosive resistant than ferrite, but still corrosive. This material can be austenitic (see next type) at high temperatures. At the high temperature, carbon can be dissolved in the fcc austenite, which in turn is quenched to form a bcc martenitic structure. So the steel is austenitized, quenched, then stress relief tempered.

Basic properties

1. Moderate corrosion resistance
2. Can be hardened by heat treatment and therefore high strength and hardness levels can be achieved
3. Poor weldability
4. Magnetic

Common uses

1. Knife blades
2. Surgical instruments
3. Shafts
4. Spindles
5. Pins

Advantages

- Increase in strength
- More corrosive resistant than ferritic
- Ability to hold an "edge"
- Good for impact
- Good up to 300 ksi when hardened.

Disadvantages

May be susceptible to red rust when annealed for machining or fabrication. Cost of material is 50% times more than the ferritic stainless steels.

4.6.4 Precipitation-Hardening Steels

These steels have been formulated so that they can be supplied in a solution treated condition, (in which they are machinable) and can be hardened, after fabrication, in a single low temperature "aging" process.

Basic properties

1. Moderate corrosion resistance
2. Very high strength
3. Good weldability
4. Good magnetic propertie

Common uses

Shafts, pumps and valves.

4.6.5 Duplex Stainless Steels

These are stainless steels containing relatively high chromium (between 18 and 28%) and moderate amounts of nickel (between 4.5 and 8%). The nickel content is insufficient to generate a fully austenitic structure and the resulting combination of ferritic and austenitic structures is called duplex. Most duplex steels contain molybdenum in a range of 2.5–4%.

Basic properties

1. High resistance to stress corrosion cracking
2. Increased resistance to chloride ion attack
3. Higher tensile and yield strength than austenitic or ferritic steels
4. Good weldability and formability

Common uses

1. Marine applications, particularly at slightly elevated temperatures
2. Desalination plant
3. Heat exchangers
4. Petrochemical plant

How stainless steel resists corrosion?

If iron and chromium are exposed to oxygen, it is the chromium that reacts to form an oxide. Due to its high chromium content, stainless steel forms a very thin layer of chromium (III) oxide as soon as the surface is exposed to the oxygen in the atmosphere. The layer of oxide is so thin that the metal can still shine through it, but it is thick enough to prevent the oxygen and water attacking the metal underneath and so no corrosion takes place.

The protection is permanent because even if the protective layer is scratched, the chromium in the steel will react with oxygen in the air to immediately re-form the protective layer.

Table 4.7. Other forms of corrosion protection

Protection	*How It is Applied*	*Uses*
Galvanising	Coating with a layer of zinc. Protects even when scratched	Car bodies
Chromium plating	Coating with a layer of chromium. Protection lost when scratched	Pipes and ornamental work
Painting	Covering with a layer of paint. Protection lost when scratched	Large structures such as ships and buildings
Organic coating	Covering with a layer of plastic	Electrical and office equipment
Tin lating	Coating with a layer of tin. Protection lost when scratched	Food and drink cans

4.7 TOOL AND DIE STEELS

Tool steels are characterized by high hardness and abrasion resistance coupled in many instances with resistance to softening at elevated temperatures. These properties are attained with high carbon and alloy content.

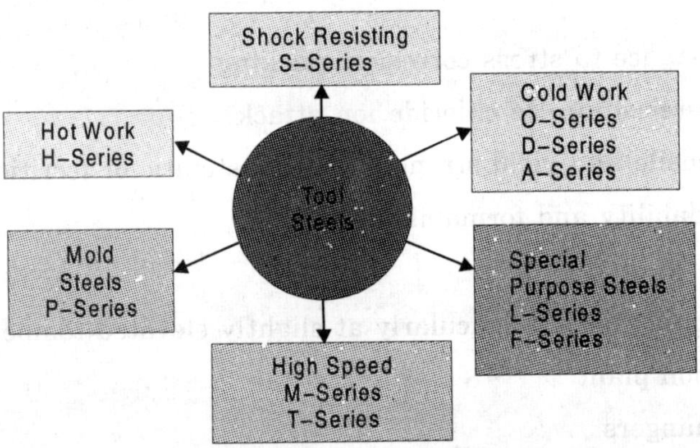

Fig. 4.3 Types of tool steel.

Table 4.8. Various tool steel and its designation

Tool Steel Type	*Prefix*	*Specific Types*
Cold Work	W = Water Hardening	W1, W2, W5
	O = Oil Hardening	O1, O2, O6, O7
	A = Medium alloy Air Hardening	A2, A4, A6, A7, A8, A9, A10, A11
	D = High Carbon, High Chromium	D2, D3, D4, D5, D7
Shock Resisting	S	S1, S2, S4, S5, S6, S7
Hot Work	H	H10–H19 Chromium types H20–H39 Tungsten types

			H40–H59 Molybdenum types
High Speed	M		Molybdenum types (M1, M2, M3–1, M3-2, M4, M6, M7, M10, M33, M34, M36, M41, M42, M46, M50
	T		Tungsten types (T1, T4, T5, T6, T8, T15)
Mold Steels	P		P6, P20, P21
Special Purpose	L and F series		L2, L6

Table 4.9. Various alloy tool steel and its application

Alloy	*Characteristics*	*Applications*
A2 A6	Air hardening, cold work steel, high wear resistance, superior toughness, excellent non-deforming properties, readily machined.	Intricate die shapes, thread rolling dies and slitters, blanking and forming dies, rolls, punches, gages, shear blades, cams, cutters broaches.
D2 D3 D6 D7	Air hardening, cold work steel, great hardness, very high wear resistance, non-deforming.	Blanking and deep drawing dies, gages, punches, rolls, shear knives, cold forming dies, thread rolling dies, stamping, spindles.
L6	Low alloy—special purpose steel, high wear resistance and toughness.	Bearings, rollers, clutch plates, feed fingers, chuck parts, spindles, wrenches, cams, collets, jigs.
M2 M4	High speed tool steel, best general purpose tool steel, excellent resistance to wear with toughness.	Cutting tools (all kinds), taps, chasers, reamers, broaches, counterbores.
O1 O2 O7	Oil hardening, cold work steel, general purpose steel. Good abrasive and wear resistance. Good machinability.	All cold forming and shearing applications.
S1 S2 S4 S5 S7	Shock resisting tool steels, high strength, moderate wear resistance. Primarily oil-hardening. Withstands repeated and severe impacts.	Chisels, rivet sets, hammers, punches, stamps, mandrels, knockout pins, grippers, chipping tools, hot-working tools (for repetitive high-impact applications, all types of severe service).

One problem that exists in discussing the metallurgy of tool steels is that, since there are six major categories of tool steels, it is difficult to make statements that apply to all these steels. The following are some of the characteristics of tool steels:

1. Composition and physical properties vary significantly (some tool steels have compositions that fit into the composition ranges of carbon and alloy steels, but

most tool steels have alloy concentrations that are significantly higher than the carbon and alloy steels).

2. One important factor that should be kept in mind is that the alloy additions do not improve corrosion resistance even though some grades have as much chromium as stainless steels. The reason for this is that alloy elements are usually combined with carbon to form carbides.
3. The most significant metallurgical difference between tool steels and the other steels is their microstructure. A fully hardened carbon steel or alloy steel would have only martensite as the predominant phase. Most tool steels have a hardened structure of martensite and alloy carbides.
4. Require special heat treatment processes.
5. Higher cost than alloy steels.
6. Better hardenability than most carbon and alloy steels.
7. High heat resistance.
8. Easier to heat treat.
9. More difficult to machine than carbon and alloy steels.
10. Most tool steels are sold as hot-finished shapes such as rounds and bars.
11. Cold-finished sheets are not available because it is difficult to cold roll or cold finish these materials.

4.7.1 Cold Work Tool Steels (W, O, A, D-types)

Cold work tool steels are used for gages, blanking, drawing and piercing dies, shears, forming and banding rolls, lathe centers, mandrels, broaches, reamers, taps, threading dies, plastic molds, knurling tools.

Water Hardening Tool Steels (W-Series)	*Oil Hardening Tool Steels (O-Series)*	*Medium Alloy Air Hardening Steels* (A-Series)	*High Carbon High Chromium Steels* (D-Series)
Essentially these are carbon steels with 0.60 to 1.10% carbon. Lowest cost tool steels. Soft core (for toughness) with hard shallow layer (for wear resistance). Use of W-series steels is declining.	0.90 to 1.45% carbon with Mn, Si, W, Mo, Cr. They contain graphite in the hardened structure along with martensite. (Graphite acts as a lubricator and also makes machining easier. Tungsten forms tungsten carbide which improves the abrasion resistance and edge retention in cutting devices.	5 to 10% alloying elements (Mn, Si, W, Mo, Cr, V, Ni) to improve the hardenability, wear resistance, toughness.	All D-series contain 12% Cr and over 1.5% C. Air or oil quench. Low distortion, high abrasion resistance.

4.7.2 Hot Work Tool Steels (H-series)

There are about 12 hot-worked tool steels. They are categorized by major alloying elements into three subgroups.

1. Chromium types
2. Tungsten types
3. Molybdenum types

These steels are used in extrusion dies, forging dies, die casting, hot shear blades, plastic molds, punches and dies for piercing shells, hot press, etc.

4.7.3 Shock Resisting Tool Steels (S-series)

These steels have 0.45 to 0.55% carbon. The alloys, silicon, and nickel are ferrite strengtheners. Chromium increases wear resistance and hardenability. The S-series of tool steels were originally developed for chisel-type applications, but the number of alloys in this category has evolved to include steels with a broad range of tool applications. This class of steels has a very good shock resistant qualities with excellent toughness.

They are used in form tools, chisels, punches, cutting blades, springs, trimming, and swaging dies, concrete and rock drills, bolt cutters.

4.7.4 Mold Tool Steels (P-series)

These steels have 0.10 to 0.35% carbon. They show high toughness. The low carbon mold steels cannot be quench hardened. The carbon and alloy content is low to allow hubbing of mold details. The desired mold shape is pressed into the steel with a hub that is usually made from a high-speed steel. Thus mold cavities can be made without machining. Hubbed cavities are then carburized to make a production injection molding cavity.

4.7.5 High-Speed Tool Steels (M and T-series)

These are the classes of steel that deep harden, retain that hardness at elevated temperatures, and have high resistance to wear and abrasion. The carbon content of these steels vary from 0.85% to 1.50%.

4.7.5.1 M-type

The M-type tool steels are high in molybdenum content and are used for lathe centers, blanking dies, hot forming dies, lathe cutting tools, drills, taps, etc. They are used in almost all cutting tools.

4.7.5.2 T-type

The T-type high speed tool steels with high carbon content have high wear resistance and very high hardness. The ones with lower carbon content are tougher but not as hard as the former group. As the amount of tungsten increases, the toughness decreases. This class of tool material has a substantial amount of wear-resistant carbides in a very high heat resistant matrix. These steels are used in machine cutting tools such as tool bits, milling cutters, taps, reamers, drills, broaches. In some instances it is used where high temperature structural steel is needed.

4.7.6 Special Purpose Tool Steels (L and F-series)

The L-type steels are low alloy steels with about 1% Cr that makes them a good low cost substitute for cold work steels. The F-type steels are high in carbon tungsten. They have high wear resistance, good toughness, and medium hardenability. The L-type steels are used in gages, broaches, drills, taps, threading dies, ball and roller bearings, clutch plates, knurls, files. The F-type steels are used as finish machining tools. They have good wear resistance and will maintain a sharp cutting edge. They may be used in dies, cutting tools, form tools, knives, etc.

4.8 HIGH STRENGTH LOW ALLOY STEELS

Some types of steel are specifically for use in fabricating large structures. They are called **'high-strength low alloy'** or **HSLA** steels. These steels are:

- Much stronger and tougher than ordinary carbon steels
- Ductile
- Highly formable
- Weldable

highly resistant to corrosion—which is important since the structure may be in place for a long time.

HSLA Steel Cars, Trucks and Bridges

The increased strength of HSLA steels means that structures can be built that contain less steel and are therefore lighter than they otherwise would be. This is an important feature for cars and trucks because it leads to fuel economy and to less damage to road surfaces. It is also important in the design of bridges since it means that the center spans can be longer and need fewer supporting beams.

HSLA Steel TV Masts

An interesting advantage of HSLA steels is seen in the construction of tall television transmitter masts. The extra strength of the steel means that the sections making up the mast can be thinner and more stable because they offer less resistance to the wind.

The Durability of HSLA Steels

The extra strength of HSLA steel makes it more durable and gives it a longer useful life span. It is therefore selected for use in street lighting poles, oil storage tanks and earth moving equipment.

The Steel Angel

One type of HSLA steel is called COR-TEN because it is particularly resistant to corrosion. It can be exposed to the atmosphere in its 'bare' condition which eliminates the need and cost of painting and re-painting.

Why HSLA steels are strong?

The starting point in achieving the desirable properties of structural steels is to get the composition of the alloy right. The extra strength can be achieved through various combinations of alloying elements which means that there can be some choice in the other properties that the steel will have.

A typical HSLA steel will contain about 0.15% carbon, 1.65% manganese and low levels (under 0.035%) of phosphorous and sulphur and additions of other elements:

Table 4.10. Addition of alloy element into HSLA

Element	*Percentage Added*	*Effect on Properties*
Copper	0.2–1.5	Improves atmospheric corrosion resistance
Nickel	At least half of the copper content	Benefits surface quality
Niobium	0.02	Increased tensile strength and yield point
Nitrogen	0.003–0.012	Contributes to strength and can improve weldability
Vanadium	Up to 0.12	Increases strength without reducing weldability

Chromium, molybdenum, silicon and zirconium may also be added.

Microstructure of HSLA Steels

The strength of all steels, including HSLA steels, comes from their microstructure. Strength is increased by:

- Increasing the amount of pearlite
- Increasing the fineness of the grains structure
- Increasing the amount of hard precipitate.

This is usually achieved by rolling the steel at low hot rolling temperatures.

4.9 MARAGING STEELS

The **18% Ni**-maraging steels, which belong to the family of iron-base alloys, are strengthened by a process of martensitic transformation, followed by age or precipitation hardening. Precipitation hardenable stainless steels are also in this group.

Maraging: derived from a combination of ***mar***tensite and ***age***-harden*ing*.

(*a*) Extra-low carbon content (wt.% C < 0.03)

(*b*) "Soft" martensite ⇒ **good formability**

(*c*) Little volume change on cooling from austenite ⇒ low residual stress

(*d*) High wt.% of Ni (Typically 13 to 25 wt.% Ni)

(*e*) 100% martensite on air cooling after soaking at ~ 816 °C

(*f*) Substitutional elements added to produce *age hardening* in iron-nickel martensite (E.g. Ti, Mo, Co, V, Nb, W, Al, Cu)

(*g*) Hardening is through intermetallic precipitates.

Maraging steels work well in electro-mechanical components where ultra-high strength is required, along with good dimensional stability during heat treatment.

Designation

The standard designation for maraging steels is: ***XX***Ni(*YYY*)

where ***XX*** represents the wt.% Ni (rounded to a whole number) and *YYY* represents the yield strength in the age-hardened condition in *psi*.

XX is typically **18** but higher and lower values are also encountered.

Example: a 18 Ni (200) steel is a maraging steel with 18 wt.% Ni and a yield strength of 200 psi.

4.9.1 Tempering of Maraging Steels

Tempering as an operation of heat treatment has been well known from the Middle Ages. It is used with martensite-quenched alloys. The processes of tempering will be considered here for steels only, since steels constitute an overwhelming majority of all marensite-hardenable alloys.

Maraging steels are carbonless **Fe-Ni** alloys additionally alloyed with cobalt, molybdenum, titanium and some other elements. A typical example is an iron alloy with **17–19% Ni, 7–9% Co, 4.5–5% Mo** and **0.6–0.9% Ti.** Alloys of this type are hardened to martensite and then tempered at 480–500°C. The tempering results in strong precipitation hardening owing to the precipitation of inter-metallic from the martensite, which is supersaturated with the alloying elements. By analogy with the precipitation hardening in aluminium, copper and other non-ferrous alloys, this process has been termed ageing, and since the initial structure is martensite, the steels have been called maraging.

The structure of commercial maraging steels at the stage of maximum hardening can contain partially coherent precipitates of intermediate metastable phases $\mathbf{Ni_3Mo}$ and $\mathbf{Ni_3Ti}$. Ni_3Ti phase is similar to hexagonal—carbide in carbon steels. Of special practical value is the fact that particles of intermediate intermetallics in maraging steels are extremely disperse, which is mainly due to their precipitation at dislocations.

The structure of maraging steels has a high density of dislocations, which appear on martensitic rearrangement of the lattice. In lath (untwined) martensite, the density of dislocations is of an order of 10^{11}—10^{12} cm^{-2}, *i.e.*, the same as in a strongly strain-hardened metal. In that respect the substructure of maraging steel (as hardened) differs appreciably from that of aluminium, copper and other alloys which can be quenched without polymorphic change.

It is assumed that the precipitation of intermediate phases on tempering of maraging steels is preceded with segregation of atoms of alloying elements at dislocations. The atmospheres formed at dislocations serve as centers for the subsequent concentration stratification of the martensite, which is supersaturated with alloying elements.

In maraging steels the dislocation structure that forms in the course of martensitic transformation, is very stable during the subsequent heating and practically remains unchanged at the optimum temperatures of tempering (480–500°C). Such a high density of dislocations during the whole course of tempering may be due to an appreciable extent, to dislocation pinning by disperse precipitates.

A long holding in tempering at a higher temperature (550°C or more) may coarsen the precipitates and increase the interparticle spacing, with the dislocation density being simultaneously reduced. With a long holding time, semi coherent precipitates of intermediate intermetallics are replaced with coarser incoherent precipitates of stable phases such as $\mathbf{Fe_2Ni}$ or $\mathbf{Fe_2Mo}$.

At increased temperatures of tempering (above 500°C), maraging steels may undergo the reverse martensitic transformation, since the as point is very close to the optimum temperatures of tempering. The formation of austenite is then accompanied with the dissolution of the intermetallics that have precipitated from the phase.

Properties of Maraging Steel

Several desirable properties of maraging steels are:

- Ultra-high strength at room temperature
- Simple heat treatment, which results in minimum distortion
- Superior fracture toughness compared to quenched and tempered steel of similar strength level
- Low carbon content, which precludes decarburization problems
- Section size is an important factor in the hardening process
- Easily fabricated
- Good weldability.

These factors indicate that maraging steels could be used in applications such as shafts, and substitute for long, thin, carburized or nitrided parts, and components subject to impact fatigue, such as print hammers or clutches.

Variations of Properties in Maraging Steels

The dependence of mechanical properties of maraging steels on the temperature of tempering is of the same pattern as that for all precipitation-hardenable alloys, *i.e.*, the strength properties increase to a maximum, after which softening takes place. By analogy with ageing, the stages of hardening and softening tempering may be separated in the process.

The hardening effect is caused by the formation of segregates at dislocations and, what is most important, by the formation of partially coherent precipitates of intermediate phases of the type $\mathbf{Ni_3Ti}$ or $\mathbf{Ni_3Mo}$. The softening is due, in the first place, to replacement of disperse precipitates having greater inter-particle spacing and, in the second place, to the reverse martensitic transformation which is accompanied by the dissolution of intermetallics in the austenite.

The ultimate strength of maraging steels increases on tempering roughly by 80% and the yield limit, by 140%, *i.e.*, the relative gain in strength properties is not greater than in typical age-hardening alloys, such as beryllium bronze or aluminium alloy **Grade 1915,** but the absolute values of ultimate and yield strength on tempering of maraging steels reach record figures among all precipitation hardening alloys. This is mainly due to the fact that maraging steels have a very high strength (**Rm = 1100 MPa**) in the initial (as-hardened) state.

The high strength of maraging steels on tempering at 480–500°C for 1–3 hours may be explained by the precipitation of very disperse semi coherent particles of the size and interparticle spacing of an order of 10^3 nm in the strong matrix, these intermetallic precipitates also possessing a high strength. Thus, with the same dispersity of precipitates as that of G. P. zones in precipitation, hardening non-ferrous alloys, maraging steels possess an appreciably higher ultimate strength (**Rm = 1800–2000 MPa**).

As compared with martensite-hardenable carbon-containing steels, carbonless maraging steels show, for the same strength, a substantially greater resistance to brittle fracture, which is their most remarkable merit. On tempering to the maximum strength, the ductility indices and impact toughness, though diminish somewhat, still remain rather high. The high ductility of the carbonless matrix and the high dispersity of uniformly distributed intermetallic precipitates are responsible for a very high resistance to cracking, which is the most valuable property of modern high-strength structural materials.

The properties of maraging steels clearly indicate that these steels have many potential applications in mechanical components of electro-mechanical data processing machines. Use of these steels in shafts that require good dimensional control following heat treatment should be pursued for two reasons. First, maintaining dimensions should be easier because quenching and tempering are not necessary. Second, wear data indicate that equivalent or better wear resistance is obtained from the maraging steel than from the more commonly used shaft materials.

Impact-fatigue strength of **18% Ni**-maraging steels indicates that these steels could be used in repeated impact loading situations. The good fracture toughness, compared to that of quenched and tempered alloy steels at the same strength level, indicates possible use in high-impact low-cycle load applications.

Finally, due to the relatively low temperature of aging, the use of the maraging steels for long, thin parts should be considered. Here, their use as a replacement for some case hardened or nitrided components is indicated that the potential application should be carefully studied.

Applications of Maraging Steels

- Aerospace
  1. Rocket motor cases
  2. Jet engine and helicopter drive shafts
  3. Aircraft landing gears
  4. Hinges for swing-wings
  5. Shock absorbers on Lunar Rover!
- Automotive
  1. Drive shafts
  2. Connecting rods
  3. Engine valves
- Tooling
  1. Extrusion rams
  2. Machine tool gears
  3. Al and Zn casting dies
  4. Index plates
  5. Rolls
  6. Splined shafts

Advantages of Maraging Steels

1. No quenching needed
2. Good dimensional stability during heat treatment

3. Workable and machinable in the martensitic condition
4. Can hot- and cold-work
5. Good weldability
6. Can nitride or nitrocarburize during maraging
7. Very good combination of strength and toughness, typical $\sigma_y = 2000$ MPa
8. Strength maintained to typically 500°C

Disadvantages

1. Expensive
2. Uses Co–a "strategic" metal with limited sources of supply and volatile pricing, Cobalt-free grades have been developed.
3. Fatigue strength and wear resistance not as good as might be expected for their σ_y and K_{Ic}.

4.10 CAST IRON AND IT'S CLASSIFICATION

The term "**cast iron**" designates an entire family of metals with a wide variety of properties. It is a generic term like steel which also designates a family of metals. Steels and cast irons are both primarily iron with carbon (C) as the main alloying element. Steels contain less than 2% and usually less than 1% C, while all cast irons contain more than 2% C. About 2% is the maximum C content at which iron can solidify as a single phase alloy with all of the C in solution in austenite. Thus, the cast irons by definition solidify as heterogeneous alloys and always have more than one constituent in their microstructure.

In addition to C, cast irons also must contain appreciable silicon (Si), usually from 1–3%, and thus they are actually iron-carbon-silicon alloys. The high C content and the Si in cast irons make them excellent casting alloys. Their melting temperatures are appreciably lower than for steel. Molten iron is more fluid than molten steel and less reactive with molding materials. Formation of lower density graphite in the iron during solidification reduces the change in volume of the metal from liquid to solid and makes production of more complex castings possible. Cast irons, however, do not have sufficient ductility to be rolled or forged.

Cast irons may often be used in place of steel at considerable cost savings. The design and production advantages of cast iron include:

- Low tooling and production cost
- Good machinability without burring
- Ability to cast into complex shapes
- Excellent wear resistance and high hardness (particularly white cats irons)
- High inherent damping capabilities

The properties of the cast iron are affected by the following factors

- Chemical composition of the iron
- Rate of cooling of the casting in the mold (which depends on the section thickness in the casting)
- Type of graphite formed (if any)

The various types of cast iron cannot be designated by chemical composition because of similarities between the types. Table lists typical composition ranges for the most frequently determined elements in the five generic types of cast iron.

4.10.1 Types of Cast Iron

Major types of cast iron are shown below

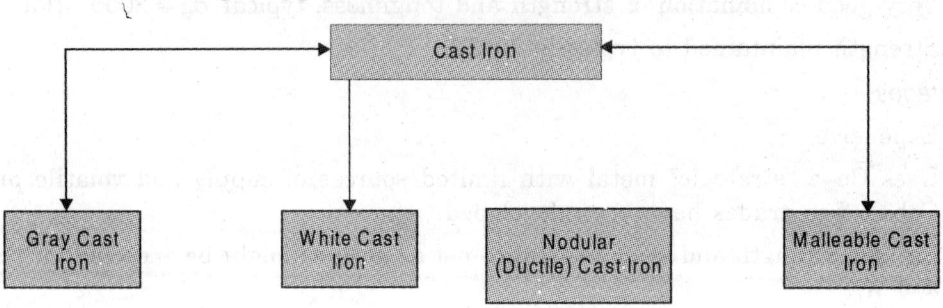

Fig 4.4. Types of cast iron.

Table 4.11. Range of compositions for typical unalloyed cast irons

Percent (%) *Type of Iron*	*Carbon*	*Silicon*	*Manganese*	*Sulphur*	*Phosphorus*
Gray	2.5–4.0	1.0–3.0	0.2–1.0	0.02–0.25	0.02–1.0
Ductile	3.0–4.0	1.8–2.8	0.1–1.0	0.01–0.03	0.01–0.1
Compacted Graphite	2.5–4.0	1.0–3.0	0.2–1.0	0.01–0.03	0.01–0.1
Malleable (Cast White)	2.0–2.9	0.9–1.9	0.15–1.2	0.02–0.2	0.02–0.2
White	1.8–3.6	0.5–1.9	0.25–0.8	0.06–0.2	0.06–0.2

There is a sixth classification for commercial purposes—the high-alloy irons. These have a wide range in base composition and also contain major quantities of other elements. The presence of certain minor elements also is vital to the successful production of each type of iron. For example, nucleating agents, called inoculants; are used in the production of gray iron to control the graphite type and size. Trace amounts of bismuth and tellurium are used in the production of malleable iron, and the presence of a few hundredths of a percent magnesium (Mg) causes the formation of the spheroidal graphite in ductile iron.

In addition, the composition of an iron must be adjusted to suit particular castings. Small castings and large castings of the same grade of iron cannot be made from the same composition of metal. For this reason, most iron castings are purchased on the basis of mechanical properties rather than composition. The common exception is for castings that require special properties such as corrosion resistance or elevated temperature strength.

The various types of cast iron can be classified by their microstructure. This classification is based on the form and shape in which the major portion of the C occurs in the iron. This system provides for five basic types: gray iron, ductile iron, malleable iron, Compacted Graphite Iron (CGI) and white iron. Each of these types may be moderately alloyed or heat treated without changing its basic classification. The high-alloy irons, generally containing over 3% of added alloy, also can be individually classified as gray or ductile iron or white, but the high-alloy irons are classified commercially as a separate group.

4.10.2 Gray Iron

When the composition of the molten iron and its cooling rate are appropriate, the "C" in the iron separates during solidification and forms separate graphite flakes that are interconnected within each eutectic cell. The graphite grows edgewise into the liquid and forms the characteristic flake shape. When gray iron is broken, most of the fracture occurs along the graphite, thereby accounting for the characteristic gray color of the fractured surface. Because the large majority of the iron castings produced are of gray iron, the generic term, cast iron, is often improperly used to mean gray iron specifically.

Gray cast iron is by far the oldest and most common form of cast iron. As a result, it is assumed by many to be the only form of cast iron and the terms "cast iron" and "gray iron" are used interchangeably. Unfortunately the only commonly known property of gray iron- brittleness- is also assigned to "cast iron" and hence to all cast irons. Gray iron, named because its fracture has a gray appearance. It contains carbon in the form of flake graphite in a matrix which consists of ferrite, pearlite or a mixture of the two. The fluidity of liquid gray iron, and its expansion during solidification due to the formation of graphite, have made this metal ideal for the economical production of shrinkage-free, intricate castings such as motor blocks.

Fig. 4.5 Gray iron.

The flake-like shape of graphite in gray iron exerts a dominant influence on its mechanical properties. The graphite flakes act as stress raisers which may prematurely cause localized plastic flow at low stresses, and initiate fracture in the matrix at higher stresses. As a result, gray iron exhibits no elastic behavior but excellent damping characteristics, and fails in tension without significant plastic deformation. The presence of graphite flakes also gives gray iron excellent machinability and self-lubricating properties.

The properties of gray iron are influenced by the size, amount and distribution of the graphite flakes, and by the relative hardness of the matrix metal around the graphite. These factors are controlled mainly by the C and Si contents of the metal and the cooling rate of the casting. Slower cooling and higher C and Si contents tend to produce more and larger graphite flakes, a softer matrix structure and lower strength. The flake graphite provides gray iron with unique properties such as excellent machinability at hardness levels that produce superior wear-resisting characteristics, the ability to resist galling and excellent vibration damping.

The amount of graphite present, as well as its size and distribution, are important to the properties of the iron. Whenever possible, it is preferable to specify the desired properties rather than the factors that influence them.

Advantages of Gray Cast Iron

1. Graphite acts a s a chip breaker and a tool lubricant.
2. Very high damping capacity.
3. Good dry bearing qualities due to graphite.
4. After formation of protective scales, it resists corrosion in many common engineering environments.

Disadvantages

1. Brittle (low impact strength) which severely limits use for critical applications.
2. Graphite acts as a void and reduces strength. Maximum recommended design stress is 1/4 of the ultimate tensile strength. Maximum fatigue loading limit is 1/3 of fatigue strength.
3. Changes in section size will cause variations in machining characteristics due to variation in microstructure.
4. Higher strength gray cast irons are more expensive to produce.

4.10.3 Ductile Iron

Ductile iron, also referred to as nodular iron or spheroidal graphite iron, was patented in 1948. After a decade of intensive development work in the 1950s, ductile iron had a phenomenal nine-fold increase in use as an engineering material during the 1960s, and the rapid increase in commercial application continues today.

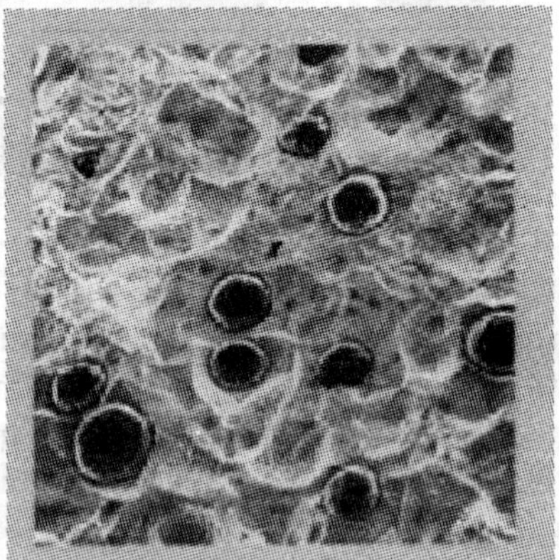

Ductile Iron

Fig 4.6 Ductile iron.

This structure is developed from the melt. The carbon forms into spheres when cerium, magnesium, sodium, or other elements are added to a melt of iron with a very low sulphur content that will inhibit carbon from forming. The control of the heat-treating process can yield pearlitic, ferritic, martensitic matrices into which the carbon spheres are embedded.

An unusual combination of properties is obtained in ductile iron because the graphite occurs as spheroids rather than as individual flakes as in gray iron. This mode of solidification is obtained by adding a very small, but specific, amount of Mg to molten iron of a proper composition. The base iron is severely restricted in the allowable contents of certain minor elements that can interfere with the graphite spheroid formation. The added Mg reacts with the sulfur and oxygen in the molten iron and changes the way the graphite is formed. Control procedures have been developed to make the processing of ductile iron dependable.

The high "C"and "Si" content of ductile iron provide the casting process advantages, but the graphite spheroids have only a nominal influence on the mechanical properties of the metal. Ductile iron, like malleable iron, exhibits a linear stress-strain relation, a considerable range of yield strengths and, as its name implies, ductility. Castings are made in a wide range of sizes with sections that can be either very thin or very thick.

The different grades are produced by controlling the matrix structure around the graphite either as-cast or by subsequent heat treatment. Only minor compositional differences exist among the regular grades, and these adjustments are made to promote the desired matrix microstructures. Alloy additions may be made to ductile iron to assist in controlling the matrix structure as-cast or to provide response to heat treatment. Special analysis ductile irons and high-alloy ductile irons provide unusual properties for special applications.

The *advantages* of ductile cast iron which have led to its success are numerous, but they can be summarized easily-versatility and high performance at low cost. Other members of the ferrous casting family may have superior individual properties which might make them the material of choice in some applications, but none have the versatility of ductile cast iron, which often provides the designer with the best combination of overall properties. This is especially evident in the area of mechanical properties where ductile cast iron offers the designer the option of selecting high ductility, with grades guaranteeing more than 18% elongation (as high as 25%), or high strength. Austempered ductile iron offers even greater mechanical and wear resistance, providing tensile strengths exceeding 230 psi.

In addition to cost advantages offered by all castings, ductile cast iron, when compared to steel and malleable cast iron, also offers further cost savings. Like most commercial cast metal, steel and malleable cast iron decrease in volume during solidification, and as a result, require feeders and risers to offset the shrinkage and prevent the formation of internal or external shrinkage defects. Ductile cast iron offers significantly low shrinkage during casting. In the case of large castings produced in rigid molds, it does not require feeders. In other cases, it requires feeders that are much smaller than those used for malleable cast iron and steel. This reduced requirement for feed metal increases the productivity of ductile cast iron and reduces its material and energy requirements, resulting in substantial cost savings. The use of the most common grades of ductile cast iron "as-cast" eliminates heat treatment costs, offering a further advantage.

Ductile cast iron is used for many structural applications, particularly those requiring strength and toughness combined with good machinability and low cost. The automotive and agricultural industries are the major users of ductile iron castings. Because of economic advantage and high reliability, ductile iron is used for such critical automotive parts as crankshafts, engine connecting rods, idler arms, wheel hubs, truck axles, front wheel spindle supports, disk brake calipers, suspension system parts, power transmission yokes, high temperature applications for turbo housing and manifolds, and high security valves for many applications. The cast iron pipe industry is another major user of ductile iron.

4.10.4 Compacted Graphite Iron

CGI became commercially available as dependable methods for its production were developed. Its graphite occurs as blunt flakes that are interconnected within each cell. This graphite structure and the resulting properties of the iron are intermediate between gray and ductile irons. The compacted graphite shape has been known for some time and also has been called quasiflake, aggregated flake, seminodular and vermicular graphite.

Is production is similar to that for ductile iron in requiring close metallurgical control and rare earth element additions, but it also requires another alloying element such as titanium to minimize the formation of sphercidal graphite. CGI retains much of the castability of gray iron, but has a higher tensile strength and some ductility. Its matrix structure can be adjusted by alloying or heat treatment.

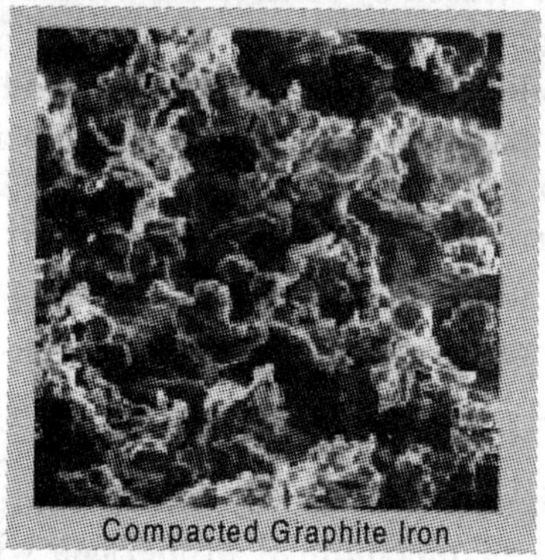

Fig. 4.7 Compacted graphite iron.

4.10.5 Malleable Iron

This type of iron is characterized by having the majority of its C content occur in the microstructure as irregularly shaped nodules of graphite. This form of graphite is called temper carbon because it is formed in the solid state during heat treatment. The iron is cast as a white iron of a suitable chemical composition.

If cast iron is cooled rapidly, the graphite flakes needed for gray cast iron do not get a chance to form. Instead, white cast iron forms. This white cast iron is reheated to about 1700°F for long periods of time in the presence of materials containing oxygen, such as iron oxide. At the elevated temperatures cementite (Fe_3C) decomposes into ferrite and free carbon. Upon cooling, the combined carbon further decomposes to small compact particles of graphite (instead of flake—like graphite seen in gray cast iron). If the cooling is very slow, more free carbon is released. This free carbon is referred to as temper carbon, and the process is called malleableizing.

After the castings are removed from the mold, they are given an extended heat treatment starting at a temperature above 1650°F (900°C). This causes the iron carbide to dissociate and the free carbon precipitates in the solid iron as graphite. The rapid solidification rate that is necessary to form the white iron limits the metal thickness in the casting that is practical for the malleable iron process.

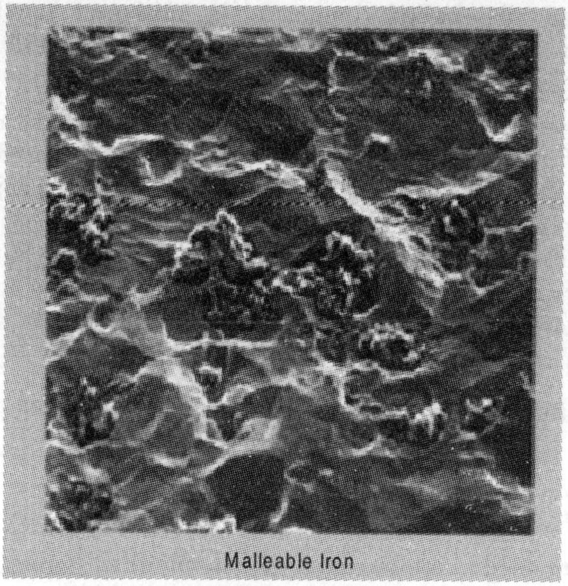

Fig. 4.8 Malleable iron.

A wide range of mechanical properties can be obtained in malleable iron by controlling the matrix structure around the graphite. Pearlitic and martensitic matrices are obtained both by rapid cooling through the critical temperature and with alloy additions. Malleable irons containing some combined carbon in the matrix often are referred to as pearlitic malleable, although the microstructure may be martensitic or a spheroidized pearlite.

Malleable cast iron is used for connecting rods and universal joint yokes, transmission gears, differential cases and certain gears, compressor crankshafts and hubs, flanges, pipe fittings and valve parts for railroad, marine and other heavy-duty applications.

Advantages

1. Excellent machinability
2. Significant ductility
3. Good shock resistance properties.

Disadvantages

The major disadvantage is shrinkage. Malleable cast iron decreases in volume during solidification, and as a result, requires attached reservoirs (feeders and risers) of liquid metal to offset the shrinkage and prevent the formation of **internal or external shrinkage defects.**

4.10.6 White Iron

White cast iron is unique in that it is the only member of the cast iron family in which carbon is present only as carbide. Due to the absence of graphite, it has a light appearance. The presence of different carbides, depending on the alloy content, makes white cast irons extremely hard and abrasion resistant but very brittle. An improved form of white cast iron is the chilled cast iron.

If the composition of the iron is appropriate or the cooling rate of the metal is sufficiently rapid during solidification, the metal will solidify with the C combined with iron as iron carbide. This compound, also called cementite, is hard and brittle and dominates the microstructure of white iron. Thus, white iron is hard and brittle and has a white crystalline fracture because it is essentially free of graphite.

White iron has a high compressive strength and excellent wear resistance, and it retains its hardness for limited periods even up to a red heat. It can be produced in selected areas of a casting-such as on the periphery of a cam-by causing localized rapid solidification of the iron. White iron at the surface of a casting is called chill. It is produced by making that portion of the mold-where the white iron is desired-of a material that can extract heat very rapidly, such as iron or graphite. White iron does not have the easy castability of other irons because its solidification temperature is generally higher, and it solidifies with C in its combined form as iron carbide.

4.10.7 High Alloy Irons

This classification includes high-alloy white irons, high-alloy gray irons and high-alloy ductile irons. Malleable irons are not heavily alloyed because this interferes with the metallurgy of the malleable process.

High-alloy irons are used in applications with demanding requirements such as extreme abrasive wear, heat or corrosion-resistance. These irons also are employed when unusual physical properties, such as low thermal expansion or nonmagnetic properties, are desired.

High-alloy iron castings are produced by foundries that specialize in their production because over 30% of alloy content requires the use of special melting facilities, casting techniques and quality control. The special property requirements of high-alloy irons are often too difficult to establish and verify for specification, so these irons are usually specified by their chemical composition. Mechanical property requirements also may be specified where these are important. The high-alloy irons are classified by the type of unusual service conditions for which they are used.

Table 4.12. Grades of cast iron and its constituents

	Major Constituents in Weight %						
Grade	*Carbon*	*Chromium*	*Manganese*	*Molybdenum*	*Nickel*	*Silicon*	*Copper*
1018	0.18						
1045	0.45						
4140	0.4	1	0.8	0.2			
5120	0.2	0.8	0.8			0.23	
8620	0.2	0.5	0.8	0.2	0.55		
431 SS	0.2	15–17	0.8		1.25–2.5	0.23	
Ductile Cast Iron	3.6–3.8		0.15–1			1.8–2.8	.15–1
Grey Cast Iron	3.25–3.5		0.5–0.9			1.8–2.3	
White Cast Iron	2.4–2.8		0.1	2	0.5	1	1.2
Austempered Ductile Iron	3.7		0.28	0.25	2	2.5	0.8

4.11 COPPER AND COPPER ALLOYS

Copper, the most noble of the metals in common use, has excellent resistance to corrosion in the atmosphere and in fresh water. In sea-water, the copper nickel alloys have superior resistance to corrosion coupled with excellent anti-fouling properties.

Copper cladding of wooden hulled warships, introduced by the Royal Navy in the 18th century to prevent damage by wood-boring insects and worms such as the teredo, was discovered to prevent bio-fouling by weed and moluscus. This meant that ships could stay at sea for long periods without cleaning. Nelson's successful blockade tactics and subsequent victory at Trafalgar was partly due to the superior speed of his clean-hulled ship.

The addition of nickel to copper improves its strength and durability and also the resistance to corrosion, erosion and cavitation in all natural waters including sea-water and brackish, treated or polluted waters. The alloys also show excellent resistance to stress-corrosion cracking and corrosion fatigue. The added advantage of resistance to bio-fouling, gives a material ideal for application in marine and chemical environments for ship and boat hulls, desalination plant, heat exchange equipment, sea-water and hydraulic pipelines, oil rigs and platforms, fish farming cages, sea-water intake screens, etc.

Minerals of Copper

Mineral	*Composition*	*Wt % Copper*	*Colour*	*Luster*
Native copper	Cu	100.00	Copper red	Metallic
Cuprite	Cu_2O	88.8	Red	Adamantine to earthy
Chalcocite	Cu_2S	79.9	Dark grey	Metallic
Covellite	CuS	66.4	Indigo blue	
Bornite	Cu_5FeS_4	63.3	Golden brown to copper red	Metallic
Malachite	$CuCO_3Cu(OH)_4$	57.5	Bright green	Silky to earthy
Azurite	$2CuCO_3Cu(OH)_2$	55.3	Blue	Vitreous to adamantine
Antlerite	$Cu_3SO_4(OH)_4$	53.7	Green	
Chrysocolla	$CuSiO_32H_2O$	36.2	Bluish green, sky blue, turquoise	Vitreous to earthy
Chalcopyrite	$CuFeS_2$	34.6	Golden yellow	Metallic to opaque

Basic Properties of Coppers

Copper is an excellent electrical conductor. Most of its uses are based on this property or the fact that it is also a good thermal conductor. However, many of its applications also rely on one or more of its other properties. For example, it wouldn't make very good water and gas pipes if it were highly reactive. We look at these other properties:

1. A good electrical conductor
2. A good thermal conductor

3. Corrosion resistant
4. Anti bacterial
5. Easily joined
6. Ductile
7. Tough
8. Non-magnetic
9. Attractive colour
10. Easy to Alloy
11. Recyclable
12. Catalytic
13. Thermal conductor.

Corrosion Resistant

Copper is low in the reactivity series. This means that it doesn't tend to corrode. Again, this is important for its use for pipes, electrical cables, saucepans and radiators. However, it also means that it is well suited to decorative use. Jewellery, statues and parts of buildings can be made from copper, brass or bronze and remain attractive for thousands of years.

Antibacterial

Copper is a naturally hygienic metal that slows down the growth of germs such as E-coli (the "burger bug"), MRSA (the hospital "superbug") and legionella. This is important for applications such as food preparation, hospitals, coins , door knobs and plumbing systems.

Easily Joined

Copper can be joined easily by soldering or brazing. This is useful for pipe work and for making sealed copper vessels.

Ductile

Copper is a **ductile** metal. This means that it can easily be shaped into pipes and drawn into wires. Copper pipes are lightweight because they can have thin walls. They don't corrode and they can be bent to fit around corners. The pipes can be joined by soldering and they are safe in fires because they don't burn or support combustion.

Tough

Copper and copper alloys are tough. This means that they were well suited to being used for tools and weapons. Imagine the joy of ancient man when he discovered that his carefully formed arrowheads no longer shattered on impact.

The property of toughness is vital for copper and copper alloys in the modern world. They do not shatter when they are dropped or become brittle when cooled below 0°C.

Non Magnetic

Copper is non magnetic and non sparking. Because of this, it is used in special tools and military applications.

Attractive Colour

Copper and its alloys, such as brass, are used for jewellery and ornaments. They have an attractive golden colour which varies with the copper content. They have a good resistance to tarnishing making them last a long a time.

Alloys Easily

Copper can be combined with other metals to make alloys. The most well known are brass and bronze. Although copper has excellent electrical and thermal properties, it needs to be hardened and strengthened for many industrial applications. It is therefore mixed with other metals and melted. The liquid metals form a solution which, when they solidify, are called alloys. Some copper alloys are :

- **brass:** copper + zinc
- **bronze:** copper + tin
- **cupro nickel:** copper + nickel

The alloys are harder, stronger and tougher than pure copper. They can be made even harder by hammering them—a process called **work hardening.**

Recyclable

Copper can be recycled without any loss of quality. 40% of the world's demand is met by recycled copper.

Catalytic Compounds

Copper can act as a catalyst. For example, it speeds up the reaction between zinc and dilute sulphuric acid. It is found in some enzymes, one of which is involved in respiration. So it really is a vital element.

Thermal Conductor

Copper is a good conductor of heat. This means that if you heat one end of a piece of copper, the other end will quickly reach the same temperature. Most metals are pretty good conductors; however, apart from silver, copper is the best.

It is used in many heating applications because it doesn't corrode and has a high melting point. The only other material that has similar resistance to corrosion is stainless steel. However, its thermal conductivity is 30 times worse than copper's.

Availability

The copper-nickel alloys are single phased throughout the full range of compositions and many standard alloys exist within this range, usually with small additions of other elements for special purposes. The two most popular of the copper rich alloys contain 10 or 30% of nickel. Some manganese is invariably present in the commercial alloys as a deoxidant and desulphurizer; it improves working characteristics and additionally contributes to corrosion resistance in sea-water. Other elements which may be present singly or in combination are:

Iron, added (up to about 2%) to the alloys required for marine applications. It confers resistance to impingement attack by flowing sea-water. The initial development of the optimum compositions of the copper-nickel-iron alloys in the 1930's has been described by G. L. Bailey. This work was to meet naval requirements for improved corrosion-resistant materials for tubes, condensers and other applications involving contact with sea water. Throughout the publication the term "copper-nickel" refers in fact to copper-nickel-iron alloys.

Chromium, can be used to replace some of the iron content and at one percent or more provides higher strength. It is used in a newly-developed 30% nickel casting alloy (IN-768)*. A low-chromium 16% nickel wrought alloy (C72200)† has been developed in the USA.

Niobium, can be used as a hardening element in cast versions of both the 10% and 30% nickel alloys (in place of chromium). It also improves weldability of the cast alloys.

Silicon, improves the casting characteristics of the copper-nickel alloys and is used in conjunction with either chromium or niobium.

Tin, confers an improved resistance to atmospheric tarnishing and at the 2% level is used with 9% nickel to produce the alloy C72500†. This has useful spring properties and is used in the electronics industry. It is not recommended for marine applications.

*INCO Designation† American Society for Testing and Materials (ASTM) unified numbering system designation.

Table 4.13. Common classification of copper alloys

Name	*Alloying Elements*
Coppers	Cu
Brasses	Cu-Zn
Leaded brasses	Cu-Zn-Pb
Tin brasses	Cu-Zn-Sn-Pb
Phosphor bronzes	Cu-Sn-P
Leaded phosphor bronzes	Cu-Sn-Pb-P
Copper-phosphorus and copper-silver-phosphorus alloys	Cu-P-Ag
Aluminum bronzes	Cu-Al-Ni-Fe-Si-Sn
Silicon bronzes	Cu-Si-Sn
Copper-nickels	Cu-Ni-Fe
Nickel silvers	Cu-Ni-Zn

Uses of Copper and Its Alloys

1. Used in large amounts by the electrical industry in the form of wire, copper is second only to silver in electrical conductance.
2. Since it resists corrosion from the air, moisture and sea water, copper has been widely used in coins.
3. Copper is also used to make water pipes and jewellery, as well as and other items.
4. Hydrated copper sulfate ($CuSO_4{\cdot}H_2O$), also known as blue vitrol, is the best known copper compound. It is used as an agricultural poison, as an algicide in water purification and as a blue pigment for inks.
5. Cuperic chloride ($CuCl_2$), another copper compound, is used to fix dyes to fabrics.
6. Cuprous chloride ($CuCl$) is a poisonous white powder that is chiefly used to absorb carbon dioxide (CO_2).
7. Copper cyanide ($CuCN$) is commonly used in electroplating.

4.12 BRASS

Brasses are alloys of copper and zinc (generally 5 to 40%), and may contain small amounts of other alloying elements. Most are available in a range of forms and can be fabricated by casting, forging, stamping, rolling, extrusion and machining.

They fall into two classes, the **alpha alloys** with less than 37% zinc which are ductile and can be cold worked and the **alpha/beta or duplex alloys** which are harder and stronger with limited cold ductility.

Brass, usually copper alloyed with zinc, is easily shaped, stamped and deep drawn. It has fair electrical conductivity, excellent forming and drawing properties and good strength.

Different grades of brass, with different amounts of zinc, have different characteristics in surface smoothness, corrosion-resistance, ease and quality of machining, response to plating, ductility levels, chemical and temperature limits. In general, brass is impervious to most common conditions, except for prolonged exterior exposure and substantial abrasion. It tends to yellow from high temperatures. We are often called upon to machine and deep draw brass for decorative items.

Lead can be added as an alloying element resulting in a brass that can be rapidly machined and produces minimal tool wear. Additions of aluminium, iron and manganese to brass improve strength, whilst silicon additions improve wear resistance. Lead brasses have excellent machining qualities and can be blanked, sheared, sawed and milled.

Chemical Formula —— Cu/Zn Alloys.

Key Properties

- High ductility (alpha alloys)
- Can be hot worked
- Hardness and brittleness increase with increasing beta alloy formation (*i.e.*, as zinc content increases above 37% zinc)
- Aesthetically pleasing colour.

Applications

High pressure gas valves

High pressure gas valves are commonly made from high tensile brass containing small additions of aluminium, iron or manganese.

Plumbing systems

Dezincification resistant brass is used for fittings in valves, connectors and taps in pump and plumbing systems. This particular alloy contains a small addition of arsenic and is specially heat treated so that the composition is homogeneous as water in some countries will attack zinc rich areas of the metal.

Marine applications

Additions of tin or aluminium to either alpha or duplex brasses improves corrosion resistance in sea and brackish waters for applications such as propellers.

Gilding metals

Brass containing 10 to 20% zinc has a very similar colour to gold. Hence, this composition is often used for costume jewellery and architectural applications.

Other applications

Heat exchangers, springs, car radiators, fasteners, hot formed parts, extruded sections, forgings, condenser tubes, architectural, sections, pressure tubing, bearings, bushes, ornamental features, and gearwheels.

4.13 BRONZE

Traditional bronze is a copper alloy with up to 10% tin. The tin in bronze makes it more resistant to wear than unalloyed copper. Bronzes today are usually stronger and more resistant to corrosion than brass. Bronze was also stronger than iron, another common metal of the era, and quality steels were not available until thousands of years later. Nevertheless the bronze age gave way to the iron age as the shipping of tin around the Mediterranean ended during the major population migrations around 1200–1100 BC, which dramatically limited supplies and raised prices. Bronze was still used to a considerable extent during the iron age, but for many purposes the weaker iron was sufficiently strong to serve in its place. As an example, Roman officers were equipped with bronze swords while foot soldiers had to make do with iron blades.

Contemporary bronzes are typically copper alloys that may contain silicon, manganese, aluminium, lead, iron and other elements, with or without tin.

The variations in bronze composition significantly affect its characteristics. Wearability, machinability, corrosion-resistance and ductility for deep drawing are often considered.

Bronze is the most popular metal for top quality bells and cymbals, and also for cast metal sculpture (see bronze sculpture). Common bronze alloys often have the unusual and very desirable property of expanding slightly just before they set, thus filling in the finest details of a mould.

Bronze also has very little metal-on-metal friction, which made it invaluable for the building of cannons where iron cannonballs would otherwise stick in the barrel. Bronze is still widely used today for springs, bearings, bushings and similar roles, and is particularly common in the bearings on small electric motors. Phosphor bronze is thought particularly suited to precision-grade bearings and springs.

Bronze parts are typically used for bearings, clips, electrical connectors and springs. The evans company can stamp and deep draw from these alloys cost effectively, using high speed transfer and progressive presses.

Combro, or commercial bronze, is 90–10, or **90% copper—10% tin**. It is frequently the least expensive, most easily obtained grade of bronze.

Aluminium bronze is a **copper-aluminium (6–8%) alloy** that may contain iron, nickel, and/or silicon for greater strength. It is used for tools and, because it will not spark when struck, for parts to be used around flammable materials. Aluminium bronze is frequently used for aircraft and automobile engine parts, gears, propellers, air pumps, slide valves etc.,

Manganese bronze is actually a brass containing manganese. The composition is **Zinc—35%, Manganese—5% and remaining Copper.**

It is often used for ship propellers because it is strong and resists saltwater corrosion. Worm gears are made from this alloy.

Phosphor Bronze containing phosphor added to increase the strength, ductility of casting. It has good wearing qualities and high elasticity. Composition is

Tin—9–10%, Phosphorous—0.1–0.3% and remaining 87–90% Copper.

Used to manufacture bearing, wormwheels, linings, lead screw etc.,

Silicon Bronze has good corrosion resistance and high strength material. Composition is

Silicon—3% Manganese/Zinc—1% and remaining Copper.

Used for tanks, stoves etc., and where ever good strength and corrosion resistance are required.

Beryllium Bronze has high yield point, High fatigue strength, and good corrosion resistance alloy. Composition is

Beryllium—2.25% and copper—97.75%

Used to make heavy duty electricalswitches, cams, bushes etc.,

4.14 GUN METAL

It is an alloy of copper, tin and zinc in the order of 88%–10%–2%. The zinc is added to clean the metal and to increase its flow. It is strong and resistant to corrision by water and atmosphere. It is used in casting boiler fittings, bearing, bushes etc.

4.15 COPPER/NICKEL ALLOYS (Cu/Ni)

Cupronickel is an alloy of copper, nickel and strengthening impurities, such as iron and manganese.

Background

Sometimes called cupro-nickels, there exists a range of different copper nickel alloys that possess different properties and hence are suited to a range of different applications. Some of the better known copper nickel alloys include:

- Copper with 10% nickel
- Copper with 30% nickel
- Copper with 25% nickel with 0.05–0.4% manganese
- Copper with 45% nickel (also known as **constantan**)

All copper nickel alloys consist of only one phase as the copper nickel binary system exhibits complete solid solubility.

Key Properties

Properties vary with composition, however, some properties are outlined below.

Copper 90/10 and Copper 70/30

- Outstanding resistance to corrosion, particularly sea water
- 70/30 is stronger and has superior resistance to impingement corrosion
- Good resistance to bio-fouling, with the 90/10 alloy being slightly superior compared to the 70/30 alloy.

Copper rich alloys are

- Ductile
- Can be hardened only by cold working
- Good corrosion resistance
- Good strength
- Low temperature co-efficient of electrical resistance

The nickel content in these alloys also enables them to retain their strength at elevated temperatures compared to copper alloys without nickel.

Physical Properties

Table 4.14. Physical properties of cupro-nickel

	Units	*90–10*	*70–30*	*66–30–2–2*
Density	kg/dm^3	8.90	8.95	8.86
Melting Range	°C	1100–1145	1170–1240	
Specific Heat	J/kg °K	377	377	377
Thermal Conductivity	W/m°K	50	29	25
Co-efficient. of Linear Expansion 10–300°C	10^{-6}/°K	17	16	15.5
Electrical Resistivity	microhm. cm	19	34	50
Modulus of Elasticity	GPa	135	152	156
Modulus of Rigidity	GPa	50	56	

The effect of alloying additions to Cu-Ni are

Manganese is invariably present in the commercial alloys as a de-oxidant and de-sulfurizer; it improves working characteristics and additionally contributes to corrosion resistance in seawater.

Iron is added (up to about 2%) to the alloys required for marine applications. It confers resistance to impingement attack by flowing seawater and increases the strength. The initial development of the optimum compositions of the copper-nickel-iron alloys took place in the 1930's. This work was done to meet naval requirements for improved corrosion-resistant materials for tubes, condensers and other applications involving contact with seawater. Throughout the term "copper-nickel (Cu-Ni)" refers in fact to copper-nickel-iron alloys.

Chromium can be used to replace some of the iron content and at one percent or more provides higher strength. It is used in a 30% nickel casting alloy (IN-768)

Niobium can be used as a hardening element in cast versions of both the 10% and 30% nickel alloys (in place of chromium). It also improves weldability of the cast alloys.

Silicon improves the casting characteristics of the Cu-Ni alloys and is used in conjunction with either chromium or niobium.

Tin confers an improved resistance to atmospheric tarnishing and at 2% is used with 9% nickel to produce the alloy C72500. This alloy has useful spring properties and is used in the electronics industry. It is not often recommended for marine applications.

Uses

1. Cupronickel does not corrode in seawater, because its electronegativity is adjusted to be neutral with regard to seawater. Because of this it is used for marine hardware, and sometimes for the propellers, crankshafts and hulls of premium tugboats, fishing boats and other working boats.
2. The most ubiquitous use, from the point of view of the average person, is that most of the silver-coloured modern circulation coins are cupronickel. A typical mix is 75% copper, 25% nickel, and a trace amount of manganese. In the past true silver coins were debased with cupronickel.
3. It is used in thermocouples, and a 55% copper/45% nickel alloy is used to make very accurate resistors.
4. Due to the fact that the 90/10 alloy requires no surface protection and hence gives extra safety, this alloy is being increasingly employed for brake and hydraulic suspension systems and cooling systems in cars and commercial vehicles.
5. Due to the very low temperature co-efficient of electrical resistivity, the copper with 45% nickel alloy is used for resistance wire in high precision resistors. This property allows the resistor to operate at almost exactly the same resistance regardless of temperature.
6. Also used in cooling circuits, ammunition, seawater corrosion-resistant assemblies, condenser tubes.

4.16 ALUMINIUM AND ALUMINIUM ALLOYS

Pure aluminium is soft, ductile, corrosion resistant and has a high electrical conductivity, see Table 4.16. In consequence it is widely used for foil and conductor cables, but alloying with other elements is necessary to provide the higher strengths needed for other applications.

Table 4.15. Typical properties for aluminium

Property	*Value*
Atomic Number	13
Atomic Weight (g/mol)	26.98
Valency	3
Crystal Structure	Face centered cubic
Melting Point (°C)	660.2
Boiling Point (°C)	2480
Mean Specific Heat (0–100°C) (cal/g.°C)	0.219
Thermal Conductivity (0–100°C) (cal/cms. °C)	0.57
Co-efficient of Linear Expansion (0–100°C) ($\times 10^{-6}$/°C)	23.5
Electrical Resistivity at 20°C (μΩcm)	2.69
Density (g/cm^3)	2.6898
Modulus of Elasticity (GPa)	68.3
Poissons Ratio	0.34

Aluminium's Properties

Pure aluminium is a silvery-white metal with many desirable characteristics. It is light, nontoxic (as the metal), nonmagnetic and non-sparking.

1. It is decorative. It is easily formed, machined, and cast. Alloys with small amounts of copper, magnesium, silicon, manganese, and other elements have very useful properties.
2. Strength depends on purity. 99.996 percent pure aluminium has a tensile strength of about 49 megapascals (MPa), rising to 700 MPa following alloying and suitable heat treatment.
3. Although not found free in nature, Aluminium is an abundant element in the earth's crust.
4. A key property is low density. Aluminium is only one-third the weight of steel.
5. Aluminium and most of its alloys are highly resistant to most forms of corrosion. The metal's natural coating of aluminium oxide provides a highly effective barrier to the ravages of air, temperature, moisture and chemical attack.
6. Aluminium is a superb conductor of electricity. This property allied with other intrinsic qualities has ensured the replacement of copper by aluminium in many situations.
7. Aluminium is non-magnetic and non-combustible, properties invaluable in advanced industries such as electronics or in offshore structures.
8. Aluminium is non-toxic and impervious, qualities that have established its use in the food and packaging industries since the earliest times.
9. Other valuable properties include high reflectivity, heat barrier properties and heat conduction. The metal is malleable and easily worked by the common manufacturing and shaping processes.

4.16.1 Aluminium Alloy Classification

The classification provides for:

Table 4.16. Classification of aluminium alloy

1XXX	Aluminium of 99% minimum purity
2XXX	Aluminium-copper alloys
3XXX	Aluminium-manganese alloys
4XXX	Aluminium-silicon alloys
5XXX	Aluminium-magnesium alloys
6XXX	Aluminium-magnesium-silicon alloys
7XXX	Aluminium-zinc-magnesium alloys
8XXX	Miscellaneous alloys, e.g., aluminium-lithium alloys

Alloys fall into two main groups. The work-hardening alloys, where strength is achieved by the amount of "cold work" applied to the alloy, e.g., by rolling, and heat-treatable or precipitation hardening alloys, where the strength and properties are achieved by heat treatments of varying complexity.

4.16.2 Designation of Alloys

This standardization according to the standards of aluminium association is given. In this system, the aluminium alloys of foundry are grouped by their principal elements of addition. One uses a number with four digits with a point separating the two last.

Table. 4.17. Aluminium alloy designation

Code	*Elements of Addition*
1xx.x	Less than 1% (aluminium with 99,00% or more)
2xx.x	Copper
3xx.x	Silicon, with an addition of copper and/or magnesium
4xx.x	Silicon
5xx.x	Magnesium
7xx.x	Zinc
8xx.x	Tin
9xx.x	Other elements
6xx.x	Series not used

Al/Cu Alloys

The foundry seldom uses the alloys which contain only copper, because of their bad flow. This property can however, be improved by the addition of silicon. One can nevertheless obtain good hot properties by carrying out additions of nickel and magnesium.

Alloys Al/Si, Al/Si/Mg and Al/Si/Cu

The Al/Si alloys are used. Their contents of If vary from 5 to 20 %. the very great majority of these alloys present an eutectic or hypoeutectic composition. The composition of eutectic is 12, 7% of silicon. The alloys of these series show a very good flow and resist corrosion well. Silicon present in the eutectic component has an acicular morphology normally. However, an addition of sodium or strontium makes it possible to modifythis morphology. Silicon becomes fibrous then. The addition of magnesium (from 0, 3 to 1%) to the Al/Si alloys makes it possible to improve their mechanical properties considerably. The Al/Si/Mg alloys are indeed setting by controlled precipitation of the compound Mg_2 if and of its transitory forms.

The addition of copper (from 3 to 5%) improves the mechanical properties of the Al/Si alloys. In this case, the addition of magnesium improves their response to the thermal treatments. The alloys Al/Si/Cu eutectics have a good hot behaviour and a low dilation co-efficient. One uses them in particular for the manufacture of pistons or cylinder heads, in the internal combustion engines.

Al/Mg Alloys

The excellent corrosion resistance in marine atmosphere is the selection criterion of this series. Resistance to sea water is also very good. On the other hand, their coulability is poor.

Al/Zn/Ni Alloys

These alloys are difficult to run. Their low flow and their tendency to cracking and porosity are the causes. On the other hand, they are self-quenching and age naturally at the ambient temperature. Their properties become thus maximum after approximately one or two months. The cooling affects their mechanical properties little. By consequent, those do not vary according to the thickness of the cast parts.

4.17 ALUMINIUM ALLOY STRENGTHENING

Strengthening can be by

- Solid Solution Strengthening
- Age Hardening I-Precipitation
- Age Hardening II-Strengthening
- Strain Hardening

4.17.1 Solid Solution Strengthening

The substitution of solute atoms for aluminium ones distorts the crystal lattice, hinders dislocation mobility and hence strengthens the alloy. This section looks at how the properties of aluminium can be improved by solid solution strengthening.

The first we explains that in order to be effective solid solution strengtheners, alloy additions must satisfy two criteria:

1. High RT solid solubility;
2. Atomic misfit to create local compressive or tensile strains

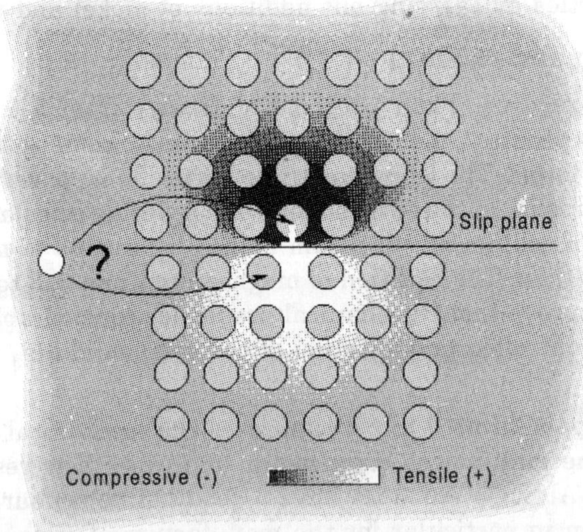

Fig. 4.9 Solid solution strengthening mechanism.

4.17.2 Age Hardening I-Precipitation

The strongest aluminium alloys (2xxx, 6xxx and 7xxx) are produced by age hardening. In this section the user can learn how a fine dispersion of precipitates can be formed by appropriate heat treatment. The strengthening that results from this is covered in the following section, *Age Hardening II-Strengthening.*

The section starts with a review of the major requirement for an alloy system to respond to this form of hardening, namely a significant decrease in solid solubility of one or more of the alloying elements with decreasing temperature. This is followed by an overview of the 3 main stages of heat treatment, *i.e.*, solution heat treatment, quenching and ageing. The formation of a non-equilibrium **supersaturated solid solution** by **quenching** is contrasted to the type of equilibrium structure that might form if the (hypothetical) alloy were slowly cooled.

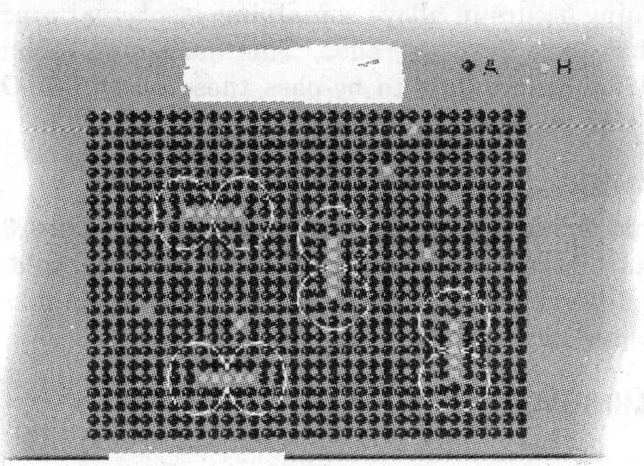

Fig. 4.10 Age hardening I-precipitation.

A general model for decomposition is given, followed by details of the precipitation sequences in 4 specific alloy systems: Al-Cu, Al-Cu-Mg, Al-Mg-Si and Al-Zn-Mg.

Having described the types of metastable precipitates that might form during ageing, the section then goes on to look at the thermodynamic and kinetic bases for their formation in preference to the direct precipitation of the equilibrium phase.

The kinetics of metastable precipitate formation are also illustrated using Time-Temperature-Transformation (TTT) diagrams. An example of such a diagram is used in an exercise designed to help the student understand some of the key concepts relating to precipitate formation. This in turn leads to the concept of metastable solvuses.

The section is rounded off by a look at the formation of **Precipitate Free Zones** (PFZs) and includes an exercise in which the user is asked to minimise the width of a PFZ in a hypothetical alloy by manipulating the heat treatment.

4.17.3 Age Hardening II-Strengthening

Having studied the formation of precipitates in the previous section, this section goes on to look at how they actually contribute to the overall strengthening of the alloy. The 3 main mechanisms are:

- Coherency strain hardening;
- Chemical hardening;
- Dispersion hardening.

Coherency strain hardening results from the interaction between dislocations and the strain fields surrounding GP zones and/or *coherent* precipitates. The software illustrates how an optimum precipitate spacing exists at which the strengthening effect is maximized.

Chemical hardening results from the increase in applied stress required for a dislocation to cut through a *coherent* (or *semi-coherent*) precipitate. This in turn depends on a number of factors, including (*i*) the extra **interfacial area**—and hence energy—between precipitate and matrix; (*ii*) the possible creation of an **Anti-Phase Boundary** (APB) within an ordered precipitate and (*iii*) the change in separation distance between dissociated dislocations due to different stacking fault energies of matrix and precipitate. The 3 contributions are illustrated by interactive graphics.

Dispersion hardening occurs in alloys containing *incoherent* precipitates or particles—*i.e.*, typically those that have been overaged. This hardening results from the increased shear stress required for dislocations to by-pass these obstacles. Orowan bowing is one mechanism by which this might be achieved.

4.17.4 Strain Hardening

Wrought alloys that do not respond to age hardening (e.g., 1xxx, 3xxx, 5xxx) are usually strengthened by strain hardening. This generally involves cold-working at ambient temperatures, at which the multiplication of dislocations occurs at a faster rate than they are destroyed by dynamic recovery.

4.18 USES OF ALUMINIUM

Aerospace

Aluminium is the primary aircraft material, comprising about 80 percent of an aircraft's unladen weight. The standard Boeing 747 jumbo jet contains approx. 75,000 kg of aluminium. Because the metal resists corrosion, some airlines don't paint their planes, saving several hundred kgs of weight.

Automotive

1. The use of aluminium for truck and automobile engine blocks and cylinder heads, heat exchangers, transmission housings, engine parts and automobile wheels has risen steadily over the last decade.
2. The use of aluminium reduces noise and vibration. Its use significantly improves vehicle handling.
3. A high proportion of end of life vehicle scrap is recycled.
4. Wheels and bumper reinforcements help improve safety.
5. Aluminium absorbs kinetic energy. In a vehicle crash involving a largely aluminium vehicle a high proportion of the shock is absorbed by the structure, not the vehicle occupants.
6. It is estimated that 90 percent of trailer trucks have aluminium bodies, as do long-distance buses and cargo containers.
7. Aluminium does not rust like steel does. An aluminium vehicle body outlasts a steel chassis and tractor unit by three or four times. Aluminium does not react with most common materials, so it can haul many bulk cargoes, including coal, chemicals and food, without harm.
8. Aluminium components can cut 1,800 kilograms from the weight of a tractor-trailer truck. Thus such a truck can carry a bigger load without exceeding weight limits. Over the vehicle's life, there will be a saving of from six to twelve times the energy it takes to produce the primary aluminium it incorporates.

9. On smaller commercial vehicles, aluminium bodies may weigh 45 percent less than steel bodies, so more can be carried on a smaller chassis, which reduces costs.

Pharmaceutical Uses of Aluminium

1. Aluminium hydroxide is widely used as an antacid to relieve gastric irritation and assist in the healing of peptic ulcers. It has good acid neutralising capacity and also has the ability to absorb and reduce the activity of pepsin.
2. Soluble aluminium compounds have been used for many years as antiperspirants. Aluminium chloride was the first compound used as an antiperspirant although currently aluminium chlorohydrate which is much less acidic, is the major antiperspirant compound. The action mechanism is still under investigation but it appears to act by forming a plug of aluminium hydroxide within the sweat duct.
3. In 1926 alum-precipitation diphtheria toxoid was discovered to have greater antigenic properties (*i.e.*, stimulating the production of antibodies) than the toxoid alone. The enhancement of diphtheria toxoid by the adjuvant (beneficial additive) aluminium hydroxide is typical of the use of an aluminium salt to increase the level and duration of immunity afforded by a vaccine. Aluminium salts are the most widely used type of adjuvant due to its reputation for safety in humans.

Aluminium in Water

1. Aluminium performs a valuable role in the treatment of water.
2. Aluminium sulphate (alum) is widely used in the purification of waste water as well as water from rivers, lakes and reservoirs. It is a flocculating agent with the capacity to coagulate and trap solid matter which may be floating in the water; such as algae and other organic and non-organic matter. During the process a fine precipitate is formed which removes many contaminants, including the spores of dangerous pathogens. Before leaving the treatment plant the water is filtered to remove the flocculate and the vast majority of the aluminium.
3. At present there is a WHO guideline for the maximum level of aluminium in drinking water of 0.2 mg total aluminium per litre. This is essentially set for the visual effect and taste. No health based criteria have been proposed for aluminium levels in drinking water by the World Health Organization.

Electrical Applications

Aluminium or aluminium alloy electrical conductors are now widely used in the following areas:

1. Overhead lines
2. Electrical energy distribution and transport cables
3. Energy cables for industrial use

Aluminium is particularly suited to these uses because of its high electrical conductivity, low weight and good resistance to corrosion.

Almost all electric lights, motors, appliances and power systems depend on a vast grid of aluminium wire. Around the world most high-voltage overhead transmission and distribution lines and many underground lines are made of aluminium. Aluminium replaced copper in high-voltage transmission lines after 1945 and today is the most economical way to transmit electric power.

Aluminium weighs only one-third as much as copper and one kilogram of aluminium can carry twice as much electricity as one kilogram of copper. Aluminium power lines are therefore lighter and require fewer, and lighter support structures.

Aluminium power lines can be made of single-strand wires, of many wires stranded together or, for maximum strength, of aluminium strands wrapped around a steel core.

Aluminium is also widely used in "switchyards" or substations where electricity is stepped down to lower voltages for local distribution. Many substations are almost all aluminium.

4.19 BEARINGS: AN INTRODUCTION

Bearings are needed whenever one part of a machine slides against another. Bearings can be classified as providing *sliding* or *rolling contact.*

A sliding bearing typically uses a lubricant to reduce friction between the sliding surfaces. A shaft and bushing bearing is known as a *journal bearing*.

The fluid lubricant forms a film between the sliding surfaces so that there is no contact between solid components. This kind of bearings are known as **fluid film bearings.**

Rolling contact bearings are often referred to **antifriction bearings.** Antifriction bearings, as their name implies, minimize friction by removing any possible sliding between bearing surfaces and replacing all contacts with rolling interfaces.

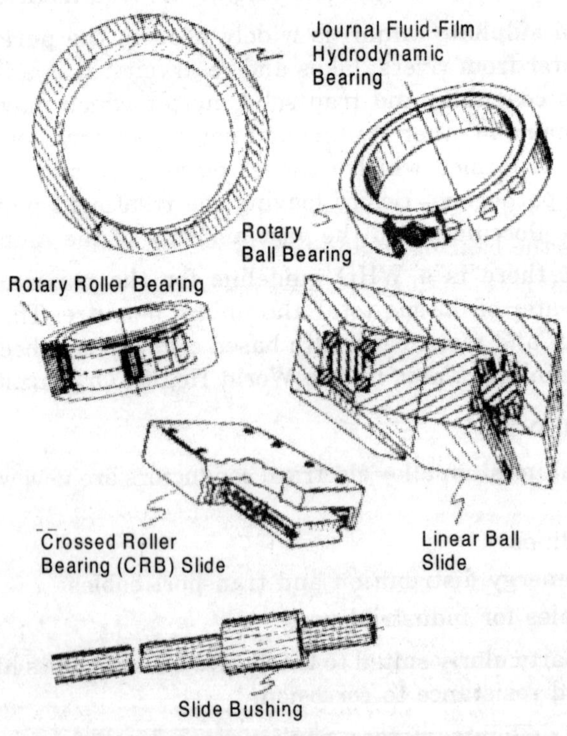

Fig. 4.11 Types of bearings.

Fluid Film Bearings

Historically speaking, fluid film bearings were the first type of rotary bearing to appear simply because they are more simple than rolling-contact bearings. Early sliding bearings were almost certainly first made from wood after the invention of the wheel in prehistoric times, and these were lubricated with grease derived from animal fat. Metal wheel journal bearings followed. When the industrial revolution began in the eighteenth century, machine rotational speeds reached a point where lubricated metal journal bearings became hydrodynamically isolated so that there was no metal-to-metal contact. The initial discovery was certainly by accident, but soon an empirical methodology was developed followed by the science of tribology related to journal bearings.

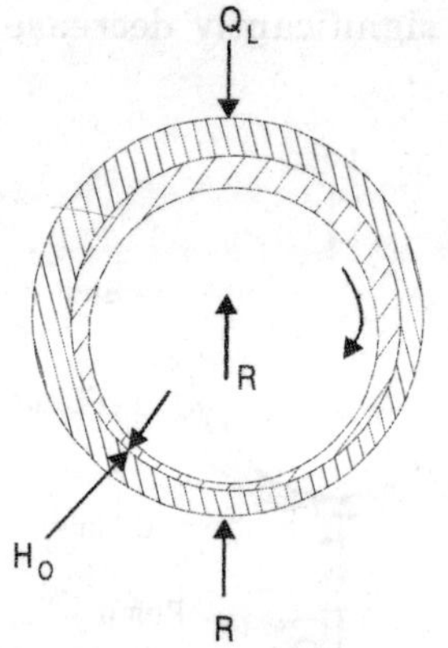

Fig. 4.12 A journal bearing has hydrodynamic lubricating layer.

When a journal bearing begins rotating, there is very little lubricant between the hole and shaft at the contact point, H_0, and rubbing occurs. Therefore much friction needs to be overcome when starting a hydrodynamic journal bearing. When the bearing has reached sufficient speed, the lubricant begins to wedge into the contact area and hydrodynamic lift is attained.

Various ways have been devised for keeping a journal bearing lubricated. The lubricant often cools and cleans the bearing in addition to its lubrication function. For instance, in a siphon wick lubrication arrangement, as illustrated below, gravity provides the pressure head needed to keep the lubricant flowing to the bearing surface.

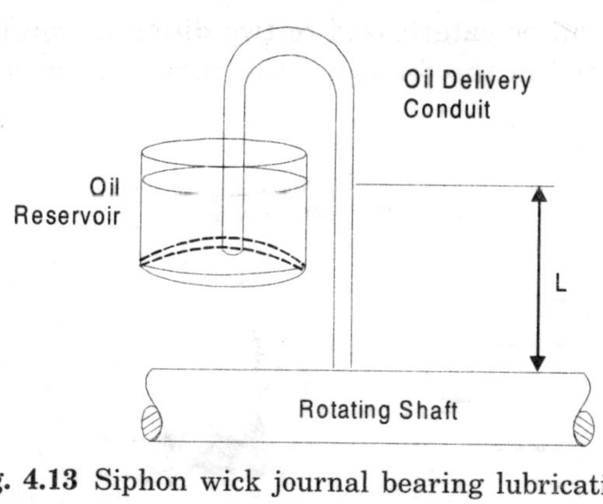

Fig. 4.13 Siphon wick journal bearing lubrication.

Another method of delivering lubricant can be done by a capillary wick, as illustrated below. The necessary pressure head is developed through capillary action within the fibers of a textile wick, as with the phenomenon of a candle wick.

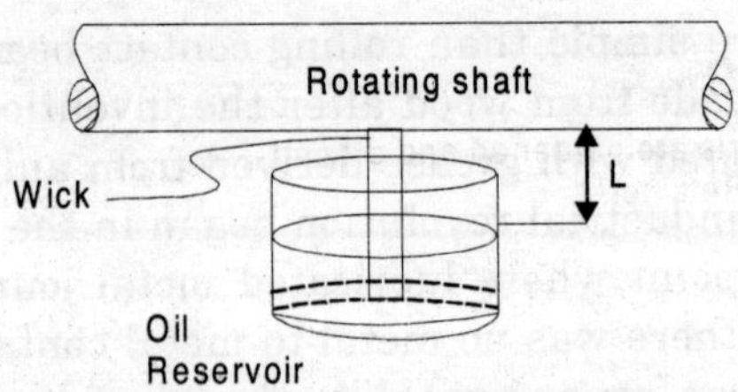

Fig. 4.14 Capillary wick lubrication method.

For applications that require significantly decrease the amount of starting friction, a hydraulic lift can be introduced.

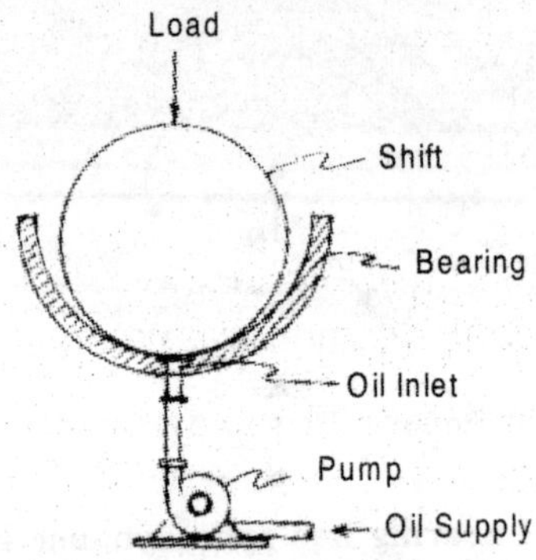

Fig. 4.15. Hydraulic lift lubricated journal bearing.

Hydraulic lift journal bearings have been successfully applied to slow-moving, heavy rotating masses such as those found in steel rolling and paper mills.

Antifriction Bearings

An *antifriction bearing*, also known as a *rolling contact bearing*, is justified over a journal or fluid film bearing when very little friction is needed for low differential surface speeds. Of course, the extra mechanical complexity of antifriction bearings drives up their cost when compared to similar journal bearings.

Antifriction bearings can be categorized to two different configurations: axial ball and roller bearings, as illustrated in the following two figures respectively.

Rotary Axial Ball Bearing

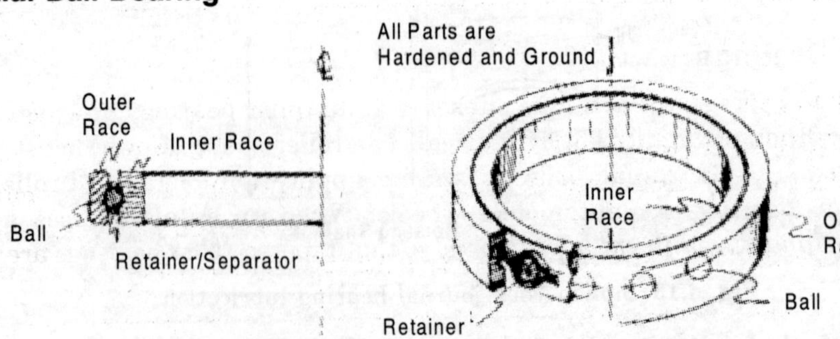

Fig. 4.16 A typical rotary axial ball bearing.

Rotary Axial Roller Bearing

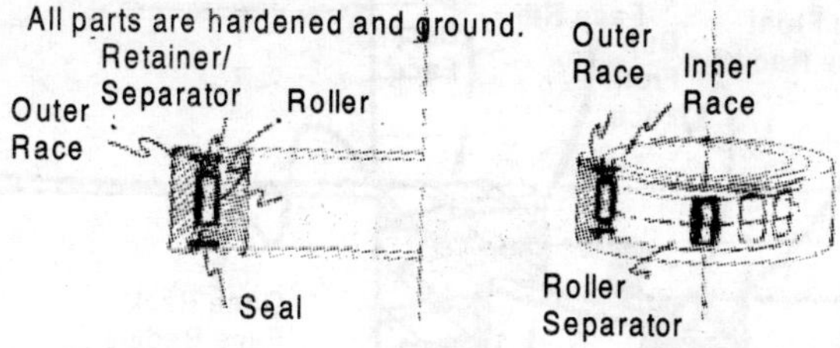

Fig. 4.17 A typical rotary axial roller bearing.

Thrust Bearings

Thrust bearings do what their name implies: they provide load capacity axially while still rotating.

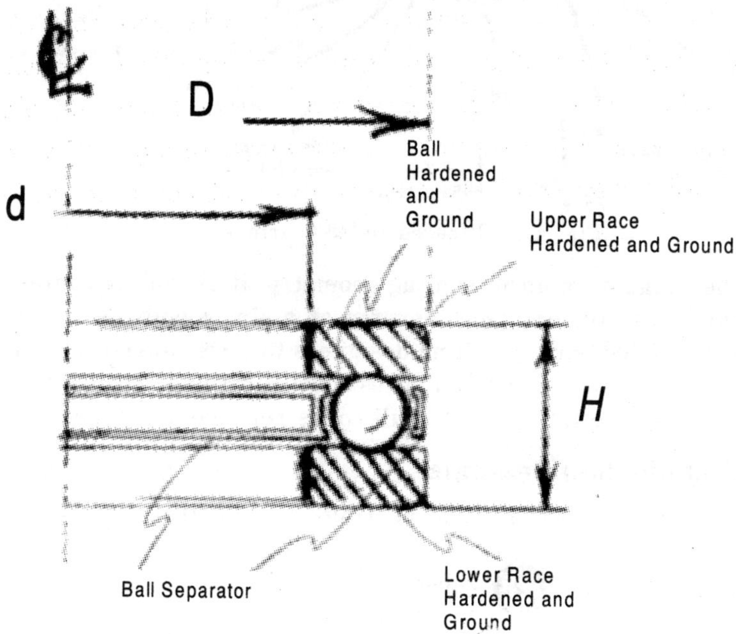

Fig. 4.18 Rotary thrust ball bearing.

Tapered Roller Bearings

Tapered roller bearings are a unique subset of axial roller bearings in which the rollers are tapered rather than straight right cylindrical. The roller shape allows thrust loads to be withstood in addition to the radial loads. A familiar application for tapered roller bearings is the central hub bearings for automobile wheels. When an auto traverses a turn, the wheels must *withstand a significant lateral force*, so that tapered roller bearings are necessary.

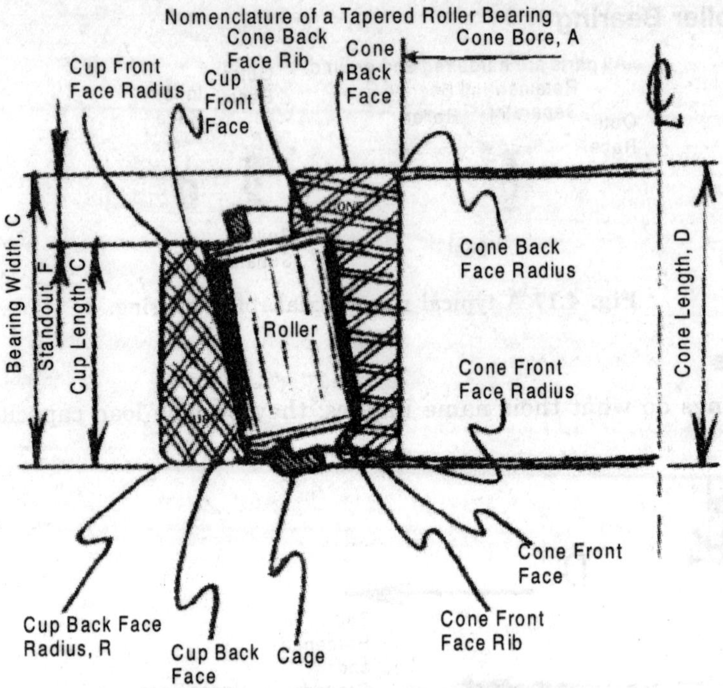

Fig. 4.19 Tapered roller bearings.

Tapered roller bearings have an intriguing geometry. If all rolling-contact surfaces are projected out to form cones, all cone tips converge at a single point on the central axis of the bearing. This fact enabled early machine designers to have tapered bearings fabricated without CNC equipment. The following two figures show how tapered roller bearing geometry is derived. Note how it is intuitive how the full cones roll about one another.

Nomenclatures of Antifriction Bearings

Various rolling elements of antifriction bearings are illustrated in the figure below.

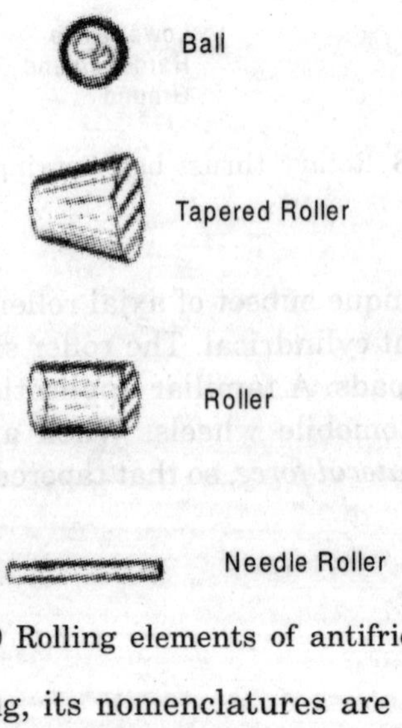

Fig. 4.20 Rolling elements of antifriction bearings.

For a typical axial bearing, its nomenclatures are annotated below.

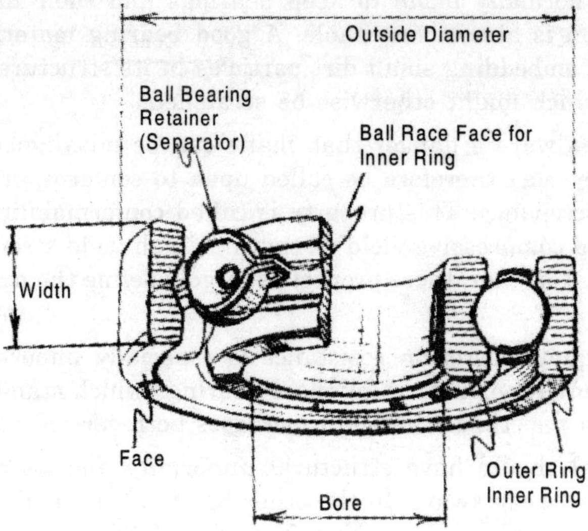

Fig. 4.21 Axial ball bearing nomenclatures.

Material Properties

Many millions of bearings operate successfully in the boundary and mixed-film modes for their entire service lives. The only penalty this entails is an increase in friction compared to hydro-dynamically lubricated bearings and a consequently higher energy expenditure. Bearing life, however, will depend very heavily on the choice of bearing material. Even hydrodynamic bearings pass through boundary and mixed-film modes during start-up, and shut down, or when faced with transient upset conditions. This means that material selection is an important design consideration for all sleeve bearings, no matter what their operating mode. The general attributes of a good bearing material are:

- A low co-efficient of friction versus hard shaft materials,
- Good wear behavior against steel journals (scoring resistance),
- The ability to absorb and discard small contaminant particles (embedibility),
- The ability to adapt and adjust to the shaft roughness and misalignment (conformability),
- High compressive strength,
- High fatigue strength,
- Corrosion resistance,
- Low shear strength (at the bearing-to shaft interface),
- Structural uniformity, and
- Reasonable cost and ready availability.

A material's inherent frictional characteristics are extremely important during those periods, however, brief, when the bearing operates in the boundary mode. A low co-efficient of friction is one factor in a material's resistance against welding to, and therefore scoring, steel shafts. Frictional co-efficients for bronze alloys against steel range between 0.08 and 0.14. During wear, or when there is absolutely no lubricant present, the frictional co-efficient may range from about 0.12 to as high as 0.18 to 0.30. By comparison, the frictional co-efficient during wear for aluminum on steel is 0.32 and for steel on steel it is 1.00.

While efforts are normally made to keep bearings and their lubricants clean, some degree of contamination is almost inevitable. A good bearing material should be able to compensate for this by embedding small dirt particles in its structure, keeping them away from the steel shaft, which might otherwise be scratched.

Likewise, there is always a danger that shafts can be misaligned, or not be perfectly smooth. A bearing alloy may therefore be called upon to conform, or "wear-in" slightly to compensate for the discrepancy. This property is called conformability: it is related to the material's hardness and compressive yield strength. A high yield strength is also related to good fatigue resistance. Together, these properties largely define the material's load-carrying capacity.

The need for adequate corrosion resistance is especially important in bearings that operate in aggressive environments, or for those bearings which stand idle for long periods of time. Good corrosion resistance therefore increases both service life and shelf life.

A bearing material should have structural uniformity and its properties should not change as surface layers wear away. On the other hand, alloys such as the leaded bronzes are used because they provide a lubricating film of lead at the bearing/journal interface. Lead has a low shear strength, and is able to fill in irregularities in the shaft and act as an emergency lubricant if the oil supply is temporarily interrupted.

Finally, a bearing material should be cost-effective and available on short notice. No single bearing material excels in all these properties and that is one of the reasons bearing design always involves a compromise. However, the bronze bearing alloys provide such a broad selection of material properties that one of them can almost always fit the needs of a particular design.

Bearing Materials

The bearing rings and rolling elements of rolling bearings are subjected to repetitive high pressure with a small amount of sliding. The cages are subjected to tension and compression and sliding contact with the rolling elements and either or both of the bearing rings.

Therefore, the materials used for the rings, rolling elements, and cages require the following characteristics :

Material characteristics required for bearing rings and rolling elements:

- High rolling contact fatigue strength
- High hardness
- High wear resistance
- High dimensional stability
- High mechanical strength

Characteristics required for cage material: High wear resistance, High dimensional stability, High mechanical strength

Other necessary characteristics, such as easy production, shock and heat resistance, and corrosion resistance, are required depending on individual applications.

White Metal (BABBITT METALS)

The first tin base white-metal was produced, and patented, by Isaac Babbitt and today white-metals are sometimes loosely referred to as babbitt metals.

It contains 88% tin, 8% antimony, and 4% copper. It is a soft metal with low co-efficient of friction and has low strength too. It is most common metal used in bearing along with cast iron where the bearing subject to high pressure and load.

Lead base and Tin base

There are two main varieties of white-metal, tin-base and lead-base. In Britain the tin-base alloys are preferred for all except the mildest duties. Tin-base alloys are cleaner, they do not oxidise or dross so easily when molten, they are less viscous when molten and therefore flow more readily. The solidification shrinkage is less and segregation less likely, so that they are more easily handled in the lining shop. Their ductility is greater and their mechanical properties are retained to a greater extent as temperature increases and, finally, resistance to corrosion by oil products is excellent. They are however, more costly. Tin-base white metals are generally understood to contain no lead but it is not uncommon to find up to 0.35% permitted in alloys of this type to facilitate the use of reclaimed scrap metals. Hoyt consider that lead in a high tin-base whitemetal is an impurity and that it can be a distinct disadvantage where maximum reliability is required. The presence of lead results in the formation of a peritectic complex melting at 185°C. This is 40°C lower than the bulk of the alloy and leads to reduced strength and 'wiping'. Among the reasons for the superiority of Hoyt alloys are the use of virgin metals, themselves selected for freedom from impurities and the strictest control which is exercised over material selection and process conditions during alloying.

Copper Base alloy

They are most important bearing alloys. These are harder and stronger than white metals (lead base and tin base) and are used.

Cadmium Base Alloy

It contains 95% Cadmium and 5% silver. It is used for medium loaded bearing subjected to high temperature.

Materials for Bearing Rings and Rolling Elements

Primarily, high carbon chromium bearing steel is used for the bearing rings and rolling elements. Most NSK bearings are made of SUJ2 among the JIS steel types, while the larger bearings generally use SUJ3. The chemical composition of SUJ2 is approximately the same as AISI 52100 specified in the USA, DIN 100 Cr6 in Germany, and BS 535A99 in England.

For bearings that are subjected to very severe shock loads, carburized low-carbon alloy steels such as chrome steel, chrome molybdenum steel and nickel chrome molybdenum steel, are often used. Such steels, when they are carburized to the proper depth and have sufficient surface hardness, are more shock-resistant than normal, through-hardened bearing steels because of the softer energy-absorbing core.

NSK uses highly pure vacuum-degassed bearing steel containing a minimum of oxygen, nitrogen, and hydrogen compound impurities. The rolling fatigue life of bearings has been remarkably improved using these materials combined with the appropriate heat treatment.

For special-purpose bearings, high-temperature bearing steel, which has superior heat resistance, and stainless steel, which has good corrosion resistance, may be used.

REVIEW QUESTIONS

1. What is steel?
2. Classify various kinds of steel and explain each in brief.
3. Explain the effects of alloying elements on steel.

4. Explain the different mechanical properties of steel.
5. What is stainless steel and explain it in brief ?
6. Classify different types of stainless steel.
7. How stainless steel resist corrosion?
8. Classify tool steel and explain each in brief.
9. What is HSLA steel?
10. Why HSLA steels are strong?
11. What is maraging steel and explain in brief?
12. What are the properties of maraging steel?
13. Explain different application of maraging steel.
14. What is cast iron and how it is classified?
15. Explain grey cast iron in brief.
16. Explain ductile cast iron in brief.
17. Explain CGI cast iron in brief.
18. Explain malleable cast iron in brief.
19. Explain white cast iron in brief.
20. What are the properties of copper?
21. What are the uses of copper?
22. What is brass and what are its properties?
23. What is bronze and explain it in brief?
24. What is gun metal?
25. Explain copper-nickel alloy.
26. Explain the properties of aluminium.
27. How aluminium is classified?
28. Discuss different aluminium alloys in brief.
29. Explain different strengthening mechanism.
30. Discuss various bearing alloys.

5

CHAPTER

MECHANICAL PROPERTIES AND TESTING

5.1 PLASTIC DEFORMATION

When a material is stressed below its elastic limit, the resulting deformation or strain is temporary. Removal of stress results in a gradual return of the object to its original dimensions. When a material is stressed beyond its elastic limit, plastic or permanent deformation takes place, and it will not return to its original shape by the application of force alone. The ability of a metal to undergo plastic deformation is probably its most outstanding characteristic in comparison with other materials. All shaping operations such as stamping, pressing, spinning, rolling, forging, drawing, and extruding involve plastic deformation of metals. Various machining operations such as milling, turning, sawing, and punching also involve plastic deformation. Plastic deformation may take place by :

- Slip
- Twinning
- Combination of slip and twinning.

5.2 DEFORMATION BY SLIP

If a single crystal of a metal is stressed in tension beyond its elastic limit, it elongates slightly, a step appears on the surface indicating relative displacement of one part of the crystal with respect to the rest, and the elongation stops. Increasing the load will cause another step. It is as if neighboring thin sections of the crystal had slipped past one another like a sliding cards on a deck. Each successive elongation requires a higher stress and results in the appearance of another step, which is actually the intersection of a slip plane with the surface of the crystal. Progressive increase of the load eventually causes the material to fracture.

Slip occurs in directions in which the atoms are most closely packed, since this requires the least amount of energy.

Fig. 5.2 shows that when the plastic deformation is due to slip, the atoms move a whole inter-atomic space (moving from one corner to another corner of the unit cell). This means that overall lattice structure remains the same. Slip is observed as thin lines under the microscopes and these lines can be removed by polishing.

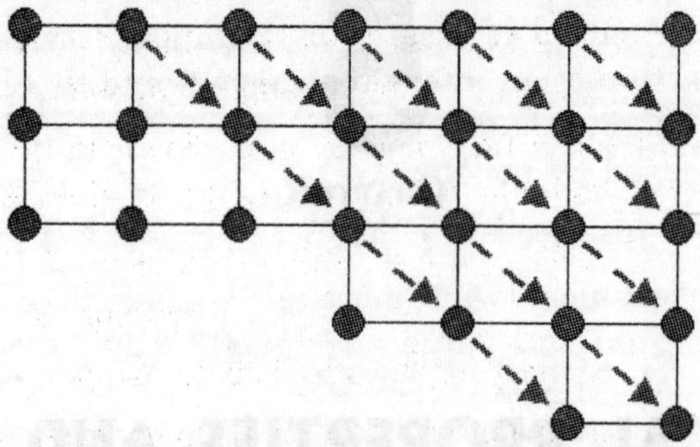

Fig. 5.1 The effect of slip on the lattice structure.

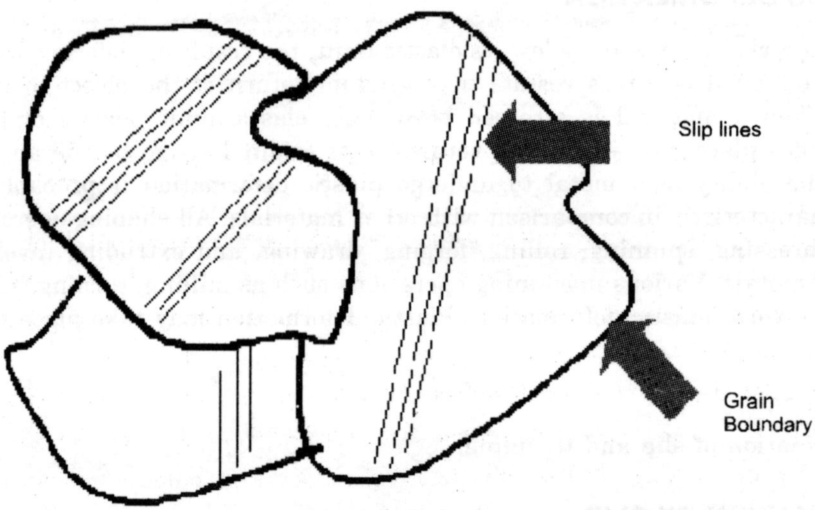

Fig. 5.2 Slip appears as thin lines under the microscope.

Fig. 5.3 Slip lines in copper.

5.3 DEFORMATION BY TWINNING

When mechanical deformation is created by twinning, the lattice structure changes. The atoms move only a fraction of an inter-atomic space and this leads to a rearrangement of the lattice structure. Twinning is observed as wide bands under the microscope. These wide bands cannot be removed by polishing.

Two kinds of twins are of interest to the metallurgists:

1. Deformation or mechanical twins, most prevalent in close packed hexagonal metals (magnesium, zinc, iron with large amount of ferrite)
2. Annealing twins, most prevalent in F.C.C. (Face centered cubic) metals (aluminum, copper, brass, iron with austenite).These metals have been previously worked and heat treated. The twins are formed because of a change in the normal growth mechanism.
3. The behavior of twinning in tin is called as **cry of tin**
4. The behavior of twinning in iron is known as **Neumann bands**

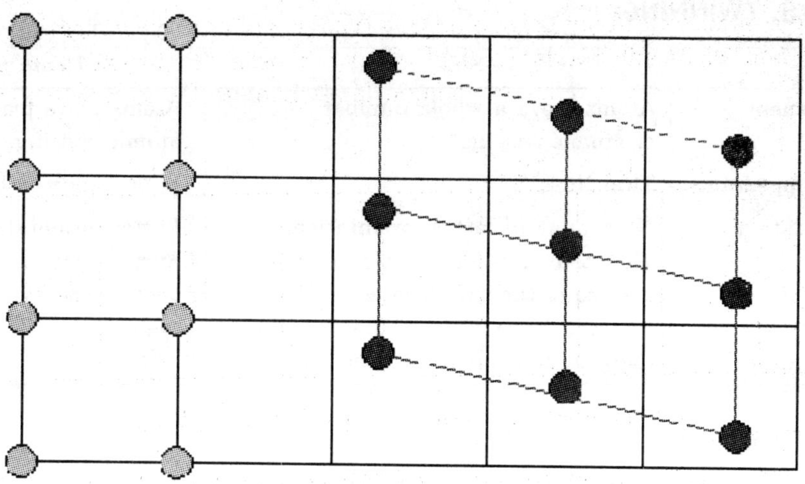

Fig. 5.4 The effect of twinning on the lattice structure.

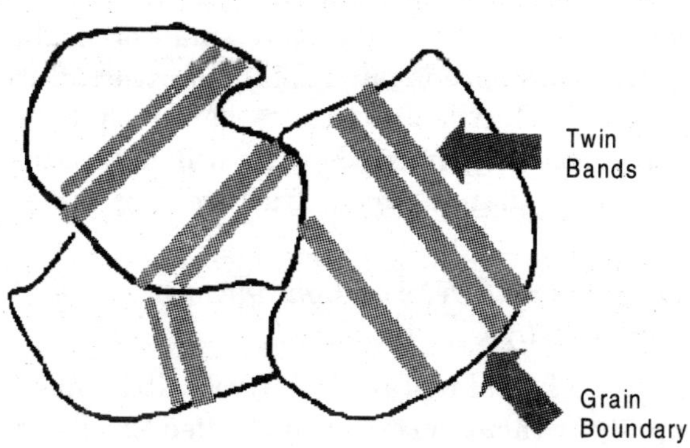

Fig. 5.5 Twin band~

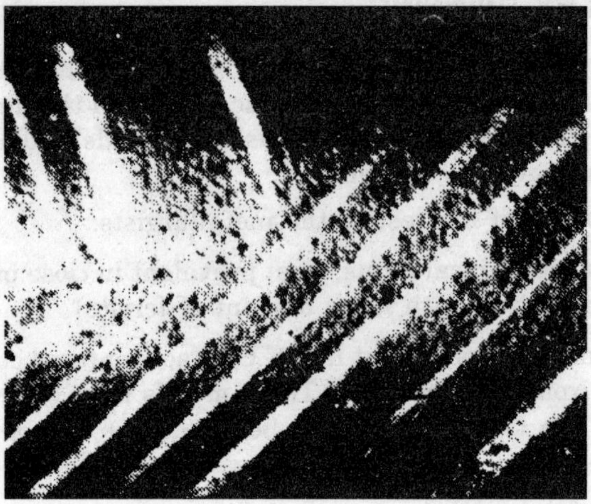

Fig. 5.6 Twin bands in zinc.

5.4 SLIP VS. TWINNING

	Slip	*Twinning*
Atomic movement	Atoms move a whole number of atomic spacing.	Atoms move fractional atomic spacing.
Microscopic appearance	Thin lines	Wide bands or broad lines
Lattice orientation	No change in lattice orientation. The steps are only visible on the surface of the crystal and can be removed by polishing. After polishing there is no evidence of slip.	Lattice orientation changes. Surface polishing will not destroy the evidence of twinning.

5.5 FRACTURE

Depending on the ability of material to undergo plastic deformation before the fracture two fracture modes can be defined-ductile or brittle metals can fail by ductile or brittle fracture. Metals that can sustain substantial plastic strain or deformation before fracturing exhibit *ductile fracture.* Usually a large part of the plastic flow is concentrated near the fracture faces. Metals that fracture with a relatively small or negligible amount of plastic strain exhibit *brittle fracture.* Cracks propagate rapidly. Brittle failure results from *cleavage* (splitting along definite planes). Ductile fracture is better than brittle fracture, because ductile fracture occurs over a period of time, where as brittle fracture is fast, and can occur (with flaws) at lower stress levels than a ductile fracture. Fig. 5.8 shows the basic types of fracture.

Ductile fracture–*extensive plastic deformation ahead of crack Crack is "stable": resists further extension unless applied stress is increased.*

Brittle fracture–ceramics, ice, cold metals: Relatively little plastic deformation Crack is "unstable": propagates rapidly without increase in applied stress.

5.5.1 Brittle Fracture

Basically, brittle fracture is a rapid run of cracks through a stressed material. The cracks usually travel so fast that you can't tell when the material is about to break. In other words, there is very little plastic deformation before failure occurs. In most cases, this is the worst type of fracture because you can't repair visible damage in a part or structure before it breaks.

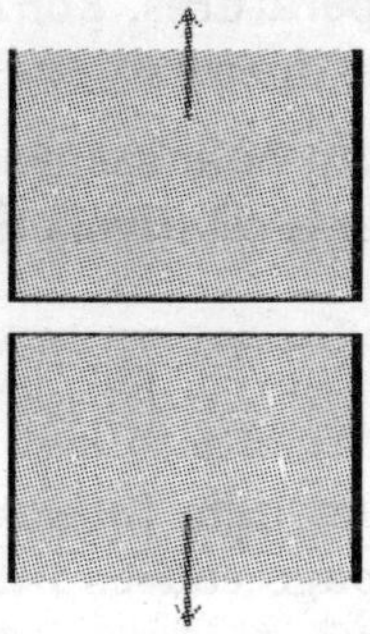

Fig. 5.7 Brittle fracture (Limited dislocation mobility).

In brittle fracture, the cracks run close to perpendicular to the applied stress. This perpendicular fracture leaves a relatively flat surface at the break. Besides having a nearly flat fracture surface, brittle materials usually contain a pattern on their fracture surfaces. Some brittle materials have lines and ridges beginning at the origin of the crack and spreading out across the crack surface.

The materials, like some steels have back to back V-shaped markings pointing to the origin of the crack. These V-shaped markings are called chevrons. Very hard or fine grained materials have no special pattern on their fracture surface, and amorphous materials like ceramic glass have shiny smooth fracture surfaces.

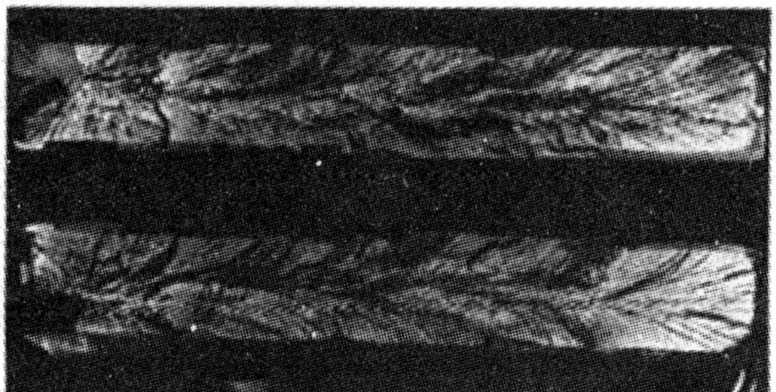

Fig. 5.8(a) Brittle fracture.

5.5.2 Ductile to Brittle Transition (DBT)

In fracture, there are many shades of gray. Brittle fracture and ductile fracture are fairly general terms describing the two opposite extremes of the fracture spectrum. The first and foremost factor is temperature. Basically, at higher temperatures the yield strength is lowered and the fracture is more ductile in nature. On the opposite end, at lower temperatures the yield strength is greater and the fracture is more brittle in nature. This relationship with temperature has to do with atom vibrations. As temperature increases, the atoms in the material vibrate with greater frequency and amplitude. This increased vibration allows the atoms under stress to slip to new places in the material (*i.e.*, break bonds and form new ones with other atoms in the material). This slippage of atoms is seen on the outside of the material as plastic deformation, a common feature of ductile fracture.

As temperature decreases a ductile material can become brittle.Ductile-to-brittle transition alloying usually increases the ductile-to-brittle transition temperature. FCC metals remain ductile down to very low temperatures. For ceramics, this type of transition occurs at much higher temperatures than for metals.

The ductile-to-brittle transition can be measured by impact testing: the impact energy needed for fracture drops suddenly over a relatively narrow temperature range -temperature of the ductile-to-brittle transition.

When temperature decreases however, the exact opposite is true. Atom vibration decreases, and the atoms do not want to slip to new locations in the material. So when the stress on the material becomes high enough, the atoms just break their bonds and do not form new ones. This decrease in slippage causes little plastic deformation before fracture. Thus, we have a brittle type fracture.

At moderate temperatures (with respect to the material) the material exhibits characteristics of both types of fracture. In conclusion, temperature determines the amount of brittle or ductile fracture that can occur in a material.

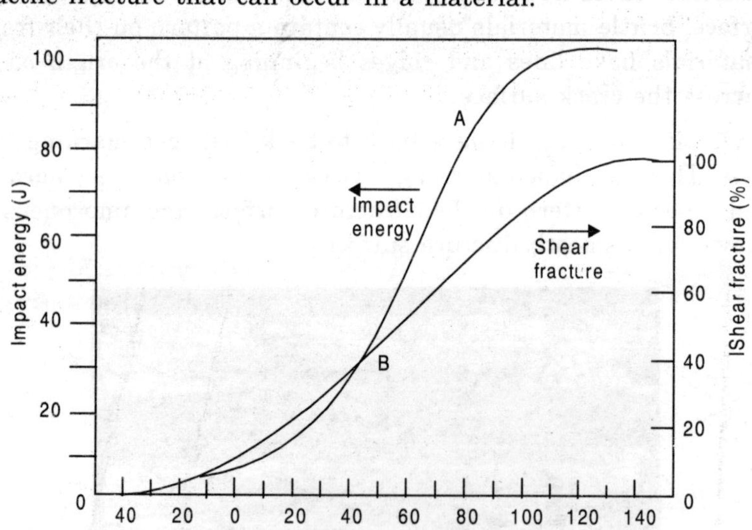

Fig. 5.8(b) Effect of temperature on impact energy and percentage of shear fracture.

Another factor that determines the amount of brittle or ductile fracture that occurs in a material is dislocation density. The higher the dislocation density, the more brittle the fracture will be in the material. The idea behind this theory is that plastic deformation comes from the movement of dislocations. As dislocations increase in a material due to stresses above the materials yield point, it becomes increasingly difficult for the dislocations to move because they pile into each other. So a material that already has a high dislocation density can only deform but so much before it fractures in a brittle manner. The last factor is grain size. As grains get smaller in a material, the fracture becomes more brittle. This phenomenon is due to the fact that in smaller grains, dislocations have less space to move before they hit a grain boundary. When dislocations cannot move very far before fracture, then plastic deformation decreases. Thus, the material's fracture is more brittle.

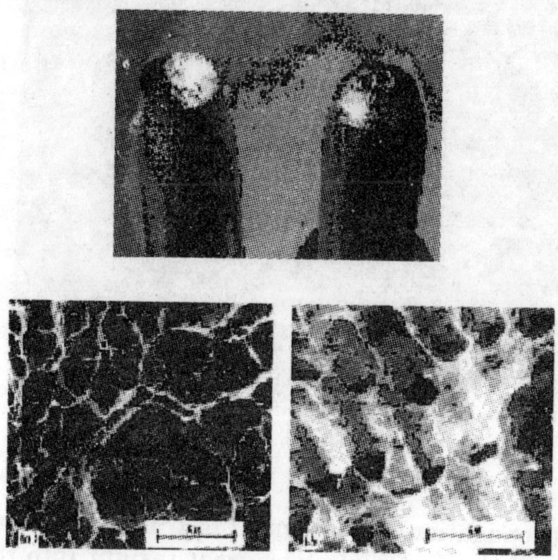

Fig. 5.9 Cup/Cone fracture in aluminium.

One of the most important and key concepts in the entire field of Materials Science and Engineering is fracture. In its simplest form, fracture can be described as a single body being separated into pieces by an imposed stress. For engineering materials there are only two possible modes of fracture, ductile and brittle. In general, the main difference between brittle and ductile fracture can be attributed to the amount of plastic deformation that the material undergoes before fracture occurs. Ductile materials demonstrate large amounts of plastic deformation while brittle materials show little or no plastic deformation before fracture. Fig. 5.10 a tensile stress-strain curve, represents the degree of plastic deformation exhibited by both brittle and ductile materials before fracture.

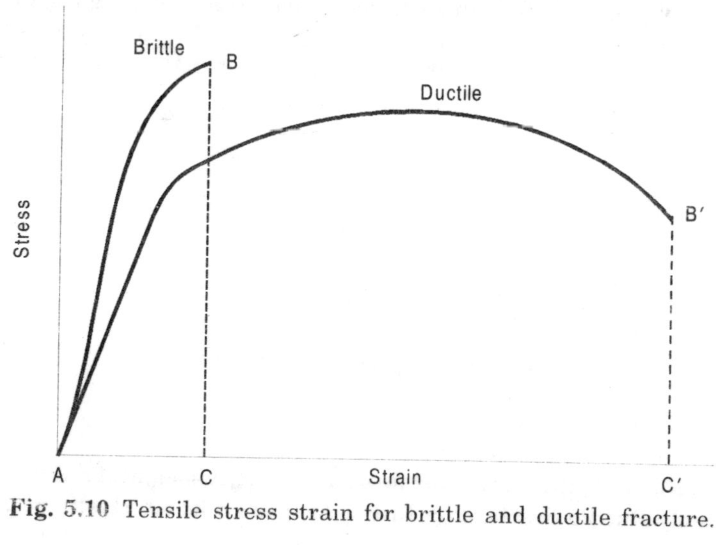

Fig. 5.10 Tensile stress strain for brittle and ductile fracture.

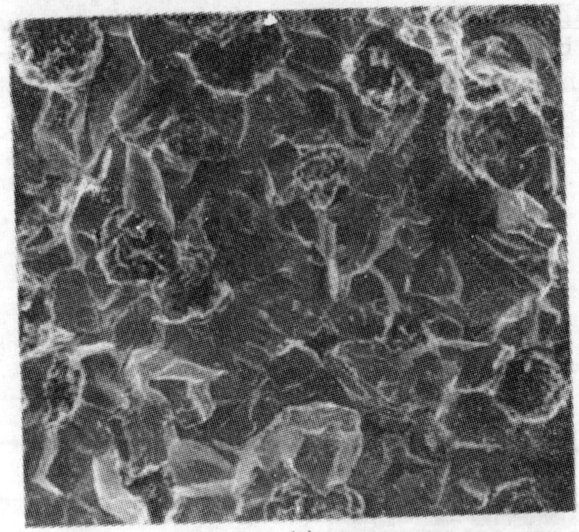

(a)

Fig. 5.11 Ductile cast iron transgranular surfaces.

Crack initiation and propagation are essential to fracture. The manner through which the crack propagates through the material gives great insight into the mode of fracture. In ductile materials (ductile fracture), the crack moves slowly and is accompanied by a large amount of plastic deformation. The crack will usually not extend unless an increased stress is applied. On the other hand, in dealing with brittle fracture, cracks spread very rapidly with little or no plastic deformation. The cracks that propagate in a brittle material will continue to grow and increase in magnitude once they are initiated. Another important mannerism of crack propagation is the way in which the advancing crack travels through the material. A crack that passes through the grains within the material is undergoing Transgranular fracture. However, a crack that propagates along the grain boundaries is termed an intergranular fracture. Fig. 5.11 shows a scanning electron fractograph of ductile cast iron, examining a transgranular fracture surface.

On both macroscopic and microscopic levels, ductile fracture surfaces have distinct features. Macroscopically, ductile fracture surfaces have larger necking regions and an overall rougher appearance than a brittle fracture surface. Fig. 5.12 (below) shows the macroscopic differences between two ductile specimens (a,b) and the brittle specimen (c).

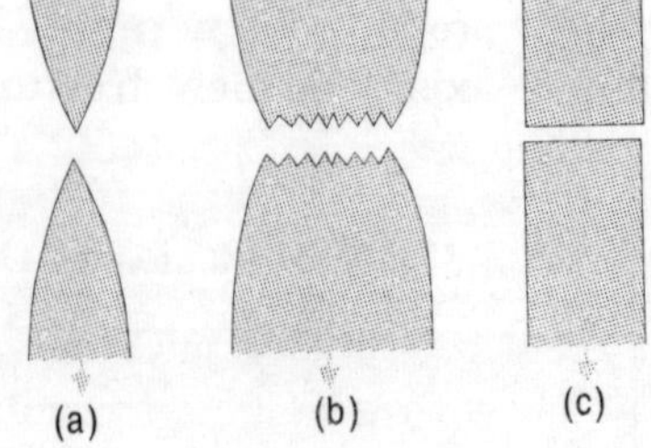

Fig. 5.12 (*a*) Highly Ductile Fracture in which the specimen necks down to a point (*b*) Moderately Ductile Fracture (*c*) Brittle Fracture without plastic deformation.

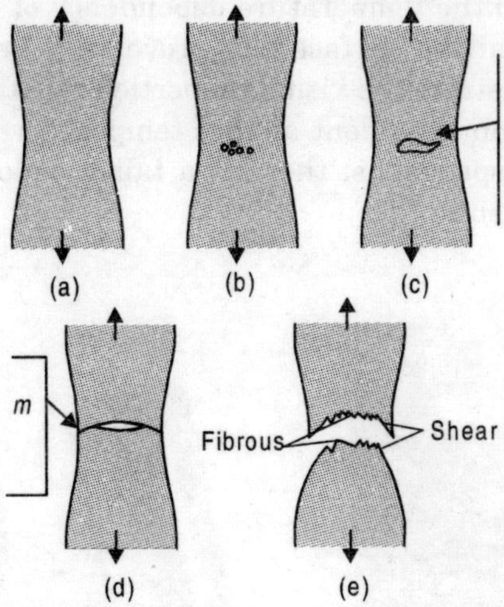

Fig. 5.13 (*a*) Necking (*b*) Cavity formation (*c*) Cavity Coalescence to form a crack (*d*) Crack propagation (*e*) Fracture.

On the microscopic level, ductile fracture surfaces also appear rough and irregular. The surface consists of many microvoids and dimples. Fig. 5.14 demonstrates the microscopic qualities of ductile fracture surfaces.

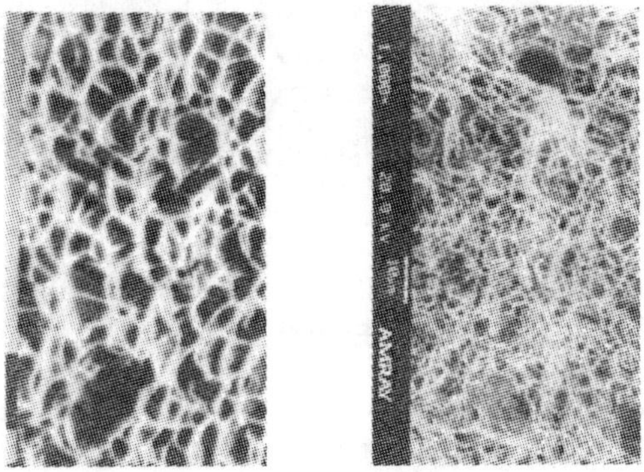

Fig. 5.14 Microscopic quality of ductile fracture surfaces.

The failure of many ductile materials can be attributed to cup and cone fracture. This form of ductile fracture occurs in stages that initiate after necking begins. First, small microvoids form in the interior of the material. Next, deformation continues and the microvoids enlarge to form a crack. The crack continues to grow and it spreads laterally towards the edges of the specimen. Finally, crack propagation is rapid along a surface that makes about a 45° angle with the tensile stress axis. The new fracture surface has a very irregular appearance. The final shearing of the specimen produces a cup type shape on one fracture surface and a cone shape on the adjacent connecting fracture surface, hence the name, cup and cone fracture. Fig. 5.15 shows cup and cone, and brittle fracture in aluminium.

The Charpy and Izod tests measure the impact energy of a specimen. By using an apparatus and impacting a specimen with a weighted pendulum hammer the impact energy can be measured. A primary use of the Charpy and Izod tests is to determine if a material experiences brittle to ductile transition with decreasing temperature. Brittle to ductile transition is directly related to the temperature dependency of the impact energy absorbed. Also an examination of the failure surface can prove very beneficial. If a section of the failure surface seems to demonstrate the visual properties of both brittle and ductile fracture, then brittle to ductile transition is evident at that temperature range. It is very important to remember that with most specimens, there is a fairly wide band of temperatures that support brittle to ductile transition.

Fig. 5.15 (*a*) Cup and Cone Fracture in aluminium (*b*) Brittle fracture in mild steel.

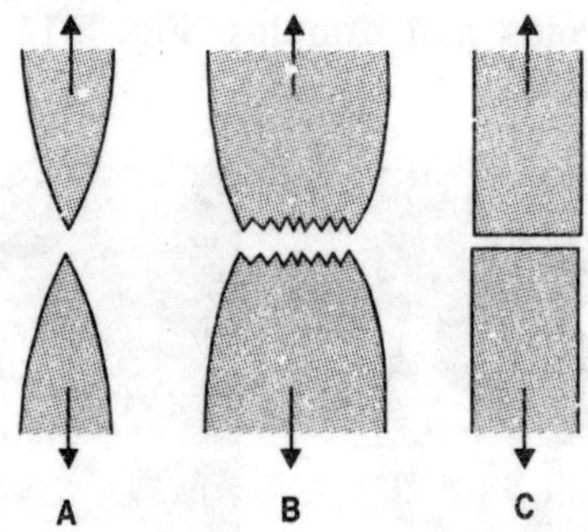

Fig. 5.16 Brittle to ductile.

In most design situations a material that demonstrates ductile fracture is usually preferred for several reasons. First and foremost, brittle fracture occurs very rapidly and catastrophically without any warning. Ductile materials plastically deform, thereby slowing the process of fracture and giving ample time for the problem to be corrected. Second, because of the plastic deformation, more strain energy is needed to cause ductile fracture. Next, ductile materials are considered to be "forgiving" materials, because of their toughness you can make a mistake in the use, design of a ductile material and still the material will probably not fail. Also, the properties of a ductile material can be enhanced through the use of one of the strengthening mechanisms. Strain hardening is a perfect example, as the ductile material is deformed more and more its strength and hardness increase because of the generation of more and more dislocations. Therefore, in engineering applications, especially those that have safety concerns involved, ductile materials are the obvious choice. Safety and dependability are the main concerns in material design, but in order to attain these goals there has to be a thorough understanding of fracture, both brittle and ductile. Understanding fracture and failure of materials will lead the materials engineer to develop safer and more dependable materials and products.

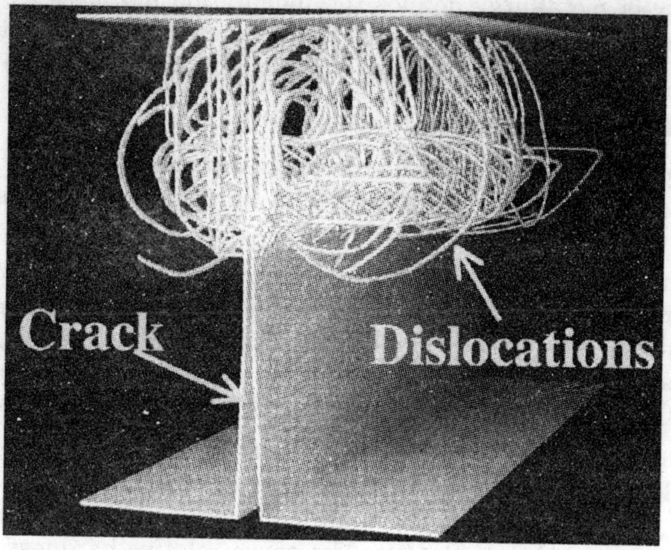

Brittle

Fig. 5.17 Brittle-ductile transition.

5.5.3 Ductile Fracture-Applications

- Ductile materials - extensive plastic deformation and energy absorption ("toughness") before fracture.
- Brittle materials - little plastic deformation and low energy absorption before fracture.
  - A. Very ductile, soft metals (e.g. Pb, Au) at room temperature, other metals, polymers, glasses at high temperature.
  - B. Moderately ductile fracture, typical for ductile metals
  - C. Brittle fracture, cold metals, ceramics.

5.6 MECHANICAL PROPERTY TESTING

Hardness is the property of a material that enables it to resist plastic deformation, usually by penetration. However, the term hardness may also refer to resistance to bending, scratching, abrasion or cutting.

What is Hardness?

The Metals Handbook defines hardness as "Resistance of metal to plastic deformation", usually by indentation. However, the term may also refer to stiffness or temper, or to resistance to scratching, abrasion, or cutting. It is the property of a metal, which gives it the ability to resist being permanently, deformed (bent, broken, or have its shape changed), when a load is applied. The greater the hardness of the metal, the greater resistance it has to deformation.

In mineralogy the property of matter commonly described as the resistance of a substance to being scratched by another substance. In metallurgy hardness is defined as the ability of a material to resist plastic deformation.

The dictionary of metallurgy defines the indentation hardness as the resistance of a material to indentation. This is the usual type of hardness test, in which a pointed or rounded indenter is pressed into a surface under a substantially static load.

5.6.1 Measurement of Hardness

Hardness is not an intrinsic material property dictated by precise definitions in terms of fundamental units of mass, length and time. A hardness property value is the result of a defined measurement procedure.

Hardness of materials has probably long been assessed by resistance to scratching or cutting. An example would be material B scratches material C, but not material A. Alternatively, material A scratches material B slightly and scratches material C heavily. Relative hardness of minerals can be assessed by reference to the Moh's Scale that ranks the ability of materials to resist scratching by another material.

Similar methods of relative hardness assessment are still commonly used today. An example is the file test where a file tempered to a desired hardness is rubbed on the test material surface. If the file slides without biting or marking the surface, the test material would be considered harder than the file. The above relative hardness tests are limited in practical use and do not provide accurate numeric data or scales particularly for modern day metals and materials.

The usual method to achieve a hardness value is to measure the depth or area of an indentation left by an indenter of a specific shape, with a specific force applied for a specific time. There are three principal standard test methods for expressing the relationship between hardness and the size of the impression, these being Brinell, Vickers, and Rockwell. For practical and calibration reasons, each of these methods is divided into a range of scales, defined by a combination of applied load and indenter geometry. There are three types of tests used with accuracy by the metals industry; they are the Brinell hardness test, the Rockwell hardness test, and the Vickers hardness test. Since the definitions of metallurgic ultimate strength and hardness are rather similar, it can generally be assumed that a strong metal is also a hard metal. The way the three of these hardness tests measure a metal's hardness is to determine the metal's resistance to the penetration of a non-deformable ball or cone. The tests determine the depth which such a ball or cone will sink into the metal, under a given load, within a specific period of time. The followings are the most common hardness test methods used in today's technology:

1. Rockwell hardness test
2. Brinell hardness
3. Vickers
4. Knoop hardness
5. Shore.

5.6.2 Brinell Hardness

Brinell hardness is determined by forcing a hard steel or carbide sphere of a specified diameter under a specified load into the surface of a material and measuring the diameter of the indentation left after the test. The Brinell hardness number, or simply the Brinell number, is obtained by dividing the load used, in kilograms, by the actual surface area of the indentation, in square millimeters. The result is a pressure measurement, but the units are rarely stated.

Fig. 5.18 Brinell hardness tester.

The Brinell hardness test uses a desk top machine to press a 10 mm diameter, hardened steel ball into the surface of the test specimen. The machine applies a load of 500 kilograms for soft metals such as copper, brass and thin stock. A 1500 kilogram load is used for aluminium castings, and a 3000 kilogram load is used for materials such as iron and steel. The load is usually applied for 10 to 15 seconds. After the impression is made, a measurement of the diameter of the resulting round impression is taken. It is measured to plus or minus 0.05 mm using a low-magnification portable microscope. The hardness is calculated by dividing the load by the area of the curved surface of the indention, (the area of a hemispherical surface is arrived at by multiplying the square of the diameter by 3.14159 and then dividing by 2). To make it easier, a calibrated chart is provided, so with the diameter of the indentation the corresponding hardness number can be referenced. A well structured Brinell hardness number reveals the test conditions, and looks like this, "75 HB 10/500/30" which means that a Brinell Hardness of 75 was obtained using a 10 mm diameter hardened steel with a 500 kilogram load applied for a period of 30 seconds. On tests of extremely hard metals a tungsten carbide ball is substituted for the steel ball. Among the three hardness tests discussed, the Brinell ball makes the deepest and widest indentation, so the test averages the hardness over a wider amount of material, which will more accurately account for multiple grain structures, and any irregularities in the uniformity of the alloy.

5.6.3 Rockwell Hardness Test Method

The Rockwell Hardness test is a hardness measurement test based on the net increase in depth of impression as a load is applied. Hardness numbers have no units and are commonly given in the R, L, M, E and K scales. The higher the number in each of the scales means the harder the material.

Hardness has been variously defined as resistance to local penetration, scratching, machining, wear or abrasion, and yielding. The multiplicity of definitions, and corresponding multiplicity of hardness measuring instruments, together with the lack of a fundamental definition, indicates that hardness may not be a fundamental property of a material, but rather a composite one including yield strength, work hardening, true tensile strength, modulus of elasticity, and others. In the Rockwell method of hardness testing, the depth of penetration of an indenter under certain arbitrary test conditions is determined. The indenter may either be a steel ball of some specified diameter or a spherical diamond-tipped cone of 120° angle and 0.2 mm tip radius, called Brale. The type of indenter and the test load determine the hardness scale (A, B, C, etc).

A minor load of 10 kg is first applied, which causes an initial penetration and holds the indenter in place. Then, the dial is set to zero and the major load is applied. Upon removal of the major load, the depth reading is taken while the minor load is still on. The hardness number may then be read directly from the scale.

The hardness of ceramic substrates can be determined by the Rockwell hardness test, according to the specifications of ASTM E-18. This test measures the difference in depth caused by two different forces, using a dial gauge. Using standard hardness conversion tables, the Rockwell hardness value is determined for the load applied, the diameter of the indentor, and the indentation depth.

The hardness testing of plastics is most commonly measured by the Rockwell hardness test or Shore (Durometer) hardness test. Both methods measure the resistance of the plastic toward indentation. Both scales provide an empirical hardness value that doesn't correlate to other properties or fundamental characteristics. Rockwell hardness is generally chosen for 'harder' plastics such as nylon, polycarbonate, polystyrene, and acetal where the resiliency or creep of the polymer is less likely to affect the results.

The results obtained from this test are a useful measure of relative resistance to indentation of various grades of plastics. However, the Rockwell hardness test does not serve well as a predictor of other properties such as strength or resistance to scratches, abrasion, or wear, and should not be used alone for product design specifications.

The Rockwell hardness tester to measure the hardness of metal measures resistance to penetration like the Brinell test, but in the Rockwell case, the depth of the impression is measured rather than the diametric area. With the Rockwell tester, the hardness is indicated directly on the scale attached to the machine. This dial like scale is really a depth gauge, graduated in special units. The Rockwell hardness test is the most used and versatile of the hardness tests.

For soft materials such as copper alloys, soft steel, and aluminium alloys a 1/16" diameter steel ball is used with a 100 kilogram load and the hardness is read on the "B" scale. In testing harder materials, hard cast iron and many steel alloys, a 120 degrees diamond cone is used with up to a 150 kilogram load and the hardness is read on the "C" scale. The Rockwell test uses two loads, one applied directly after the other. The first load, known as the "minor", load of 10 kilograms is applied to the specimen to help seat the indenter and remove the effects, in the test, of any surface irregularities. In essence, the minor load creates a uniformly shaped surface for the major load to be applied to. The difference in the depth of the indentation between the minor and major loads provides the Rockwell hardness number. There are several Rockwell scales other than the "B" & "C" scales, (which are called the common scales). The other scales also use a letter for the scale symbol prefix, and many use a different sized steel ball indenter. A properly used Rockwell designation will have the hardness number followed by "HR" (Hardness Rockwell), which will be followed by another letter which indicates the specific Rockwell scale. An example is 60 HRB, which indicates that the specimen has a hardness reading of 60 on the B scale. There is a second Rockwell tester referred to as the "Rockwell Superficial Hardness Tester". This machine works the same as the standard Rockwell tester, but is used to test thin strip, or lightly carburized surfaces, small parts that might collapse under the conditions of the regular test. The superficial tester uses a reduced minor load, just 3 kilograms, and has the major load reduced to either 15 or 45 kilograms depending on the indenter, which are the same ones used for the common scales. Using the 1/16" diameter, steel ball indenter, a "T" is added (meaning thin sheet testing) to the superficial hardness designation. An example of a superficial Rockwell hardness is 15T-22, which indicates the superficial hardness as 22, with a load of 15 kilograms using the steel ball. If the 120 diamond cone were used instead, the "T" would be replaced with "N".

The Rockwell hardness test method consists of indenting the test material with a diamond cone or hardened steel ball indenter. The indenter is forced into the test material under a preliminary minor load *F0* (Fig. 5.19 *a*) usually 10 kgf. When equilibrium has been reached, an indicating device, which follows the movements of the indenter and so responds to changes in depth of penetration of the indenter is set to a datum position. While the preliminary minor load is still applied an additional major load is applied with resulting increase in penetration (Fig. 5.19 *b*). When equilibrium has again been reach, the additional major load is removed but the preliminary minor load is still maintained. Removal of the additional major load allows a partial recovery, so reducing the depth of penetration (Fig. 19 *c*). The permanent increase in depth of penetration, resulting from the application and removal of the additional major load is used to calculate the Rockwell hardness number.

$$HR = E - e$$

Where,

F0 = preliminary minor load in kgf

F1 = additional major load in kgf

F = total load in kgf

e = permanent increase in depth of penetration due to major load F1 measured in units of 0.002 mm

E = a constant depending on form of indenter: 100 units for diamond indenter, 130 units for steel ball indenter

HR = Rockwell hardness number

D = diameter of steel ball

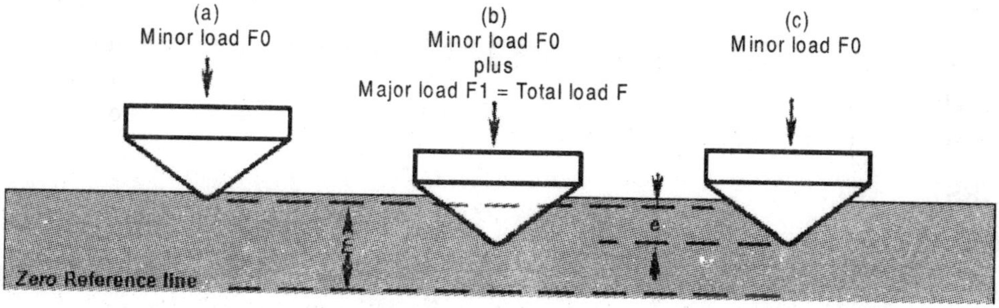

Fig. 5.19 Rockwell principle.

Rockwell Hardness Scales

Scale	Indenter	Minor Load F0 kgf	Major Load F1 kgf	Total Load F kgf	Value of E
A	Diamond cone	10	50	60	100
B	1/16" steel ball	10	90	100	130
C	Diamond cone	10	140	150	100
D	Diamond cone	10	90	100	100
E	1/8" steel ball	10	90	100	130
F	1/16" steel ball	10	50	60	130
G	1/16" steel ball	10	140	150	130
H	1/8" steel ball	10	50	60	130
K	1/8" steel ball	10	140	150	130
L	1/4" steel ball	10	50	60	130
M	1/4" steel ball	10	90	100	130
P	1/4" steel ball	10	140	150	130
R	1/2" steel ball	10	50	60	130
S	1/2" steel ball	10	90	100	130
V	1/2" steel ball	10	140	150	130

Typical Application of Rockwell Hardness Scales

HRA . . . . Cemented carbides, thin steel and shallow case hardened steel

HRB . . . . Copper alloys, soft steels, aluminium alloys, malleable irons, etc

HRC . . . . Steel, hard cast irons, case hardened steel and other materials harder than 100 HRB

HRD . . . Thin steel and medium case hardened steel and pearlitic malleable iron

HRE . . . . Cast iron, aluminium and magnesium alloys, bearing metals

HRF . . . Annealed copper alloys, thin soft sheet metals

HRG . . . . Phosphor bronze, beryllium copper, malleable irons HRH . . . . Aluminium, zinc, lead

HRK . . . . }

HRL . . . . }

HRM . . . . } . . . . Soft bearing metals, plastics and other very soft materials

HRP . . . . }

HRR . . . . }

HRS . . . . }

HRV . . . . }

Advantages of the Rockwell hardness method include the direct Rockwell hardness number readout and rapid testing time. Disadvantages include many arbitrary non-related scales and possible effects from the specimen support anvil (try putting a cigarette paper under a test block and take note of the effect on the hardness reading! Vickers and Brinell methods don't suffer from this effect).

5.6.4 Vicker Hardness

It is the standard method for measuring the hardness of metals, particularly those with extremely hard surfaces: the surface is subjected to a standard pressure for a standard length of time by means of a pyramid-shaped diamond. The diagonal of the resulting indention is measured under a microscope and the Vickers Hardness value read from a conversion table.

Vickers hardness is a measure of the hardness of a material, calculated from the size of an impression produced under load by a pyramid-shaped diamond indenter. Devised in the 1920s by engineers at Vickers, Ltd., in the United Kingdom, the diamond pyramid hardness test, as it also became known, permitted the establishment of a continuous scale of comparable numbers that accurately reflected the wide range of hardnesses found in steels.

The indenter employed in the Vickers test is a square-based pyramid whose opposite sides meet at the apex at an angle of 136°. The diamond is pressed into the surface of the material at loads ranging up to approximately 120 kilograms-force, and the size of the impression (usually no more than 0.5 mm) is measured with the aid of a calibrated microscope.

The Vickers hardness test method consists of indenting the test material with a diamond indenter, in the form of a right pyramid with a square base and an angle of 136° between opposite faces subjected to a load of 1 to 100 kgf. The full load is normally applied for 10 to 15 seconds. The two diagonals of the indentation left in the surface of the material after removal of the load are measured using a microscope and their average calculated. The area of the sloping surface of the indentation is calculated. The Vickers hardness is the quotient obtained by dividing the kgf load by the square mm area of indentation.

The Vickers test is reliable for measuring the hardness of metals, and also used on ceramic materials. The Vickers testing method is similar to the Brinell test. Rather than using the Brinell's steel ball type indenter, and have to calculate the hemispherical area of impression, the Vickers machine uses a penetrator that is square in shape, but tipped on one corner so it has the appearance of a playing card "diamond". The Vickers indenter is a 136 degrees square-based diamond cone, the diamond material of the indenter has an advantage over other indenters because it does not deform over time and use. The impression left by the Vickers penetrator is a dark square on a light background. The Vickers impression is more easily "read" for area size than the circular impression of the Brinell method. Like the Brinell test, the Vickers number is determined by dividing the load by the surface area of the indentation ($H = P/A$). The load varies from 1 to 120 kilograms. To perform the Vickers test, the specimen is placed on an anvil that has a screw threaded base. The anvil is turned raising it by the screw threads until it is close to the point of the indenter. With start lever activated, the load is slowly applied to the indenter. The load is released and the anvil with the specimen is lowered. The operation of applying and removing the load is controlled automatically.

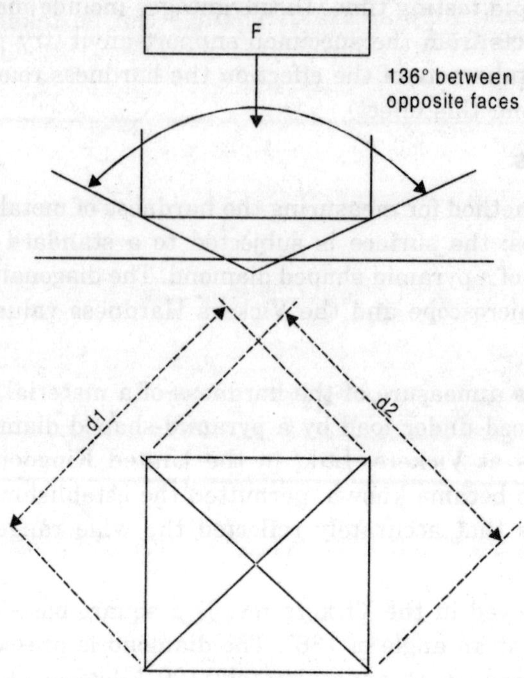

Fig. 5.20(a) Vickers hardness.

Several loadings give practically identical hardness numbers on uniform material, which is much better than the arbitrary changing of scale with the other hardness machines. A filar microscope is swung over the specimen to measure the square indentation to a tolerance of plus or minus 1/1000 of a millimeter. Measurements taken across the diagonals to determine the area, are averaged. The correct Vickers designation is the number followed "HV" (Hardness Vickers). The advantages of the Vickers hardness test are that extremely accurate readings can be taken, and just one type of indenter is used for all types of metals and surface treatments. Although thoroughly adaptable and very precise for testing the softest and hardest of materials, under varying loads, the Vickers machine is a floor standing unit that is rather more expensive than the Brinell or Rockwell machines.

F = load in kgf

d = arithmetic mean of the two diagonals, $d1$ and $d2$ in mm

HV = Vickers hardness

$$HV = \frac{2F \sin \frac{136°}{2}}{d^2}$$

$$HV = 1.854 \frac{F}{d^2} \text{ approximately.}$$

When the mean diagonal of the indentation has been determined the Vickers hardness may be calculated from the formula, but is more convenient to use conversion tables. The Vickers hardness should be reported like 800 HV/10, which means a Vickers hardness of 800, was obtained using a 10 kgf force. Several different loading settings give practically identical hardness numbers on uniform material, which is much better than the arbitrary changing of scale with the other hardness testing methods. The advantages of the Vickers hardness test are that extremely accurate readings can be taken, and just one type of indenter is used for all types of metals and surface treatments. Although thoroughly adaptable and very precise for testing the softest and hardest of materials, under varying loads, the Vickers machine is a floor standing unit that is more expensive than the Brinell or Rockwell machines.

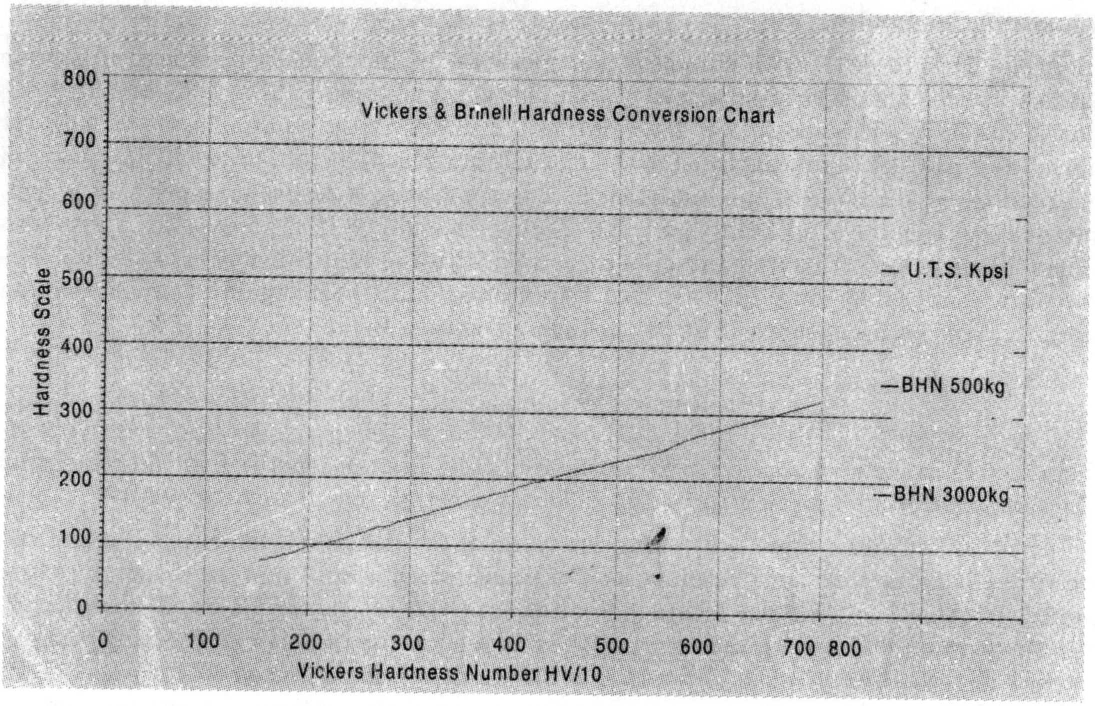

Fig. 5.20(b) Vicker Vs Brinell conversion chart.

5.6.5 Knoop Hardness

The relative micro hardness of a material is determined by the Knoop indentation test. In this test, a pyramid-shaped diamond indenter with apical angles of 130° and 172°30' (called a Knoop indenter) is pressed against a material. Making a rhombohedra impression with one diagonal seven times longer than the other. The hardness of the material is determined by the depth to which the Knoop indenter penetrates.

This test method was devised in 1939 by F. Knoop and colleagues at the National Bureau of Standards in the United States. By using lower indentation pressures than the Vickers hardness test, which had been designed for measuring metals, the Knoop test allowed the hardness testing of brittle materials such as glass and ceramics.

The diamond indenter employed in the Knoop test is in the shape of an elongated four-sided pyramid, with the angle between two of the opposite faces being approximately 170° and the angle between the other two being 130°. Pressed into the material under loads that are often less than one kilogram-force, the indenter leaves a four-sided impression about 0.01 to 0.1 mm in size. The length of the impression is approximately seven times the width, and the depth is 1/30 the length. Given such dimensions, the area of the impression under load can be calculated after measuring only the length of the longest side with the aid of a calibrated microscope. The final Knoop hardness (HK) is derived from the following formula:

$$HK = 14.229\ (F/D^2),$$

with F being the applied load (measured in kilograms-force) and D^2 the area of the indentation (measured in square millimetres). Knoop hardness numbers are often cited in conjunction with specific load values.

ASTM D-1474 deals with standard test methods for indentation hardness of organic coatings. In this test, Knoop hardness determinations are made at 23 ± 2° C and 50 ± 5% relative humidity. The specimens are equilibrated under these conditions for at least 24 hours. They are then rigidly attached to the movable stage so that the surface to be measured is normal to the direction of the indentation. The apparatus is preset to apply a 25 g load. The time the indentor is in contact with the specimen should be 18 ± 0.5 seconds. The length of the long diagonal of the impression is measured with the filar micrometer eyepiece. The procedure is repeated until at least five impressions have been made at widely spaced locations. The Knoop hardness number is then calculated by

$$KHN = \frac{0.0025}{l^2 C_P}$$

where 0.0025 is the load applied in kg to the indentor, l is the length of the long diagonal of the indentation in mm, and Cp is the indentor constant, equal to 7.028×10^{-2}.

ASTM D-785 is the standard test for determining the Rockwell hardness of plastics and electrical insulating materials. A minor load of 10 kg, which is built into the machine, is first applied without shock. Within 10 seconds after applying the minor load and immediately after set position if obtained, the major load is applied on the specimen. The major load is removed 15 seconds after its application. The Rockwell hardness is read off the scale on the machine. Care should be taken in choosing the proper scale, as Rockwell hardness values are reported as a letter, indicating the scale, and a number, indicating the reading.

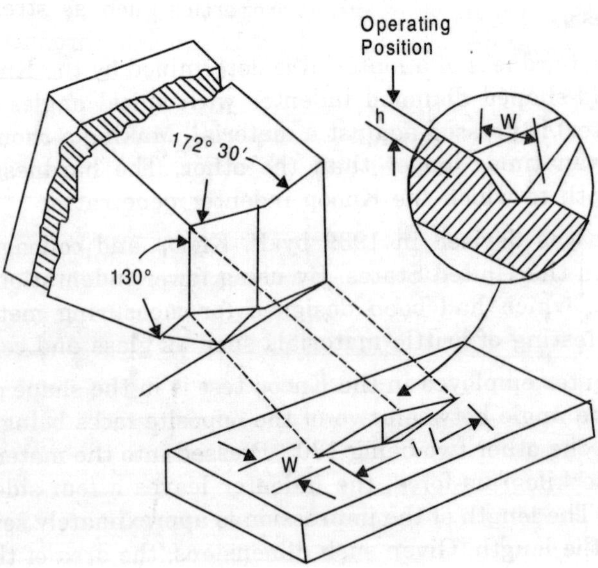

Fig. 5.21 Knoop hardness.

Shore

The shore scleroscope measures hardness in terms of the elasticity of the material. A diamond-tipped hammer in a graduated glass tube is allowed to fall from a known height on the specimen to be tested, and the hardness number depends on the height to which the hammer rebounds; the harder the material, the higher the rebound .

Shore hardness is a measure of the resistance of material to indentation by 3 spring-loaded indenter. The higher the number, the greater the resistance.

The hardness testing of plastics is most commonly measured by the Shore (Durometer) test or Rockwell hardness test. Both methods measure the resistance of the plastic toward indentation. Both scales provide an empirical hardness value that doesn't correlate to other properties or fundamental characteristics. Shore hardness, using either the shore A or shore D scale, is the preferred method for rubbers/elastomers and is also commonly used for 'softer' plastics such as polyolefins, fluoropolymers, and vinyls. The shore A scale is used for 'softer' rubbers while the shore D scale is used for 'harder' ones. The shore A hardness is the relative hardness of elastic materials such as rubber or soft plastics can be determined with an instrument called a shore A durometer. If the indenter completely penetrates the sample, a reading of 0 is obtained, and if no penetration occurs, a reading of 100 results. The reading is dimensionless.

The shore hardness is measured with an apparatus known as a Durometer and consequently is also known as 'Durometer hardness'. The hardness value is determined by the penetration of the Durometer indenter foot into the sample. Because of the resilience of rubbers and plastics, the hardness reading may change over time - so the indentation time is sometimes reported along with the hardness number. The ASTM test number is ASTM D2240 while the analogous ISO test method is ISO 868.

The results obtained from this test are a useful measure of relative resistance to indentation of various grades of polymers. However, the Shore Durometer hardness test does not serve well as a predictor of other properties such as strength or resistance to scratches, abrasion, or wear, and should not be used alone for product design specifications.

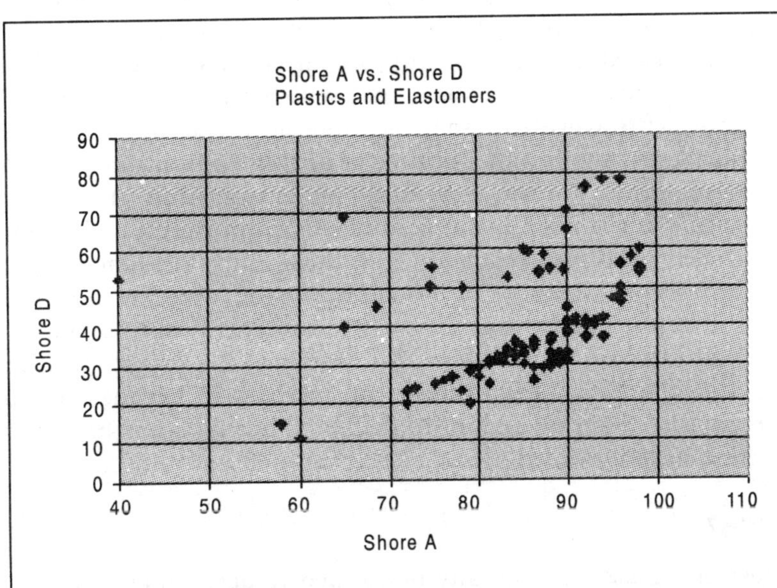

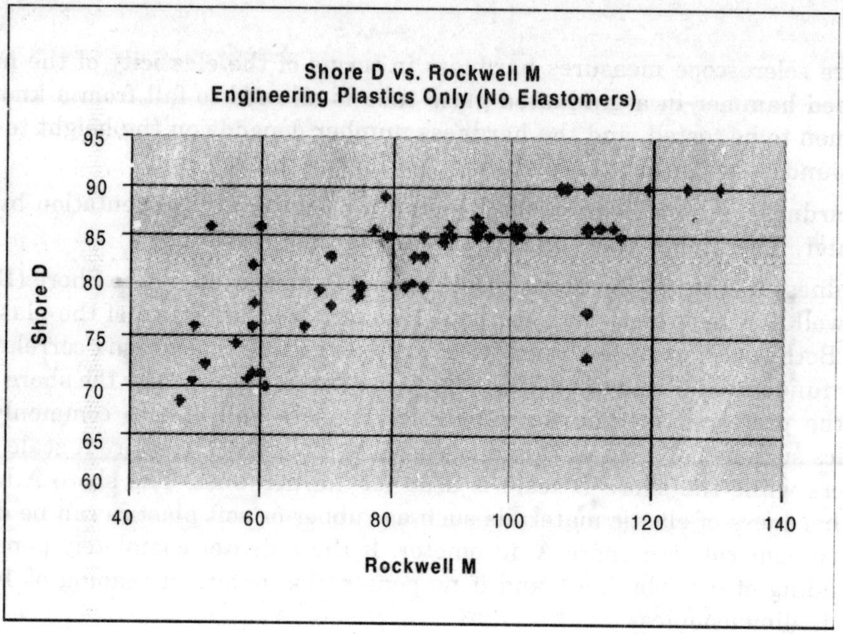

Mohs Hardness

Mohs hardness is defined by how well a substance will resist scratching by another substance. It is a rough measure of the resistance of a smooth surface to scratching or abrasion, expressed in terms of a scale devised (1812) by the German mineralogist Friedrich Mohs. The Mohs hardness of a mineral is determined by observing whether its surface is scratched by a substance of known or defined hardness.

To give numerical values to this physical property, minerals are ranked along the Mohs scale, which is composed of 10 minerals that have been given arbitrary hardness values. The minerals contained in the scale are shown in the table; also shown are other materials that approximate the hardness of some of the minerals. As is indicated by the ranking in the scale, if a mineral is scratched by orthoclase but not by apatite, its Mohs hardness is between 5 and 6. In the determination procedure it is necessary to be certain that a scratch is actually made and not just a "chalk" mark that will rub off. If the species being tested is fine-grained, friable, or pulverulent, the test may only loosen grains without testing individual mineral surfaces; thus certain textures or aggregate forms may hinder or prevent a true hardness determination. For this reason the Mohs test, while greatly facilitating the identification of minerals in the field, is not suitable for accurately gauging the hardness of industrial materials such as steel or ceramics. (For these materials a more precise measure is to be found in the Vickers hardness or Knoop hardness;) Another disadvantage of the Mohs scale is that it is not linear; that is, each increment of one in the scale does not indicate a proportional increase in hardness. For instance, the progression from calcite to fluorite (from 3 to 4 on the Mohs scale) reflects an increase in hardness of approximately 25 percent; the progression from corundum to diamond, on the other hand (9 to 10 on the Mohs scale), reflects a hardness increase of more than 300 percent.

5.7 TENSILE TEST

The tensile test of a metal is generally performed to determine:

1. Proportional and elastic limit.
2. Yield point.
3. Ultimate tensile strength.
4. Percentage elongation and reduction of area.

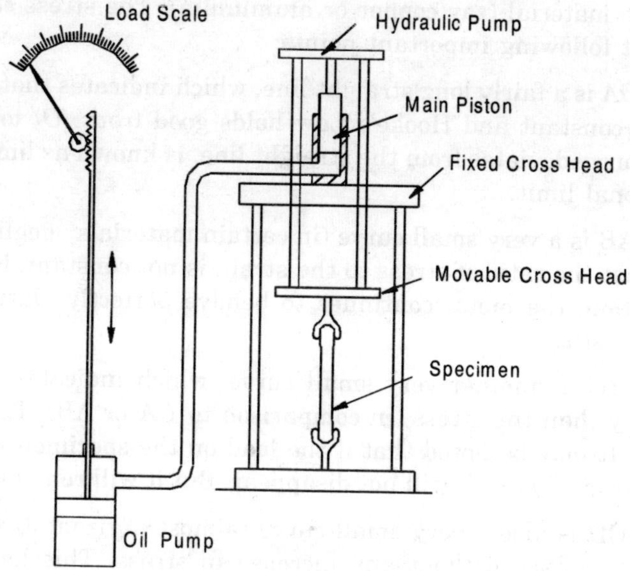

Fig. 5.22 Universal testing machine.

The results obtained by the tensile test are widely used in the design of materials for structures and other purposes. In this test, the test piece is pulled out at a constant rate by gradually increasing the axial pull, till the rupture takes place.

The tensile test for a ductile material is, generally, carried out with the help of a universal testing machine on the specimen made from the material to be tested.

The schematic working arrangement of a universal testing machine is shown in Fig. 5.22. The specimen is held in the jaws of the machine. And load is applied gradually by a hydraulic press, which is measured from the pressure developed inside the cylinder. The function of the oil pump is to supply of oil under pressure to the hydraulic cylinder. The load reading is noted directly from the load scale.

The dimension and form of the specimen varies according to the size and shape of the material to be tested and the main objective in view. The test carried out on a specimen having uniform cross-section throughout the gauge length.

The Bureau of Indian Standards (previously Indian Standards Institute) has recommended several sizes of the specimen. But the standard practice is to use a specimen whose gauge length in mm,

$$L_0 = 5.65\sqrt{A_0}$$

$$= 5.0\ d_0$$

A_0 = area of cross-section in mm^2, and

d_0 = diameter of the specimen in mm.

It means for a gauge length of 50 mm, the specimen diameter should be 10 mm.

The tensile load is gradually increased and the corresponding extensions are recorded. Now a graph is plotted with stresses along the vertical axis and the corresponding strains along the horizontal axis. If we draw a curve passing through the vicinity of all such points, we shall obtain a curve as shown in Fig. 5.23. Such a graph is known as stress-strain diagram for a ductile material (say copper or aluminium). The stress-strain diagram gives us information about following important points:

1. The graph *OA* is a fairly long straight line, which indicates that the ratio of a stress to strain is constant and Hooke's Law holds good from *(O)* to *(A)*. The point *(A)*, where the curve deviates from the straight line, is known as limit of proportionality or proportional limit.
2. The graph AB is a very small curve (in certain materials* negligible length), which indicates that the ratio of stress to the strain is not constant, but slightly changes. In this portion, the metal continues to behave perfectly elastic. The point *(B)* is known as elastic.
3. The graph BC is another very small curve, which indicates the strain increases more quickly than the stress (in comparison to *OA* or AB). The point *(C)* is called yield point. It may be noted that if the load on the specimen is removed, then the elongation from (B) to (C) will not disappear. But it will remain as a permanent set.
4. The graph CD is also a very small curve (almost horizontal) which indicates that the strain increases without any increase in stress. This happens as there is a sudden elongation of the specimen due to creep, without any appreciable increase in stress. During this ductile elongation of the specimen cross-sectional area gets reduced uniformly in proportion length.
5. The graph is an upward curve, which indicates that the specimen regains strength, and higher values of stresses are required for higher strains. The graph rises up to the maximum limit indicated by the point (E). The stress, corresponding to the point (£), is known as ultimate tensile stress or tenacity, which is a measure of tensile strength of a material. The work done stretching the specimen is transferred, largely, into heat and the specimen becomes hot.
   - At this point the elongation of a different materials is different. But in the case of a mild steel specimen, the elongation is about 2%.
   - In wrought iron, the points A and *B* are, practically, the same point. But in rolled aluminium, these points exist separately.
6. The graph *EF* is a downward curve, which indicates that a neck is formed, which decreases the cross-sectional area of the specimen. Now it requires lesser load to continue extension till fracture takes place at *F*.

A little consideration will show, that less stress is necessary to break away the specimen. The stress corresponding to the point *(F)* is known as breaking stress. The breaking stress, *i.e.,* the stress at point *(F)* is less than that the point *E.* This statement appears to be somewhat misleading. But it is true because the formation of a neck takes place at point *E,* which reduces cross-sectional area of the specimen. It causes the specimen to fail suddenly at a point *F.* If for each value of strain, between the points *D* and *F,* tensile load is divided by the reduced cross-sectional area at the narrowest part of the neck, then the stress-strain

curve will follow the line stress-strain curve shown by the dotted line *DG* is called true curve. Similarly the curve shown by the line *DF* is called the nominal curve or engineering curve. In actual practice, it is the engineering stress-strain curve, used for all applications.

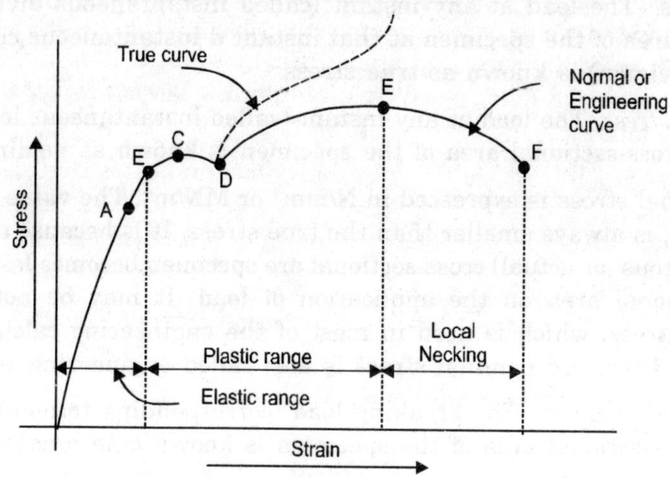

Fig. 5.23 Stress Vs strain.

As a matter of fact, the greater value of angle φ will represent the material to be more elastic. The higher position of yield point (C) will represent the material to be more hard. The higher position of the point (£) will represent the material to be more strong. Similarly, the position of the load (point *F*) will represent the brittleness or toughness of the material.

It may be noted that the stress-strain curve gives a valuable information about mechanical properties of a metal. The following terms are important in the tensile test of a specimen:

1. *Elastic stress.* The elastic load (corresponding to point *B*) divided by the original cross-sectional area of the specimen is known as elastic stress. Mathematically the elastic stress,

$$\sigma_0 = \frac{\text{Elastic load}}{\text{Original cross-sectional area}} = \frac{P_0}{A_0}$$

The elastic stress is expressed in N/mm^2 or MN/m^2 etc.

2. *Working stress.* It is the stress, which is used by the engineers for their structures or machine components. The working stress is kept much below the elastic stress, and is also known as safe stress.

3. *Yield stress.* The yield load (corresponding to point C) divided by the original cross-sectional area of the specimen is known as yield stress. Mathematically, the yield stress,

$$\sigma_y = \text{(yield load)/original corss sectional area}$$

4. *Ultimate stress.* The ultimate load (corresponding to point E) divided by the original cross-sectional area of the specimen is known ultimate stress.The ultimate stress is also called ultimate tensile stress, the maximum stress or tenacity. It is expressed in N/mm^2 or MN/m^2.

5. *Factor of safety.* The ratio of ultimate stress to the working stress is known as factor of safety.

These days, the value of factor of safety for structural steel is taken as 2 or 2.5. But in the case of cast iron, concrete, wood etc., the value factor of safety is taken as 4 to 5.

6. *True stress.* The load at any instant (called instantaneous divided by the cross-sectional area of the specimen at that instant d instantaneous cross-sectional area of the specimen) is known as true stress.

7. *Nominal stress.* The load at any instant (called instantaneous load) divided by the original cross-sectional area of the specimen is known as nominal stress.

   The nominal stress is expressed in N/mm^2 or MN/m^2. The value of nominal stress, in tension, is always smaller than the true stress. It is because of the fact that the instantaneous (or actual) cross-sectional are specimen becomes less than the original cross-sectional area on the application of load. It may be noted that it is the nominal stress, which is used in most of the engineering calculations for design purposes. Therefore nominal stress is also called engineering stress.

8. *True breaking stress.* The breaking load (corresponding to point F divided by the final cross-sectional area of the specimen is known true breaking stress.

9. *Nominal breaking stress.* The breaking load (corresponding to point F)divided by the original cross-sectional area of the specimen is known as nominal breaking stress.

10. *Percentage elongation.* The elongation or increase in length divided by the original length of the specimen, expressed as per cent, is known as percentage elongation.

11. *Percentage reduction of area.* The reduction in cross-sectional divided by the original cross-sectional area of the specimen, expressed as percent, is known as percentage reduction of area. It is evident from the above relation that the percentage reduction area depends upon the original diameter and diameter of the specimen at any instant. In other words, it does not depend upon the gauge length.

12. *Uniform elongation.* The increase in length of the specimen, when it loaded up to the limit of proportionality (corresponding to point *A*) is uniform throughout its gauge length. However, as the applied load is increased, beyond the limit of proportionality, the area of cross-section starts reducing due to the permanent deformation of the material. Therefore the elongation produced in the specimen is no longer uniform beyond the limit of proportionality.

13. *Total elongation.* The total increase in length of the specimen measured immediately after its fracture, is known as total elongation. It may be noted that elongation of the specimen after fracture is not uniform throughout its gauge length. It is because of the fact that elongation in the region of neck is more than that in the remaining portion of the specimen.

5.8 CHARPY AND IZOD TEST

Two standard tests, the Charpy and Izod, measure the impact energy (the energy required to fracture a test piece under an impact load), also called the notch toughness.

Impact Fracture Testing (testing fracture characteristics under high strain rates). In standard testing, such as tensile and flexural testing, the material absorbs energy slowly. In real life, materials often absorb applied forces very quickly: falling objects, blows, collisions, drops, etc. The purpose of impact testing is to simulate these conditions. Izod and Charpy methods are used to investigate the behavior of specified specimens under specified impact stresses, and to estimate the brittleness or toughness of specimens. They should not be used as a source of data for design calculations on components. Information on the typical behavior of a material can be obtained by testing different types of test specimens prepared under different conditions, varying notch radius and test temperatures.

Both tests are performed on a pendulum impact machine. The specimen is clamped in a vice; the pendulum hammer with a hardened steel striking edge with specified radius is released from a predefined height, causing the specimen to shear from the sudden load. The residual energy in the pendulum hammer carries it upwards: the difference in the drop height and return height represents the energy to break the test bar. The test can be carried out at room temperature, or at lower temperatures to test cold-temperature embrittlement.

Impact values cannot be considered absolute unless the geometry of the test equipment and specimen conform to the end-use requirement. The relative ranking of materials may be expected to be the same between two test methods if the mode of failure and impact velocities.

Impact loading differs from quasi-static loading in that a load is applied over a very short time instead of being introduced gradually at some constant rate. This causes significant changes in the observed material properties from those associated with normal static tests. In the case of impact loading the effects measured are of a dynamic nature, with vibration and possibly fracture being observed.

There are two methods of impact testing in common use: Charpy or Izod Method:

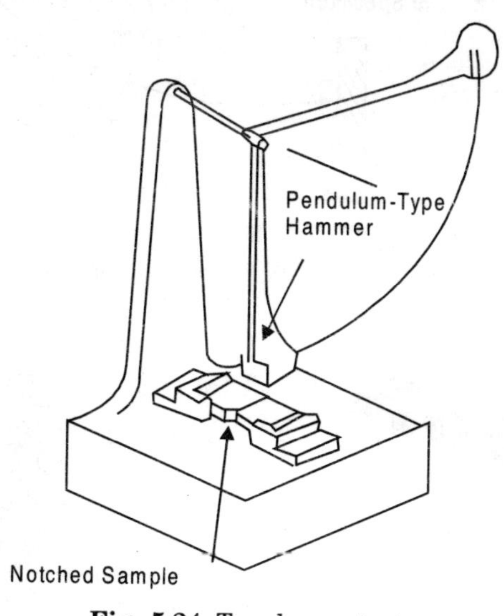

Fig. 5.24 Toughness test.

The quality known as *toughness* describes the way a material reacts under sudden impacts. It is defined as the work required to deform one cubic inch of metal until it fractures. Toughness is measured by the Charpy test or the Izod test. Both of these tests use a notched sample. The location and shape of the notch are standard. The points of support of the sample, as well as the impact of the hammer, must bear a constant relationship to the location of the notch. The tests are conducted by mounting the samples as shown in Fig. 5.24 and allowing a pendulum of a known weight to fall from a set height. The maximum energy developed by the hammer is 120 ft-lb in the Izod test and 240 ft-lb in the Charpy test. By properly calibrating the machine, the energy absorbed by the specimen may be measured from the upward swing of the pendulum after it has fractured the material specimen as shown in Fig. 5.24. The greater the amount of energy absorbed by the specimen, the smaller the upward swing of the pendulum will be and the tougher the material is.

Material Toughness Test: Indication of toughness is relative and applicable only to cases involving exactly this type of sample and method of loading. A sample of a different shape will yield an entirely different result. Notches confine the deformation to a small volume of metal that reduces toughness. In effect, it is the shape of the metal in addition to the material composition that determines the toughness of the material.

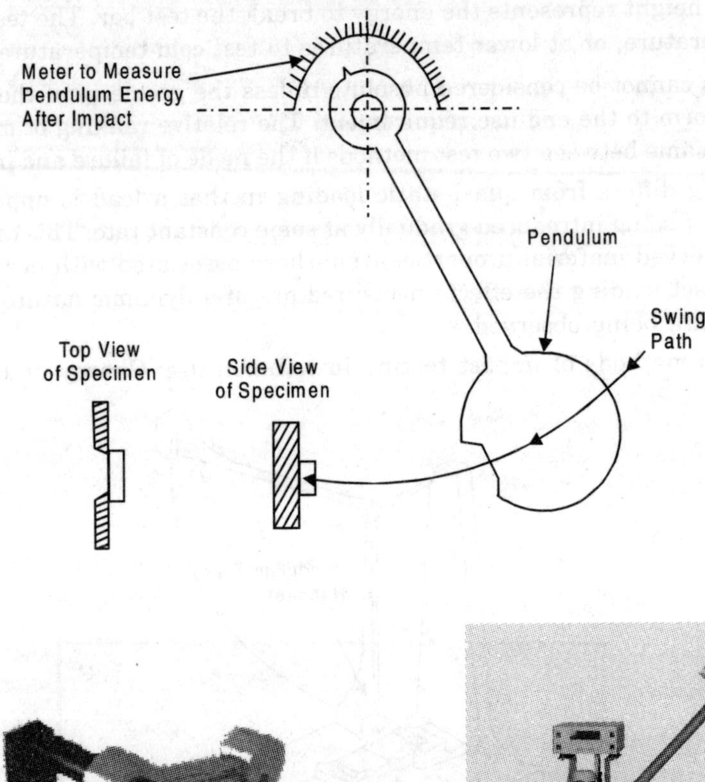

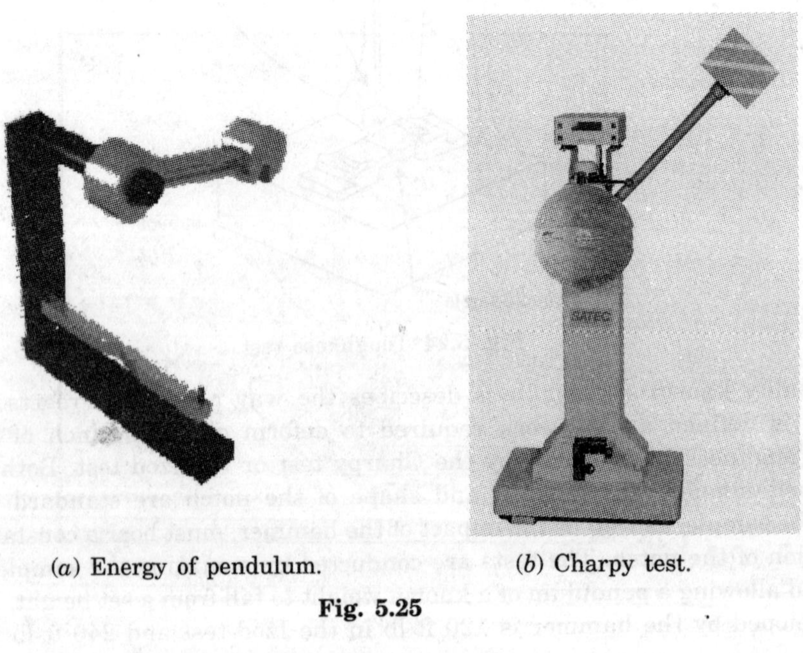

(*a*) Energy of pendulum. (*b*) Charpy test.

Fig. 5.25

The test method generally utilized in the USA is ASTM D256. The result of the Izod test is reported in energy lost per unit of specimen thickness (such as ft-lb/in or J/cm) at the notch ('t' in graphic at right). Additionally, the results may be reported as energy lost per unit cross-sectional area at the notch (J/m^2 or ft-lb/in^2). In Europe, ISO 180 methods are used and results reported based only on the cross-sectional area at the notch (J/m^2).

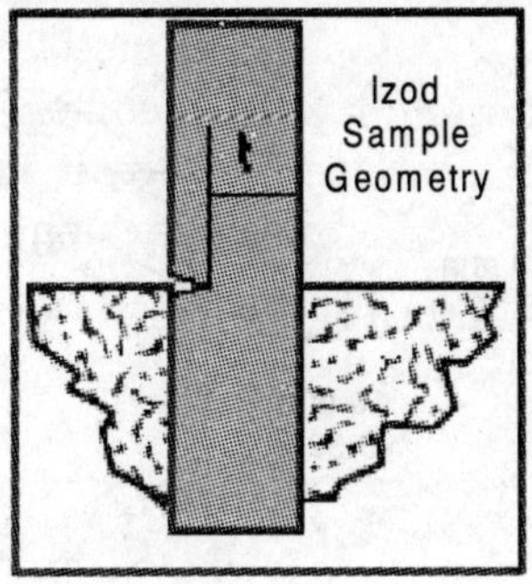

Fig. 5.26 Izod test.

A pendulum swings on its track and strikes a notched, cantelevered plastic sample. The energy lost (required to break the sample) as the pedulum continues on its path is measured from the distance of its follow through. Sample thickness is usually 1/8 in. (3.2 mm) but may be up to 1/2 in. (12.3 mm)

Materials that are sensitive to the stress concentrations at the notch ('notch-sensitive') will perform poorly in the notched izod test. Engineers use this knowledge to avoid designs with high stress concentrations such as sharp corners or cutouts. Unnotched specimens are also frequently tested via the Izod impact method to give a more complete understanding of impact resistance.

Izod impact tests are commonly run at low temperatures–down to – 40°F (– 40°C) or occasionally lower-to help gauge the impact resistance of plastics used in cold environments.

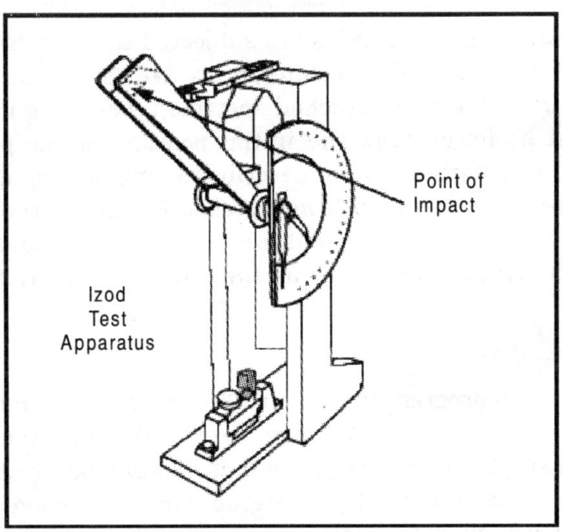

Fig. 5.27 Izod apparatus.

The impact resistance of a given grade of polymer is a function of the base resin plus the presence of any impact modifiers (such as elastomers) and reinforcing agents that may be added by the manufacturer/compounder. Environmental factors, in additional to temperature, also play a role in impact resistance. For example, nylons (polyamides) generally experience higher impact strength in the conditioned state (in equilibrium with atmospheric moisture) than in a dry-as-molded state.

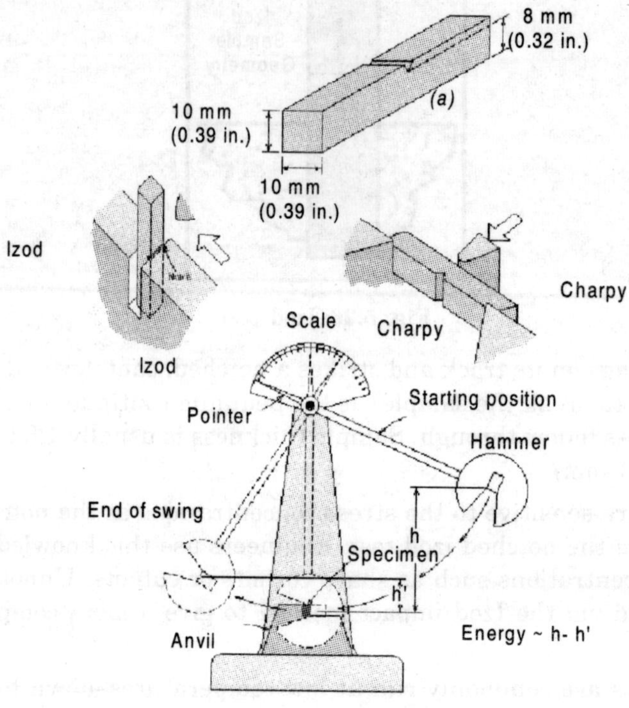

Fig. 5.28 Impact test.

The Notched Bar test, where specimens are subjected to axial, bending or torsion loads using specialized testing machines. The technique involves swinging a weight of W from a certain specified height h to strike the notched specimen, breaking it as it passes through, and arriving at a height h', lower than the initial position of the pendulum. The energy expended in rupturing the specimen can be described using the equation U = W(h-h'). The other testing method uses specimens with no notches for the purpose of obtaining either stress–strain diagrams of material specimens under loads or load-distortion diagrams of structural members or composite structures as they are completely fractured in testing.

5.9 FATIGUE TEST

Fatigue can be defined as progressive fracture. It can occur when a material is subjected to a repeated or cyclic stress, such as a vibration (*see* Oscillation). Even when the maximum stress is less than the elastic limit, failure of the material can occur after even a short time. With some metals, such as titanium alloys, fatigue can be avoided by keeping the cyclic stress below a threshold level. No deformation is apparent during fatigue, but small-localized cracks develop and propagate in the material until a crack exceeds a critical length. Factor of safety, in engineering, the ratio of the calculated strength of a member or piece of material to the predicted structural demand that will be made upon it when the member is part of the structure. For example, if a structural member is six times as strong as is necessary to withstand the greatest computed stress that the member will incur as part of the structure, the factor of safety is 6. Factors of safety of 1.5 to 8 are common in civil engineering; however, where reduction in weight is of great importance, factors as low as 1 may be used in experimental designs, with additional strength added where tests show the necessity for it. In computing the factor, engineers make allowance for defects and variations in materials, repeated reversals of and abnormal increases in stress, and differences in opinion in the evaluation of the strength of materials. It will be described briefly later.

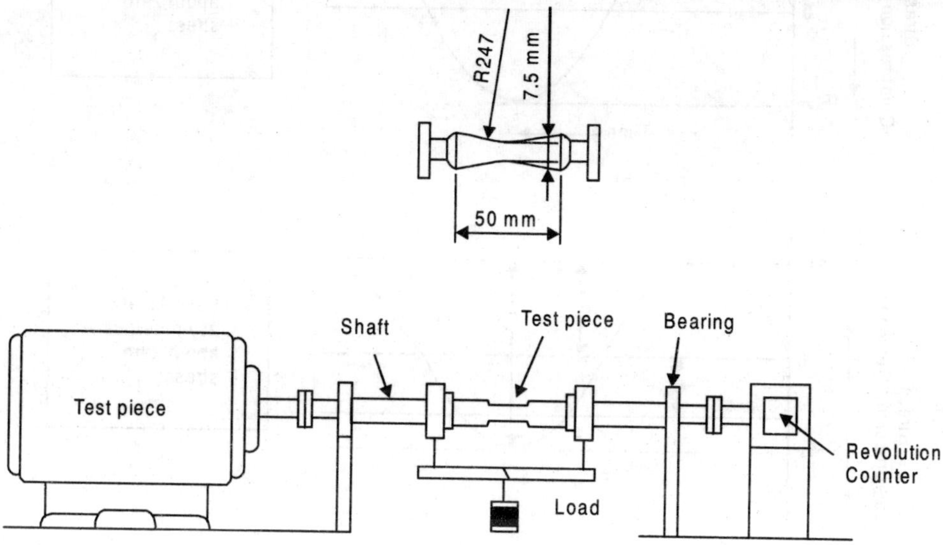

Fig. 5.29 Fatigue test.

Failure under Fluctuating/Cyclic Stresses

Under fluctuating / cyclic stresses, failure can occur at loads considerably lower than tensile or yield strengths of material under a static load: Fatigue estimated to causes 90% of all failures of metallic structures (bridges, aircraft, machine components, etc.)

Fatigue failure is brittle-like (relatively little plastic deformation)—even in normally ductile materials. Thus sudden and catastrophic!

Applied stresses causing fatigue may be axial (tension or compression), flexural (bending) or torsional (twisting).Fatigue failure proceeds in three distinct stages:

- ❖ Crack initiation in the areas of stress concentration (near stress raisers)
- ❖ Incremental crack propagation
- ❖ Final catastrophic failure.

Fatigue: Cyclic Stresses (II)

Cyclic stresses are characterized by maximum, minimum and mean stress, the range of stress, the stress amplitude, and the stress ratio

Mean Stress $\sigma_m = (\sigma_{max} + \sigma_{min})/2$

Range of Stress, $\sigma_r = (\sigma_{max} - \sigma_{min})/2$

Stress Amplitude: $\sigma_a = \sigma_r/2$

Stress Ratio, R= $\sigma_{min}/\sigma_{max}$

Remember the convention that tensile stresscs are positive,compressive stresses are negative.

Fatigue: Cyclic Stresses (I)

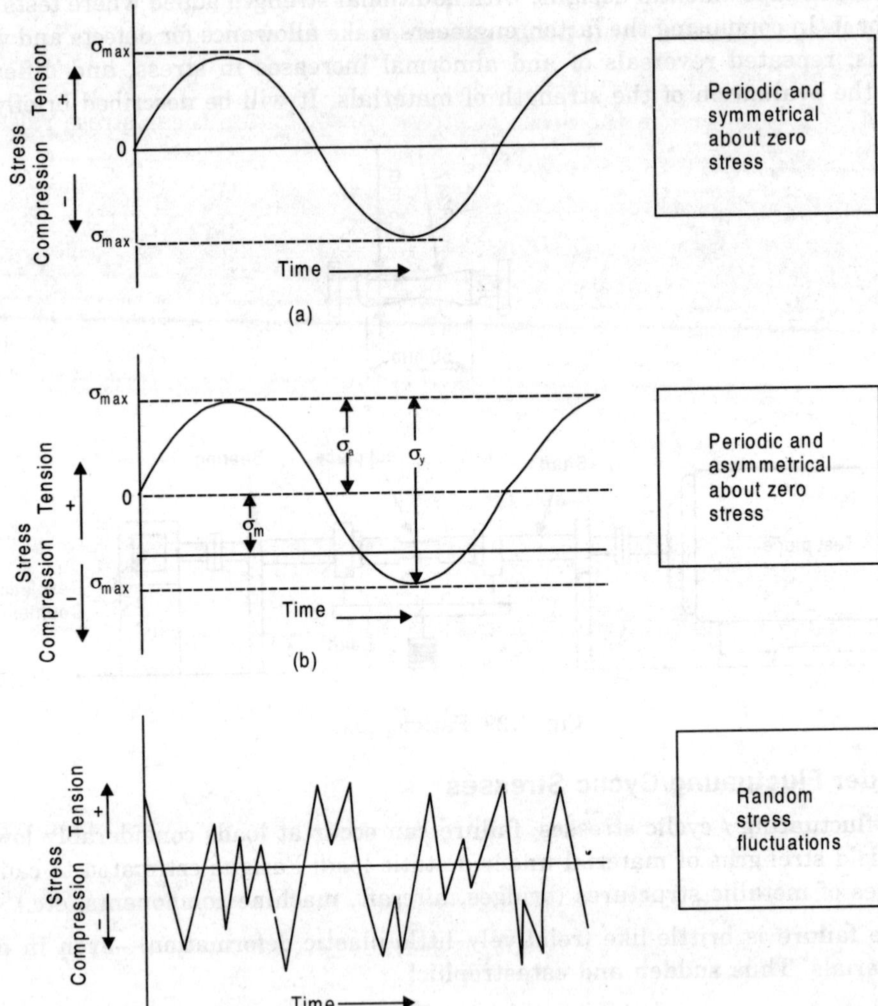

Fig. 5.30 Fatigue cyclic stress.

Fatigue: S-N curves (I) (stress-number of cycles to failure)

Fatigue properties of a material (S-N curves) are tested in rotating-bending tests in fatigue testing apparatus:(Result is commonly plotted as S (stress) vs. N (number of cycles to failure).

1. Low cycle fatigue: high loads, plastic and elastic deformation.
2. High cycle fatigue: low loads, elastic deformation (N >10^5).
3. Fatigue limit (endurance limit) occurs for some materials.
4. Some Fe and Ti alloys. In this case, the S-N curve becomes horizontal at large N.

5. The fatigue limit is a maximum stress amplitude below which the material never fails, no matter how large the number of cycles.
6. In most alloys, S decreases continuously with N. In these cases the fatigue properties are described by fatigue strength: stress at which fracture occurs after specified number of cycles (e.g. 107) Fatigue life: Number of cycles to fail at specified stress level.

Fatigue: Crack initiation and propagation (I)

Three stages of fatigue failure:

1. Crack initiation in the areas of stress concentration (near stress raisers)
2. Incremental crack propagation
3. Final rapid crack propagation after crack reaches critical size.

The total number of cycles to failure is the sum of cycles at the first and the second stages:

$$N_f = N_i + N_p$$

Where,

N_f : Number of cycles to failure

N_i : Number of cycles for crack initiation

N_p : Number of cycles for crack propagation

High cycle fatigue (low loads): N_i is relatively high. With increasing stress level, N_i decreases and N_p dominates.

Fatigue: Crack initiation and propagation (II)

Crack initiation at the sites of stress concentration (micro cracks, scratches, indents, interior corners, dislocation slip steps, etc.). Quality of surface is important.

Crack propagation

Stage I: Initial slow

Propagation along crystal planes with high resolved shear stress. Involves just a few grains, and has flat fracture surface.

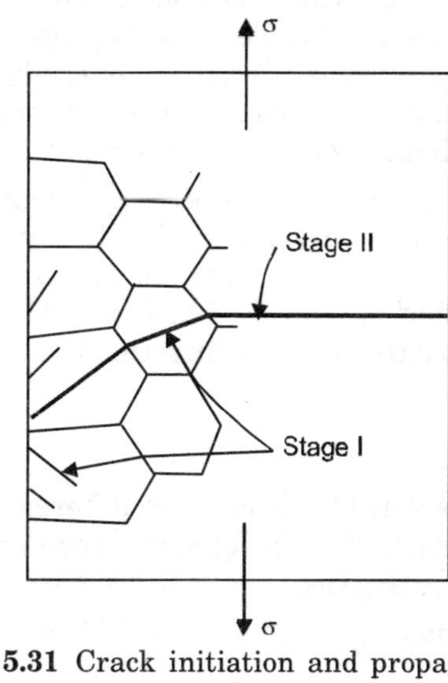

Fig. 5.31 Crack initiation and propagation.

Stage II: Faster propagation perpendicular to the applied stress. Crack grows by repetitive blunting and sharpening process at crack tip. Rough fracture surface. Crack eventually reaches critical dimension and propagates very rapidly.

Factors that affect fatigue life

- Magnitude of stress (mean, amplitude...)
- Quality of the surface (scratches, sharp transitions and edges).
- Environmental effects
- Thermal fatigue. Thermal cycling causes expansion and contraction, hence thermal stress, if component is restrained.

Solutions

1. Polishing (removes machining flaws etc.)
2. Introducing compressive stresses (compensate for applied tensile stresses) into thin surface layer by "Shot Peening"- firing small shot into surface to be treated
3. High-tech solution-ion implantation, laser peening
4. Case Hardening-create C-or N-rich outer layer in steels by atomic diffusion from the surface. Makes harder outer layer and also introduces compressive stresses
5. Optimizing geometry-avoid internal corners, notches etc.
6. Eliminate restraint by design
7. Use materials with low thermal expansion coefficients
8. Decrease corrosiveness of medium, if possible add protective surface coating
9. Add residual compressive stresses.

5.10 CREEP

Creep is the slow change in the dimensions of a material due to prolonged stress; most common metals exhibit creep behavior. In the creep test, loads below those necessary to cause instantaneous fracture are applied to the material, and the deformation over a period of time (creep strain) under constant load is measured, usually with an extensometer or strain gauge. In the same test, time to failure is also measured against level of stress; the resulting curve is called stress rupture or creep rupture. Once creep strain versus time is plotted, a variety of mathematical techniques is available for extrapolating creep behavior of materials beyond the test times so that designers can utilize thousand-hour test data, like predicting ten-thousand-hour behavior. For example, steel cables used to support suspension bridges; otherwise the bridge would gradually sag with time. Creep is generally more of a problem at higher temperatures. Advances in jet engines for airplanes have been made possible by the development of super alloys that have extraordinary resistance to creep at high stresses and temperatures.

A material that yields continually under stress and then returns to its original shape when the stress is released is said to be viscoelastic; this type of response is measured by the stress-relaxation test. A prescribed displacement or strain is induced in the specimen and the load drop-off as a function of time is measured. Various viscoelastic theories are available that permit the translation of stress-relaxation test data into predictions about the creep behavior of the material.

Mechanisms of Creep

Different mechanisms are responsible for creep in different materials and under different loading and temperature conditions. The mechanisms include :

- Stress-assisted vacancy diffusion
- Grain boundary diffusion

- ❖ Grain boundary sliding
- ❖ Dislocation motion
- ❖ Different mechanisms result in different values of n, Qc.

Creep Importance

Some machine components are subjected to stresses during lengthy periods of time. For example, rotary components of jet engines such as blades and disks, experience stresses due to centrifugal force. In addition, the hot combustion gases that flow through a jet engine cause the temperature to be very high. In fact, in some cases it may reach levels as high as 80% of the melting temperature of the materials the engine components are made of. The data from creep tests on many different materials, which are collected in databases, along with the exact knowledge of the service stress and temperature conditions help designers in the choice of the suitable material for a given component and in the prediction of its lifetime under those conditions.

Under what circumstances does creep occur?

In order for creep to happen, two main conditions must be fulfilled:

1. the material must be subjected to some stress,
2. the temperature must be sufficiently high.

In fact, the movement of dislocations and the diffusion of vacancies and atoms, which are responsible for creep, occur more readily as the temperature increases. Every single material has its own "low" and "high" temperature regions. The temperature is high when the effects of diffusion become appreciable. For example, 300°C is a high temperature for aluminium, but it's not for nickel-base super alloys. Usually, half of the melting temperature, taken on an absolute scale (degrees Kelvin), is considered as marking the transition between the "low" and the "high" temperature regimes.

The magnitudes of stress and temperature determine the time necessary for a specimen to achieve a certain amount of permanent creep deformation and eventually to fail.

How does the creep test setup look like?

The setup for creep and stress rupture tests is pretty simple. It consists of a frame, a furnace in which the specimen is kept at the desired temperature, and an electric motor that applies the load on the test sample by means of a spring and load bars. In older machines the stress is applied using weights. A lever system takes care of translating the applied weight into the suitable stress on the specimen. The temperature is controlled by a thermocouple that is applied directly on the specimen, whereas the load is monitored by a load cell. The specimen is fitted with an LDT (Linear Displacement Transducer) for continuous monitoring of its elongation, if required.

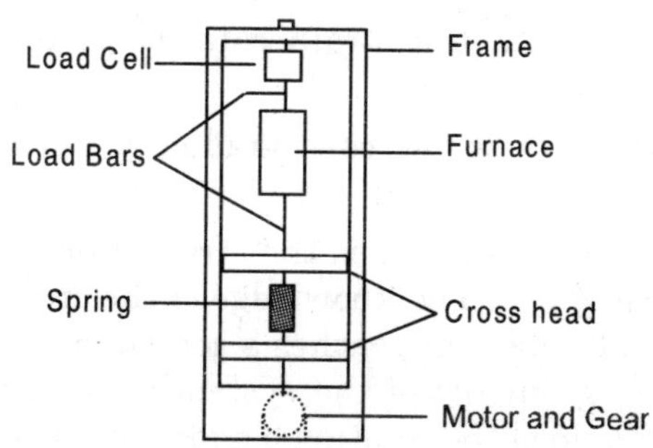

Content of the Furnace

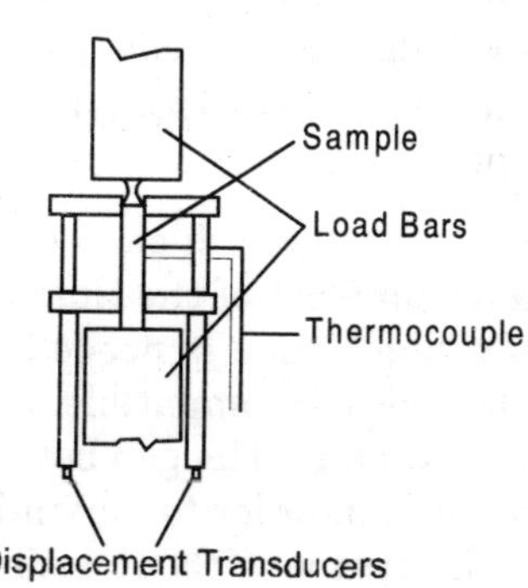

Creep test setup

How to perform a creep test?

To determine creep properties, a material is subjected to prolonged constant tension or compression loading at constant elevated temperature. Deformation is recorded at specified time intervals and a creep vs. time diagram is plotted. Slope of curve at any point is creep rate. If failure occurs, it terminates the test and the time for rupture is recorded. If specimen does not fracture within the test period, creep recovery may be measured.

What kind of tests do we carry out in order to assess the creep behavior of a material? There are two kinds of tests that are of interest to engineers. These are the creep test and the stress rupture test. Both types of tests require similar setups.

When a creep test is performed, the specimen is subjected to a given stress and temperature that are kept constant throughout the test. Its elongation is monitored continuously up to the point where it fractures. In order to be able to verify that stress and temperature do not vary during the test, they are also monitored continuously. The elongation is then plotted as a function of elapsed time.

The slope of the curve is the so-called strain rate. A creep curve usually exhibits three distinct sections:

— **section I:** where the strain rate stabilizes and hence decreases (primary or transient creep),

— **section II:** where the curve is linear, *i.e.*, the strain rate (slope of the curve)is constant and minimum (secondary or steady state creep),

— **section III:** where the strain rate starts to increase gradually until the sample fractures (tertiary creep).

The part of the curve which is of interest to designers is the straight one. Steady state creep often takes up most of the time in a creep test. The knowledge of the creep rate allows to estimate how much time is needed until a component reaches a certain deformation and, for example, becomes incompatible with the geometry of the system it is part of. The jet engine is a good example. The gap between the tip of the rotating blades and the engine casing has to be very small in order to maximize the engine efficiency in that the amount of gas that flows through the engine without acting on the blades is kept as small as possible. However, if a blade elongates too much as a result of creep, it ends up scraping against the inner wall of the casing causing serious damage. Jet engine manufacturers and users don't want this to happen! If, however, the creep rate of the material is known along with the lifetime already spent by the blades, these can be replaced before the irreparable happens.

The stress rupture test is easier to perform because it does not require a continuous monitoring of the specimen elongation. With this test one basically wants to know how long it takes for a specimen to break at a given stress and temperature.

What are the mechanisms that govern creep?

There are different mechanisms that control creep, depending on the applied stress and on the temperature at which the test is performed. These involve dislocation motion and diffusion of vacancies and interstitials.

- ❖ Dislocation glide is determined by dislocations moving conservatively along their glide planes. It occurs if the stress is high enough for the dislocations to overcome obstacles in the lattice.

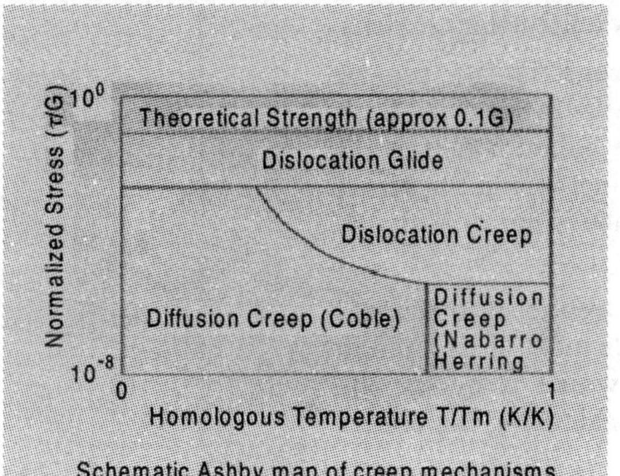

Schematic Ashby map of creep mechanisms.

- ❖ Dislocation creep is the movement of dislocations outside their glide plane and is assisted by diffusion of vacancies. It occurs only at relatively high temperatures, *i.e.*, when the influence of diffusion becomes significant.

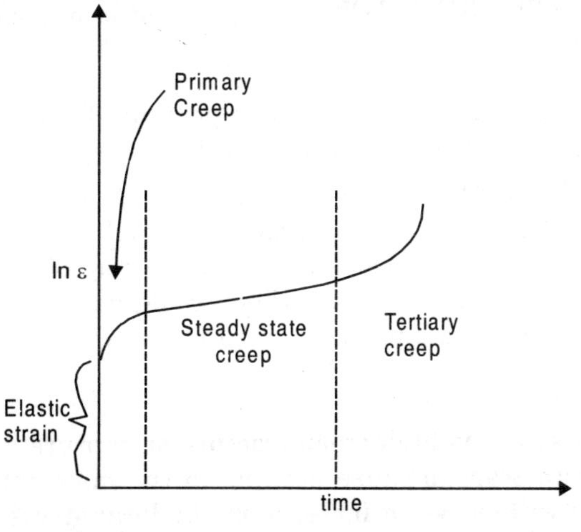

Fig. 5.32 Strain Vs. time creep behavior.

- Diffusion creep occurs at relatively low stress. The deformation of the material is due to the flow of atoms and vacancies that causes them to rearrange themselves along the direction of load. At lower temperatures the diffusion occurs mainly along easier paths, such as *e.g.,* grain boundaries (Coble creep), whereas at high temperatures, atoms and vacancies diffuse across the bulk of the material (Nabarro-Herring creep).
- Grain boundary sliding is also an important mechanism. In order to maintain continuity within the creeping material, the grains must rearrange themselves and they can do so only by sliding along each other. Moreover, grain boundary sliding is important as, in the third part of the creep experiment, it determines the onset of fracture.

There are plots, whose idea was developed by Ashby, from which the active mechanism at a given stress and temperature can be read. Every material has its own plot (or map).

Note: The abscissa in Fig. 5.33 has been exaggerated in the primary and tertiary regions.

As stated above creep is the plastic deformation of a material at a high homologous temperature below a material's yield stress. The effect of increasing the stress and temperature on the above curve is shown below.

As demonstrated above a material deforming by creep spends most of its time in the steady state region which is by far the dominant region when considering the effects of creep.

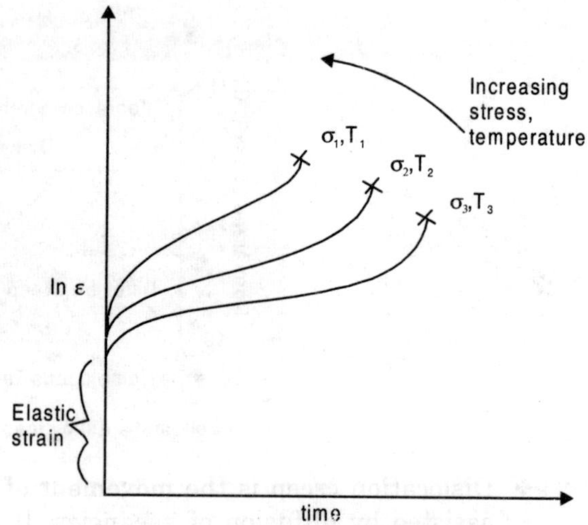

Fig. 5.33 Strain Vs. time creep behavior effect of temperature and stress.

Primary Creep

In the first region of the above graph is named the primary creep region. This region is characterized by the following equation.

$$\epsilon_{p0} = \beta . t^{1/3}$$

Primary creep strain is usually less than one percent of the sum of the elastic, steady state, and primary strains. The mechanism in the primary region is the climb of dislocations that are not pinned in the matrix.

Since the amount of initial strain of a material is due to the number of dislocations initially present, the primary region is strongly dependent on the history of the material. If the material had been heavily worked before the creep test, there would have been many more dislocations present and the characteristics of the primary creep region would have been much different.

Tertiary Creep

When the amount of strain is high creep fracture or rupture will occur. In the tertiary region the high strains will start to cause necking in the material just as in the uni-axial tensile test. This necking will cause an increase in the local stress of the component which further accelerates the strain. Eventually the material will pull apart in a ductile fracture around defects in the solid. These defects could be precipitates at high temperatures or grain boundaries at lower temperatures.

In any case the importance of the tertiary region to normal operation and creep design criteria is minimal. In the figure, the time scale of the tertiary region is greatly expanded for the purpose of clarity. Considering the small amount of time in addition to the fact that the tertiary region develops a plastic instability similar to necking, operating in the tertiary region is not feasible. Therefore it is a conservative estimate to approximate the end of serviceable life of any component to coincide with the end of the steady state creep region. Only under accident conditions may the extra time in the tertiary region may be useful to consider.

Steady State Creep

The second region of the above graph is the steady state region. This region is so named because the strain rate is constant. In this region the rate of strain hardening by dislocations is balanced by the rate of recovery.

When the homologous temperature of a creep sample is between 0.3 and 0.7 of its melting temperature, the mechanism of creep is dislocation climb. This is the climb of dislocation jogs that impede the normal motion of the dislocation. This dislocation climb mechanism can be described by the following equation.

$$\frac{\mathrm{E}_{ss}}{\mathrm{E}_e} = \mathrm{A}.\left(\frac{\sigma}{\sigma_e}\right)^m .e^{-\frac{\mathrm{H}}{k\mathrm{T}}}$$

Note: Where H is the activation energy for diffusion. A is a constant, and sigma are the applied stresses.

When higher temperatures are applied and the temperature is above 0.7 of the melting temperature, a different mechanism takes place. In this region the creep is analogous to viscous flow. In this region the mechanism of the creep is diffusion of atoms from one place to another. This type of creep can be described by:

$$\frac{\mathrm{E}_{ss}}{\mathrm{E}_e} = \frac{1}{d_e^2}\cdot\frac{\sigma}{\sigma_g}\cdot e^{-\frac{\mathrm{H}}{k\mathrm{T}}}$$

Note: Where d_g is the diameter of the grains in the material, and H' is the diffusion activation energy. The above relation indicate that as grain size increases the creep rate decreases.

Two mechanisms of diffusion creep have been proposed. One mechanism by Coble proposes that the diffusion of atoms occurs along the grain boundaries of the material. Coble proposed this process because diffusion is easier along grain boundaries. This is due to the fact that vacancies are more common in the grain boundary than in the bulk. Since more vacancies are present, atoms will have more sites to jump to during diffusion which means the activation energy for diffusion will be less in the grain boundary than in the bulk. Another mechanism proposed by Herring and Nabarro suggests that the atomic diffusion takes place in the bulk, even though the activation energy for diffusion in the bulk is higher.

At higher temperatures in the homologous temperature region of 0.7 and above the bulk diffusion model dictates the creep performance. This is due to the larger number of diffusional paths in the bulk, as compared with the relatively few paths for diffusion along the grain boundaries. So, at high homologous temperatures in the 0.7 and above range the Herring-Nabarro model dominates due to the large number of paths for diffusion.

At lower temperatures, but still above homologous temperature of 0.7, thc Coble model dominates the creep behavior. In this case the temperature is low enough that diffusion in the bulk is not activated due to its the relatively high activation energy. In the grain boundary diffusion is activated since the activation energy for diffusion along a grain boundary is lower.

In either case for these high temperature applications large grains are necessary to reduce the creep rate because they reduce the number of grain boundaries and increase the bulk diffusional distances.

Creep is a time-dependent and permanent deformation of materials when subjected to a constant load at a high temperature (> 0.4 Tm). Examples: turbine blades, steam generators.

1. Instantaneous deformation, mainly elastic.
2. Primary/transient creep. Slope of strain vs. time decreases with time: work-hardening.
3. Secondary/steady-state creep. Rate of straining is constant: balance of work-hardening and recovery.
4. Tertiary. Rapidly accelerating strain rate up to failure: formation of internal cracks, voids, grain boundary separation, necking, etc.

Failure Parameters of creep Behavior

The stage secondary/steady-state creep is of longest duration and the steady-state creep rate. It is the most important parameter of the creep behavior in long-life applications.

Another parameter, especially important in short-life creep situations, is time to rupture, or the rupture lifetime, tr.

Steady State Creep Rate

$$\varepsilon_s = \Delta\varepsilon / \Delta t$$

Stages of creep

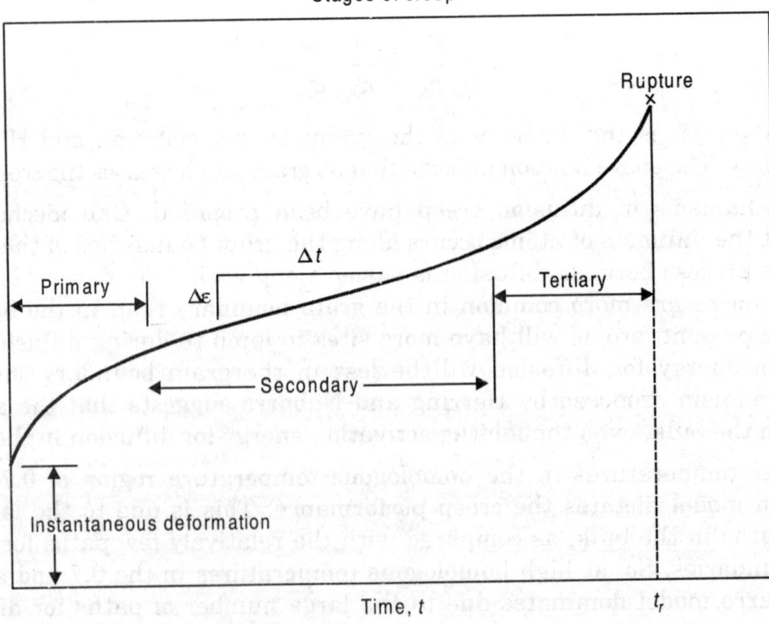

Fig. 5.34 Stages of creep.

6

CHAPTER

NON METALLIC MATERIALS

6.1 INTRODUCTION

A polymer is a large molecule comprised of repeating structural units joined by covalent bonds. Poly comes the Greek word for "many" and mer comes from the Greek word for "parts".

6.2 PHYSICAL PROPERTIES OF A POLYMER

The physical properties of a polymer material are largely determined by:

- molecular weight
- strength of intermolecular forces
- regularity of the polymer structure
- flexibility of the polymer molecule.

A list of physical properties might include:

- melting point
- boiling point
- solubility
- melt viscosity
- tensile strength.

Melting point—The melting point of a polymer does not occur over a sharp temperature range (1–2°C) as is observed for small organic molecules. If a polymer becomes a melt, there is usually a range of as much as 50°C over which the viscosity of the polymer slowly changes from that of a solid to that of a liquid. Note that for a polymer to melt, a polymer must be a thermoplastic.

Using the term "melting point" is misleading, because polymers never "melt". The term "softening point" is sometimes used. A polymer does have a glass transition temperature (Tg) and a crystalline melt temperature (Tm). The glass transition temperature refers to a point where there is a change in polymer molecular chain motion which has drastic effects on strength. Tg is sometimes called the "glass-rubber" transition. The crystalline melt temperature (Tm) is higher than Tg, and at Tm the crystalline domains of a polymer melt to become amorphous.

Tensile strength—Tensile strength measures how difficult it is to break a substance when stress is applied to pull it apart. Tensile strength generally increases with molecular weight. An instron grips a sample and pulls it apart. The instron creates a plot of where the y-axis is the force exerted between the two grips, and the x-axis is the separation distance between the two clamps. Usually, the electronics cause the Instron to increase the distance between the two clamps (pulling) at a constant rate, and the force or "strength" required is measured. This is somewhat analogous to when you were a little kid at the supermarket, and you pulled down on a scale in the produce section, and watched the scale readout increase.

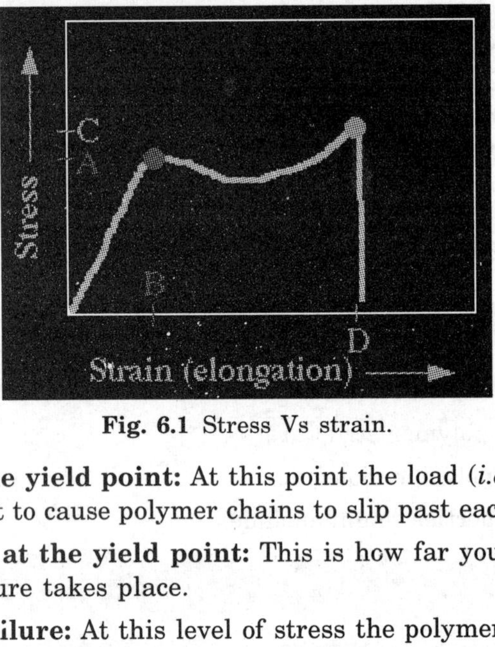

Fig. 6.1 Stress Vs strain.

- A—**Stress at the yield point:** At this point the load (*i.e.*, the force of the tensile pull) is sufficient to cause polymer chains to slip past each other, and yield occurs.
- B—**Elongation at the yield point:** This is how far you can stretch the polymer before yield failure takes place.
- C—**Stress at failure:** At this level of stress the polymer molecules can no longer maintain cohesive integrity and the sample breaks.
- D—**Elongation at failure:** This is how much the sample can stretch before failure occurs. Elongation Failure is often reported as follows: a 10 cm specimen that breaks at 15 cm is reported as a sample with 50% elongation. For this test you take a sample and clamp it with 10 cm between the two clamps, and then pull. Thus, you would need a sample with a length of 10 cm plus twice whatever length is required to go between the clamps.

Strengthening Mechanism of Polymers

Sometimes it is required to produce polymers, which are rigid and resistant to corrosive chemicals and temperature. Though there are many strengthening mechanisms of polymers, yet the followings are important from the subject point of view:

1. *Crystallisation.* This mechanism makes the polymers to attain regularity in their atomic or molecular arrangements. It depends upon the orientation of the chains.

2. *Cross-linking.* This mechanism ties the chains of molecules together by covalent bonds. It depends upon chemical reactions rather than chain orientations. The cross linking

is strongly affected by temperature, *i.e.,* it gets accelerated by the increase in temperature and is not reversible.

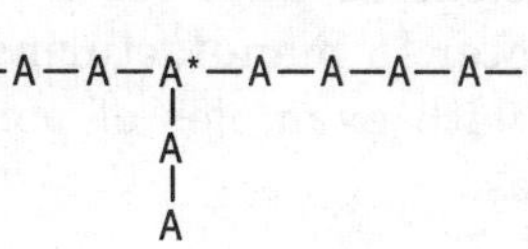

3. *Chain-stiffening.* This mechanism can be used to produce *stiffness* chains through a number of methods. One of the methods is 'hang' the bulky groups of atoms on the chain to restrict bending. Certain polymers are instrinsically stiff. In such polymers, chains cannot bend but can twist on its bonds. Similarly some monomers, which have ring shaped structure, are inherently rigid.

Shape of the Polymer

As a matter of fact, the shape of a polymer affects, to a great extent, resistance to its plastic deformation. It has been observed that the symmetrical polymers have greater resistance to the plastic deformation; it has been observed that of symmetrical polymers. It is due to the fact, that the chain molecules, in unsymmetrical polymers, are held together by greater forces of attraction than those of symmetrical polymers. Moreover, it is difficult for the chain molecules to slip over one another. For example, polyvinyl chloride polymer is an unsymmetrical polymer and the polyethylene is a symmetrical polymer. Therefore polyvinyl chloride has a greater resistance to the plastic deformation than that of polyethylene.

Degree of Polymerization

The number of repetitive units (or mers) present in one molecule of a polymer is known as degree of polymerization and is abbreviated as D.P. It has been observed that the substance, in which the value of D.P. is less than 20 are liquids at room temperature. Similarly, the substances in which the value of D.P. is less than 100 are greasy at room temperature. And the substances in which the D.P. is more than 1000 are solids at room temperature.

Temperature of Polymer

It has been observed that at very low temperature, the polymers are hard, rigid and glass like materials. They give limited elastic deformation and fracture in a brittle manner. But as the temperature of polymer is increased, above the room temperature, it gradually deforms under the applied load. Moreover, when the load is removed, it recovers back to its original shape and size, after a certain time. This type of behaviour in a polymer, is known as visco-electric behaviour. It exists below a certain temperature known as glass transition temperature. When the temperature of the polymer is further increased, it undergoes an irrecoverable plastic deformation under the applied load. But "may be noted that the polymer is still in a solid form at these temperatures", is type of behaviour exists below a certain temperature known as flow temperature or melting temperature of the polymer. Above this temperature, polymers is present in its liquid form. For example, polymers such as polyethylene, polyvinyl chloride, etc. are well above their glass transition temperature even at room temperatures.

6.3 TYPE OF POLYMER

Polymers can be classified as addition polymers or condensation polymers. This comes from a time when it was simple enough to ask "Did you break a double bond to make your polymer (addition polymerization) or did you eliminate a by-product such as water, methanol, or hydrogen chloride (condensation polymerization)". There is good reason to segregate polymers into these two classifications because the method of polymerization dictates what problems the engineer will encounter in manufacturing the product. This will be discussed in more detail further on, along with examples of polymers that fit neither classification such as epoxies and polyurethanes.

6.3.1. Condensation Polymer

A condensation polymer can be defined as a polymer in which the structural unit contains fewer atoms than the monomer or monomers from which the polymer is derived. There must be an elimination of a by-product, usually water. As an example, a polyester may be obtained from the reaction of a diol with a diacid. (Polymer chemists abbreviate "dicarboxylic acid" to "diacid").

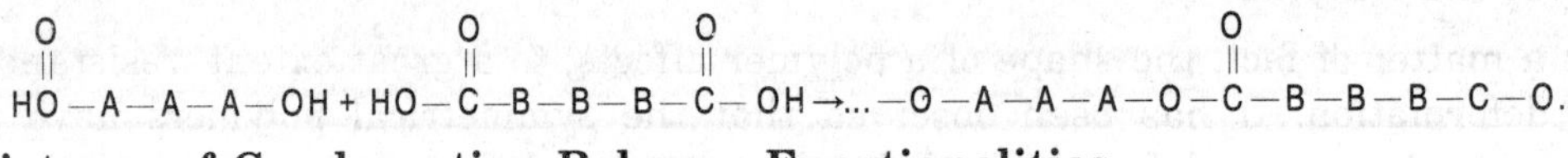

Pictures of Condensation Polymer Functionalities

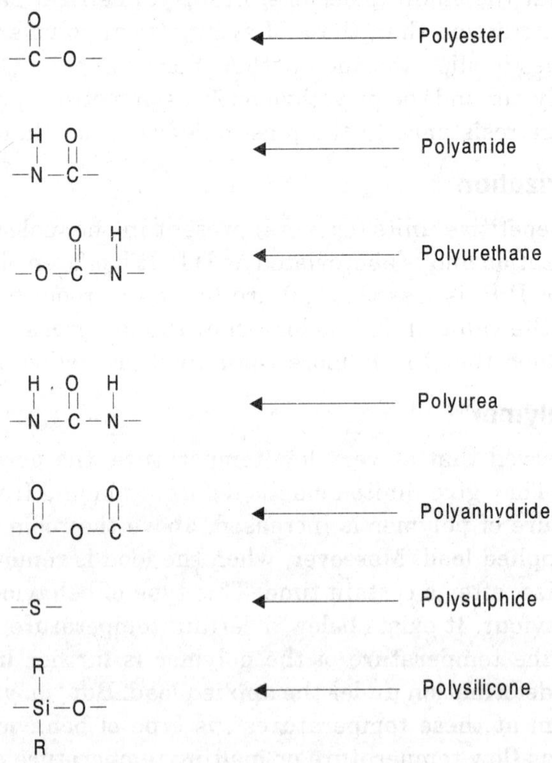

6.3.2 Chain Polymerization

1. Any two molecular species can react
2. Monomer disappears early in the reaction
3. Polymer molecular weight rise steadily throught the reaction
4. All types of molecular species are present at any stage.

6.4 POLYPROPYLENE (PP)

Polypropylene is prepared from propylene (the official IUPAC name is propene) which comes from the cracking process.

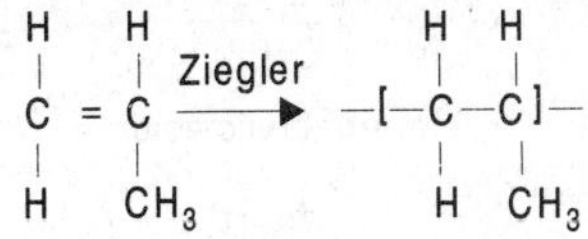

propylene poly (propylene)

Propylene is cheaper than ethylene because of its stability factor.

The free radical process is not used for the production of polypropylene from propylene because of the extensive transfer of hydrogen's to the propagating centers which results in a resonance stabilized alkyl radical which has little tendency to react with another monomer molecule.

$$R^* + CH_2{-}CH = CH_2 \rightarrow RH + [CH_2{-}CH = CH_2 \leftrightarrow CH_2 = CH{-}CH_2] \text{ or } CH_2 \ldots CH \ldots CH_2$$

Advantages of the Ziegler process include better control of the tacticity. The product isolated is mostly isotactic.

Physical Properties of Polypropylene

- The physical properties of polypropylene resemble those of high density polyethylene (HDPE).
- Increased softening point (over PE, probably—ask in class for a confirmation).
- More prone to attack by oxidizing agents on the tertiary hydrogen.
- Higher melting point (165°C) than the rest of hydrocarbon polymers.
- High degree of crystallinity.
- Solubility (or the lack thereof :) similar to PEs.
- Better weather aging (this is includes exposure to water, sunlight, and corrosive salts, etc.).

Applications include the plastic bottle industry and injection molding transportation film.

6.5 ETHYLENE PROPYLENE RUBBER (EPR)

Ethylene Propylene Rubber is prepared in the presence of Zeigler Natta catalyst system. EPR rubber can be thought of as polypropylene with pendent methyl groups missing wherever ethylene monomers were incorporated into the EPR chain.

Polyisobutylene is made from isobutylene as follows:

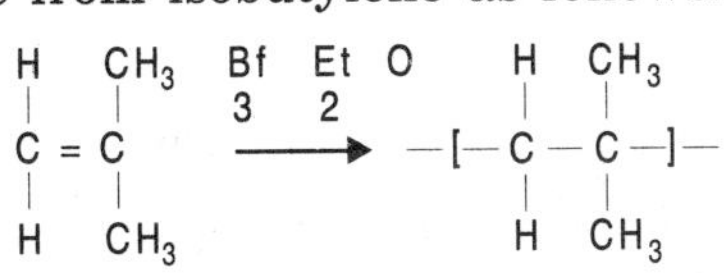

The polymerization is best carried out at temperatures from – 40°C to room temperature. This is a cationic polymerization process. It is more resistant to oxidation than EPR because there are no tertiary hydrogens. There is a cure problem, though. For curing some diene monomer such as isoprene (1–3%) is added. Cross linking can be done with sulphur.

Acrylic polymers are based on acrylic acid and its homologenes and their derivatives. The principle commercial acrylic polymers are polymerized from the following monomers:

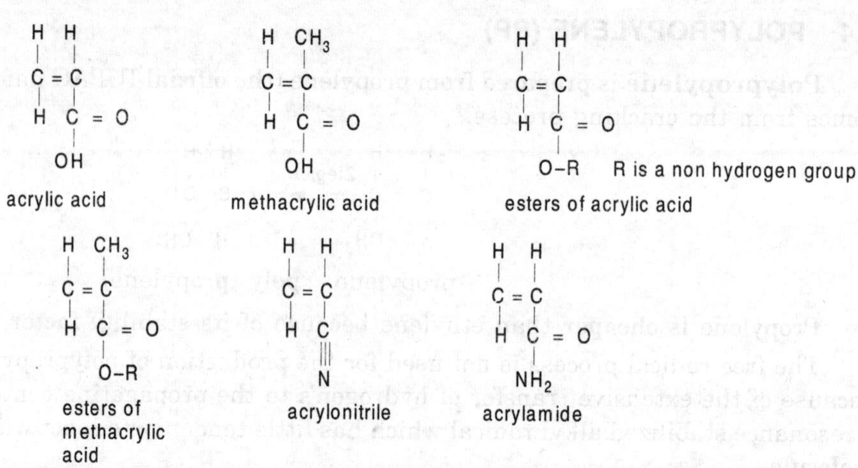

acrylic acid; methacrylic acid; esters of acrylic acid (R is a non hydrogen group); esters of methacrylic acid; acrylonitrile; acrylamide

From the above it seems to be suggested that acrylamide and acrylonitrile are in the acrylic family. The polymer encyclopedia gives separate coverage for acrylamide and acrylonitrile. Perhaps it is more appropriate to say acrylamide and acrylonitrile are similar to acrylics, than to say they are acrylics. Applications of acrylics include coatings, textiles, plastics, and plexiglass.

6.6 POLYETHYLENE TEREPHTHALATE (PET)

Polyethylene terephthalate (PET) and polybutylene terephthalate (PBT) are the most common thermoplastic polyesters. They are similar to PA6 and PA66 in many respects but with much lower water absorption. However, they are prone to hydrolysis, and prolonged contact with water at temperatures as low as 50°C has a detrimental effect on properties.

PET is used in the manufacture of biaxially oriented film and bottles, the latter suitable for carbonated drinks. The purpose of the orientation is to enhance rigidity, strength and toughness and also to improve barrier properties, which allows thinner bottles to be made.

PBT displays a good combination of stiffness and toughness and can withstand continuous service at 120°C. The most important grades are those reinforced with glass. Applications for PBT include electrical connectors, pump components, and gears, as well as under bonnet and exterior parts for cars.

Synthesis of Polyethylene Terephthalate (PET)—from ethylene glycol and terephthalic acid feedstocks.

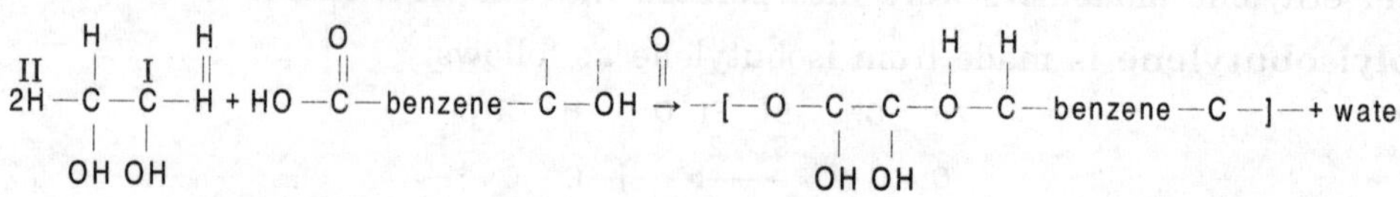

In an alternate scheme, the diacid above is replaced with the corresponding dimethyl ester:

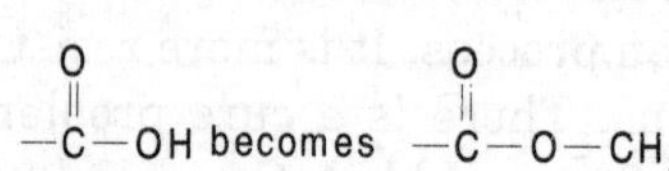

and methanol is given off instead of water.

Poly Ethylene Terephthalate (PET) or Terylene (Polyesters)

This polymer is the most notable example of a polyester which contains the ester linkage and is a condensation polymer made by elimination of water between molecules of 1,2-ethanediol (ethylene glycol—antifreeze) and terephthalic acid (benzene-1,4-dicarboxylic acid).

PET can be manufactured into a wide variety of different forms—as thin films it is the base of magnetic tape, as thicker film it is used for "boil-in-bag" food packaging, a thicker layer is used for soft-drink bottles and oven ready trays for convenience foods, and in the fibrous form it can be woven into polyester materials, e.g., Terylene, Crimplene or Dacron.

A look at the structure of PET shows that there are no hydrogen atoms attached to the oxygen atoms so there is no possibility of hydrogen bonding between polymer chains. The inter-chain attractions in polyesters are of **van der Waals** and **dipole-dipole** nature between the C=O or **carbonyl** groups. Polyester is stronger than polyethene (van der Waals only) but less strong than nylon (van der Waals + hydrogen bonds + dipole-dipole.

Properties of PET

- Colorless, rigid, easily crystallized. For fiber production, the molten polymer is extruded through spinnerets into air at room temperature. The filaments produced cool rapidly and the material is amorphous and weak. The filaments are then heated above the glass transition temperature, and molecular orientation and crystallinity are induced (via the application of a tensile stress—stretching, to use the venacular).
- The temperature is raised to 200°C and the tension applied at that temperature leads to maximum possible crystallinity allowed by thermodynamic law. This insures the best possible dimensional stability. To summarize the above: (1) extrusion, (2) orientation, (3) stabilization. Amorphous PET is transparent and has good impact strength (this helps when you drop your soda bottle). Crystalline PET is probably opaque, or at least translucent. Crystalline PET has high strength, good creep resistance, and a high surface hardness.

6.7 CHEMICAL REACTIONS OF PE

Chlorination of Polyethylene—PE may be halogenated in solution using solvents such as carbon tetrachloride, chloroform, and chloro benzene at temperatures from 45 to 75°C. There is a comment in the notes that suggests that light or peroxides are added. Up to 30% chlorine can be added. The chlorination reduces the crystallinity of PE.

Chlorosulphonated Polyethylene—PE may be chlorinated in the presence of chlorine and a small amount of sulphur dioxide to make chlorosulphonated polyethylene.

From the notes it appears that this produces polyethylene with the following functional groups:

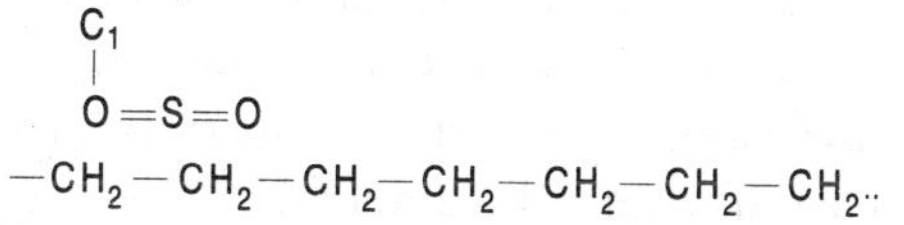

6.8 PEEK

PEEK has outstanding chemical resistance, nearly as good as fluoropolymers such as FEP/PFA/PTFE. PEEK is also an FDA approved material. PEEK is good in steam, up to 550°F, even when stainless steel has a problem in this environment. "Down hole" drilling applications are excellent for PEEK. PEEK has great impact strength. It is used in the compressor industry for poppets, seats, and valve plates. PEEK has low moisture absorption. PEEK has high temperature capability 600°F (low load). We recommend PEK for even higher temperatures. Carbon fiber PEEK has proven itself for the chemical processing industry as a bearing for butterfly valves. In the liquid chromatography market, it's purity and resistance to concentrated acetic acid makes PEEK the preferred material of construction. PEEK is inherently V-O due to oxygen index of 35% (1/8").

These semi-crystalline polymers have excellent mechanical properties, good thermal stability and good chemical resistance. Despite a Tg of 145°C, the continuous service rating of PEEK is 250°C. PEEK is inherently fire retardant. It is easier to burn a hole through an aluminium sheet than through one made from PEEK. These materials are, however, very expensive and difficult to process.

They find application in high temperature wire covering and printed circuit boards. Fibre reinforced grades are used in demanding applications that include valves, pumps and missile nose cones.

6.9 PMMA

- Hard, rigid, transparent (very clear to see through)
- Softening point at 125°C
- Tougher than polystyrene but less tough than ABS (acrylobutylstyrene) polymer
- Absorbs very little visible light but there is a 4% reflection at each polymer-air interface for normal incident light.

Strictly speaking, the term "absorbance" applies only to radiation that is trapped and then usually re-emitted at a lower frequency (heat rather than light). If you are standing on the other side of a polymer sheet, and you want light to come through the polymer so you can see what is on the other side, than the problem of reflectance must be considered. Since 4% of the light reflects back at the air/polymer interface, and then another 4% is lost at the polymer air interface, only 92% of the light makes it through (so says the notes, actually, since 4% of 96 is 3.84, and 96–3.84 = 92.16, you get 92.16% of the light, assume the 4% number is accurate to 4.00%, anyhow).

- PMMA is a polar material and has a rather high dielectric constant and power factor.
- a good electrical insulator at low frequencies but less satisfactory at higher frequencies.
- good water resistance.
- PMMA prepared by free radical polymerization is amorphous and is therefore soluble in solvents with similar solubility parameters such as benzene, toluene, chloroform, methylene chloride, esters, ethyl acetate, and amyl acetate.
- PMMA has good resistance to alkalis (sodium hydroxide, etc.), aqueous inorganic salts (the Pacific Ocean) and dilute acids.

- PMMA has a better resistance to hydrolysis than PMA probably by virtue of the shielding of the methyl group.
- PMMA's outstanding good outdoor weather resistance is marketably superior to other thermoplastics.
- when heated about 200°C, decomposition becomes appreciable and at 350–450°C, a nearly quantitative yield of monomer is readily obtained. Thus, the recovery of monomer from scrap is feasible.
- because it's a thermoplastic, it can be molten and molded (at 100 to 150°C) into anything we want.
- a syndiotactic polymer can be polymerized. At lower temperatures, the stereochemistry of the polymer can be controlled by means of the solvent.

6.10 NYLONS

Nylon 6 is a major commercial nylon.

Nylons can be prepared from:

. Reaction of a diamine with dicarboxylic acid

The self condensation of aminoacid

The ring opening polymerization of lactam

Nylons are distinguished based on the number of carbon atoms in the starting material. Note that the seven member ring structure shown below, caprolactam, has six carbon atoms:

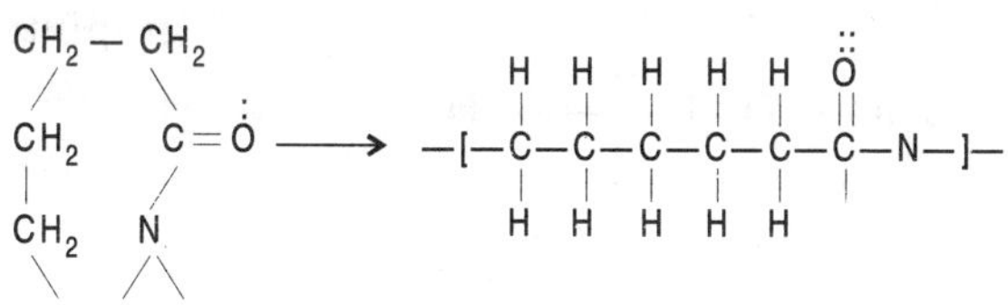

6.11 POLY VINYL ALCOHOL (PVA)

A good trick question on a test would be "Show the addition polymerization of poly vinyl alcohol". PVA is not prepared via addition polymerization because of the following keto-enol tautomerism:

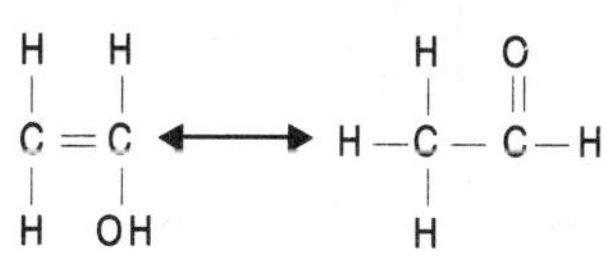

Poly vinyl alcohol is prepared by the hydrolysis of poly vinyl acetate.

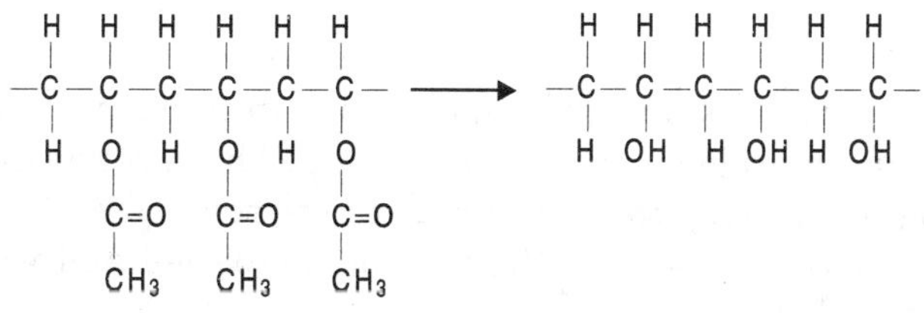

PVAc is hydrolyzed by treating an alcoholic solution of PVAc with aqueous acid or alkali. Acid hydrolysis results in traces of the acid in the polymer which are difficult to remove and which promote polymer instability. Alkali hydrolysis results in the contamination of the product by large amounts of sodium acetate which are hard to remove and have little intrinsic value. These difficulties are avoided by using small amounts of base as catalyst. From the notes, the alcoholysis of PVAc in methanol in the presens of sodium methoxide, might be an example of this. The best method involve making solution from suspension polymers.

Poly vinyl alcohol has substantial head-to-tail tacticity. The treatment of poly vinyl alcohol with HIO_4 shows

A reduced solution viscosity, which indicates a decrease in molecular weight which in turn is attributed to oxidation cleavage of the polymer chain which would only occur at head-to-head linkages, so there are some head-to-head linkages, but the calculations indicate head-to-head constitutes only 1–2%. Poly vinyl alcohol is soluble in highly polar solvents such as DMSO, DMF, and water.

6.12 POLY VINYL CHLORIDE (PVC) AND RELATED POLYMERS

Vinyl chloride is prepared from acetylene and ethylene.

Preparation of acetylene:

$$CaO + 3C \longrightarrow CaC_2 + CO$$

if CaO + 3C simply means "react calcium oxide with graphite carbon".

$$CaC + 2H_2O \longrightarrow \underset{\text{acetylene}}{H—C \equiv C—H} + Ca(OH)_2$$

or

$$2CH_4 \xrightarrow{\text{thermal cracking}} H—C \equiv C—H + 3H_2$$

Ethylene can be prepared from ethane by cracking:

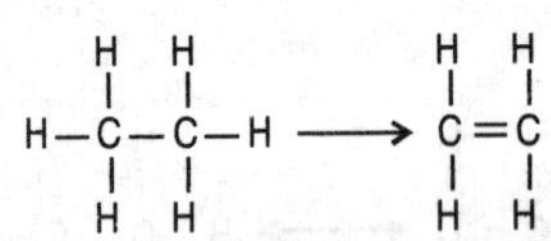

and vinyl chloride can be prepared from acetylene:

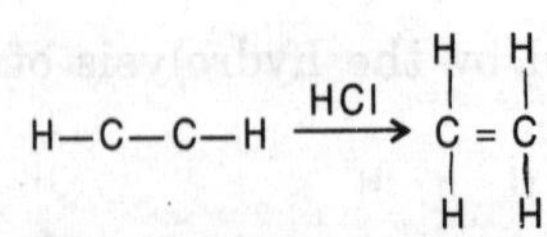

The reaction is carried out in the vapor phase in a multi-tubular reactor packed with a catalyst of mercuric chloride on activated charcoal. The reaction is highly exothermic, thus cooling must be applied to keep the temperature between 100 and 180°C. Pressures between 5 and 10 atm are used. Gas\es from the reactor are cooled and washed in aqueous NaOH to remove unreacted HCl.

The product is then liquified by cooling to –40°C and pure vinyl chloride is obtained by fractional distillation. Vinyl chioride is colorless, with a boiling point of –14°C, a pleasant sweet odor, and it does not need an inhibitor for storage.

Caution!—vinyl chloride is a possible carcinogen, and it is toxic.Preparation of vinyl chloride from ethylene:

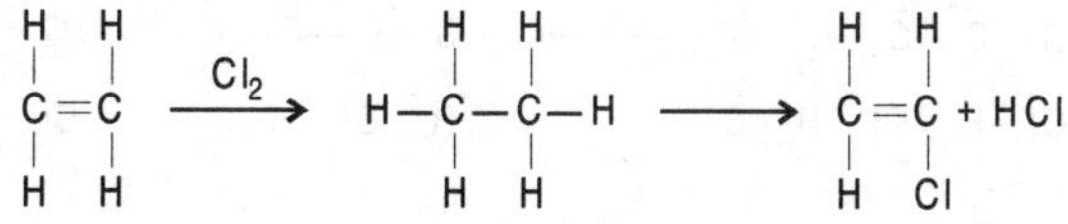

ethylene 1,2-dichloroethane chloroethene

In the above, the gases of ethylene and chloride are allowed to react in a solvent. A metal catalyst, ferric chloride, is used, and the reaction temperature is kept down to avoid formation of highly chlorinated compounds.

The 1,2-dichloroethane is dehydrochlorinated by passing it at 500°C and at 3 atm pressure over a catalyst of Kaolin. The gases are quenched in a stream of unreacted 1,2-dichloroethane (the notes use the name ethylene dichloride), and gases which do not condense are scrubbed with water to recover HCl. Vinyl chloride is obtained from the liquid mixture by distillation at 5 atm pressure and purified by redistillation. Preparation of vinyl chloride from ethylene is more expensive and the engineer must worry about the recovery of HCl.

The preparation of poly vinyl chloride is mainly done by suspension polymerization, carried out batchwise in a stirred reactor, jacketed for heating and cooling. The reaction is run at 50 to 100°C and the pressure must be 100 psi. Once the reaction is completed, the pressure is essentially gone (*i.e.*, the monomer is all polymerized).

This reaction requires monomer, water, surfactant, and stirring of the initiator. The shape of the polymer particles depends on the suspending agent used. The syndiotacticity of PVC may be increased by polymerizing below –40°C, using highly active. In (indium) and the result is a more brittle product. Atactic PVC has better qualities for Commercial applications.

Properties of Poly Vinyl Chloride

- *PVC is colorless and rigid.*
- *PVC has a high P and low S point (huh?).*
- *PVC has a higher D and power factor than polyethylene.*
- *The high chlorine content of PVC renders it flame retarding.*
- *The glass transition temperature of 50–60°C precludes the use of PVC for hot water pipes (the hot water would take the polymer into the rubbery transition and over time there could be dimensional distortion.*

PVC is soluble in proton acceptor solvents such as THF, esters, and MEK

- *PVC is unaffected by mild acids, basic materials and water.*
- *Exposure to temperatures above 70°C and exposure to UV light.*
- *Have adverse effects on its properties.*
- *PVC is attacked by strong oxdizing agents.*

PVC can be plasticized with DSP aryl phosphates (tritolyl phosphate), esters of aliphatic aciesd (dibuytlsebocate), epoxidized oil (soybean oil), 40–60 parts of plasticizer per 100 parts of polymer. Unplasticized PVC is outstanding for its anti-corrosion ability.

Exposure to UV light or heat leads to degradation vi dehydrochlorination or oxidation.

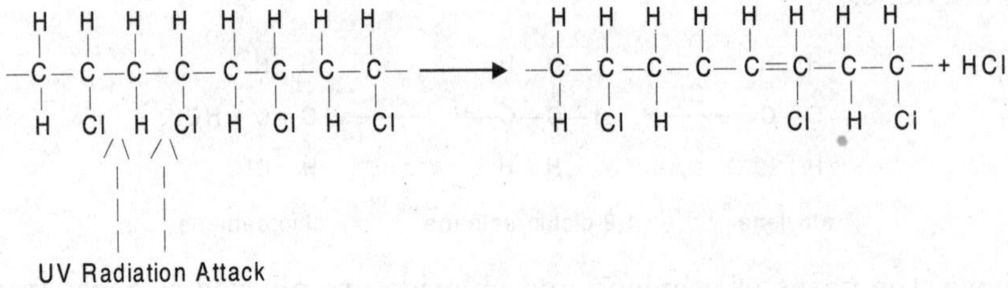

Dehydrochlorination can occur until all chlorine atoms are gone. The above reaction leads to a yellowing of the plastic.

A Stabilizing agent is added to interfere with the degradation process.

Low temperature chlorination of PVC—If PVC is chlorinated, via exposure to chlorine gas in a 50°C chloroform solution, and illumination.

(UV I guess, possibly just visible—I need to look this up), then chlorines attack hydrogens on the methylene groups [methylene is–CH_2–].

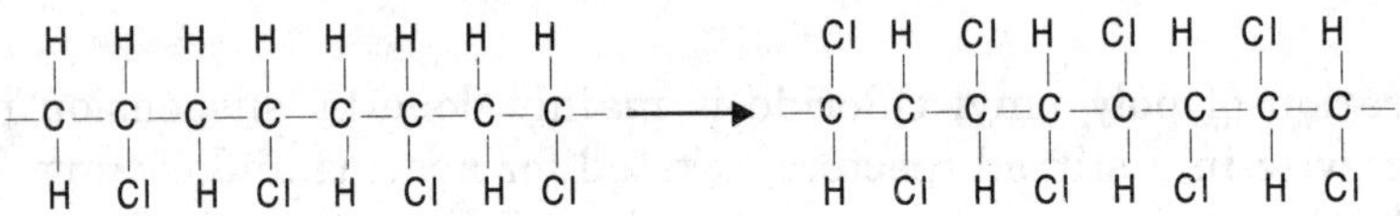

High Temperature Chlorination of PVC

- Conducted in solution at 100°C
- Substitution occurs extensively at the

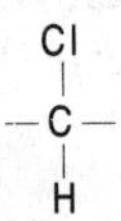

- Group and chain scission also occurs
- Soluble in low cost solvents such as acetone, butylacetate, and methylene chloride
- Useful for adhesives, protective coatings, spinning fibres, and chemical filter cloth
- Low softening point, low impact strength
- Poor color stability.

Vinylidene chloride copolymers (5–12% vinylidene chloride)—The properties are similar to the poly vinyl chloride-co-vinyl acetate copolymer. Poly vinyl choride-co-vinylidene chloride is used for calendering applications and filler polymer in rigisols.

Acrylonitrile copolymer (60% VC and 40% AN)—Used for nonflammable fibres, and industrial garments.

Olefin copolymers (3–10% ethylene or propylene)—Used for blow-moulded bottles.

Vinylidene chloride production

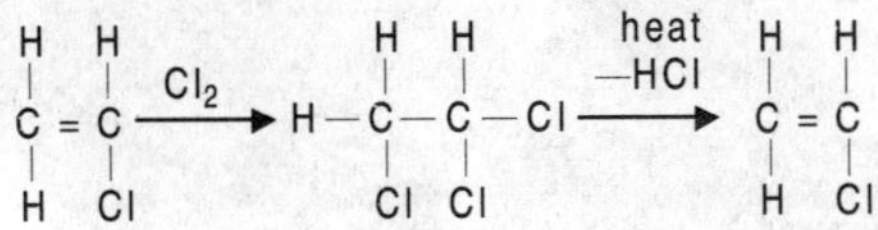

The liquid phase chlorination of vinyl chloride at 30 to 50°C under pressure (the first arrow reaction shown above—the second arrow reaction probably requires heat).

or

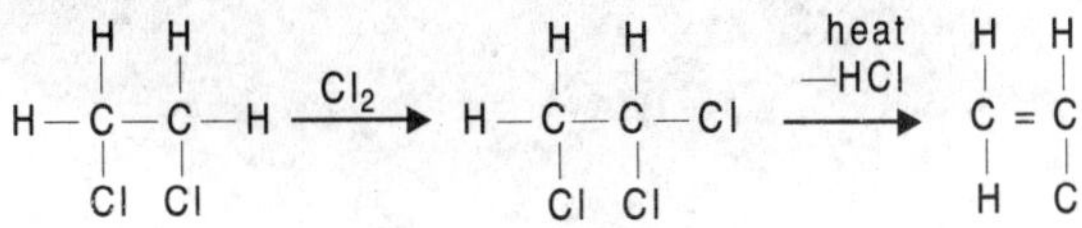

The liquid phase chlorination of ethylene dichloride (the second arrow reaction probably requires heat).

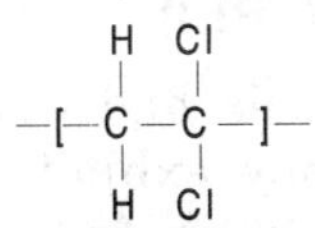

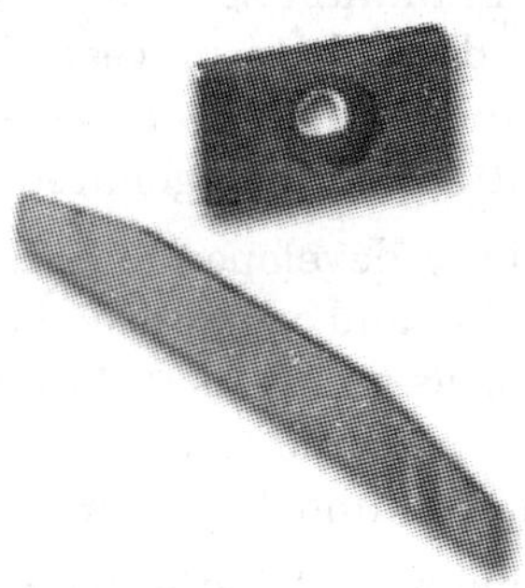

Fig. 6.2 PVC.

Applications include filaments, car upholstery, garden chair fabrics, toughness, chemical resistance, and packing films. The main uses of poly vinylidene chloride-co-acrylonitrile copolymers include coatings for materials such as cellophane, paper, and polyethylene.

6.13 PI-POLYIMIDE

Aurum, originally developed by NASA, is a relatively new member of the high performance plastics family. Aurum is the finest injection moldable, bearing material available in the general market today. Aurum has 600°F capabilities, and high load/low friction properties not duplicated with other injection moldable materials. Aurum has high viscosity and requires higher performance injection molding machines to mold it properly. The best properties are achieved by processing at elevated melt and mold temperatures.

6.14 PAI-POLYAMIDIMIDE

Torlon is an early member of the high performance plastics family. Torlon® is a high strength, high temperature (500 degrees F max) polymer that is injection, and oven "cured"

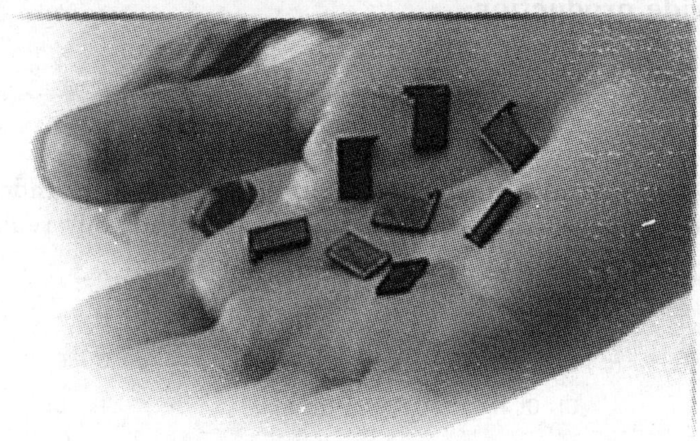

Fig. 6.3 PAI.

Thermoplastic Polyimides (PI, PAI, PEI)

Polyimides (PI) are noted for their high temperature performance, retaining their mechanical properties to 250°C. They exhibit low flammability and smoke emission characteristics and offer the lowest minimum service temperature of thermoplastics. They are relatively expensive and can be difficult to process. Thermoplastic polyimide requires high temperatures and pressures and is usually processed by autoclave or compression moulding. They are susceptible to attack by halogenated solvents.

Polyamideimide (PAI) was initially developed as a high temperature enamel but was later modified for processing by injection and compression techniques. No other commercially available unreinforced thermoplastic is as strong as PAI over its operating range. Applications include valves, bearings, gears, electrical connectors and jet engine parts. If wear resistance is important, grades filled with graphite and PTFE are available.

Polyetherimides (PEI) are amorphous, high performance thermoplastics with a continuous use temperature of around 170°C. PEI resins can also be melt processed using typical equipment for high volume production. The strength, creep and impact properties of PEIs make them ideal for under bonnet components. They are also used in high temperature switchgear and electrical connectors. A number of medical equipment components are manufactured using PEIs, taking advantage of their excellent resistance to repeated sterilisation using steam, autoclave, gamma radiation or ethylene oxide. Microwave cookware is another application.

6.15 PPS-POLYPHENYLENE SULPHIDE

PPS, polyphenylene sulphide (Ryton by Chevron Phillips Chemical Company, Fortron® by Ticona) is the oldest material in the high performance, injection-moldable category.

Non-filled grades are used exclusively as coatings. With the addition of glass and carbon fibers, minerals, and PTFE fillers, PPS becomes a very suitable molding material. Initially, PPS was promoted as a replacement for thermosetting materials. While no known solvents attack PPS, strong reducing agents will attack the material, and high temperature water will act as a solvent on the binder which bonds glass-fiber to the polymer (some grades).

Fig. 6.4 PPS.

PPS is generally used in applications where high temperature and chemical resistance are required. A continuous use temperature of 428°F and short term properties at 500°F allow PPS to be used in automotive, electronic (solderability), and may OEM applications.

6.16 COMPOSITE MATERIALS

Materials comprising two or more different materials bonded together having combined properties of constituents are called composites.

6.16.1 Agglomerated Materials

The materials, in which the particles are condensed together to form an integral **mass,** are known as agglomerated materials. A common example of agglomerated materials is cement concrete, which is formed by mixing coarse aggregate, fine aggregate, cement and water in different proportions. Other useful agglomerated material is grinding wheel (abrasive material) which is formed by mixing asphalt, stone and resin of different sizes. Some other useful agglomerated materials are cemented carbide tools and ceramics. The cemented carbide tools are manufactured by agglomerating small particles of hard tungsten carbide with alloys of cobalt and nickel. These alloys act as a binder between the tungsten carbide particles. Combining a ceramic material and metal through various processes produces the cermets. In this process, the mixture of ceramic material and metal is taken in the form of powder, which is mixed, pressed and finally sintered to produce a composite material. In cermets, the metal provides high toughness and thermal shock resistance. The ceramic materials provide high refractoriness and creep resistance. They have high abrasion resistance, excellent chemical stability and machinability etc.

Important Terms in Agglomerated Materials

Following are the important terms, which are frequently used in the study of agglomerated materials:

1. Particle size 2. Packing factor 3. Density and porosity.

Particle Size

It has been observed that most of the particles used in agglomerated materials are not perfect spheres. As a result of this, it is, usually, difficult to measure the exact particle size of an agglomerated material. In most of the cases, the variation in spherical shape is quite common. In order to have the particle size of the various constituent materials, the particles are made. To pass through standard size screens, which have a fixed number of openings per square centimeter.

It may be noted from the practical point of view that it is not sufficient to depend upon the average size of an aggregate, as the aggregate mixture will be composed of a varying range of screen sizes.

Packing Factor

The term 'packing factor' may be defined as the ratio of true volume of the total constituent materials to the bulk volume of the agglomerate materials. It has been observed that whenever uniformity sized material packed into a large mass, a considerable amount of porosity exists with in the body, whose value depends upon the size and shape of the material. Mathematically packing factor,

$$\text{P.F} = \text{True Value/Bulk Volume}$$

Where true volume is the total volume actually occupied by all the particles **and the bulk volume is the total** volume of the agglomerated material.

It will be interesting to know that, from practical point of view, it is always desirable to increase the packing factor of an agglomerated material. It is achieved by the following two ways:

1. By using the non-spherical particles with matching surfaces.
2. By mixing particles of different sizes.

Density and Porosity

We have already discussed in the last article that a considerable lot of porosity exists within the body of an agglomerated material. It has been observed that this porosity is due to open or closed pores. It will be interesting to know that the open pores are the vacant spaces, between the packed particles, which are interconnected with one another :

$$\textbf{True Density} = \textbf{Mass /True Volume}$$

$$\textbf{Bulk Density} = \textbf{Mass/Bulk Volume}$$

Though there are a number of agglomerated materials these days, yet the following are important from the subject point of view:

1. Cements **2. Cement concrete.**

Cements

The cement is one of the agglomerated materials, which is one of the most commonly used material of construction work these days. It is manufactured by a partial fusion of a mixture containing clay, limestone and oxides of silicon, aluminum, iron and often magnesium. This mixture is heated to a temperature of about 1450°C. At this temperature, the material sinters and partially fuses into bails known as clinkers. The clinkers are then cooled and grounded into a very fine powder and some gypsum is also added to it. The resulting product is cement, commonly known as portland cement. The main constituents of cement are tricalcium silicate (C_3S), dicalcium silicate (C_2S), tricalcium aluminate (C_3A) and tetra allumino-ferrite (C_4Af).

Setting and Hardening of Cement

We know that water is always added to the cement, before it is used in the construction work. It has been observed that the water reacts chemically with the surface of cement grains and produces a gelatinous material called 'gel'. It serves as a cementing material between the grains. With the passage of time, hardening of this material takes place due to loss of water.

$$C_3A + \longrightarrow C_3A.6H_2O$$

All the above-mentioned reactions are known as exothermic as they liberate energy in the form of heat. This heat is known as heat of hydration. The rate at which the setting and hardening takes place, depends upon the amount of heat of hydration. It has been observed that the tricalcium silicate (C_3A) requires about 30 days to attain 70 per cent of its ultimate strength.

Cement Concrete

It is a mixture of cement, sand, brick ballast or stone ballast and water in different proportions. On hardening, the mixture forms a stone like material known as cement concrete. It has been observed that the cement and water form a paste, which binds the aggregates to a permanent mass after hardening. The sand, which is usually known as fine aggregate, is required to fill the voids present between the ballast. The brick or stone ballast is commonly known as coarse aggregate.

The purpose for the addition of water, to the mixture, is to produce hydrates and make it more workable. The strength of cement concrete depends upon the water-cement ratio. It has been observed that if the water-cement ratio is too low, the trapped air in the mixture cannot be removed. This produces porosity in the concrete mixture, which decreases its strength. On the otner hand, if the water-cement ratio is too high, the bonding in the mixture is imperfect. Thus optimum water-cement ratio is required to produce optimum strength. Sometimes, some chemicals are also added to the cement concrete to reduce porosity at the optimum water-cement ratio and to avoid failure of the structure.

It will be interesting to know that the cement concrete produces excellent resistance to compressive stress, shear stress and abrasion. The limitations of cement concrete are low tensile strength shrinkage and expansion etc. The above limitations are removed by laying the cement concrete with steel to form reinforced cement concrete.

Composites are materials consisting of fillers in the form of inorganic, organic fibre or powder as well as metallic powders of relatively high strength and modulus embedded in or bonded to a matrix with distinct interface (boundaries) between them. Most usual fillers are fibres. Both fillers and matrix retain their physical and chemical identities, in that they produce a combination of properties that cannot be achieved with either of the constituent acting alone.

Most widely used composites are Fibre Reinforced Plastics (FRP). In general, fibres are the principal load-carrying members, while the surrounding matrix keeps them in the desired location and orientation, acts as a load transfer medium between them and protects environmental damage due to exposure to elevated temperature and humidity, for example. But even though fibres provide reinforcement for the matrix, the latter serves a number of useful functions in a fibre-reinforced composite material.

Among the main uses of fibre reinforced composites are various types of glass, carbon as well as Kelvar 49. Other fibres such as boron, silicon carbide and Al_2O_3 are used in limited quantities. All these fibres can be incorporated into a matrix either in continuous lengths or in discontinuous (chopped) lengths.

Again, there are some mineral fillers which are also now well known to be used either alone or in combination with fibres. The most widely used fillers are carbonates ($CaCO_3$, chalk, limestone), clay, mica, microsphere (ceramics), minerals (silicates), organics (hull, shell and wood flour, corn cobs), silicones (sand, quartz) talc, cork, etc.

The matric model may be polymer, a metal or a ceramic. A variety of chemical compositions and micro structural arrangements are possible in each matrix category.

Advantages and disadvantages of polymer composite over metal matrix.

Some fibre reinforcement composites have better strength and modulus than may traditional metals.

Fibre reinforcement composites have:

1. (*a*) Low specific gravity.

   (*b*) Strength/weight ratio and modulus/weight ratio are superior to those of other materials.

   (*c*) Fatigue strength/weight ratio as well as fatigue damage tolerance of many composite laminates are excellent.

   For these reasons fibre reinforced composites are used as major structural materials and are used as a substitute in aerospace, automotive and other industries.

2. Traditional structural materials, such as steel and Al alloys, are considered isotropic since they exhibit nearly equal properties in all directions. However, fibre reinforced composites strength strongly depends on the direction of fibre orientation. The highest strength is in the longitudinal direction of fibre axis and minimum at 90°C with the fibre axis. Similar angular departure is observed for other physical and mechanical properties, such as co-efficient of thermal expansion, thermal conductivity and impact strength.
3. The design of fibre reinforced structure is difficult compared to a metal structure, mainly due to the difference in properties in directions.
4. In addition to the directional dependence of properties, there are a number of other differences between structural metals and fibre reinforced composites. For example, metal generally shows yielding and plastic deformation. FRC are elastic in their tensile strength (stress-strain characteristics). Moreover mechanism of damage development and growth in metal and composite structure are also quite different.
5. Co-efficient of thermal expansion for many fibre-reinforced composites are much lower than those of metals. As a result, composite structures may exhibit a better dimensional stability over a wide temperature range.

Applications

There are numerous applications of composites. However, we give only major areas of application: (1) Aircraft (2) Space (3) Automotive (4) Sporting goods and (5) Marine engineering.

1. Aircraft and Military Applications

Major applications of fibre-reinforced composites are in this field due to low weight at higher speed and increased payloads. Carbon fibres either alone or in hybridization with Kelvar fibres, have become the primary material in many wing, fuselage (body of aircraft) and empannage components. Nowadays, substantial amounts of carbon and Kelvar 49 fibre reinforced composites are used in secondary structures of many commercial aircrafts. A pioneering example of the use of composite material is found in a business aircraft in which carbon and Kelvar 49 fibres—epoxy composites—accounting for over 70% of the aircraft's weight.

Fibre reinforced epoxies are used in rotor blades in commercial and military helicopters. Besides low weight this composite can be tailor-made for any design of the blade.

Fibre reinforced composites are selected in missile structures for low weight which increases the missile range and payload capacity.

2. Space Applications

Low weight is the main reason in space applications. In space shuttles, for example, total weight saving by FRC is 12 KN per vehicle. Among various applications of the space shuttle are boron fibre-reinforced aluminium tubes, aluminium honeycomb in combination with a fibre-reinforced-epoxy-facesheets for the payload bay door; Kelvar 49 reinforced epoxy pressure vessels.

Another important property of FRC for space application is dimensional stability over a wide range of temperature. Good mechanical properties and dimensional stability have lead c-fibre reinforced epoxies to be used for artificial satellites. Space telescope support structure are also made from FRC.

3. Automotive Applications

Application of fibre-reinforced composites in the automotive industry can be classified into three groups:

- Body components
- Chassis components, and
- Engine components.

External body components, such as hood or door panels, require :

- High stiffness
- Damage tolerance
- Class A surface finish and appearance.

Resins used are: Polyurethane due to the flexible nature. Underbody components such as radiator support, bumper reinforcement beams, doorframe, etc. where glass is not important —E glass—polyester Sheet Molding Compound (SMC) composite worked well.

Among Chassis components, the first major structural application of FRC was the corvette rear leaf spring with E-gloss-Epoxy composite to replace steel spring and saved 80% of the weight. Research is going on to industrially replace drive shafts and road wheels by FRC.

The application of fibre-reinforced composites in engine components is still in the development stage. Fatigue failure at very high temperatures pose the greatest challenge in these applications. Development of high temperature polymers and metal matrix composites would find a breakthrough in this region.

The manufacturing and design of FRC materials for automotive applications are very different from that of aircraft and they are:

- Volume of production Automotive production is much more than aircraft. When labour oriented hand laying method is popular for aircraft production, high speed methods of fabrication, such as compression molding, filament winding and extrusion are mostly used for automotive industry.
- Again cost is also a factor. In aircraft, when Kelvar 49 and c-fibre were found to be very useful, but the high cost of such filler compared to the low cost of E-glass, found limited application of c-fibre and Kelvar in automobiles. In automobiles, E-glass with polyester or vinylester is found more promising. But the cost factor remains still vital—so till now mild steel (low carbon) which is less expensive than FRC is still popular in many automotive applications.

4. Sports Goods Applications

There is another major field where FRC is finding more and more market potential. The advantage of using FRC in sports goods are:

- Weight reduction
- Vibration damping
- Design flexibility.

The applications include:

- Tennis rackets
- Racket ball rackets
- Golf club shafts
- Fishing rods
- Bicycle framework
- Snow and water skis
- Ski poles, pole vault poles
- Hockey sticks
- Surfboards
- Helmets and others.

Weight reduction is achieved by substituting c-fibre-reinforced epoxiers for metals.

Faster damping of vibration of carbon or boron fiber reinforced expoxiers and urethane materials are very popular in tennis rackets. Similar applications are in ski industries due to light weight and damping vibration, shock and low temperature resistance.

5. Marine Applications

Glass-fibre-reinforced polyester laminates have found wide use in marine applications. Recently Kevlar 49 fibre is replacing glass fibre in some of these applications because of its higher tensile strength-weight and modulus-weight ratios than glass fibre. Among the application areas are boat hulls, docks, frames, etc. The main advantages are:

- Weight reduction
- Acceleration
- Maneuverability
- Fuel efficiency.

Use of particular composites.

When FRC finds more and more applications, particulate composites are also finding greater market particularly in low strength, decorative items, mostly for indoor applications. It is replacing mostly ceramics, wood as well as plywood industries.

Such particulate composites which are poor in strength, but are cheap, easy to fabricate and can be obtained in a variety of designs and colours (appearance), finding applications in areas like domestic applications as ceiling material, floor tiles, cooking utensils and furniture. Recent breakthroughs make use of these composites also in light structural applications.

6.17 CERAMICS

Ceramics and glasses are inorganic, nonmetallic materials consisting of metallic and nonmetallic elements bonded primarily with ionic and covalent bonds. These high strength bonds give rise to the special characteristics of these materials. They occupy a unique place in the spectrum of engineered materials offering many desirable alternatives to the metals and polymers in common usage.

Ceramics are closely associated with our everyday life. Of them, functional ceramics are distinguished from conventional ceramics (chinaware) and called "fine ceramics" or "engineering ceramics". Of the functions of ceramics, "mechanical" and "thermal" performances are targeted for some structural materials. Among the ceramic materials in this group, representative ones are usually of the Al_2O_3 (alumina) system, SiC (silicon carbide) system, Si_3N_4 (silicon nitride) system, and ZrO_2 (zirconia) system.

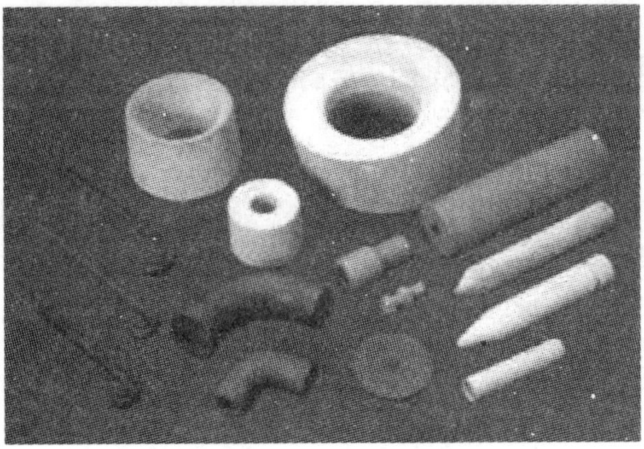

Fig. 6.5 Ceramic materials.

Low to moderate density compared to metals

High modulus of elasticity (stiffness)

Good strength retention at elevated temperatures

Resistant to high temperature creep

Dimensional stability

High compressive strength

Low to moderate tensile and shear strength

High hardness

Corrosion and oxidation resistant

Good electrical insulation properties

Wide range of thermal conductivity

Wide range of thermal expansion co-efficient

Brittle

Low impact strength

Sensitive to thermal shock.

6.18 ALUMINIUM OXIDE, Al_2O_3

Alumina is the most cost effective and widely used material in the family of engineering ceramics. The raw materials from which this high performance technical grade ceramic is made are readily available and reasonably priced, resulting in good value for the cost in fabricated alumina shapes. With an excellent combination of properties and an attractive price, it is no surprise that fine grain technical grade alumina has a very wide range of applications.

6.18.1 Key Properties

Hard, wear-resistant

Excellent dielectric properties from DC to GHz frequencies

Resists strong acid and alkali attack at elevated temperatures

Good thermal conductivity

Excellent size and shape capability

High strength and stiffness.

Available in purity ranges from 94%, an easily metallizable composition, to 99.5% for the most demanding high temperature applications.

6.18.2 Typical Uses

Aluminum oxide, commonly referred to as alumina, possesses strong ionic inter-atomic bonding giving rise to it's desirable material characteristics. It can exist in several crystalline phases which all revert to the most stable hexagonal alpha phase at elevated temperatures. This is the phase of particular interest for structural applications alpha phase alumina is the strongest and stiffest of the oxide ceramics. Its high hardness, excellent dielectric properties, refractoriness and good thermal properties make it the material of choice for a wide range of applications.

High purity alumina is usable in both oxidizing and reducing atmospheres to 1925°C. Weight loss in vacuum ranges from 10^{-7} to 10^{-6} g/cm^2. sec over a temperature range of 1700° to 2000°C. It resists attack by all gases except wet fluorine and is resistant to all common reagents except hydrofluoric acid and phosphoric acid. Elevated temperature attack occurs in the presence of alkali metal vapors particularly at lower purity levels.

The composition of the ceramic body can be changed to enhance particular desirable material characteristics. An example would be additions of chrome oxide or manganese oxide to improve hardness and change color. Other additions can be made to improve the ease and consistency of metal films fired to the ceramic for subsequent brazed and soldered assembly.

6.19 BORON NITRIDE (BN)

Boron nitride is a white solid material in the as produced hot pressed form. It is a low porosity solid. It is easily machined into complex shapes using standard carbide tooling. The material is anisotropic in its electrical and mechanical properties due to the platy hexagonal crystals and their orientation during the hot press consolidation.

Key Properties

High thermal conductivity

Low thermal expansion

Good thermal shock resistance

High electrical resistance

Low dielectric constant and loss tangent

Microwave transparency

Non toxic

Easily machined—non abrasive and lubricious

Chemically inert

Not wet by most molten metals.

Typical Uses

Electronic parts—heat sinks, substrates, coil forms, prototypes

Boron doping wafers in silicon semiconductor processing

Nuclear applications (has a high neutron capture cross-section)

Vacuum melting crucibles

CVD crucibles

Microcircuit packaging

Sputtering targets

High precision sealing, brazing, and metallizing fixtures

Microwave tubes

Horizontal caster break rings

Low friction seals

Plasma arc insulators

High temperature furnace fixtures and supports.

Boron nitride is often referred to as "white graphite" because it is a lubricious material with the same platy hexagonal structure as carbon graphite. Unlike graphite, BN is a very good electrical insulator. It offers very high thermal conductivity and good thermal shock resistance. BN is stable in inert and reducing atmospheres up to 2800°C, and in oxidizing atmospheres to 850°C.

Three grades are commonly used, including a boric oxide binder system, a calcium borate binder system, and a pure diffusion bonded grade. The boric oxide containing material (Grade BO) absorbs moisture, which causes swelling and property degradation. The calcium borate containing material (Grade CA) is moisture resistant. The pure BN material (Grade XP) contains no binders and is used for extremes of temperature and where purity is important. The boric oxide material is the most commonly used grade.

Fused silica is a non-crystalline (glass) form of silicon dioxide (quartz, sand). Typical of glasses, it lacks long range order in its atomic structure. It's highly cross linked three dimensional structure gives rise to it's high use temperature and low thermal expansion co-efficient.

Key Properties

Near zero thermal expansion

Exceptionally good thermal shock resistance

Very good chemical inertness

Can be lapped and polished to fine finishes

Low dielectric constant

Low dielectric loss

Good UV transparency.

Typical Uses

High temperature lamp envelopes

Temperature insensitive optical component supports

Lenses, mirrors in highly variable temperature regimes

Microwave and millimeter wave components

Aeronautical radar windows.

High purity sand deposits provide the raw material for bulk refractory grade, which is electric arc melted at extremely high temperatures. Optical and general purpose fused silica rods and tubing are drawn from a melt made from high purity chemicals. Fiber optic purity is made by thermal decomposition of high purity gaseous silica containing chemicals. The glass may be clear or translucent, in which case it is often referred to as fused quartz. The glass has very high viscosity, and this property allows the glass to be formed, cooled and annealed without crystallizing. Fused silica glass is a very low thermal expansion material, and so is extremely thermal shock resistant. The material is also chemically inert up to moderate temperatures except to hydrofluoric acid, which dissolves silica. It will devitrified above about 1100°C in the presence of contaminants such as sodium, phosphorus and vanadium, with the formation of cristobalite crystals which destroy the properties of the glass. The dielectric properties are stable up through gigahertz frequencies.

6.20 SILICON CARBIDE (SIC)

Silicon carbide is the only chemical compound of carbon and silicon. It was originally produced by a high temperature electro-chemical reaction of sand and carbon. Silicon carbide is an excellent abrasive and has been produced and made into grinding wheels and other abrasive products for over one hundred years. Today the material has been developed into a high quality technical grade ceramic with very good mechanical properties. It is used in abrasives, refractories, ceramics, and numerous high-performance applications. The material can also be made an electrical conductor and has applications in resistance heating, flame igniters and electronic components. Structural and wear applications are constantly developing.

Key Properties

Low density

High strength

Low thermal expansion

High thermal conductivity

High hardness

High elastic modulus

Excellent thermal shock resistance

Superior chemical inertness.

Typical Uses

Fixed and moving turbine components

Suction box covers

Seals, bearings

Ball valve parts

Hot gas flow liners

Heat exchangers

Semiconductor process equipment.

Silicon carbide is composed of tetrahedra of carbon and silicon atoms with strong bonds in the crystal lattice. This produces a very hard and strong material. Silicon carbide is not attacked by any acids or alkalis or molten salts up to 800°C. In air, SiC forms a protective silicon oxide coating at 1200°C and is able to be used up to 1600°C. The high thermal conductivity coupled with low thermal expansion and high strength give this material exceptional thermal shock resistant qualities. Silicon carbide ceramics with little or no grain boundary impurities maintain their strength to very high temperatures, approaching 1600°C with no strength loss. Chemical purity, resistance to chemical attack at temperature, and strength retention at high temperatures has made this material very popular as wafer tray supports and paddles in semiconductor furnaces. The electrical conduction of the material has lead to its use in resistance heating elements for electric furnaces, and as a key component in thermistors (temperature variable resistors) and in varistors (voltage variable resistors).

6.21 ACRYLONITRILE BUTADIENE STYRENE (ABS)

Styrene acrylonitrile copolymers have been available since the 1940's and while its increased toughness over styrene made it suitable for many applications, its limitations led to the introduction of a rubber (butadiene) as a third monomer and hence was born the range of materials popularly referred to as ABS plastics. These became available in the

1950's and the variability of these copolymers and ease of processing has led to ABS becoming the most popular of the engineering polymers.

Terluran is the ABS from BASF: special Terluran grades and Terluran standard are ideal materials wherever superlative surface quality, colorfastness and luster are required. Terluran's properties are superior to those generally expected from an ABS, even where comparable products require costly modification. Terluran is an extremely cost-effective material for components with stringent service requirements, or where there is weight-saving potential.

ABS polymers are amorphous polymers readily synthesized by adding styrene and acrylonitrile to a polybutadiene latex. In the resulting polymer, some Styrene Acrylonitrile (SAN) is grafted on to the polybutadiene backbone chain while the remainder of the SAN forms a continuous matrix. It is the SAN grafted onto the polymer chains that makes the two phases compatible. This essentially gives ABS its strength and toughness. A wide range of ABS materials can be formulated from different combinations of the above three components. It is particularly important to take into account the tendency ABS polymers have to creep, particularly at elevated temperatures. ABS materials also have poor solvent resistance, but they have high impact strength and lend themselves to processing by injection molding.

Applications of ABS include: computer and household appliance housings, crash helmets and electroplated bathroom furniture.

Applications

Because of its good balance of properties, toughness/strength/temperature resistance coupled with its ease of molding and high quality surface finish, ABS has a very wide range of applications. These include domestic appliances, telephone handsets computer and other office equipment housings, lawn mower covers, safety helmets, luggage shells, pipes and fittings. Because of the ability to tailor grades to the property requirements of the application and the availability of electroplatable grades ABS is often found as automotive interior and exterior trim components.

Current Case Studies

Automotive

Automotive construction places particularly high requirements on the materials used. Under extreme stresses they have to be dimensionally stable and must not warp, even when faced with great temperature variations.

E&E

Electrical and electronics industries increasingly require surfaces which are not only highly scratch- and wear-resistant but also decorative and easy to maintain. ABS's excellent antistatic performance is a particular advantage here.

Office Equipment

Attractive products with elegant design and high quality create a feeling of well-being at home and in the office. ABS can create exciting and varied color schemes. Grades can also be electroplated, emboss-stamped or metallized. Depending on the molding equipment used. Surfaces can be matt, glossy or satin.

Polyphenylene Oxide (PPO)

PPO is a high strength, tough and heat resistant polymer, but in the unmodified state it is extremely difficult to process. It is also relatively expensive. Fortunately, it is miscible with polystyrene, and the resulting amorphous blends are easily processed and cheaper than PPO, with little loss in mechanical properties. Stiffness and strength are approximately 50% higher than high impact ABS, with similar creep behavior. Modified PPO grades are also self extinguishing when ignited. Resistance to solvents is poor, a characteristic of styrene-based polymers. As well as glass fibre reinforced grades, these materials are available in structural foam grades.

Modified PPOs are used for electrical fittings, car fascia panels, TV components, and computer housings. Foamed modified PPO is particularly suited to the last example.

6.22 O'-SIALON

O'-Sialon is a unique class of non-oxide ceramic which incorporates grains of silicon carbide held by a matrix of O'-Sialon. This results in a product that exhibits high strength at both room temperature and working temperature. It also gives longer life meaning less change-overs and less down time. No expensive and time consuming coatings are required because O'-Sialon is non-wetting to molten aluminum and its alloys.

Property

- Open porosity
- Modulus of rupture

- CTE, linear 20°C
- Thermal conductivity
- Density.

Maximum Service Temperature, Air Property	*Units*	*Value*
	Mechanical	
Density	gm/cc	3.10–3.24
Hardness	Knoop kg/mm^2	1600–1800
Tensile Strength	kpsi	65
Modulus of Elasticity	psi × 10^6	42
Flexural Strength	kpsi	110
Compressive Strength	kpsi	500–510
Poisson's Ratio	–	.28
Fracture Toughness	MPa m$^{1/2}$	5.5–7.5
	Thermal	
Co-efficient of Thermal Expansion	$\times 10^{-6}$/°C	2.7–3.0
Thermal Conductivity	W/m°K	20–25
Specific Heat	cal/g°C	0.12
Max. Working Temp.	°C	1200
Shock Resistance	°C diff.	915
	Electrical	
Dielectric Strength	ac V/mil	–
Dielectric Constant	(at 1 MHz)	–
Volume Resistivity	ohm-cm^2/cm	–

Applications

- Dosing tubes
- Riser tubes
- Heater protection tubes
- Thermocouple protection tubes.

Advantages

- Excellent oxidation resistance
- Non-wetting to aluminum and its alloys
- Good thermal shock
- Good abrasion resistance
- Chemically inert.

6.23 ZIRCONIA PSZ

Zirconia is best known among ceramics as being **both hard and fracture-tough at**

room temperature. Additionally, its fine (sub-micron) grain size enables **excellent surface finishes and the ability to hold a sharp edge.**

Although it retains many properties including corrosion resistance at extremely high temperatures, zirconia does exhibit structural changes that may limit its use to perhaps only 500°C. It also **becomes electrically conductive** as this temperature is approached.

Zirconia is commonly blended with either MgO, CaO, or Yttria as a stabilizer in order to facilitate transformation toughening. This induces a partial cubic crystal structure instead of fully tetragonal during initial firing, which remains metastable during cooling. Upon impact, the tetragonal precipitates undergo a stress induced phase transformation near an advancing crack tip. This action expands the structure as it absorbs a great deal of energy, and is the cause of the high toughness of this material. Reforming also occurs dramatically with elevated temperature and this negatively affects strength along with 3–7% dimensional expansion. The amount of tetragonal can be controlled by additions of the blends above to balance toughness against loss of strength.

Cubic Zirconia: This single crystal optically clear form of ZrO_2 has a relatively low fracture toughness and strength, but very high thermal shock resistance.

Zirconia PSZ: Cream colored blends with approximately 10% MgO, called partially stabilized zirconia (PSZ), are high in toughness, and retain this property to elevated temperatures. They are somewhat lower in cost but also have larger grain structure.

Important Laminated Materials

Though there are a number of laminated materials these days, yet the following are important from the subject point of view: (1) Plywood (2) Tufnol.

Plywood

It is produced by binding together an odd number of thin layers (called plies) of fine wood by a resin under pressure. These plies are laid in such a way that alternate layers have their grain structure at right angles to each other. The number of plies, usually, range from 3 to 7. But in special cases, the number of plies may be more. The plywood has the advantage over the ordinary wood, that it is less liable to warp. Moreover, it is equally strong in all directions.

Tufnol

It is produced by combining a laminated material having layers of woven textiles with a thermosetting resin. In the composite material, the resin provides the necessary appearance and rigidity, while the woven textile provides the necessary strength.

6.24 REINFORCED MATERIALS

The materials, which are produced by combining some suitable material to provide additional strength which does not exist in a single material, are known as reinforced materials. The common example of reinforced material is Reinforced Cement Concrete (RCC). Glass-fibre reinforced plastic etc.

6.25 IMPORTANT REINFORCED MATERIALS

Though there are a number of reinforced materials these days, yet the following are important from the subject point of view :

1. Reinforced cement concrete.
2. Nylon reinforced rubber.
3. Glass-fibre reinforced plastic.

Reinforced Cement Concrete

It is produced by placing the steel rods (*i.e.*, reinforcement bars) in the cement concrete mixture. The resulting product, which provides excellent resistance to both the compressive and tensile stresses, is known as Reinforced Cement Concrete (RCC). It will be interesting to know that the reinforcement, being strong in tension is provided in the tensile zone. And the cement concrete, being strong in compression, is provided in compression zone. Sometimes, the reinforcement is provided in both compression and tensile zones. This is generally done when the maxim moment is very high.

Nylon Reinforced Rubber

It is commonly used in the manufacture of automobile and cycle tyres, in this composite material, the nylon thread (sometimes steel wires, glass wires etc.) provides the necessary strength and the rubber provides the necessary surface of the tyres.

Glass-fibre Reinforced Plastic

It is produced by combining glass fibre with plastic. In this composite material, the glass-fibre provides the necessary strength and the plastic reduces brittleness. The commonly used plastics are polyester resin, phenolics, silicons etc. The fibres can be employed either in the form of continuous lengths, staples or whiskers.

A complete material with desired yield strength and modulus of elasticity can be obtained by selecting the maximum number of fibres per unit volume. This will allow each fibre to take its full share of load. The fibre-reinforced composites are generally anisotropic (*i.e.*, the material has different properties in different directions). Moreover, the maximum strength of the composite is in the direction of alignment of fibres.

The following three conditions are essential to prepare a glass-fibre reinforced plastic material:

1. The co-efficient of expansion of the fibre should match closely to that of the plastic material.
2. The fibre and the plastic material should be chemically compatible with each other. This would avoid any undesirable reaction taking place between them.
3. The fibre should be stable at room temperature. And it should retain its strength' at high temperatures.

6.26 TYPE OF PLASTIC

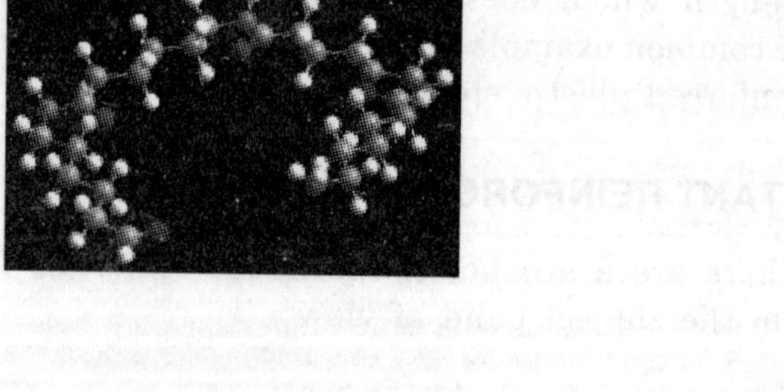

Acetals

Acetals are engineering-type thermoplastics. The acetal homopolymer is polyoxymethylene, in which methyl groups are linked together by an oxygen atom.

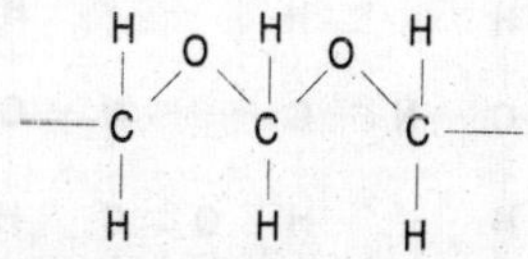

Polyoxymethylene

Mechanical and Chemical Properties

Acetals are highly crystalline. They are rigid, resilient, tough, and strong. They do not easily become brittle, even with long-term exposure to unfavorable conditions and high temperatures. Acetals cannot be dissolved by organic solvents, however, they have limited resistance to strong acids and oxidizing chemicals. Acetals absorb minimal amounts of moisture, a characteristic which enhances their high flammability.

Applications

Acetals are used in hardware components such as gears and bearings. They are also found in pumps, valves, screws, bottles, fans, paint sprayers, shower heads, tool handles, and dishes.

Acrylics

Acrylics are synthetic plastics, prepared from acrylic acids. They are polymers of the esters of acrylic acid.

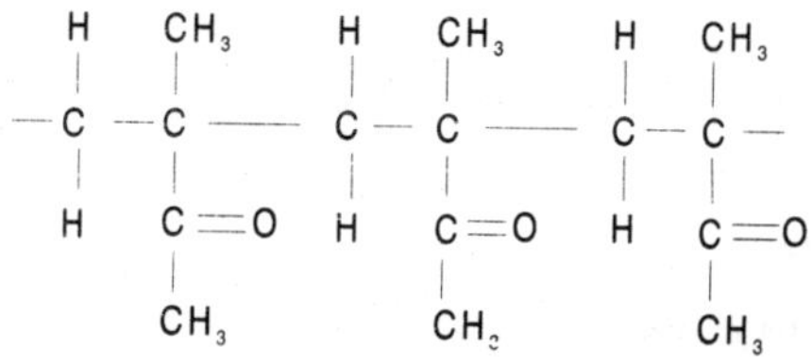

Methyl Methacrylate

Mechanical and Chemical Properties

While acrylics are clear and transmit light exceptionally well, they are also easily coloured. They can be found in all shades, including fluorescents. Their surface lustre is outstanding. Despite the fact that they have a low softening point, acrylics are weather resistant and hard. Acrylics have low moisture absorbtivity and high scratch resistance. They are susceptible to damage by certain chemicals such as gasoline and cleaning fluids, however, they will withstand non-oxidizing acids and household alkalies. Acrylic plastics are slow burning and burn with little smoke or toxicity.

Applications

Acrylics are excellent as lens material. They are used in binoculars, cameras, and eye glasses. Acrylics are also used in stop lights and car headlights. Lighting fixtures, dishes, floor waxes, carpets, piano keys, beverage dispensers, and skylights all contain acrylic plastics.

Amino Resins

Amino resins consist of melamine formaldehydes and urea formaldehydes. The molecular structure of urea formaldehyde is shown below.

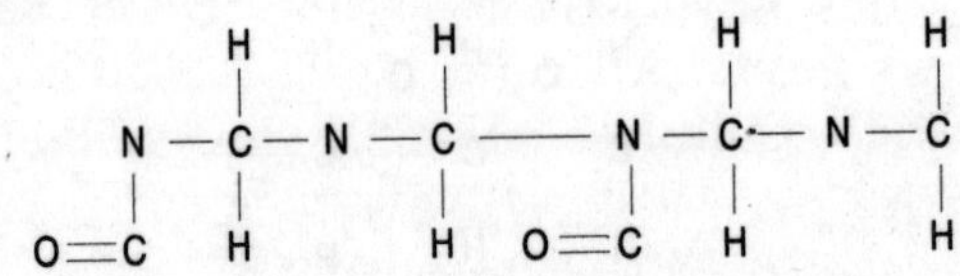

Urea Formaldehyde

Mechanical and Chemical Properties

Amino plastics are hard, scratch and stain resistant, moldable, thermally resistant, and come in a variety of translucent and opaque colours. While they are fairly strong, they are not unbreakable. They are resistant to solvents such as cleaning fluids, gasoline, and oils. Aminos will not burn or soften, even in open flame.

Applications

Amino resins are used in molding powders. Molded products of amino plastics include switch cover plates, buttons, electric mixer housings, radio cabinets, coffee makers, and door knobs. Aminos are also extremely useful as adhesives, especially in the woods industry, and as laminated lay-ups for kitchen counters. Finally, aminos are also employed as surface coatings on paper and fabric.

Cellulosics

"Cellulosics" is the general term for a group of plastics which are derived from cellulose, a natural occuring fibre which is obtained from wood pulp. The five principle cellulose plastics are:

- Cellulose acetate
- Cellulose nitrate
- Cellulose propionate
- Cellulose acetate butyrate
- Ethyl cellulose.

The molecular structure of cellulose is shown below:

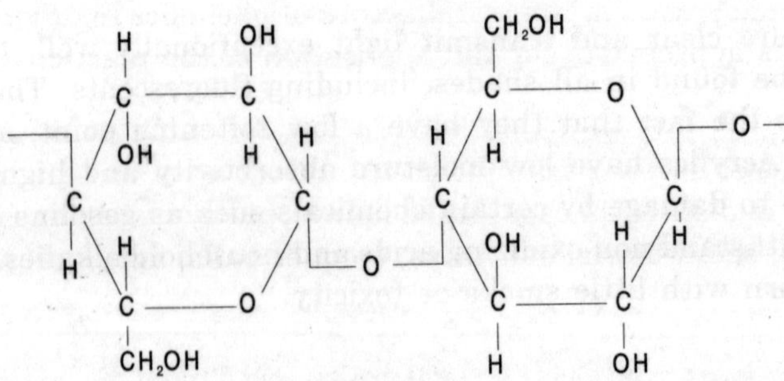

Cellulose

Various chemical groups are substituted for the hydroxy groups in glucose, with each substitution resulting in the production of one of these five plastics.

Mechanical and Chemical Properties

While each of the five cellulosics have unique properties, certain characteristics are common to all of these plastics. They are among the toughest of all the plastics, and are moderately heat resistant. They have lustrous surfaces and can be found in opaque, transluscent, and transparent forms. All cellulosics are soluble in some hydrocarbons and decompose in strong acids. Cellulose plastics are available in a wide variety of colours.

Applications

Cellulosics are used in shoe heels, eyeglass frames, toothbrush handles, pen and pencil barrels, piano keys, beads, toys, fisherperson's floats and tackle, cutlery handles, combs and steering wheels.

Phenolics

Phenolics are synthetic resins, produced by the condensation of phenol with formaldehyde in the presence of a base. The generic phenolic structure is shown below.

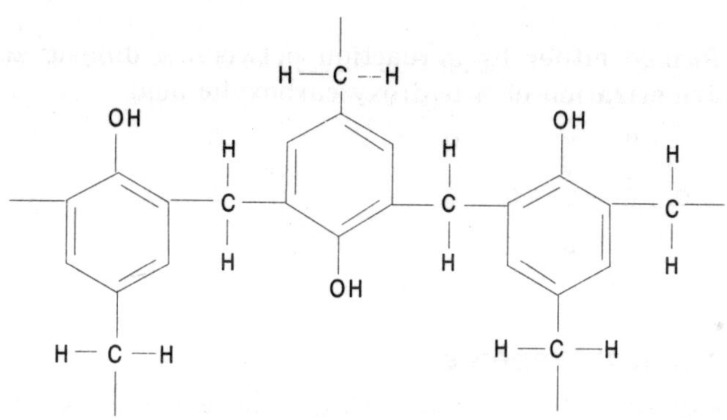

Phenolic

Mechanical and Chemical Properties

Phenolics are hard, rigid, heat resistant, and brittle. Fillers are used in order to improve their toughness. They have excellent insulating properties and are heat resistant to 260°C. They are chemically inert to most common solvents and weak acids. They absorb very little moisture. Fillers are widely used in the manufacture of phenolics in order to achieve certain desired charactertics as appropriate for the application of the plastic.

Applications

Phenolics may be used in their liquid form in laminating of veneers, fabrics, and paper. Phenolics are also used in distributor caps, brake linings, pulleys, washing machines, detergent dispensers, telephones, salad bowls, ash trays, croquet balls, and roof panels.

Polyamides

Polyamides are plastics whose structural units are linked by amide groupings. The most common type of polyamide is nylon.

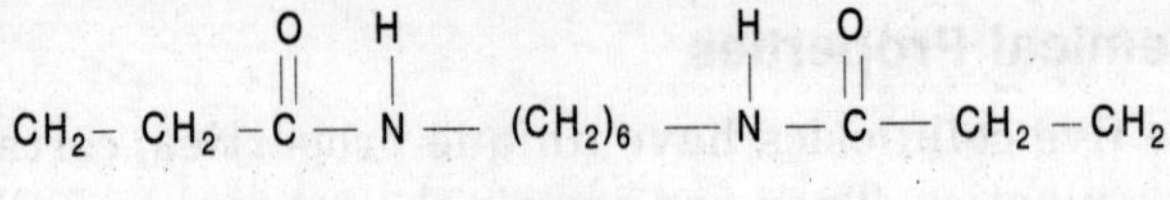

Polyamide

Mechanical and Chemical Properties

Polyamides are naturally beige or off-white, but they can be manufactured to be transparent. Polyamides can be easily molded. They are hard and brittle and resistant to abrasion, shrinkage and heat. Certains polyamides are especially flexible and impervious to impact. Polyamides are resistant to deterioration by alkalies, petroleum products, and organic solvents. Hot phenol, formaldehydes, ultraviolet light and mineral acids destroy polyamides. Most polyamides are self-extinguishing in the event of fire.

Applications

Polyamides are used in small bearings, speedometer gears, windshield wipers, water hose nozzels, football helmets, racehorse shoes, inks, clothing, parachute fabrics, rainwear, and cellophane.

Polyesters

Polyesters are formed either by a reaction between a dibasic acid and a dihydroxy alcohol or by the polymerization of a hydroxy carboxylic acid.

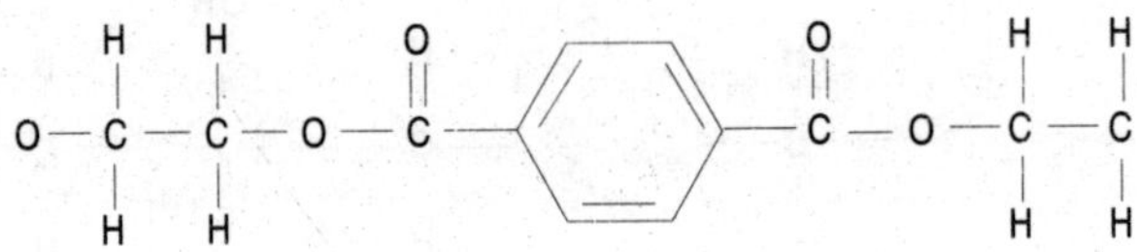

Polyester

Mechanical and Chemical Properties

Polyesters are naturally clear and colourless, however, they can be coloured and filled according to specifications. Polyesters do not show wear with exposure to poor weather conditions. They are highly resistant to chemical deterioration, withstanding most solvents, acids, and salts. Polyesters are strong and tough and range from rigid to flexible. They are also resistant to heat damage and can be made to be self-extinguishing.

Applications

The dominant uses for polyesters are in laminating and molding. Boat hulls, automobiles, and aircraft bodies all contain polyesters. Polyesters are also found in wash tubs, luggage, hammer handles, costume jewlery, and fan blades.

Polyolefins

Polyolefins are unsaturated hydrocarbons extracted from petroleum or natural gas. The structure shown below is that of a simple, straight-chain polyolefin, however, polyolefins can also be found with varying degrees of carbon chain branching.

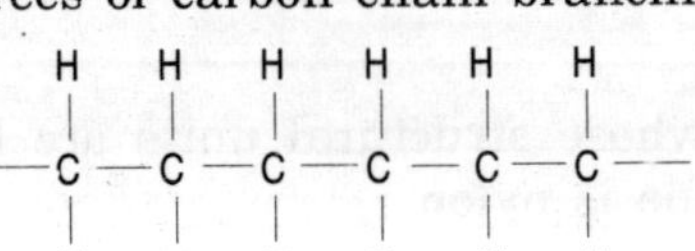

Polyolefin

Mechanical and Chemical Properties

The properties of the polyolefins depend in large part on the length and branching of their carbon chains. Short chains make brittle, waxy plastics. Longer chains produce a very tough plastic. As the density of a polyolefin increases, so do its softening temperature, gloss, and grease resistance. As the density of a polyolefin decreases, so do its crack-resistance and its permeability. Most polyolefins are resistant to attack by acids, bases, and salts. Oxidizing agents, solvents, and hydrocarbons can destroy this group of plastics. Uncoloured polyolefins are more susceptible to damage by weathering in the presence of oxygen and sunlight. Polyolefins are slow burning.

Applications

Polyolefins are used in pipe fittings, packaging films, surgical implants, wire insulation, beverage cases, trash-can liners, produce bags, canteens, and rug backing for automotive flooring.

Polyurethanes

Polyurethanes are produced by reacting diisocyanates with glycols. The molecular structure of polyurethane is shown below.

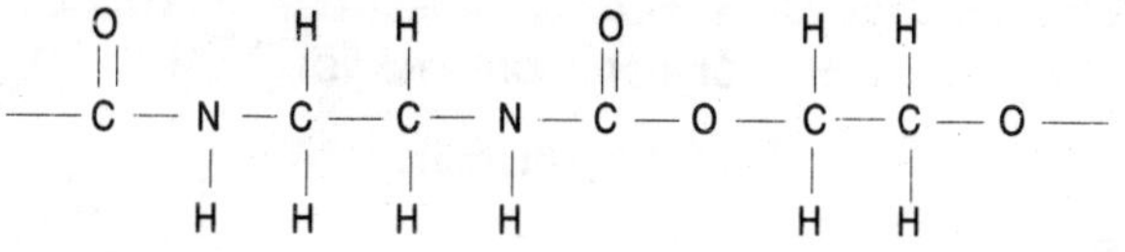

Polyurethane

Mechanical and Chemical Properties

Polyurethanes are naturally amber in colour. They are easily stretched; a property which has earned them the nickname 'elastomers'. Polyurethanes are scratch, tear, and shock resistant. They are very tough but have good cushioning properties. Polyurethanes are not easily damaged by chemicals including solvents, acids, and oils.

Applications

Polyurethanes are found in tires, gaskets, bumpers, and synthetic leather. More foamy varieties of polyurethane are used in refrigerator insulation, sponges, furniture cushioning, and life jackets.

Styrenes

Styrene plastics are made by the polymerization of styrenes. Its carbon chain is long, linear, and amorphous.

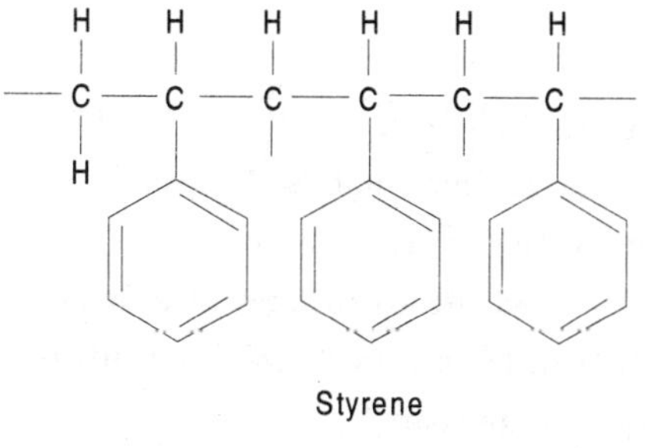

Styrene

Mechanical and Chemical Properties

Styrenes are smooth, clear, odourless, and tasteless. They can be found in a wide range of colours. They melt over a wide range of temperatures and pressures, allowing for terrific molding possibilities. They demonstrate terrific insulating properties. Styrenes are hard and brittle and show poor resistance to chemical treatments. Styrenes are limited in their amount of liquid absorption. Butadiene fillers increase the impact resistance of styrenes, making them much more versatile in their range of uses. Styrenes burn slowly.

Applications

Styrenes are widely used in disposable products including picnic utensils and food containers. They are also found in automobile interior parts, model airplane and car kits, jewellery, clock cases, place mats, envelope windows, ice buckets, and egg cartons.

Vinyls

Vinyl plastics are formed by the polymerization of chemical compounds containing the group $CH_2{=}CH{-}$.

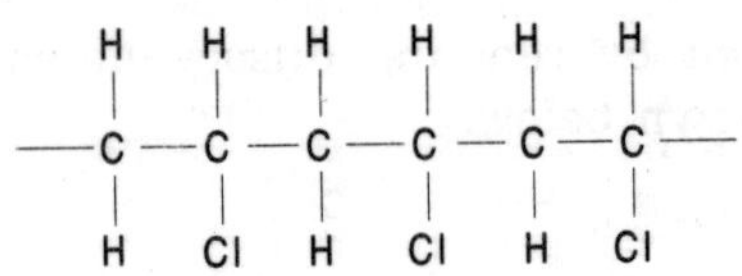

Vinyl (Halide)

REVIEW QUESTIONS

1. What is a polymer?
2. What are the properties of polymer?
3. Explain various strengthening mechanism of polymers.
4. Classify polymer.
5. What is condensation polymer and explain in brief?
6. What is PP and explain in brief?
7. What is EPR and explain in brief?
8. What is PET and explain in brief?
9. What is PEEK and explain in brief?
10. What is PMMA and explain in brief?
11. What are nylon?
12. What is poly viny alcohol?
13. What is PVC and explain in brief?
14. What is the use of stabilizing agent in PVC?
15. What is polyamide?
16. What is polyphenylene sulphide and explain in brief?
17. What are composite material and what is its uses?
18. Explains in brief about agglomerated materials.
19. What are the advantages and disadvantages of polymer composite over metal matrix?
20. What are the application of fibre-reinforced composites?
21. What are ceramics and list its uses?

22. What are boron nitride and list its uses?

23. What are silicon carbide and list its uses?

24. What are ABS and list its uses?

25. What is PPS and list its uses?

26. What is sialon and list its uses?

27. What is zirconia?

28. Explain different types of laminated materials.

29. Classify reinforced materials and discuss each in brief.

30. What are the different kinds of palstics?

7
CHAPTER

HARDENABILITY AND TESTING

7.1 INTRODUCTION

Hardenability is the ability of the Fe-C alloy to be hardened by forming martensite. Hardenability is not "hardness". It is a qualitative measure of the rate at which hardness decreases with distance from the surface because of decreased martensite content. High hardenability means the ability of the alloy to produce a high martensite content throughout the volume of specimen.

The influence of alloy composition on the ability of a steel alloy to transform to martensite for a particular quenching treatment is related to a parameter called hardenability. For every different steel alloy there is a specific relationship between the mechanical properties and the cooling rate. "Hardenability" is a term that is used to describe the ability of an alloy to be hardened by the formation of martensite as a result of a given heat treatment. Hardenability is not "hardness", which is the resistance to indentation; rather, hardenability is a qualitative measure of the rate at which hardness drops off with distance into the interior of a specimen as a result of diminished martensite content. A steel alloy that has a high hardenability is one that hardens, or forms martensite, not only at the surface but to a large degree throughout the entire interior.

7.2 HARDENABILITY

The hardenability of a steel is broadly defined as the property which determines the depth and distribution of hardness induced by quenching. Hardenability is a characteristic determined by the following factors.

- Chemical composition
- Austenite grain size
- Structure of alloy before quenching.

The hardenability is the depth and evenness of hardness of a steel upon quenching from austenite.

Thickness Considerations

The properties of heat treated steel are significantly affected by the thickness of the section. Hardening consist of heating the steel through and just above its critical range to obtain the condition of solid solution and quenching with sufficient rapidity to retain this condition. If a steel has a large thickness it is practically impossible to obtain an even temperature throughout and the middle of the section is always at a lower temperature compared to the outside surfaces. On quenching the heat is absorbed rapidly from the outside and it is impossible even with the most drastic quench processes to remove heat from the core region sufficient to obtain the desire structure. For thin sections it may be possible to obtain the desire structure throughout the section with a comparative mild quenching process.

7.3 QUENCHING

There are a number of fluids used for quenching steels listed below in order of quenching severity.

- Brine
- Water
- Oil
- Special liquids
- Air.

Note: Agitation of medium increases its quenching severity.

Soft distilled water is the preferred medium when using water for quenching carbon steels. The water should have no impurities such as oil, grease or acids as they could result in uneven hardening if they stick to the surface of the steel being hardened an provide local thermal insulation. Hard water is unsatisfactory because it may release scale as the temperature is raised. Soap is sometimes added to adjust quenching rates. Cold brine or water is used to provide the most severe quench with the consequent maximum hardness.

Oil bath quenching is used where extreme hardness is not required and where freedom from quenching shock is needed. Oils used are mainly mineral oils with the viscosity selected to suit the type of steel to be quenched. Oil cooling systems are required when significant quenching capacity is required to prevent the oil from breaking down and to maintain the quenching conditions. Air-cooling is used for mild hardening process when a tough hard pearlitic structure is required.

Vacuum Treatments

Many of the heat treatment processes can be completed in vacuum furnaces at very low pressures (high vacuums). The advantages of using vacuum furnaces are listed below:

- No surface oxidation
- Minimal distortion
- No post cleaning operations
- Near finished, machined shape prior to treatment
- Normally improved control of processes.

7.4 MEASUREMENT OF HARDENABILITY (JOMINY END QUENCH)

Hardenability is measured by the Jominy endquench test performed for standard cylindrical specimen, standard austenitization conditions, and standard quenching conditions (jet of water at specific flow rate and temperature).

The Jominy end quench test is used to measure the hardenability of a steel, which is a measure of the capacity of the steel to harden in depth under a given set of conditions. This TLP considers the basic concepts of hardenability and the Jominy test.

Knowledge about the hardenability of steels is necessary to be able to select the appropriate combination of alloy steel and heat treatment to manufacture components of different size to minimize thermal stresses and distortion. The Jominy end quench test is the standard method for measuring the hardenability of steels. This describes the ability of the steel to be hardened in depth by quenching.

Hardenability depends on the chemical composition of the steel and also be can affected by prior processing conditions, such as the austenitizing temperature. It is not only necessary to understand the basic information provided from the Jominy test, but also to appreciate how the information obtained can be used to understand the effects of alloying in steels and the steel microstructure.

Hardenability is the ability of a steel to partially or completely transform from austenite to some fraction of martensite at a given depth below the surface, when cooled under a given condition. For example, a steel of a high hardenability can transform to a high fraction of martensite to depths of several millimetres under relatively slow cooling, such as an oil quench, whereas a steel of low hardenability may only form a high fraction of martensite to a depth of less than a millimetre, even under rapid cooling such as a water quench. Hardenability therefore describes the capacity of the steel to harden *in depth* under a given set of conditions.

Steels with high hardenability are needed for large high strength components, such as large extruder screws for injection moulding of polymers, pistons for rock breakers, mine shaft supports, aircraft undercarriages, and also for small high precision components such as die-casting moulds, drills and presses for stamping coins. High hardenability allows slower quenches to be used (e.g., oil quench), which reduces the distortion and residual stress from thermal gradients.

Steels with low hardenability may be used for smaller components, such as chisels and shears, or for surface hardened components such as gears. Hardenability can be measured using the Jominy end quench test. The test sample is a cylinder with a length of 102 mm (4 inches) and a diameter of 25.4 mm (1 inch).

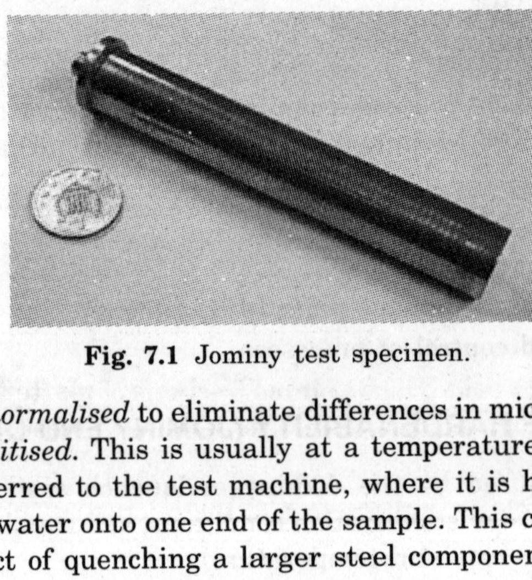

Fig. 7.1 Jominy test specimen.

The steel sample is *normalised* to eliminate differences in microstructure due to previous forging, and then *austenitised*. This is usually at a temperature of 800 to 900°C. The test sample is quickly transferred to the test machine, where it is held vertically and sprayed with a controlled flow of water onto one end of the sample. This cools the specimen from one end, simulating the effect of quenching a larger steel component in water.

Fig. 7.2 Jominy test machine.

The cooling rate varies along the length of the sample from very rapid at the quenched end, to rates equivalent to air cooling at the other end.

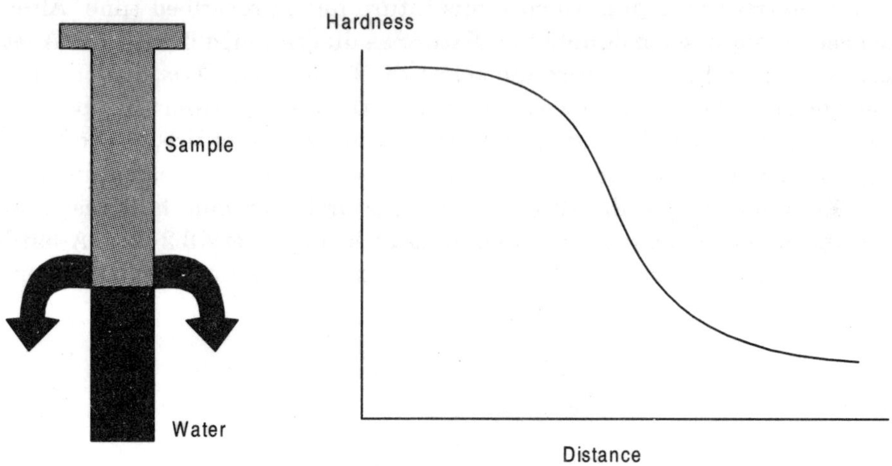

Fig. 7.3

The round specimen is then ground flat along its length to a depth of 0.38 mm (15 thousandths of an inch) to remove decarburised material. The hardness is measured at intervals from the quenched end. The interval is typically 1.5 mm for alloy steels and 0.75 mm for carbon steels.

High hardness occurs where high volume fractions of martensite develop. Lower hardness indicates transformation to bainite or ferrite/pearlite microstructures.

Jominy end quench hardness data for two steels of different hardenability can be seen in a later section of this TLP, with images of the microstructure variation along the length of the sample.

Similar tests have been developed in other countries, such as the SAC test, which uses a sample quenched from all sides by immersion in water. This is commonly used in the USA.

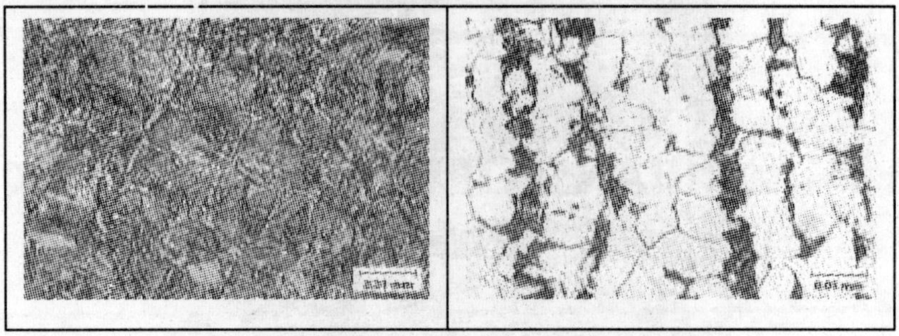

(*a*) Martensite (*b*) Ferrite/pearlite

Fig. 7.4

7.4.1 The Jominy EndQuench Test-II

One standard procedure that is widely utilized to determine hardenability is the Jominy endquench test. With this procedure, except for alloy composition, all factors that may influence the depth to which a piece hardens (*i.e.,* specimen size and shape, and quenching treatment) are maintained constant. A cylindrical specimen 25.4 mm in diameter and 100 mm long is austenitized at a prescribed temperature for a prescribed time. After removal from the furnace, it is quickly mounted in a fixture as diagrammed in Fig. 7.2. A jet of water of specified flow rate and temperature quenches the lower end. Thus, the cooling rate is a maximum at the quenched end and diminishes with position from this point along the length of the specimen. After the piece has cooled to room temperature, shallow flats 0.4 mm deep are ground along the specimen length and Rockwell hardness measurements are made for the first 50 mm along each flat (Fig. 7.3); for the first 12.8 mm, hardness readings are taken at 1.6 mm intervals, and for the remaining 38.4 mm, every 3.2 mm. A hardenability curve is produced when hardness is plotted as a function of position from the quenched end.

8

CHAPTER

ISOTHERMAL TRANSFORMATION AND CRITICAL COOLING TRANSFORMATION

8.1 INTRODUCTION

We have already discussed in the last chapter the isothermal curve for specimen, when it is cooled from the upper critical temperature to a temperature below the lower critical *point* (723°C). Now, if we cool the steel tin from the upper critical temperature to different temperatures (say 500°C, 400°C and 250°C) and plot the graphs in the same way as discussed above. We shall obtain different curves as shown in Fig. 8.1.

Now let us draw another graph with temperature along the vertical axis and time along the horizontal axis. Now let the time elapse before the beginning to the end of transformation be marked on isotherms (*i.e., constant* temperature lines) by projecting them from the isothermal curve. we draw a curve connecting all these points of the beginning and end of transformation, we shall obtain a curve as shown in figure. The diagram obtained is known as isothermal transformation diagram.

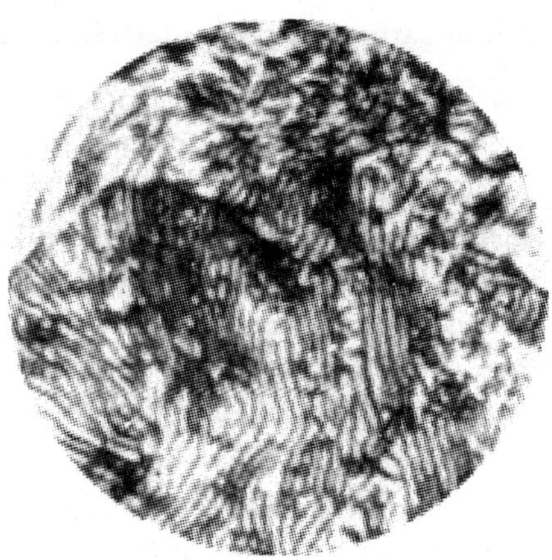

Pearlite
Ferrite = Light Areas
Cementite = Dark Areas

Fig. 8.1

8.2 PEARLITES

A mixture of alternate strips of ferrite and cementite in a single grain. The distance between the plates and their thickness is dependant on the cooling rate of the material; fast cooling creates thin plates that are close together and slow cooling creates a much coarser structure possessing less toughness. The name for this structure is derived from its mother of pearl appearance under a microscope. A fully pearlitic structure occurs at 0.8% carbon. Further increases in carbon will create cementite at the grain boundaries, which will start to weaken the steel.

$$\gamma \text{ (0.76 wt\% C)} \longrightarrow \alpha \text{ (0.022 wt\% C)} + Fe_cC \text{ (6.70 wt\% C)}$$

Consider again the iron-iron carbide eutectoid reaction which is fundamental to the development of microstructure in steel alloys. Upon cooling, austenite, having an intermediate carbon concentration, transforms to a ferrite phase, having a much lower carbon content, and also cementite. With a much higher carbon concentration, Pearlite is one microstructural product of transformation (Figure), and the mechanism of pearlite formation was discussed previously (Section) and demonstrated in Fig. 8.2.

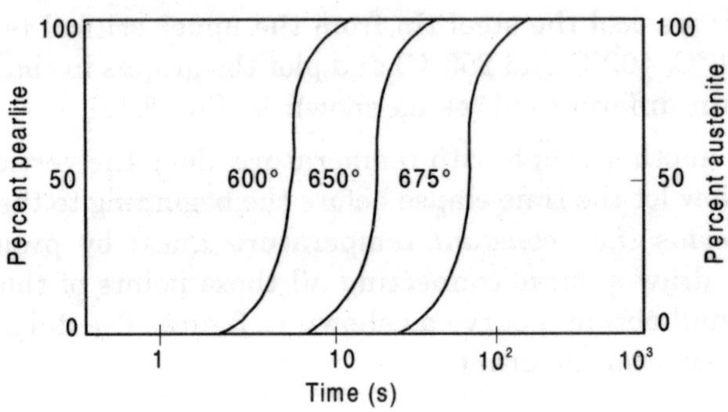

Fig. 8.2 Iron carbon alloy of eutectoid composition.

For an iron-carbon composition (0.76 wt% C) isothermal fraction reacted versus the logarithm of time for the austenite-to-pearlite transformation.

Temperature plays an important role in the rate of the austenite-to-pearlite transformation. The temperature dependence for an iron-carbon alloy of eutectoid composition is indicated in Fig. 8.2, which plots S-shaped curves of the percentage transformation versus the logarithm of time at three different temperatures. For each curve, data were collected after rapidly cooling a specimen composed of 100% austenite to the temperature indicated; that temperature was maintained constant throughout the course of the reaction.

A more convenient way of representing both the time and temperature dependence of this transformation is in the bottom portion of Fig. 8.3. Here, the vertical and horizontal axes are, respectively, temperature and the logarithm of time. Two solid curves are plotted; one represents the time required at each temperature for the initiation or start of the transformation; the other is for the transformation conclusion. The dashed curve corresponds to 50% of transformation completion. These curves were generated from a series of plots of the percentage transformation versus the logarithm of time taken over a range of temperatures. The S-shaped curve [for 675°C (1247°F)], in the upper portion of Fig. 8.3, illustrates how the data transfer is made.

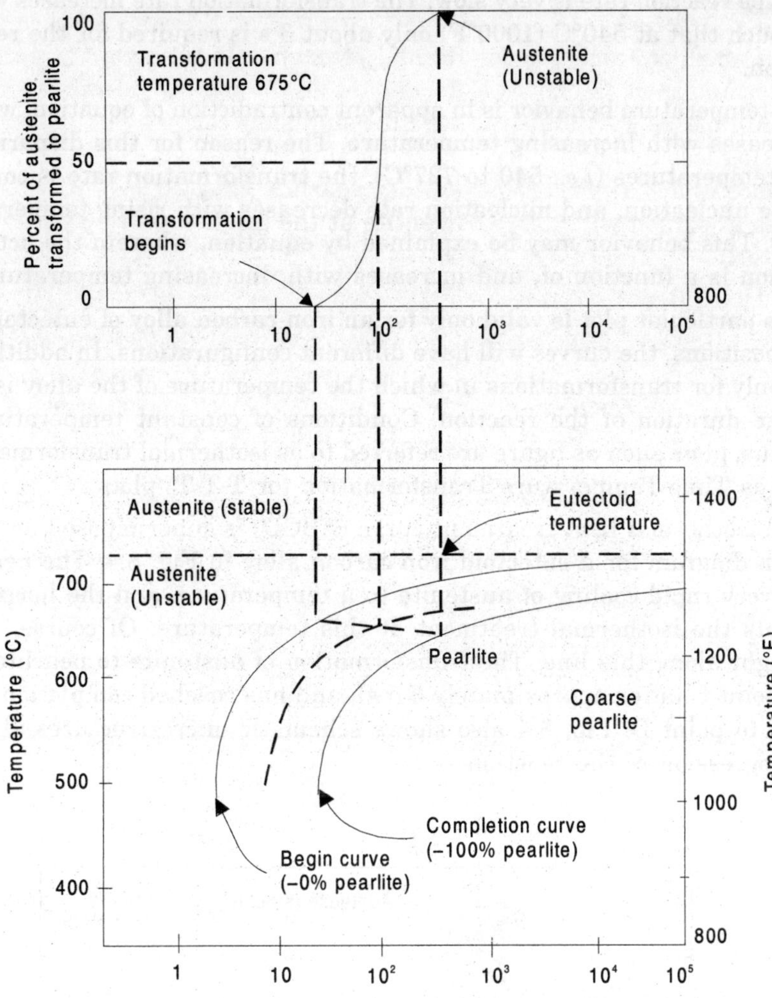

Fig. 8.3 Transformation Vs. logarithm of time measurement.

In interpreting this diagram, note first that the eutectoid temperature [727°C (1341°F)] is indicated by a horizontal line; at temperatures above the eutectoid and for all times, only austenite will exist, as indicated in the figure. The austenite-to-pearlite transformation will occur only if an alloy is super cooled to below the eutectoid; as indicated by the curves, the time necessary for the transformation to begin and then end depends on temperature. The start and finish curves are nearly parallel, and they approach the eutectoid line asymptotically. To the left of the transformation start curve, only austenite (which is unstable) will be present, whereas to the right of the finish curve, only pearlite will exist. In between, the austenite is in the process of transforming to pearlite, and thus both micro constituents will be present.

According to equation, the transformation rate at some particular temperature is inversely proportional to the time required for the reaction to proceed to 50% completion (to the dashed line in Fig. 8.4). That is, the shorter this time, the higher the rate. Thus, from Fig. 8.4, at temperatures just below the eutectoid (corresponding to just a slight degree of under cooling) very long times (on the order of 10^5 s) are required for the 50% transformation, and therefore the reaction rate is very slow. The transformation rate increases with decreasing temperature such that at 540°C (1000°F) only about 3 s is required for the reaction to go to 50% completion.

This rate-temperature behavior is in apparent contradiction of equation, which stipulates that rate increases with increasing temperature. The reason for this disparity is that over this range of temperatures (*i.e.,* 540 to 727°C), the transformation rate is controlled by the rate of pearlite nucleation, and nucleation rate decreases with rising temperature (*i.e.,* less super cooling). This behavior may be explained by equation, wherein the activation energy Q for nucleation is a function of, and increases with, increasing temperature.

First, this particular plot is valid only for an iron-carbon alloy of eutectoid composition; for other compositions, the curves will have different configurations. In addition, these plots are accurate only for transformations in which the temperature of the alloy is held constant throughout the duration of the reaction. Conditions of constant temperature are termed isothermal; thus, plots such as figure are referred to as isothermal transformation diagrams, or sometimes as Time-Temperature-Transformation (or T-T-T) plots.

An actual isothermal heat treatment curve (ABCD) is superimposed on the isothermal transformation diagram for a eutectoid iron-carbon alloy in Fig. 8.4. The near-vertical line AB indicates very rapid cooling of austenite to a temperature, and the horizontal segment BCD represents the isothermal treatment at this temperature. Of course, time increases from left to right along this line. The transformation of austenite to pearlite begins at the intersection, point C (after approximately 3.5 s), and has reached completion by about 15 s, corresponding to point D. Fig. 8.4 also shows schematic microstructures at various times during the progression of the reaction.

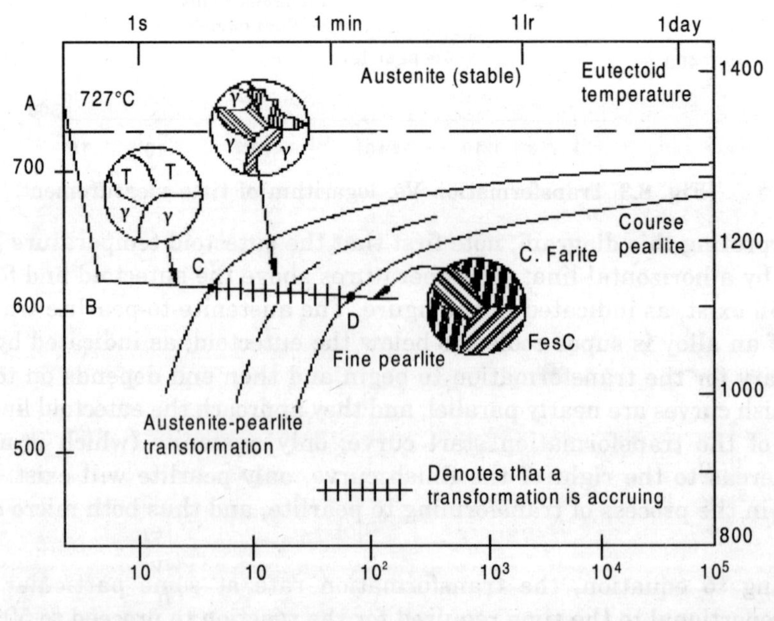

Fig. 8.4 Isothermal transformation diagram for eutectoid iron-carbon alloy.

The thickness ratio of the ferrite and cementite layers in pearlite is approximately 8 to 1. However, the absolute layer thickness depends on the temperature at which the isothermal transformation is allowed to occur. At temperatures just below the eutectoid, relatively thick layers of both the a-ferrite and Fe_3C phases are produced; this microstructure is called coarse pearlite, and the region at which it forms is indicated to the right of the completion curve on figure. At these temperatures, diffusion rates are relatively high, such that during the transformation illustrated in figure carbon atoms can diffuse relatively long distances, which result in the formation of thick lamellae. With decreasing temperature, the carbon diffusion rate decreases, and the layers become progressively thinner. The thin-layered structure produced in the vicinity of 540°C is termed fine pearlite; this is indicated in Fig. 8.4. To be discussed in section is the dependence of mechanical properties on lamellar thickness. Photomicrographs of coarse and fine pearlite for a eutectoid composition are shown in Fig. 8.4.

For iron-carbon alloys of other compositions, a proeutectoid phase (either ferrite or cementite) will coexist with pearlite, as discussed in phase diagrams. Thus additional curves corresponding to a proeutectoid transformation also must be included on the isothermal transformation diagram. A portion of one such diagram for a 1.13 wt% C alloy is shown in Fig. 8.4.

8.3 BAINITE

From the discussion of the preceding section, it would seem reasonable to expect the alternating ferrite and cementite lamellae to become thinner and thinner as the isothermal transformation temperature is lowered to below that at which fine pearlite forms. Such is not the case; other micro constituents that are products of the austenitic transformation are found to exist at these lower temperatures. One of these micro constituents is called bainite. Furthermore, depending on transformation temperature, two general types of bainite have been observed: upper and lower bainite. Like pearlite, the microstructure of each of these bainites consists of ferrite and cementite phases; however, their arrangements are different from the alternating lamellar structure found in pearlite.

For temperatures between approximately 300 and 540°C, bainite forms as a series of parallel laths (*i.e.,* thin narrow strips) or needles of ferrite that are separated by elongated particles of the cementite phase. Such is termed upper bainite, and its microstructural details are so fine that their resolution is possible only using electron microscopy. Fig. 8.5 is an electron micrograph that shows a grain of upper bainite (positioned diagonally from lower left to upper right); the various phases in this micrograph have been labeled. In addition, the phase that surrounds the bainite is martensite, the topic to which a subsequent section is addressed. Furthermore, no proeutectoid phase forms with bainite.

At lower temperatures between about 200°C and 300°C lower bainite is the transformation product. For lower bainite, the ferrite phase exists as thin plates (instead of laths as with upper bainite), and narrow cementite particles (as very fine rods or blades) form within these ferrite plates. Fig. 8.5 is an electron micrograph of lower bainite; in this micrograph, the plates of bainite appear as needlelike structures, whereas the phase that surrounds them is martensite. Furthermore, the cementite particles within these bainite plates are so small as not to be resolvable; the schematic inset shown with this micrograph represents the detailed structure of these plates.

The time-temperature dependence of the bainite transformation may also be represented on the isothermal transformation diagram. It occurs at temperatures below those at which pearlite forms; begin-, end-, and half-reaction curves are just extensions of those for the pearlitic transformation, as shown in figure, the isothermal transformation diagram for an iron-carbon alloy of eutectoid composition that has been extended to lower temperatures. All three curves are C-shaped and have a "nose" at point N, where the rate of transformation is a maximum. As may be noted, whereas pearlite forms above the nose that is, over the temperature range of about 540 to 727°C (1000 to 1341°F)—for isothermal treatments at temperatures between about 215 and 540°C (420 and 1000°F), bainite is the transformation product. Temperature regimes over which upper and lower bainites form are indicated on Fig. 8.5.

It should also be noted that pearlitic and bainitic transformations are really competitive with each other, and once some portion of an alloy has transformed to either pearlite or bainite, transformation to the other micro constituent is not possible without reheating to form austenite.

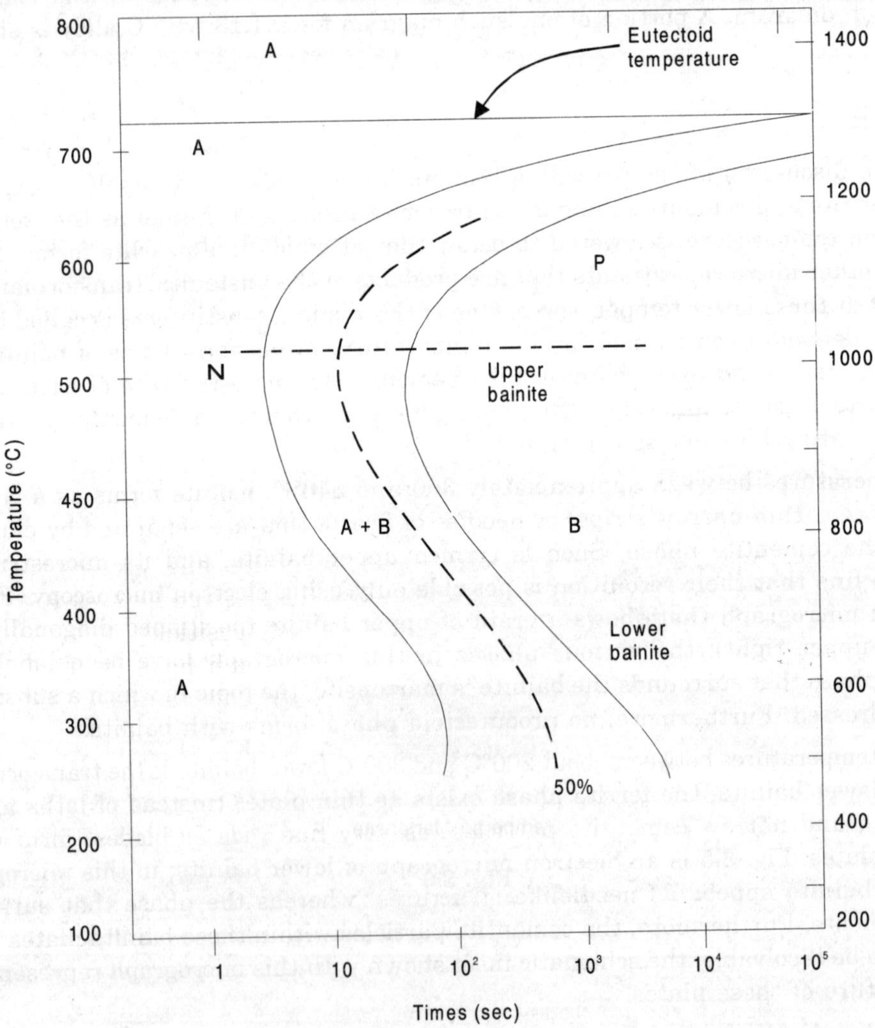

Fig. 8.5 Isothermal transformation diagram for an iron carbon alloy of eutectoid composition.

8.4 SPHEROIDITE

If a steel alloy having either pearlitic or bainitic microstructures is heated to, and left at, a temperature below the eutectoid for a sufficiently long period of time—for example, at about 700°C (1300°F) for between 18 and 24 hr yet another microstructure will form. It is called spheroidite. Instead of the alternating ferrite and cementite lamellae (pearlite), or the microstructures observed for upper and lower bainites, the Fe_3C phase appears as spherelike particles embedded in a continuous a phase matrix. This transformation has occurred by additional carbon diffusion with no change in the compositions or relative amounts of ferrite and cementite phases.

8.5 MARTENSITE

If steel is cooled rapidly from austenite, the F.C.C structure rapidly changes to B.C.C leaving insufficient time for the carbon to form pearlite. This results in a distorted structure that has the appearance of fine needles. There is no partial transformation associated with martensite, it either forms or it doesn't. However, only the parts of a section that cool fast enough will form martensite; in a thick section it will only form to a certain depth, and if the shape is complex it may only form in small pockets. The hardness of martensite is solely dependant on carbon content, it is normally very high, unless the carbon content is exceptionally low. Yet another microconstituent or phase called martensite is formed when austenit-ized iron-carbon alloys are rapidly cooled (or quenched) to a relatively low temperature (in the vicinity of the ambient). Martensite is a nonequilibrium single-phase structure that results from a diffusionless transformation of austenite. It may be thought of as a transformation product that is competitive with pearlite and bainite. The martensitic transformation occurs when the quenching rate is rapid enough to prevent carbon diffusion. Any diffusion whatsoever will result in the formation of ferrite and cementite phases.

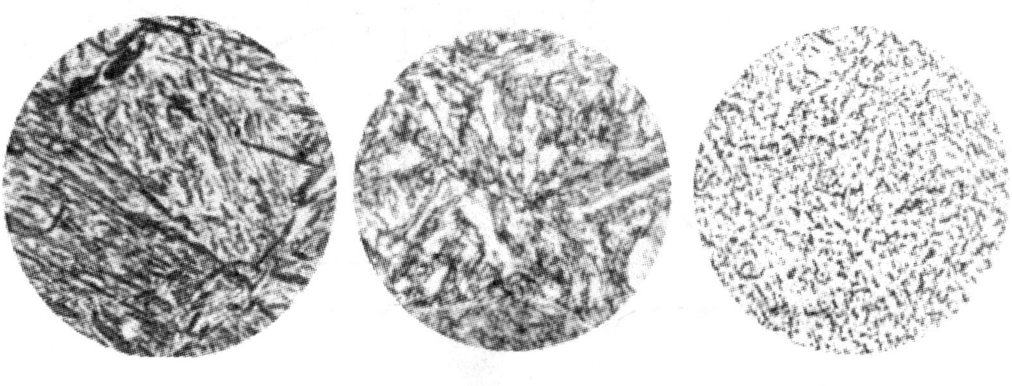

Martensite   Tempered Martensite   Heavily Tempered

Fig. 8.6

8.6 TEMPERING

The carbon trapped in the martensite transformation can be released by heating the steel below the A1 transformation temperature. This release of carbon from nucleated areas allows the structure to deform plastically and relieve some of its internal stresses. This reduces hardness and increases toughness, but it also tends to reduce tensile strength. The degree of tempering is dependant on temperature and time; temperature having the greatest influence.

8.7 ANNEALING

This term is often used to define a heat treatment process that produces some softening of the structure. True annealing involves heating the steel to austenite and holding for some time to create a stable structure. The steel is then cooled very slowly to room temperature. This produces a very soft structure, but also creates very large grains, which are seldom desirable because of poor toughness.

Normalising returns the structure back to normal. The steel is heated until it just starts to form austenite; it is then cooled in air. This moderately rapid transformation creates relatively fine grains with uniform pearlite.

Welding If the temperature profile for a typical weld is plotted against the carbon equilibrium diagram, a wide variety of transformation and heat treatments will be observed.

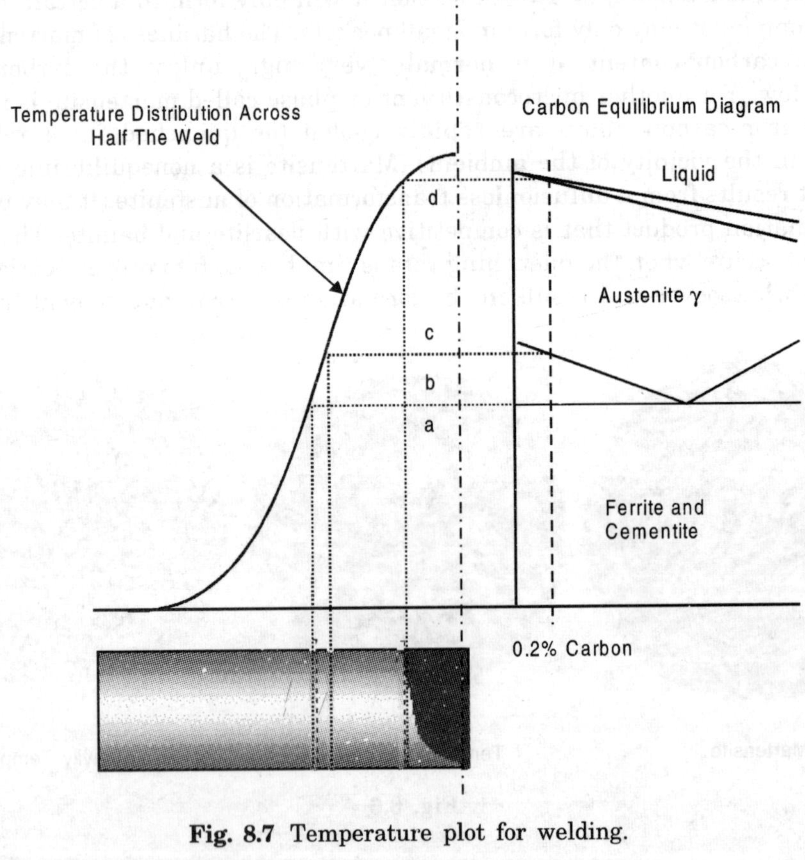

Fig. 8.7 Temperature plot for welding.

8.8 CONTINUOUS COOLING TRANSFORMATION DIAGRAMS

Isothermal heat treatments are not the most practical to conduct because an alloy must be rapidly cooled to and maintained at an elevated temperature from a higher temperature above the eutectoid. Most heat treatments for steels involve the continuous cooling of a specimen to room temperature. An isothermal transformation diagram is valid only for conditions of constant temperature, which diagram must be modified for transformations that occur as the temperature is constantly changing. A plot containing such modified beginning and ending reaction curves is termed a Continuous Cooling Transformation (CCT) diagram. Some control may be maintained over the rate of temperature change depending on the cooling environment. Two cooling curves corresponding to modcrately fast and slow rates are superimposed and labeled in Fig. 8.9 again for a eutectoid steel. The transformation starts after a time period corresponding to the intersection of the cooling curve with the beginning reaction curve and concludes upon crossing the completion transformation curve. The microstructural products for the moderately rapid and slow cooling rate curves in Fig. 8.9 are fine and coarse pearlite, respectively.

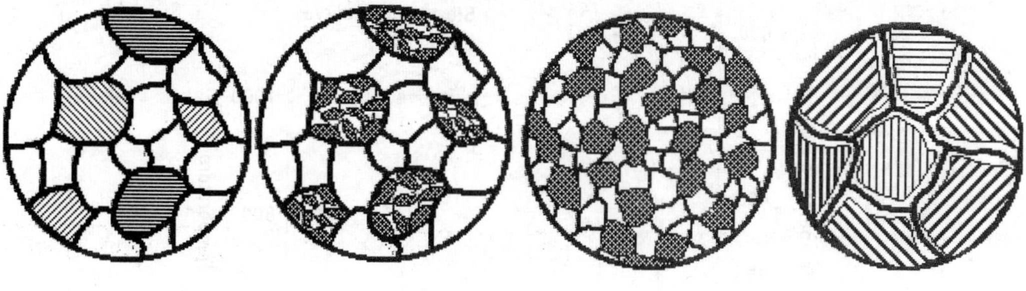

a b c d

Fig. 8.8 Temperature distribution.

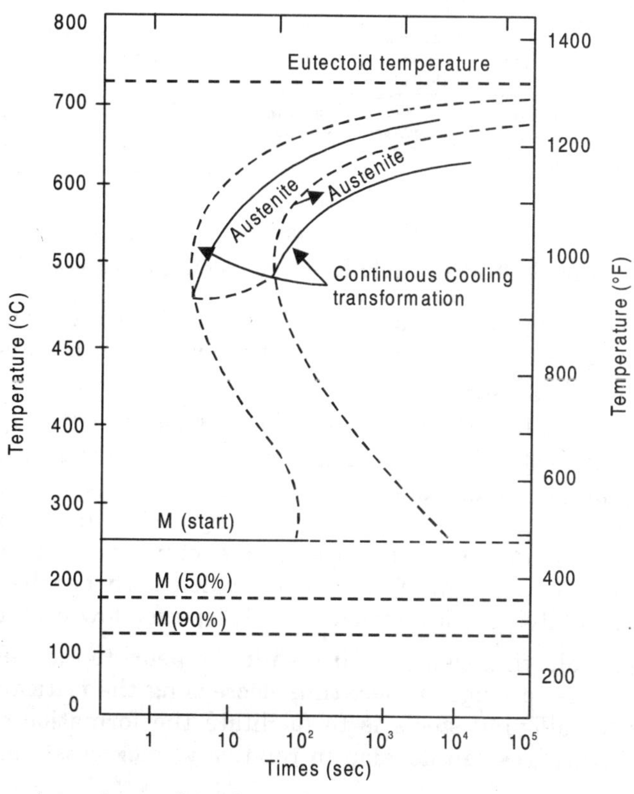

Fig. 8.9 Superimposition of isothermal and continuous cooling transformation.

Normally, bainite will not form when an alloy of eutectoid composition or, for that matter, any plain carbon steel is continuously cooled to room temperature. This is because all the austenite will have transformed to pearlite by the time the bainite transformation has become possible. Thus, the region representing the austenite-pearlite transformation terminates just below the nose as indicated by the curve AB. For any cooling curve passing through AB in Fig. 8.10, the transformation ceases at the point of intersection; with continued cooling, the unreacted austenite begins transforming to martensite upon crossing the Af (start) line.

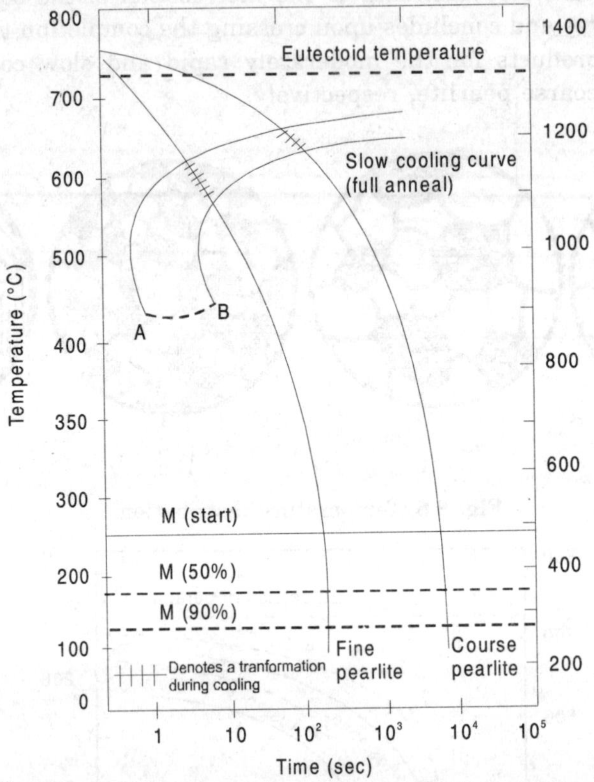

Fig. 8.10 Moderately rapid and slow cooling curve.

With regard to the representation of the martensitic transformation, the M (start), M (50%), and M (90%) lines occur at identical temperatures for both isothermal and continuous cooling transformation diagrams.

For the continuous cooling of a steel alloy, there exists a critical quenching rate, which represents the minimum rate of quenching that will produce a totally martensitic structure. This critical cooling rate, when included on the continuous transformation diagram, will just miss the nose at which the pearlite transformation begins, as illustrated in Fig. 8.11. As the figure also shows, only martensite will exist for quenching rates greater than the critical; in addition, there will be a range of rates over which both pearlite and martensite are produced. Finally, a totally pearlitic structure develops for low cooling rates.

Carbon and other alloying elements also shift the pearlite (as well as the proeutectoid phase) and bainite noses to longer times, thus decreasing the critical cooling rate. In fact, one of the reasons for alloying steels is to facilitate the formation of martensite so that totally martensitic structures can develop in relatively thick cross-sections. Fig. 8.9 shows the continuous cooling transformation diagram for the same alloy steel the isothermal transformation diagram for which is presented in figure. The presence of the bainite nose accounts for the possibility of formation of bainite for a continuous cooling heat treatment.

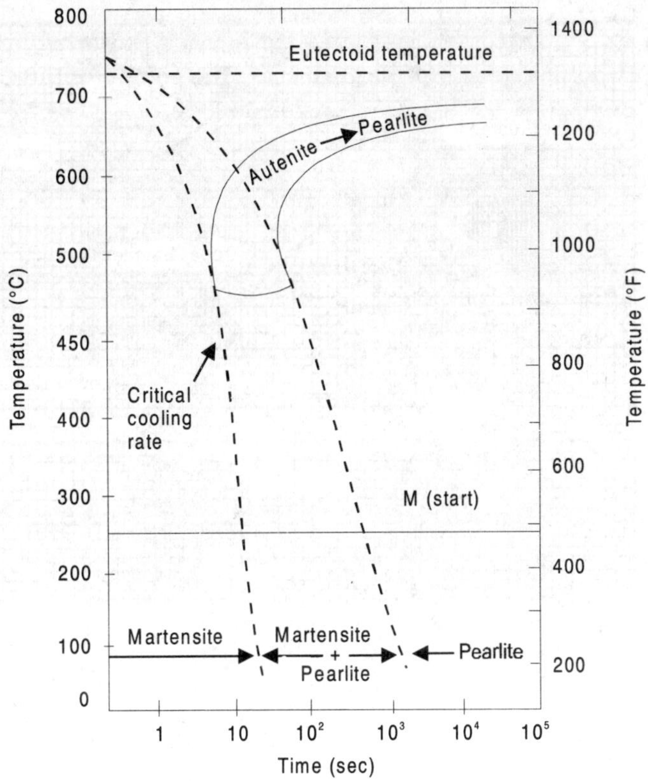

Fig. 8.11 CCTD-eutectoid iron carbon alloy.

Interestingly enough, the critical cooling rate is diminished even by the presence of carbon. In fact, iron-carbon alloys containing less than about 0.25 wt% carbon are not normally heat treated to form martensite because quenching rates too rapid to be practical are required. Other alloying elements that are particularly effective in rendering steels heat treatable are chromium, nickel, molybdenum, manganese, silicon, and tungsten; however, these elements must be in solid solution with the austenite at the time of quenching. Excessive energy consumption. Recovery and recrystallization processes are allowed to occur. Ordinarily a fine-grained microstructure is desired, and therefore, the heat treatment is terminated before appreciable grain growth has occurred. Surface oxidation or scaling may be prevented or minimized by annealing at a relatively low temperature (but above the recrystallization temperature).

Changes in Steel Structure Below Lower Critical Temperature

We have already discussed that the isothermal transformation of austenite at a temperature below the lower critical point (723°C) gives rise to the formation of a mixture composed of the ferrite and cementite. Rule depending upon the transformation temperature, the structures and properties of this ferrite-cementite mixture are substantially different. The various changes in the structures due to the transformation of austenite at different temperatures, are shown in Fig. 8.12.

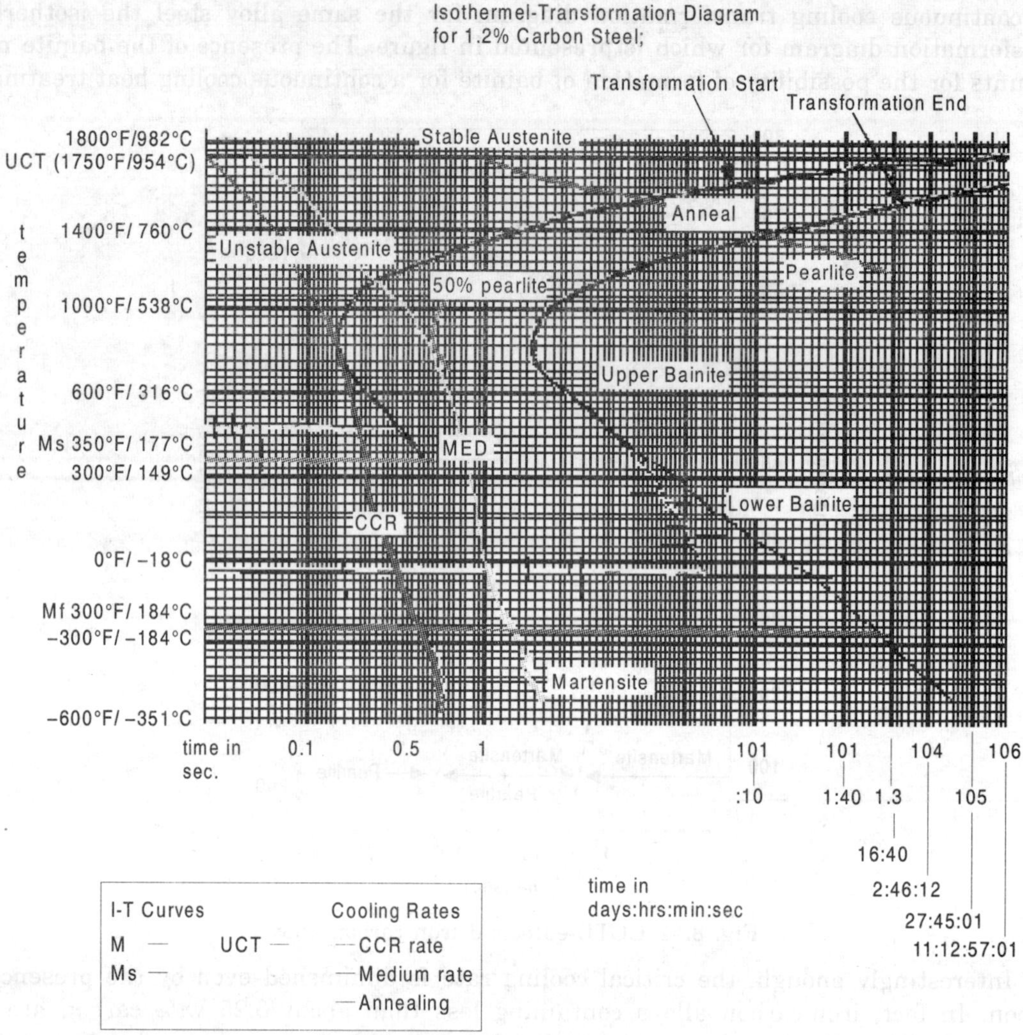

Fig. 8.12 IT diagram-cooling rates.

It has been observed that the ferrite-cementite mixture, for different temperatures, due to the transformation of austenite, primarily in the degree of dispersion (or refinement) of both phases. At lower transformation temperatures, both the phases are more dispersed. But transformation temperatures (at about 700°C) the ferrite-cementite becomes sufficiently distinct and is known as pearlite.

It has also been observed that at somewhat lower transformations temperatures (at about 650°C) the ferrite-cementite mixture is more dispersed and is known as sorbite. At still lower transformation temperatures (at 600°C) the ferrite cementite mixture becomes so dispersed that its structure can only be determined by an electronic microscope. Its structure similar to pearlite and sorbite and is known as troosite. At still more lower transformation temperature (from about 550°C to 200°C) the ferrite-cementite mixture is more dispersed and is known as accicular it has a needle like structure.

Note: The symbol M_s stands for the temperature at which the formation of martensite begins and the symbol M_f stands for the temperature at which the formation of martesite ends.

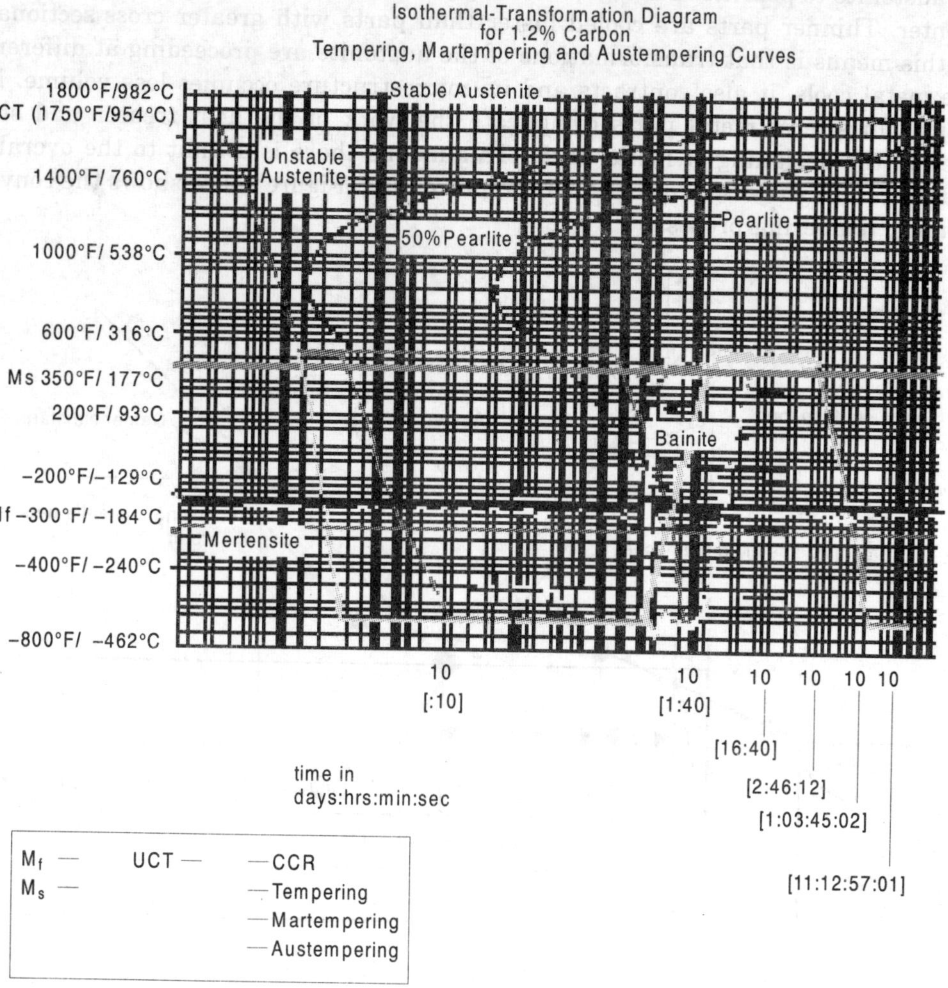

Fig. 8.13 IT diagram (tempering martempering and austempering).

However, the fast heating and cooling rates encountered in welding will have a significant influence on these temperatures, making the accurate prediction of weld metallurgy using this diagram difficult.

8.9 QUENCH AND TEMPERING PROCESSES

1. Conventional Heat, Quench and Temper process
2. Martempering
3. Austempering.

8.9.1 Conventional Heat, Quench and Temper Process

In this process, austenite is transformed to martensite as a result of rapid quench from furnace to room temperature. Then, martensite is heated to a temperature which gives the desired hardness. One serious drawback is the possibility of distorting and cracking the metal as a result of severe quenching required to form martensite without transforming any of the austenite to pearlite. During quenching process, the outer area is cooled quicker than the center. Thinner parts are cooled faster than parts with greater cross-sectional areas. What this means is that transformations of the austenite are proceeding at different rates. As the metal cools, it also contracts and its microstructure occupies less volume. Extreme variations in size of metal parts complicate the work of the heat treater and should be avoided in the designing of metal parts. This means there is a limit to the overall size of parts that can be subjected to such thermal processing. Figure below shows the conventional hardening, tempering process.

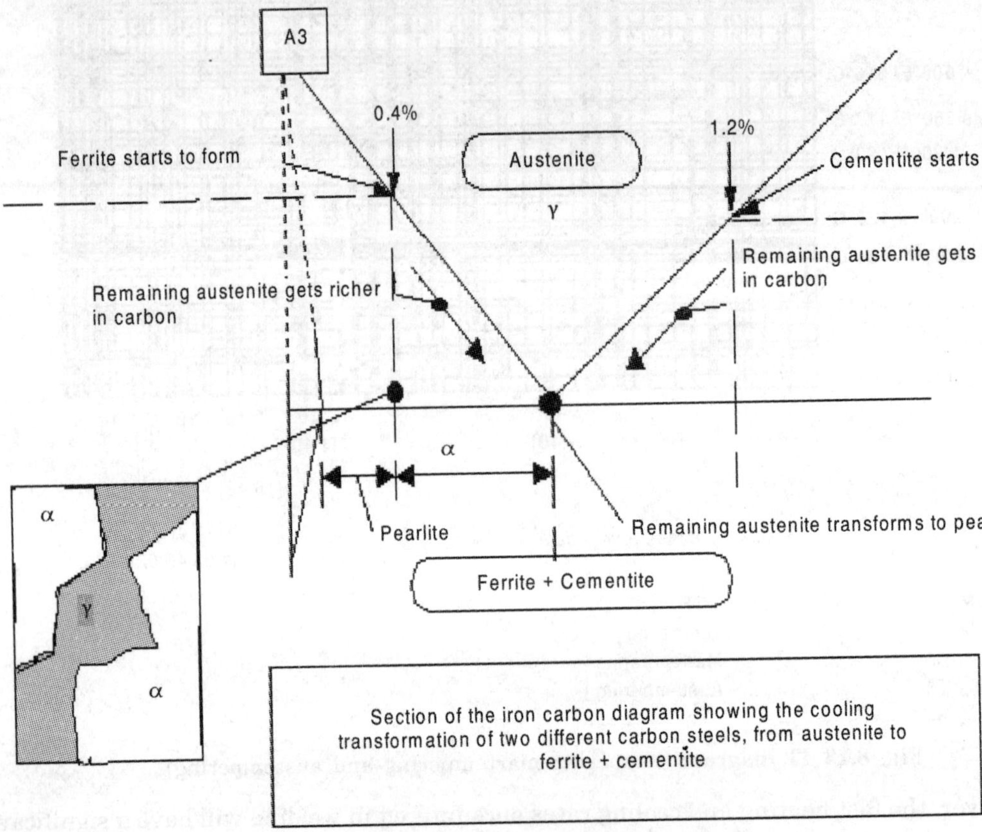

Fig. 8.14 Cooling transformation.

8.9.2 Martempering (Marquenching)

To overcome the restrictions of conventional quenching and tempering, Martempering process can be used. Martempering or marquenching permits the transformation of austenite to martensite to take place at the same time throughout the structure of the metal part. This is shown in figure below. By using interrupted quench, the cooling is stopped at a point above the martensite transformation region to allow sufficient time for the center to cool to the same temperature as the surface. Then cooling is continued through the martensite region, followed by the usual tempering.

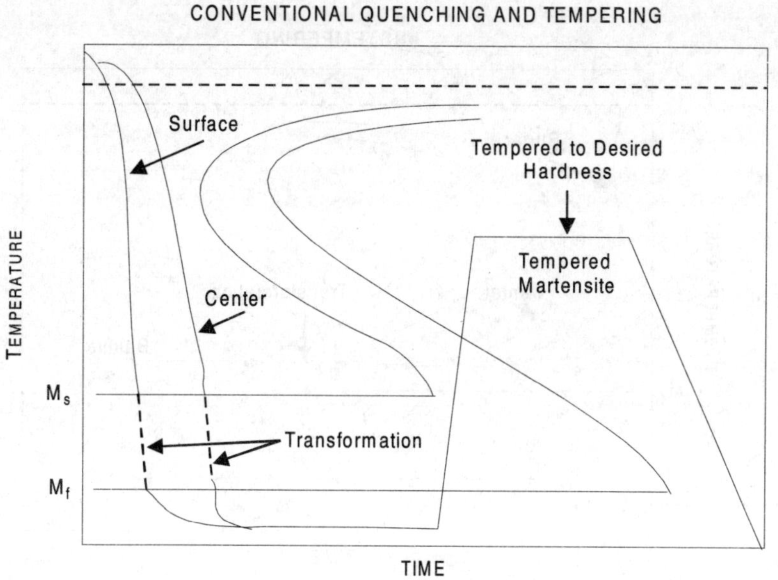

Fig. 8.15 Conventional quenching and tempering process.

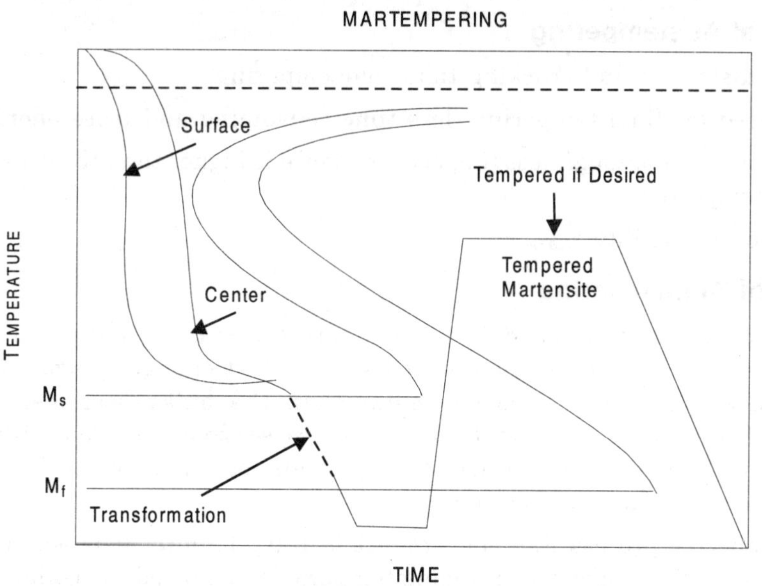

Fig. 8.16 Martempering process.

8.9.3 Austempering

This is the second method that can be used to overcome the restrictions of conventional quench and tempering. The quench is interrupted at a higher temperature than for martempering to allow the metal at the center of the part to reach the same temperature as the surface. By maintaining that temperature, both the center and the surface are allowed to transform to bainite and are then cooled to room temperature.

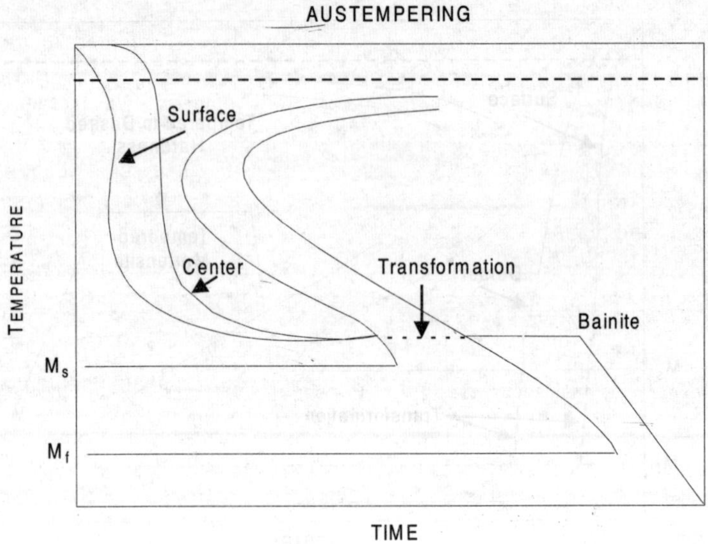

Fig. 8.17 Austempering process.

Advantages of Austempering

1. Less distortion and cracking than martempering,
2. No need for final tempering (less time consuming and more energy efficient)
3. Improvement of toughness (impact resistance is higher than the conventional quench and tempering)
4. Improved ductility

Limitations of Austempering

Austempering can be applied to parts where the transformation to pearlite can be avoided. This means that the section must be cooled fast enough to avoid the formation of pearlite. Thin sections can be cooled faster than the bulky sections. Most industrial applications of austempering have been limited to sections less than 1/2 in. thick. The thickness can be increased by the use of alloy steels, but then the time for completion of transformation to bainite may become excessive.

In austempering process, the end product is 100% bainite. It is accomplished by first heating the part to the proper austenitizing temperature followed by cooling rapidly in a salt bath which is maintained between 400 and 800°F. The part is left in the bath until the transformation to bainite is complete. The steel is caused to go directly from austenite to bainite.

GLOSSARY

Abrasion

The process of rubbing, grinding, or wearing away by friction.

Abrasive

A substance capable of grinding away another material.

Acid Steel

Steel melted in a furnace with an acid bottom and lining and under a slag containing an excess of an acid substance such as silica.

Acid-Brittleness

Brittleness resulting from pickling steel in acid; hydrogen, formed by the interaction between iron and acid, is partially absorbed by the metal, causing acid brittleness.

Activation

The changing of the passive surface of a metal to a chemically active state. Contrast with passivation.

Age Hardening

Hardening by aging, usually after rapid cooling or cold working. The term as applied to soft, or low carbon steels, relates to a wide variety of commercially important, slow, gradual changes that ake place in properties of steels after the final treatment. These changes, which bring about a condition of increased hardness, elastic limit, and tensile strength with a consequent loss in ductility, occur during the period in which the steel is at normal temperatures.

Aging

A change in properties that occurs at ambient or moderately elevated temperatures after hot working or a heat treating operation (quench aging in ferrous alloys), or after a cold working operation (strain aging). The change in properties is often, but not always, due to a phase change (precipitation), but does not involve a change in chemical composition. In a metal or alloy, a change in properties that generally occurs slowly at room temperature and more rapidly at higher temperatures.

Air Cooling

Cooling of the heated metal, intermediate in rapidity between slow furnace cooling and quenching, in which the metal is permitted to stand in the open air.

AISI Steels

Steels of the American Iron and Steel Institute. Common and alloy steels have been numbered in a system essentially the same as the SAE. The AISI system is more elaborate than the SAE in that all numbers are preceded by letters: A represents basic open-hearth alloy steel, B acid bessemer carbon steel, C basic open-hearth carbon steel, CB either acid bessemer basic open-hearth carbon steel, E electric furnace alloy steel.

Alclad

Composite sheet produced by bonding either corrosion-resistant aluminum alloy or aluminum of high purity to base metal of structurally stronger aluminum alloy. The coatings are anodic to the core so they protect exposed areas of the core electrolytically during exposure to corrosive environment.

Allotriomorph

A particle of a phase that has no regular external shape.

Allotropy

The property whereby certain elements may exist in more than one crystal structure.

Alloy

A substance having metallic properties and composed of two or more chemical elements of which at least one is a metal.

Alloy Steel

Steel containing substantial quantities of elements other than carbon and the commonly-accepted limited amounts of manganese, sulphur, silicon, and phosphorus. Addition of such alloying elements is usually for the purpose of increased hardness, strength or chemical resistance.

Alloying Element

An element added to a metal, and remaining in the metal, that effects changes in structure and properties.

Alpha Brass

A copper-zinc alloy containing up to 38% of zinc. Used mainly for cold working.

Alpha Bronze

A copper-tin alloy consisting of the alpha solid solution of tin in copper. Commercial forms contain 4 or 5% of tin. This alloy is used in coinage, springs, turbine, blades, etc.

Alpha Iron

The polymorphic form of iron, stable below 1670°F. has a body centered cubic lattice, and is magnetic up to 1410°F.

Aluminizing

Forming an aluminum or aluminum alloy coating on a metal by hot dipping, hot spraying, or diffusion.

Aluminum Killed Steel

A steel where aluminum has been used as a deoxidizing agent.

Angstrom Unit

(A) A unit of linear measure equal to 10 (–10) m, or 0.1 nm; not an accepted Si unit, but still sometimes used for small distances such as interatomic distances and some wavelengths.

Anisotropy

The characteristics of exhibiting different values of a property in different directions with respect to a fixed reference system in the material.

Annealing

Heating to and holding at a suitable temperature and then cooling at a suitable rate, for such purposes as reducing hardness, improving machinability, facilitating cold working, producing a desired microstructure, or obtaining desired mechanical, physical, or other properties.

Annealing Twin

A twin formed in a metal during an annealing heat treatment.

Anodizing (Aluminum Adic Oxide Coating),

A process of coating aluminum by anodic treatment resulting in a thin film of aluminum oxide of extreme hardness. A wide variety of dye colored coatings are possible by impregnation in process.

ASTM

Abbreviation for American Society For Testing Material. An organization for issuing standard specifications on materials, including metals and alloys.

Attenuation

The fractional decrease of the intensity of an energy flux, including the reduction of intensity resulting from geometrical spreading, absorption, and scattering.

Austempering

Quenching a ferrous alloy from a temperature above the transformation range, in a medium having a rate of heat abstraction high enough to prevent the formation of high-temperature transformation products, and then holding the alloy, until transformation is complete, at a temperature below that of pearlite formation and above that of martensite formation.

Austenitic Steel

Steel which, because of the presence of alloying elements, such as manganese, nickel, chromium, etc., shows stability of austenite at normal temperatures.

Austenitizing

Forming austenite by heating a ferrous alloy into the transformation range (partial austenitizing) or above the transformation range (complete austenitizing).

Austentite

A solid solution of one or more elements in face-centered cubic iron.

Bainite

A eutectoid transformation product of ferrite and a fine dispersion of carbide, generally formed at temperatures below 840 to 930 F (450 to 500C): upper bainite is an aggregate containing parallel lath-shape units of ferrite, produces the so-called feathery appearance in optical microscopy, and is formed at temperatures above about 660 F (350 C); lower bainite consists of individual plate-shape units and is formed at temperatures below about 660 F (350 C).

Bamboo Grain Structure

A structure in wire or sheet in which the boundaries of the grains tend to be aligned normal to the long axis and to extend completely through the thickness.

Banded Structure

Appearance of a metal showing parallel bands in the direction of rolling or working.

Banding

Inhomogeneous distribution of alloying elements or phases aligned in filaments or plates parallel to the direction of working.

Bark

Surface of metal, under the oxide-scale layer, resulting from heating in an oxidizing environment. In the case of steel, such bark always suffers from decarburization.

Bath Annealing

Is immersion is a liquid bath (such as molten lead or fused salts) held at an assigned temperature-when a lead bath is used, the process is known as lead annealing.

Bauxite

The only commercial ore of aluminum, corresponding essentially to the formula $Al_2O_3.H_2O$.

Beryllium Copper

An alloy of copper and 2–3% beryllium with optionally fractional percentages of nickel or cobalt. Alloys of this series show remarkable age-hardening properties and an ultimate hardness of about 400 Brinell (Rockwell C43). Because of such hardness and good electrical conductivity, beryllium-copper is used in electrical switches, springs, etc.

Billet

A solid semi-finished round or square product that has been hot worked by forging, rolling, or extrusion. An iron or steel billet has a minimum width or thickness of 1 1/2 in. and the cross-sectional area varies from 2 1/4 to 36 sq. in. For nonferrous metals, it may also be a casting suitable for finished or semi-finished rolling or for extrusion.

Binary Alloy

An alloy containing two elements, apart from minor impurities, as brass containing the two elements copper and zinc.

Black Annealing

A process of box annealing or pot annealing ferrous alloy sheet, strip or wire after hot working and pickling.

Blister

A defect in metal, on or near the surface, resulting from the expansion of gas in a subsurface zone. Very small blisters are called pinheads or pepper blisters.

Blister Steel

High-carbon steel produced by carburizing wrought iron. The bar, originally smooth, is covered with small blisters when removed from the cementation (carburizing) furnace.

Bloom: a semi-finished hot rolled steel product, rectangular in section, usually produced on a blooming mill but sometimes made by forging.

Bloom

A semi-finished hot rolled product, rectangular in cross section, produced on a blooming mill. For iron and steel, the width is not more than twice the thickness, and the cross-sectional area is usually not less than 36 sq. in. Iron and steel blooms are sometimes made by forging.

Blowhole

A cavity which was produced during the solidification of metal by evolved gas, which in failing to escape is held in pockets.

Blue Annealing

Heating hot rolled ferrous sheet in an open furnace to a temperature within the transformation range and then cooling in air, in order to soften the metal. The formation of a bluish oxide on the surface is incidental.

Blue Brittleness

Reduced ductility occurring as a result of strain aging, when certain ferrous alloys are worked between 300 and 700 (degrees) F. This phenomenon may be observed at the working temperature or subsequently at lower temperatures.

Body-centered

Having the equivalent lattice points at the corners of the unit cell, and at its center; sometimes called centered, or space-centered.

Brale

A diamond penetrator, conical in shape, used with a Rockwell hardness tester for hard metals.

Brasses

Copper base alloys in which zinc is the principal alloying element. Brass is harder and mechanically stronger than either of its alloying elements copper or zinc. It is formable and ductile; develops high tensile strength with cold-working and is not heat treatable.

Brazing

Joining metals by fusion of nonferrous alloys that have melting points above 800°F (425°C), but lower than those of the metals being joined. May be accomplished by a torch. Filler metal is ordinarily in rod form in torch brazing; whereas in furnace and dip brazing the work material is first assembled and the filler metal may then be applied as wire, washers, clips, bands, or may be bonded, as in brazing sheet.

Brinell Hardness Test

A common standard method of measuring the hardness of materials. The smooth surface of the metal is subjected to indentation by a hardened steel ball under pressure. The diameter of the indentation, in the material surface, is then measured by a microscope and the hardness value is read from a chart or determined by a prescribed formula.

Brittle Fracture

Fracture preceded by little or negligible plastic deformation.

Brittleness

The tendency of a metal or material to fracture without undergoing appreciable plastic deformation.

Bronze

Primarily an alloy of copper and tin, but additionally, the name is used when referring to other alloys not containing tin, for example, aluminum bronze, manganese bronze, and beryllium bronze.

Carbide

A compound of carbon with one or more metallic elements.

Carbon Equivalent

Referring to the rating of weld-ability, this is a value that takes into account the equivalent additive effects of carbon and other alloying elements on a particular characteristic of a steel. For rating of weld-ability, a formula commonly used is: $CE = C + (Mn/6) + [(Cr + Mo + V)/5] + [(Ni + Cu)/15]$.

Carbon Steel

Common or ordinary steel as contrasted with special or alloy steels, which contain other alloying metals in addition to the usual constituents of steel in their common percentages.

Carbonitriding

Introducing carbon and nitrogen into a solid ferrous alloy by holding above Ac1 in an atmosphere that contains suitable gases such as hydrocardons, carbon monocide, and ammonia. The carbonitrided alloy is usually quench hardened.

Carburizing

A process in which an austenitized ferrous material is brought into contact with a carbonaceous atmosphere having sufficient carbon potential to cause absorption of carbon at the surface and, by diffusion, create a concentration gradient.

Cartridge Brass

70% copper 30% zinc. This is one of the most widely used of the copper-zinc alloys; it is formable and ductile and possesses excellent cold-working, poor hot working and poor machining properties. Rated excellent for soft-soldering; good for silver alloy brazing or oxyacetylene welding and fair for resistance of carbon arc welding. The alloy develops high tensile strength with cold-working. Temper is obtained by cold rolling.

Case

In a ferrous alloy, the outer portion that has been made harder than the inner portion, or core.

Case Hardening

Carburizing and subsequently hardening by suitable heat-treatment, all or part of the surface portions of a piece of iron-base alloy.

Cast

(1) A term indicating in the annealed state as Cast Spring Steel Wire. (2) In reference to Bright or Polished Strip Steel or Wire, the word cast implies discoloration as a shadow. (3) A term implying a lack of straightness as in a coil set.

Cast Iron

Iron containing more carbon than the solubility limit in austenite (about 2%).

Cast Steel

Steel in the form of castings, usually containing less than 2% carbon.

Cementite

A compound of iron and carbon known as iron carbide, which has the approximate chemical formula Fe_3C containing 6.69% of carbon. Hard and brittle, it is the hard constituent of cast iron, and the normal form in which carbon is present in steel. It is magnetizable, but not as readily as ferrite.

Charpy Test

A pendulum-type single-blow impact test in which the specimen usually notched, is supported at both ends as a simple beam and broken by a falling pendulum. The energy absorbed, as determined by the subsequent rise of the pendulum, is a measure of impact strength or notch toughness.

Chatter Marks

Parallel indentations or marks appearing at right angles to edge of strip forming a pattern at close and regular intervals, caused by roll vibrations.

Chemical Polishing

Improving the specular reflectivity of a metal surface by chemical treatment.

Chromadizing (Chromodizing, Chromatizing)

Forming an acid surface to improve paint adhesion on aluminum or aluminum alloys, mainly aircraft skins, by treatment with a solution of chromic acid.

Clad Metal

A composite metal containing two or three layers that have been bonded together. The bonding may have been accomplished by co-rolling, welding, heavy chemical deposition or heavy electroplating.

Cladding

A process for covering one metal with another. Usually the surfaces of fairly thick slabs of two metals are brought carefully into contact and are then subjected to co-rolling so that a clad composition results. In some instances a thick electroplate may be deposited before rolling.

Cleavage

Fracture of a crystal by crack propagation across a crystallographic plane of low index.

Cleavage Fracture

Fracture of a grain, or most of the grains, in a polycrystalline metal by cleavage, resulting in bright reflecting facets.

Cleavage Plane

A characteristic crystallographic plane or set of planes in a crystal on which cleavage fracture occurs easily.

Columnar Structure

A coarse structure of parallel columns of grains, having the long axis perpendicular to the casting surface.

Coring

A variation of composition between the center and surface of a unit of structure (such as a dendrite, a grain or a carbide particle) resulting from non-equilibrium growth over a range of temperature.

Corrosion

Gradual chemical or electrochemical attack on a metal by atmosphere, moisture or other agents.

Corrosion Embrittlement

The severe loss of ductility of a metal resulting from corrosive attack, usually intergranular and often not visually apparent.

Corrosion Fatigue

Effect of the application of repeated or fluctuating stresses in a corrosive environment characterized by shorter life than would be encountered as a result of either their repeated or fluctuating stresses alone or the corrosive environment alone.

Creep

The flow or plastic deformation of metals held for long periods of time at stresses lower than the normal yield strength. The effect is particularly important if the temperature of stressing is above the recrystallization temperature of the metal.

Creep Limit

(1) The maximum stress that will cause less than a specified quantity of creep in a given time. (2) The maximum nominal stress under which the creep strain rate decreases continuously with time under constant load and at constant temperature. Sometimes used synonymously with creep strength.

Creep Strength

(1) The constant nominal stress that will cause a specified quantity of creep in a given time at constant temperature. (2) The constant nominal stress that will cause a specified creep react at constant temperature.

Crevice Erosion

A type of concentration-cell corrosion; corrosion of a metal that is caused by the concentration of dissolved salts, metal ions, oxygen, or other gases, and such, in crevices or pockets remote from the principal fluid stream, with a resultant building up of differential cells that ultimately cause deep pitting.

Critical Cooling Rate

The limiting rate at which austenite must be cooled to ensure that a particular type of transformation product is formed.

Critical Point

(1) The temperature or pressure at which a change in crystal structure, phase or physical properties occurs; same as transformation temperature. (2) In an equilibrium diagram, that specific combination of composition, temperature and pressure at which the phases of an inhomogeneous system are in equilibrium.

Critical Range

A temperature range in which an internal change takes place within a metal. Also termed transformation range.

Critical Strain

That strain which results in the formation of very large grains during recrystallization.

Critical Temperature

Synonymous with critical point if pressure is constant.

Crystal

(1) A physically homogeneous solid in which the atoms. ions or molecules are arranged in a three-dimensional repetitive pattern. (2) A coherent piece of matter, all parts of which have the same anisotropic arrangement of atom; in metals, usually synonymous with grain and crystallitc.

Crystalline Fracture

A fracture of a polycrystalline metal characterized by a grainy appearance. Compare fibrous fracture.

Crystallization

The formation of crystals by the atoms assuming definite positions in a crystal lattice. This is what happens when a liquid metal solidifies. (Fatigue, the failure of metals under repeated stresses, is sometimes falsely attributed to crystallization).

Cube-Centered

Metallography—(concerning space lattices)—Body-centered cubic. Refers to crystal structure.

Cup Fracture

A type of fracture in a tensile test specimen which looks like a cup having the exterior portion extended with the interior slightly depressed.

Cup Fracture (Cup-and-cone Fracture)

Fracture, frequently seen in tensile test pieces of a ductile material, in which the surface of failure on one portion shows a central flat area of failure in tension, with an exterior extended rim of failure in shear.

Cyaniding

Introducing carbon and nitrogen into a solid ferrous alloy by holding above Ac1 in contact with molten cyanide of suitable composition. The cyanided alloy is usually quench hardened.

Dead Soft Steel

Steel, normally made in the basic open-hearth furnace or by the basic oxygen process with carbon less than 0.10% and manganese in the 0.20–0.50% range, completely annealed.

Decarburization

Removal of carbon from the outer surface of iron or steel, usually by heating in an oxidizing or reducing atmosphere. Water vapor, oxygen and carbon dioxide are strong decarburizers. Reheating with adhering scale is also strongly decarburizing in action.

Dendrite

A crystal that has grown in treelike branching mode.

Deoxidizing

Removal of oxygen. In steel sheet, strip, and wire technology, the term refers to heat treatment in a reducing atmosphere, to lessen the amount of scale.

Diffusion

(1) Spreading of a constituent in a gas, liquid or solid, tending to make the composition of all parts uniform. (2) The spontaneous movement of atoms or molecules to new sites within a material.

Dislocation

A linear defect in the structure of a crystal.

Ductility

The ability of a material to deform plastically without fracturing, being measured by elongation or reduction of area in a tensile test, by height of cupping in an Erichsen test or by other means.

Duralumin

The trade name applied to the first aluminum-copper-magnesium type of age-hardenable alloy (17S), which contains nominally 4% Cu, 1/2% Mg. The term is sometimes used to include the class of wrought aluminum-copper-magnesium alloys that harden during aging at room temperature.

Elastic Limit

Maximum stress that a material will stand before permanent deformation occurs.

Electropolishing

Improving the specular reflectivity of a metal surface by electrochemical dissolution.

Elongation

In tensile testing, the increase in the gauge length, measured after fracture of the specimen within the gauge length, usually expressed as a percentage of the original gauge length.

Elongation After Fracture

In tensile testing, the increase in the gauge length measured after fracture of the specimen within the gauge length and usually expressed as a percentage of the original gauge length.

Endurance Limit

Same as fatigue limit.

Equilibrium Diagram

A graphical representation of the temperature, pressure and composition limits of phase fields in an alloy system as they exist under conditions of thermodynamical equilibrium. In condensed systems, pressure is usually considered constant.

Equiaxed Structure

A structure in which the grains have approximately the same dimensions in all directions.

Etchant

A chemical solution used to etch a metal to reveal structural details.

Eutectoid

(1) An isothermal reversible transformation in which a solid solution is converted into two or more intimately mixed solids, the number of solids formed being the same as the number of components in the system. (2) An alloy having the composition indicated by the eutectoid point on an equilibrium diagram. (3) An alloy structure of intermixed solid constituents formed by a eutectoid transformation.

Eutectoid Steel

Steel representing the eutectoid composition of the iron-carbon system, with about 0.80% to 0.83% carbon, the eutectoid temperature being about 1333 (degrees) F. Such steel in the annealed condition consists exclusively of pearlite. Steels with less than this quota of carbon are known as hypo-eutectoid and contain free ferrite in addition to the pearlite. When more carbon is present, the steel is known as hyper-eutectoid and contains free cementite. The presence of certain elements, such as nickel or chromium, lowers the eutectoid carbon content.

Face Centered (concerning cubic space lattices)

Having equivalent points at the corners of the unit cell and at the centers of its six faces. A face-centered cubic space lattice is characteristic of one of the slose-packed arrangements of equal hard spheres.

Fatigue

The phenomenon leading to fracture under repeated or fluctuating stresses having a maximum value less than the tensile strength of the material. Fatigue fractures are progressive, beginning as minute cracks that grow under the action of the fluctuating stress.

Fatigue Life

The number of cycles of stress that can be sustained prior to failure for a stated test condition.

Fatigue Limit

The maximum stress below which a material can presumable endure an infinite number of stress cycles. If the stress is not completely reversed, the value of the mean stress, the minimum stress or the stress ratio should be stated.

Fatigue Strength

The maximum stress that can be sustained for a specified number of cycles without failure, the stress being completely reversed within each cycle unless otherwise stated.

Ferrite

A solid solution of one or more elements in body-centered cubic iron. Unless otherwise designated (for instance, as chromium ferrite), the solute is generally assumed to be carbon. On some equilibrium diagrams there are two ferrite regions separated by an austenite area. The lower area is alpha ferrite; the upper, delta ferrite. If there is no designation, alpha ferrite is assumed.

Fiber or Fibre

Direction in which metals have been caused to flow, as by rolling, with microscopic evidence in the form of fibrous appearance in the direction of flow.

Flame Annealing

Annealing in which the heat is applied directly by a flame.

Flame Hardening

A process of hardening a ferrous alloy by heating it above the transformation range by means of a high-temperature flame, and then cooling as required.

Fractography

Descriptive treatment of fracture, especially in metals, with specific reference to photographs of the fracture surface. Microfractography involves photographs at low magnification; microfractography, at high magnification.

Fracture

Surface appearance of metals when broken.

Fracture Test

Nicking and breaking a bar by means of sudden impact, to enable microscopic study of the fractured surface.

Fretting (Fretting Corrosion)

Action that results in surface damage, especially in a corrosive environment, when there is relative motion between solid surfaces in contact under pressure.

Full Annealing

Used principally on iron and steel, means heating the metal to about 100 (degrees) F. above the critical temperature range, followed by soaking at this point and slow cooling below the critical temperature.

Gamma Iron

The form of iron stable between 1670 (degrees) F., and 2550 (degrees) F., and characterized by a face-centered cubic crystal structure.

Grain

An individual crystal in a polycrystalline metal or alloy, including twinned regions or subgrains if present.

Grain Boundary

Bounding surface between crystals. When alloys yield new phases (as in cooling), grain boundaries are the preferred location for the appearance of the new phase. Certain deterioration, such as season cracking and caustic embrittlement, occur almost exclusively at grain boundaries.

Grain Coarsening

A heat treatment that produces excessively large austenitic grains.

Grain Flow

Fiber like lines appearing on polished and etched sections of forgings, caused by orientation of the constituents of the metal in the direction of working during forging.

Grain Growth

An increase in the average size of the grains in polycrystalline metal or alloy, usually a result of heating at elevated temperature.

Grain Size

Average diameter of grains in the metal under consideration, or alternatively, the number of grains per unit area. Since increase in grain size is paralleled by lower ductility and impact resistance, the question of general grain size is of great significance. The addition of certain metals affects grain size, for example vanadium and aluminum ten to give steel a fine grain. The ASTM has set up a grain size standard for steels, and the McQuaid-Ehn Test has been developed as a method of measurement.

Granular Fracture

A type of irregular surface produced when metal fractures, characterized by a rough, grain like appearance as differentiated from a smooth silky, or fibrous, type. It can be sub classified into trans-granular and inter-granular forms. This type of fracture is frequently called crystalline fracture, but the implication that the metal has crystallized is completely misleading.

Graphite

The polymorph of carbon with a hexagonal crystal structure.

Graphitizing

Annealing a ferrous alloy in such a way that some or all of the carbon is precipitated as graphite.

Gray Cast Iron

A cast iron that gives a gray fracture due to the presence of flake graphite. Often called gray iron.

Hardenability

In a ferrous alloy, the property that determines the depth and distribution of hardness induced by quenching.

Hardening

Increasing the hardness by suitable treatment, usually involving heating and cooling.

Hardness

Degree to which a metal will resist cutting, abrasion, penetration, bending and stetching. The indicated hardness of metals will differ somewhat with the specific apparatus and technique of measuring. For details concerning the various types of apparatus used in measuring hardness, See Brinell Hardness, Rockwell Hardness, Vickers Hardness, Scleroscope Hardness. Tensile Strength also is an indication of hardness.

Heat Treatment

Heating and cooling a solid metal or alloy in such a way that desired structures, conditions or properties are attained. Heating for the sole purpose of hot working is excluded from the meaning of this term.

Heat-Affected Zone

That portion of the base metal which was not melted during brazing, cutting, or welding, but whose microstructure and physical properties were altered by the heat.

Homogenizing

Holding at high temperature to eliminate or decrease chemical segregation by diffusion.

Hooke's Law

Stress is proportional to strain in the elastic range. The value of the stress at which a material ceases to obey Hooke's law is known as the elastic limit.

Hot Shortness

Brittleness in metal in the hot forming range.

Hot Working

Deformation under conditions that result in recrystallization.

Hydrogen Embrittlement

A condition low ductility in metals resulting from the absorbtion of hydrogen.

Hypereutectoid Alloy

In a eutectoid system, any alloy containing more than the eutectoid concentration of solute.

Hypereutectoid Steel

A steel having more than the eutectoid percentage of carbon.

Hypoeutectic Alloy

In a eutectic system, any alloy containing less than the eutectic concentration of solute.

Hypoeutectoid Steel

Steel with less than the eutectoid percentage of carbon.

Impact Test

Test designed to determine the resistance of metal to breakage by impact, usually by concentrating the applied stress to a notched specimen.

Impurities

Elements or compounds whose presence in a material is undesired.

Inclusion

A nonmetallic material in a solid metallic matrix.

Induction Hardening

Quench hardening in which the heat is generated by electrical induction.

Isothermal Transformation (IT) Diagram

A diagram that shows the isothermal time required for transformation of austenite to commence and to finish as a function of temperature. Same as Time-Temperature-Transformation (TTT) diagram or S-curve.

Izod Test

A pendulum type of single-blow impact test in which the specimen, usually notched, is fixed at one end and broken by a falling pendulum. The energy absorbed, as measured by the subsequent rise of the pendulum, is a measure of impact strength or notch toughness.

Killed Steel

Steel deoxidized with a strong deoxidizing agent, such as silicon or aluminum, to reduce the oxygen content to such a level that no reaction occurs between carbon and oxygen during solidification.

Lamellar Tear

A system of cracks or discontinuties aligned generally parallel to the worked surface of a plate. Usually associated with a fusion weld in thick plate.

Lap

A surface defect, appearing as a seam, caused by fording over hot metal, fins, or sharp corners and then rolling or forging them into the surface, but not welding them.

Lattice

Space lattice. Lattice lines and lattice planes are lines and planes chosen so as to pass through collinear lattice points, and non-collinear lattice points, respectively.

Liquidus

In a constitutional diagram, the locus of points representing the temperatures at which various components commence freezing on cooling or finish melting on heating.

Low Brass

80% cu. A copper-zinc alloy containing 20% zinc. Is a light golden color, very ductile, suitable for cupping, drawing, forming, etc. Because of its good strength and corrosion resistance it is used for flexible metal gose, metal bellows, etc.

Luders Lines or Bands

Elongated surface markings or depressions caused by localized plastic deformation that results form discontinuous (inhomogeneous) yielding.

Machinability

The relative ease of machining a metal.

Machinability Index

A relative measure of the machinability of an engineering material under specified standard conditions.

Macrostructure

The structure of a metal as revealed by examination of the etched surface at a magnification not exceeding ten diameters.

Malleability

The property that determines the ease of deforming a metal when the metal is subjected to rolling or hammering. The more malleable metals can be hammered or rolled into thin sheet more easily than others.

Martempering

Quenching an austenitized ferrous alloy in a medium at a temperature in the upper part of the martensite range, or slightly above that range, and holding it in the medium until the temperature throughout the alloy is substantially uniform. The alloy is then allowed to cool in air through the martensite range.

Martensite

In steel, a metalstable transition phase with a body-centered-tetragonal crystal structure formed by diffusionless transformation of austenite generally during cooling between the Ms and Mf temperatures.

Matalloid

(a) Element intermediate in lustre and conductivity between the true metals and non-metals. Arsenic, antimony, boron, tellurium, and selenium, etc., are generally considered metalloids; frequently one allotropic modification of an element will be non-metallic, another metalloid in character. Obviously, no hard and fast line can be drawn. (b) In steel metallurgy, metalloid has a specialized, even if erroneous, meaning; it covers elements commonly present in simple steel; carbon, manganese, phosphorus, silicon and sulphur.

Matrix

The principal phase in which another constituent is embedded.

Mechanical Polishing

A method of producing a specularly reflecting surface by use of abrasives.

Mechanical Properties

The properties of a material that reveal its elastic and inelastic behavior where force is applied, thereby indicating its suitability for mechanical application; for example, modulus of elasticity, tensile strength, elongation, hardness, and fatigue limit.

Mechanical Twin

A twin formed in a metal during plastic deformation by simple shear of the structure.

Mechanical Working

Plastic deformation or other physical change to which metal is subjected, by rolling, hammering, drawing., etc. to change its shape, properties or structure.

Medium-Carbon Steel

Contains from 0.30% to 0.60% carbon and less than 1.00% manganese. May be made by any of the standard processes.

Melting Point

The temperature at which a pure metal, compound or eutectic changes form solid to liquid; the temperature at which the liquid and the solid are in equilibrium.

Metal

An opaque, lustrous, elemental substance that is a good conductor of heat and electricity and, when polished, a good reflector or light. Most metals are malleable and ductile and are, in general, denser than other substances.

Metal Spraying

A process for applying a coating of metal to an object. The metal, usually in the form of wire, is melted by an oxyhydrogen or oxyacetylene blast or by an electric arc and is proficted at high speed by gas pressure against the object being coated.

Metallography

The science concerning the constituents and structure of metals and alloys as revealed by the microscope.

Metalograph

An optical instrument designed for both visual observation and photomicrography of prepared surfaces of opaque materials at magnifications ranging from about 25 to about 1500 diameters.

Metastable

Possessing a state of pseudo-equilibrium that has a free energy higher than that of the true equilibrium state but from which a system does not change spontaneously.

Mf Temperature

The temperature at which martensitic transformation is essentially complete during cooling after austenitization.

Microstructure

The structure of a prepared surface of a metal as revealed by a microscope at a magnification greater than ten diameters.

Mild Steel

Carbon steel containing a maximum of about 0.25% C.

Modulus of Elasticity

A measure of the rigidity of metal. Ratio of stress, within proportional limit, to corresponding strain. Specifically, the modulus obtained in tension or compression is Young's modulus, stretch modulus or modulus of extensibility; the modulus obtained in torsion or shear is modulus of rigidity, shear modulus or modulus of torsion; the modulus covering the ratio of the mean normal stress to the change in volume per unit volume is the bulk modulus.

Ms Temperature

The temperature at which a martensitic transformation starts during cooling after austenitization.

Muntz Metal (A Refractory Alloy)

Alpha-beta brass, 60% copper and 40% zinc. Stronger than alpha-brass and used for castings and hot-worked (rolled, stamped, or extruded) products. High strength brasses are developed from this by adding other elements.

Music Wire

A polished high tensile strength cold drawn wire with higher tensile strength and higher torsional strength than any other material available. These high mechanical properties are obtained by a combination of the high carbon content, the patenting treatment and by many continuous passes through drawing dies. The high toughness characteristic of this material is obtained by the patenting. Such wire is purchased according to tensile strength, not hardness.

Natural Aging

Spontaneous aging of a supersaturated solid solution at room temperature.

Necking

Local reduction of the cross-sectional area of metal by stretching.

Needle Cutter Steel

Usually supplied quarter hard rolled, extra precision rolled with sheared edges. Carbon content 1.25-Chromium 0.15. Usually supplied in a 2 width from 0.002 to 0.035. Used for cutting the eyes of needle and milling the latch in a latch needle.

Neumann Band

A mechanical (deformation) twin in ferrite.

Nitriding

Introducing nitrogen into a solid ferrous alloy by holding at a suitable temperature (below Ac1 for ferritic steels) in contact with a nitrogenous material, usually ammonia of molten cyanide of appropriate composition. Quenching is not required to produce a hard case.

Nitriding Steel

Steel which is particularly suited for the nitriding process, that is, it will form a very hard and adherent surface upon proper nitriding (heating in a partially dissociated atmosphere of ammonia gas). Composition usually 0.20–0.40 carbon, 0.90–1.50 chromium, 0.15–1.00 molybdenum, and 0.85–1.20% aluminum.

Nodular Pearlite

Pearlite that has grown as a colony with an approximately spherical morphology.

Non-Ferrous Metals

Metals or alloys that are free of iron or comparatively so.

Non-Metallic Inclusions

Impurities (commonly oxides), sulphides, silicates or similar substances held in metals mechanically during solidification or formed by reactions in the solid state.

Normalizing

Heating a ferrous alloy to a suitable temperature above A3 or Acm and then cooling in still air to a temperature substantially below A1. The cooling rate usually is in the range 900 to1800 F/h (500 to 1000C/h).

Notch Brittleness

A measure of the susceptibility of a material to brittle fracture at locations of stress concentration. For example, in a notch tensile test a material is said to be notch brittle if its notch strength is less than its tensile strength; otherwise, it is said to be notch ductile.

Notch Sensitivity

A measure of the reduction in strength of a metal caused by the presence of stress concentration. Values can be obtained from static, impact or fatigue tests.

Nucleation

Initiation of a phase transformation at discrete sites, the new phase growing from nuclei.

Orange Peel

A pebble-grain surface which develops in forming of metals having coarse grains.

Orange Peel (effect)

A surface roughening (defect) encountered in forming products from metal stock that has a coarse grain size. It is due to uneven flow or to the appearance of the overly large grains usually the result of annealing at too high a temperature. Also referred to as pebbles and alligator skin.

Orientation (crystal)

Arrangement of certain crystal axes or crystal planes in a crystalline aggregate with respect to a given direction or plane. If there is any tendency for one arrangement to predominate, it is known as the preferred orientation; in the absence of any such preference, random orientation exists.

Overaging

Aging under conditions of time and temperature greater than those required to obtain maximum change in a certain property, so that the property is altered in the direction of the initial value.

Overheating

Heating a metal or alloy to such a high temperature that its properties are impaired. When the original properties cannot be restored by further heat treating, by mechanical working, or by combination of working and heat treating, the overheating is known as burning.

Oxidation

The addition of oxygen to a compound. Exposure to atmosphere sometimes results in oxidation of the exposed surface, hence a staining or discoloration. This effect is increased with temperature increase.

Passivation

The changing of the chemically active surface of a metal to a much less reactive state. Contrast with activation.

Patenting

A heat treatment applied to medium and high-carbon steel prior to cold drawing to wire. The treatment involves austenitization followed by isothermal transformation at a temperature that produces a microstructure of very fine pearlite.

Pearlite

A eutectoid transformation product of ferrite and cementite that ideally has a lamellar structure but that is always degenerate to some extent.

Peening

Mechanical working of metal by hammer blows or shot impingement.

Penetrant Inspection

A method of non-destructive testing for determining the existence and extent of discontinuities that are open to the surface in the part being inspected. The indications ore made visible through the use of a dye or fluorescent chemical in the liquid employed as the inspection medium.

Peritectic

An isothermal reversible reaction in which a liquid phase reacts with a solid phase to produce another solid phase.

Permalloy

Nickel alloys containing about 20 to 60% Fe, used for their high magnetic permeability and electrical resistivity.

Phase

A physically homogeneous and distincy portion of a material system.

Phase Diagram

Synonymous with constitutional diagram.

Phosphor Bronze

Copper base alloys, with 3.5 to 10% of tin, to which has been added in the molten state phosphorus in varying amounts of less than 1% for deoxidizing and strengthening purposes. Because of excellent toughness, strength, fine grain, resistance to fatigue and wear, and chemical resistance, these alloys find general use as springs and in making fittings. It has corrosion resisting properties comparable to copper.

Phosphor Bronze Strip

A copper-base alloy containing up to 10% tin, which has been deoxidized with phosphorus in varying amounts of less than 1%. Temper is imparted by cold rolling, resulting in greater tensile strength and hardness than in most copper-base alloys or either of its alloying elements copper or tin. The various tempers from One Number Hard to Ten Numbers Hard are classified in hardness by the number of B and S Gages reduction in dimension from the previous soft or as-annealed state. Phosphor bronze is not heat treatable for purposes of hardness development. It does not withstand elevated temperatures very well and should not be used in service above 225 (degrees) F. even after stress relieving treatment at 325 (degrees) to 350 (degrees) F. It has excellent electrical properties, corrosion resistant comparable to copper; great toughness and resistance to fatigue. Rated good for soft soldering, silver alloy brazing, oxyacctylene, carbon arc and resistance welding.

Pig Iron

(1) High-carbon iron made by reduction of iron ore in the blast furnace. (2) Cast iron in the form of pigs.

Plastic Deformation

Deformation that remains, or will remain, permanent after release of the stress that caused it.

Plasticity

The ability of a metal to be deformed extensively without rupture.

Polishing

Producing a specularly reflecting surface.

Polycrystalline

Comprising an aggregate of more than one crystal, and usually a large number of crystals.

Polymorphism

The ability of a material to exist in more than one crystallographic structure. Numerous metals change in crystallographic structure at transformation temperatures during heating or cooling. If the change is reversible, it is allotropy. The allotropy of iron, particularly the changes between the alpha body-centered and the gamma face centered form, is of fundamental importance in the hardening of steel.

Precipitation Hardening

Hardening caused by the precipitation of a constituent form a supersaturated solid solution.

Preferred Orientation

A condition of a polycrystalline aggregate in which the crystal orientations are not random.

Preheating

Heating before some further thermal or mechanical treatment. For tool steel, heating to an intermediate temperature immediately before austenitizing. For some nonferrous alloys, heating to a high temperature for a long time, in order to homogenize the structure before working.

Proof Stress

(1) The stress that will cause a specified small permanent set in a material. (2) A specified stress to be applied to a member or structure to indicate its ability to withstand service loads.

Quench Aging

Aging that occurs after quenching following solution heat treatment.

Quench Hardening

Hardening by austenitizing and then cooling at a rate such that a substantial amount of austenite is transformed to martensite.

Quenching

Rapid cooling.

Radiography

A nondestructive method of internal examination in which metal objects are exposed to a beam of X-ray or gamma radiation. Differences in thickness, density or absorption, caused by internal defects or inclusions, are apparent in the shadow image either on a fluorescent screen or on photographic film placed behind the object.

Recarburizing

(1) Increasing the carbon content of molten cast iron or steel by adding carbonaceous material, high-carbon pig iron or a high-carbon alloy. (2) Carburizing a metal part to return surface carbon lost in processing.

Recrystallization

A process whereby a distorted grain structure of cold worked metals is replaced by a new, stress-free grain structure as a result of annealing above a specific minimum temperature for a specific time.

Recrystallization Temperature

The approximate minimum temperature at which complete recrystallization of a cold worked metal occurs within a specified time.

Red Brass

85% Copper—A copper-zinc alloy containing approximately 15% zinc, used for plumbing pipe, hardware, condenser tubes. Because of its color, is used or vanity cases, coins, plaques, badges, etc. It is somewhat stronger than commercial bronze and is hardened more rapidly by cold working.

Red Shorness

Brittleness in steel when it is red hot.

Residual Stress

Stress present in a body that is free of external forces or thermal gradients.

Resilience

The tendency of a material to return to its original shape after the removal of a stress that has produced elastic strain.

Rockwell Hardness (Test)

A standard method for measuring the hardness of metels. The hardness is expressed as a number related to the depth of residual penetration of a steel ball or diamond cone (brale) after a minor load of 10 kilograms has been applied to hold the penetrator in position.

Self Diffusion

The spontaneous movement of an atom to a new site in a crystal of its own species.

Shear

A type of cutting operation in which the metal object is cut by means of a moving blade and fixed edge or by a pair of moving blades that may be either flat or curved.

Shear Bands (Deformation)

Bands in which deformation has been concentrated inhomogeneously in sheets that extend across regional groups of grains. Usually only one system is present in each regional group of grains, different systems being present in adhoining groups.

Shear Crack

A diagonal, transgranular crack caused by shear stresses.

Siliconizing

Diffusing silicon into solid metal, usually steel, at an elevated temperature.

Slag

A product resulting from the action of a flux on the nonmetallic constituents of a processed ore, or on the oxidized metallic constituents that are undesirable. Usually slags consist of combinations of acid oxides with basic oxides, and neutral oxides are added to aid fusibility.

Slip

Plastic deformation by irreversible shear displacement of one part of a crystal relative to another in a definite crystallographic direction and on a definite crystallographic plane.

Slip Direction

The crystallographic direction in which translation of slip takes place.

Slip Line

Trace of a slip plane on a viewing surface.

Slip Plane

The crystallographic plane on which slip occurs in a crystal.

Solid Solution

A single solid homogeneous crystalline phase containing two or more chemical species.

Solidus

In a constitutional diagram, the locus of points representing the temperatures at which various components finish freezing on cooling or begin to melt on heating.

Solute

The component of either a liquid or solid solution that is present to the lesser or minor extent; the component that is dissolved in the solvent.

Solution Heat Treatment

A heat treatment in which an alloy is heated to a suitable temperature, held at that temperature long enough to cause one or more constituents to enter into solid solution, and then cooled rapidly enough to hold these constituents in solution.

Solvent

The component of either a liquid or solid solution that is present to the greater or major extent; the component that dissolves the solute.

Solvus

In a phase or equilibrium diagram, the locus of points representing the temperature at which solid phases with various compositions coexist with other solid phases; that is, the limits of solid solubility.

Sorbite

Structure of steel, resulting from the tempering of martensite. In a truly sorbitic structure, the cementite is completely dispersed in the matrix. The trend is to call this structure tempered martensite.

Space Lattice (Crystal)

A system of equivalent points formed by the intersections of three sets of planes parallel to pairs of principal axes; the space lattice may be thought of as formed by the corners of the unit cells.

Spheroidizing

Any process of prolonged heating and slow cooling of steel which will convey the carbide content into rounded or spheroid form.

Spinning

The procedure of making sheet metal discs into hollow shapes by pressing the metal against a rotating form (spinning chuck) by a tool.

Stainless Steel

Corrosion resistant steel of a wide variety, but always containing a high percentage of chromium. These are highly resistant to corrosion attack by organic acids, weak mineral acids, atmospheric oxidation, etc.

Steel

An iron-base alloy usually containing carbon and other alloying elements. In carbon steel and low-alloy steel, the maximum carbon content is about 2.0%; in high-alloy steel, about 2.5%. The dividing line between low-alloy and high-alloy steels is generally regarded as the 5% level of total metallic alloying elements. Steel is differentiated from two general classes of iron-namely, cast irons, which have high carbon concentrations, and relatively pure irons, which have low carbon concentrations.

Strain

A measure of the relative change in the size of a body. Linear strain is the change per unit length of a linear dimension. True (or natural) strain is the natural logarithm of the ratio of the length at the moment of observation to the original gauge length. Shearing strain is the change in angle (expressed in radians) between two reference lines originally at right angles. When the term is used alone, it usually refers to linear strain in the direction of the applied stress.

Strain Aging

Aging induced by cold work.

Strain Hardening

An increase in hardness and strength caused by plastic deformation at temperatures lower than the recrystallization range.

Stress

Force per unit area. True stress denotes stress determined by measuring force and area at the same time. Conventional stress, as applied to tension and compression tests, is force divided by original area. Nominal stress is stress computed by simple elasticity formula.

Stress Relieving

Heating to a suitable temperature, holding long enough to reduce residual stresses and then cooling slowly enough to minimize the development of new residual stresses.

Stress-corrosion Cracking

Failure by cracking under combined action or corrosion and stress, either external (applied) or internal (residual). Cracking may be either intergranular or transgranular, depends on metal and corrosive medium.

Structure

The arangement of parts; in crystals, expecially, the shape and dimension of the until cell, and the number, kinds and positions of the atoms within it.

Subcritical Annealing

An annealing treatment in which a steel is heated to a temperature below the A1 temperature and then cooled slowly to room temperature.

Substitutional Solid Solution

A solid solution in which the solvent and solute atoms are located randomly at the atom sites in the crystal structure of the solution.

Substrate

The layer of metal underlying a coating, regardless of whether the layer is base metal.

Superalloy

An alloy developed for very high temperature service where relatively high stresses (tensile, thermal, vibratory, and shock) are encountered and where oxidation resistance is frequently required.

Supercooling

Cooling to a temperature below that of an equilibrium phase transformation without the transformation taking place.

Surface Hardening

A generic term covering several processes applicable to a suitable ferrous alloy that produce, by quench hardening only, a surface layer that is harder or more wear resistant than the core. There is no significant alteration of the chemical composition of the surface layer. The processes commonly used are induction hardening, flame hardening and shell hardening. Use of the applicable specific process name is preferred.

Temper (Met.)

The state of or condition of a metal as to its hardness or toughness produced by either thermal treatment or heat treatment and quench or cold working or a combination of same in order to bring the metal to its specified consistency. Each branch of the metal producing industry has developed its own system of temper designations. In flat-rolled products including sheet and strip steel, tin mill products, stainless strip, aluminum sheet and copper base alloy strip they are shown as follows.

Temper Brittleness

A reversible increase in the ductile-brittle transition temperature in steels heated in, or slowly cooled through, the temperature range from about 700° to 1100°F (375° to 575°C).

Tempering

Re-heating a quench-hardened or normalized ferrous alloy to a temperature below the transformation range and then cooling at any rate desired.

Tensile Strength

In tensile testing, the ratio of the maximum force sustained to the original cross-sectional area.

Ternary Alloy

An alloy that contains three principal elements.

Texture

In a polycrystalline aggregate, the state of distribution of crystal orientations. In the usual sense, it is synonymous with preferred orientation, in which the distribution is not random.

Thermocouple

A device for measuring temperatures by the use of two dissimilar metals in contact; the junction of these metals gives rise to a measurable electrical potential with changes in temperature.

Tinning

Coating with tin, commonly either by immersion into molten tin or by electro-deposition; also by spraying.

Tolerance Limit

The permissible deviation from the desired value.

Tool Steel

Any high carbon or alloy steel capable of being suitably tempered for use in the manufacture of tools.

Toughness

Property of resisting fracture or distortion. Usually measured by impact test, high impact values indicating high toughness.

Transformation

A constitutional change in a solid metal, e.g., the change from gamma to alpha iron, or the formation of pearlite from austenite.

Transformation Range

Temperature range over which a chemical or metallurgical change takes place.

Transition Temperature

(1) An arbitrarily defined temperature within the temperature range in which metal fracture characteristics determined usually by notched tests are changing rapidly such as from primarily fibrous (shear) to primarily crystalline (cleavage) fracture. Commonly used definitions are transition temperature for 50% cleavage fracture, 10-ft-lb transition temperature, and transition temperature for half maximum energy. (2) Sometimes also used to denote the arbitrarily defined temperature in a range in which the ductility changes rapidly with temperature.

Transition Temperature (Ductile-brittle Transition Temperature)

An arbitrarily defined temperature that lies within the temperature range in which metal fracture characteristics (as usually determined by tests of notched specimens) change rapidly, such as from primarily fibrous (shear) to primarily cleavage.

Transverse

Literally, 'across', usually signifying a direction or plane perpendicular to the direction of working.

Trepanning

A type of boring where an annular cut is made into a solid material with the coincidental formation of a plug or solid cylinder.

Triple Point

The intersection of the boundaries of three adjoining grains, as observed in a section.

Troosite

Tempered martensite that etches rapidly, usually appears dark, and is not resolved by the microscope.

Trowel Steel

Hardened and tempered spring steel. 0.90 to 1.05 carbon content. Ordinary tolerances, but rolled extra flat—Rockwell C 50. Used in the manufacture of plastering trowels.

Truss Spring Steel

Supplied cold rolled and bright annealed. Carbon content about 0.70—Manganese 0.74. Must be formed very severely and must be as free as possible from decarburization.

Twin

Two portions of a crystal having a definite orientation relationship; one may be regarded as the parent, the other as the twin. The orientation of the twin is either a mirror image of the orientation of the parent across a twinning plane or an orientation that can be derived by rotating the twin portion about a twinning axis.

Vacancy

A type of structural imperfection in which an individual atom site is temporarily unoccupied.

Widmanstatten Structure

A structure characterized by a geometric pattern resulting from the formation of a new phase on certain crystallographic planes in the parent phase. The orientation of the lattice in the new phase is related cystallographically to the orientation of the lattice in the parent phase.

Work Hardening

Same as strain hardening.

Wrought Iron

Iron containing only a very small amount of other elements, but containing 1–3% by weight of slag in the form of particles elongated in one direction, giving the iron a characteristic grain. Is more rust-resistant than steel and welds more easily.

X-Rays

Light rays, excited usually by the impact of cathode rays on matter, which have wave lengths between about 10–6 cm, and 10–9 cm; also written X-rays, same as Roentgen rays.

Yellow Brass

65% copper and 35% zinc. Also known as high brass. A copper-zinc alloy, named for its yellow hue. Formerly a very popular alloy, but now largely replaced by cartridge brass.

Yield Point

The first stress in a material less than the maximum obtainable stess at which an increase in strain occurs without an increase in stress. Also known as upper yield stress.

Young's Modulus

The co-efficient of elasticity of stretching. For a stretched wire, Young's Modulus is the ratio of the stretching force per unit cross-sectional area to the elongation per unit length. The values of Young's Modulus for metals are of the order 10(12) dynes per square cm.

INDEX

D

E

V

W

X

Y

Z